To

Roger Charles Anderson

THE SHIP

THE SHIP

An Illustrated History

Written and illustrated

by

Björn Landström

Doubleday & Company, Inc.

Garden City, New York

Introduction

The author of this book tells us in his Preface that after a long search for a really well illustrated account in any language of the development of ships from their beginnings to the present day he found that he would have to write and illustrate the book himself. Fortunately, being a serious student of the subject, a deep-water yachtsman and — above all — an exceptionally good draughtsman with a knowledge of what is needed to make a drawing suitable for reproduction, he combines in himself all the qualities required to make the resulting book a success.

One feature is particularly welcome. Mr Landström has not been content to reproduce known representations of ships or to confine himself to a series of drawings of ships as he believes they must have been, but has given us, side by side, both the originals and his interpretations of them; so that we can judge for ourselves whether these interpretations are justified. To me,

at least, this seems to be almost invariably the case.

This pairing of originals and interpretations is chiefly of value for the period before about 1650 A.D., since from then onwards our knowledge of ships is fairly complete. It must, however, be recognised that the story of the last 300 years forms a very small fraction of the whole and that the author is justified in treating it less fully than the rest, though some of us would have liked him to be less selective towards the end.

Mr Landström has been fortunate in his publishers. Many authors have found it difficult to persuade their publishers to let them treat their subject as fully as they wished, particularly in the matter of illustrations; but as far as one can judge, he has not been handicapped in that way. Altogether the book is a magnificent piece of work and both author and publishers deserve our hearty thanks for producing it.

Greenwich, March 1961
R. C. Anderson

Preface

This book is an attempt to satisfy a need. I had hoped for many years that such a book existed, and searched for it on the shelves of bookshops and public libraries. Gradually literature and illustrations began to accumulate, I made drawings in museums and from life, interviewed the experienced and knowledgeable and believed that I myself would soon be able to compile what I had lacked: a pictorial survey of the history of the ship. When I began to sort the information I had collected, however, I found enormous gaps, so I continued my studies, visited most maritime museums in Europe, rummaged in second-hand bookshops both large and small, spoke with the leading authorities on the subject. Both to my sorrow and comfort I found that there were great loopholes in the knowledge of even the wisest.

It is believed that the oldest representations we have of any vessels are roughly six thousand years old —

some believe that they are of older date, some that they are more recent. Of the very oldest pictures there are not many, and interpretation of them leaves much room for guesswork. If I am to say that this book is intended to illustrate the history of the ship over a period of six thousand years, then I must from the start admit that I, like others, have had to guess at much during the first five and a half. The basis for such guesswork has always been more or less primitive pictures, sometimes descriptions, combined with a little common sense and the knowledge that the development of the art of shipbuilding has always been slow. This is why I have included all original drawings and representations up to the seventeenth century, so that the reader himself may judge and reconstruct as he thinks best.

It is only from the middle of the seventeenth century that we really have fairly reliable and complete sources of information in the form of constructional drawings, descriptions and, above all, detailed working models. From that time on, the amount of information increases with the years, the quest for it becoming less and less necessary, until it finally is a matter of choosing from the flood. Many illustrated tomes have been and still are being written about the last days of the sailing-ship and the ships and navigation of our times.

I have chosen to give only a rough outline of the history of the last sailing-ships and power-driven vessels to keep anyway a seeming balance between the centuries, between the little we know about the long, long beginning and all we can read and see in the multitude of books from the last hundred years. In this way there will be a certain congruence between the description of the ships of our own times and those of times past. Furthermore, this book does not pretend to be anything more than a survey and an introduction.

I have chosen to present the illustrations in the form of drawings, partly because a drawing is often clearer than a photograph and partly because a drawing is easier to fit into the composition as a whole; in some cases I believe I have touched upon the secrets of certain types, while my brush or pencil followed lines which were carved or painted thousands of years ago. The reconstructions have seldom been wholly my own. Even where they seem to be revolutionary, they are based on material collected by many scholars. The bibliography lists the authors to whom my thanks are due. Some of the reconstructional drawings are accompanied by scales: the upper black in metres, the lower red in feet. People in many different countries will probably ask why this or that renowned vessel has not been included. Wiser men than I have committed national injustices and all I can say is that I have tried to follow the most important phases in the historical development of the ship regardless of nationality.

There are two wise men, two major authorities I wish to thank more than others for great help, for answering thousands of questions and for invigorating criticism: R. C. Anderson, Litt. D., President of the Trustees of the National Maritime Museum, Greenwich, and Captain S. Svensson, Conservator of Statens Sjöhistoriska Museum in Stockholm.

I also wish to thank the Director of Museo Storico Navale in Venice, Baron G. B. Rubin de Cervin, for much helpfulness and courtesy. I first visited the museum to make a closer study of two models which in all the available literature are said to be from the sixteenth century, one a three-masted vessel, sometimes erroneously called galleon, and the other a four-masted so-called *coca*. Baron Rubin de Cervin showed me and asked me to advertise that both well-known models had nevertheless been made sometime during the nineteenth century.

I further wish to express my gratitude to the Director of Museo Naval in Madrid, Rear Admiral Julio F. Guillen, and to the Director of Museo Maritimo in Barcelona, Captain José Ma Martinez Hidalgo y Terán for their kindness and information, and I am also grateful to the whole of the obliging staff of Statens Sjöhistoriska Museum in Stockholm where I have spent so many hours and days collecting information.

My sincere thanks are also due to Lieut.-Commander George P. B. Naish, National Maritime Museum, Greenwich, who has been kind enough to read the whole of the English translation and check the technical terms used.

Finally I wish to say that this book would never have existed were it not for the many years' encouragement and support I have had from my enthusiastic friend and publisher Adam Helms.

Saltsjöbaden, Sweden
January 1961
Björn Landström

In the beginning

The history of the ship begins naturally many thousands of years before the first known representation. The earliest pictures are of course primitive, but they by no means show us boats in their most primitive form. They are types which we still can find today in various corners of the world.

The first boat is often shown as a floating log with a naked ape-man as passenger, but it is certain that other animals were forced to take similar trips when rivers flooded and bore away bushes and trees long before the first being we really can call man walked the earth and navigated its waters. There is reason to believe that the first travel made by water began in like circumstances and often ended unhappily.

When man of his own free will first set out on the waters, chose and perhaps trimmed a suitable tree trunk, collected a bundle of rushes or bound branches to form a raft for the purpose, only then may we say that the first boat was made. It can have been a hundred thousand years ago, it can have been five hundred thousand.

Perhaps the discovery never spread beyond the tribe. Perhaps it took a thousand or a hundred thousand years before another man in another part of the world made the same discovery. To this day the Budumas break branches from the ambatche tree, bind them together to form a little raft and paddle with hands and feet across the bays of Lake Chad in Africa.

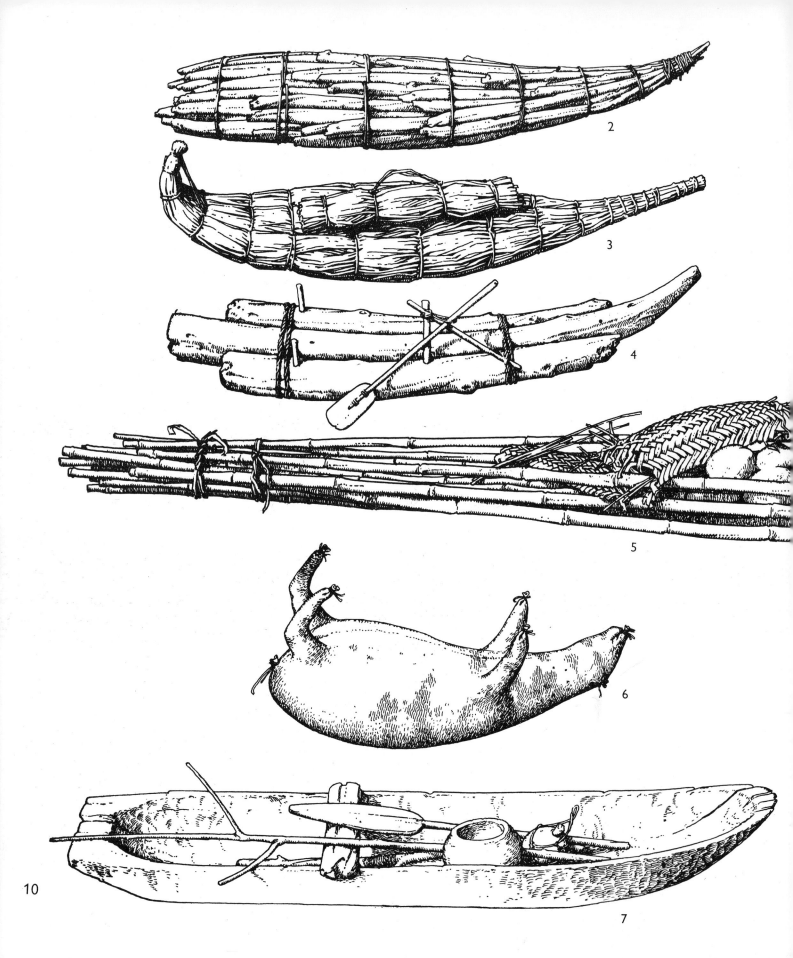

Primitive boats

Most of the primitive vessels that can have existed in prehistoric times are still to be found in use today in various parts of the world. Some were to develop and improve, others were as mature as they ever would be, lacking any possibility of development. On the White Nile people pole and paddle themselves along on a boat-like raft of ambatche branches lashed together (2), and as the raft is also called *ambatche* it may be presumed that the raft has given its name to the tree in the same way as the *balsa* of South America has given its name to the tree.

The boat-like *papyrus raft* (3) which is used both on

of the raft like a prow. It has little or no connection with the popular double canoe of today which sails under false denomination. In the Fiji Islands there is a long, buoyant *bamboo raft* (5) which consists of two layers of bamboo poles and is fitted with a railing. This is no sea-going craft and is normally only used for transport on lagoons and between nearby islands.

A relief from Nineveh of about 700 B.C. shows how men cross the Tigris swimming on inflated animal skins. The same method is still practised today in Tibet where the nomads carry the stitched and caulked skins of oxen and swine which are inflated to make buoyant boats (6) should their passage be hindered by water.

The *dug-out,* hollowed out of the trunk of the tree, was still in use at the beginning of this century in remote districts of Scandinavia, and the natives of Africa, South America and Australia continue to hollow

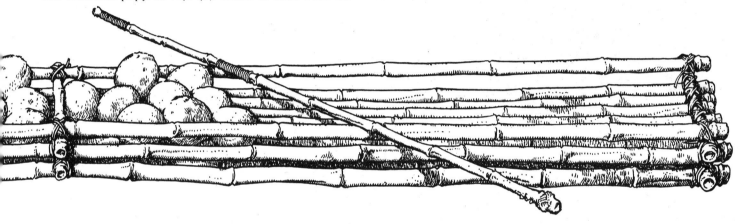

the White Nile and other African waterways has retained its appearance through the thousands of years we can follow its history. The art of building such a raft has never died as papyrus is an extremely unsubstantial material to build boats with, the life of the raft thus never being more than a few months.

The *catamaran* proper (4), found on the Coromandel Coast of India, consists of three or five logs bound together, the longest in the centre rising in the forepart

out large tree trunks with the aid of stone implements and fire (7). I believe it is very possible that the dug-out and the constructed hide boat together showed the way to all advanced shipbuilding. The primitive hide boat with skins stretched over wooden ribs is still to be found in Tibet as an alternative to the inflated bladder boat, in Greenland where it is called *umiak,* and in Britain where it is called *coracle* (8). It is used when fishing on rivers and lakes.

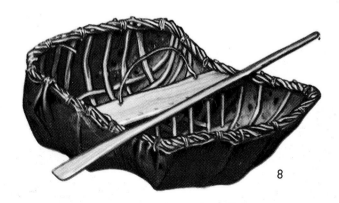

8

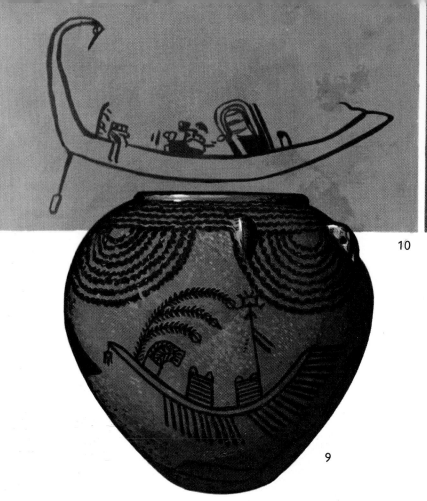

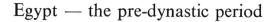

9

10

Egypt — the pre-dynastic period

The oldest pictures of boats come from Egypt. It is usually reckoned that Egypt's history under the Pharaohs began about 3400 B.C. and from that time onwards we also know a certain amount about the way man lived.

But of the tribes and peoples that inhabited the long oasis of the Nile Valley during the so-called pre-dynastic period — the period before 3400 B.C. — little is known. It is clear that they must have journeyed along and across the river on rafts or boats, and both rock-carvings and pictures on vases and in graves portray figures which can only be interpreted as types of water craft.

A small vase with red decoration has pictures which appear to be boats with many oars (9), but there are those who hold that they might just as well represent fenced-in dwelling places. A now lost mural from a grave in Hierakonpolis also showed similar figures, but there was a further picture (10) which was obviously meant to be a boat with a steering oar.

It is wellnigh impossible to fix the exact date of these pictures but it is generally agreed that they cannot be less than six thousand years old and many consider them to be much older. Of roughly the same age is the earliest known picture of a sailing craft painted on a vase (11). The carvings from the Nubian Desert showing curved, horned craft (13—14) are also accounted to be of the same indefinite age.

When we now attempt to interpret these pictures we must surely feel immediate surprise at the great similarity between the boat from Hierakonpolis (10) and the

12

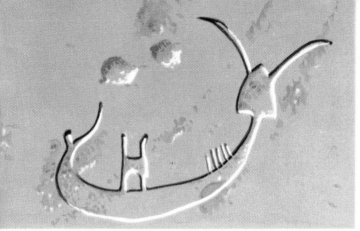

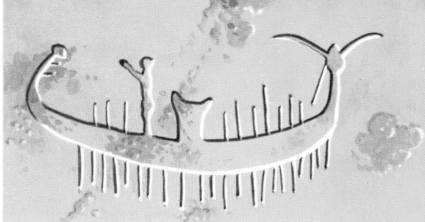

13

14

White Nile papyrus boats of our own times (3). The only real disparity is the cabin, or what anyway looks like a cabin, situated amidships — also to be seen in the Nubian Desert boats. There are some who consider these projections to be altars and explain that the carvings are ceremonial pictures of ceremonial boats, but it might just as well be a question of tents for the protection of distinguished personages or other valuable cargo in a country where the sun sits high and hot.

Even these early pictures make us suspect that the papyrus boats were spool-shaped. Whether this was to imitate the shape of the fish or whether it was the result of many thousands of years of experience is impossible to tell. Naturally the pointed prows were bent upward so that it would be easier to land on the shallow shores, and quite naturally too they helped to make the boats more buoyant and easier to manoeuvre in rapids and rough sea. On the other hand it is difficult to explain why the sterns of those early days were bent inwards so much that they came to point forwards, while the prows were kept projecting slightly outwards. This was to be characteristic of Mediterranean craft for thousands of years and we can still trace the relationship today in the small transport vessels on the lagoons of Venice for example. It seems most probable that the pre-dynastic

boats were paddled and not rowed. It was a thousand years later that pictures were made of vessels with oarsmen.

It seems fairly clear that the bull, even during prehistoric times, played an important part in the religious life of the Mediterranean peoples, and it is easy to see the crania of long-horned cattle typical of the Sudan today in the prow decorations of the Nubian boat pictures. Their purpose seems to have been to guard the vessels, to frighten away evil spirits and other adversaries, and also perhaps to be the eyes of the vessel, finding the safe passage through the sandbanks of the river.

The picture of the sailing craft also shows a hull which most reminds one of the papyrus boat. The raised portion in the stern might be an altar or a cabin, but it might also well be a platform for the helmsman just as there is a little platform in the fore for the lookout. The figure decorating the high prow could be either bird or fish, and as we shall see later a similar figurehead was to be found on the northern shores of the Mediterranean. As was to be the case with Egyptian sailing craft for the next two thousand years the mast was situated far forward, by which we understand that the sail was only used when the wind was almost directly aft.

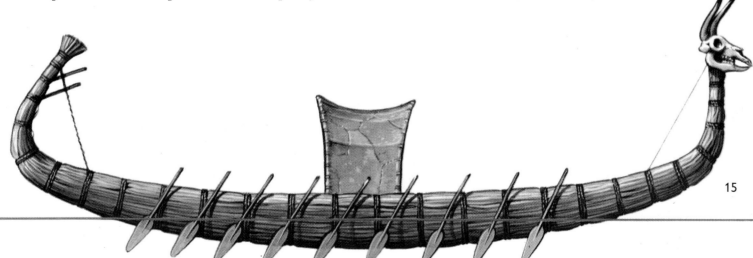

15

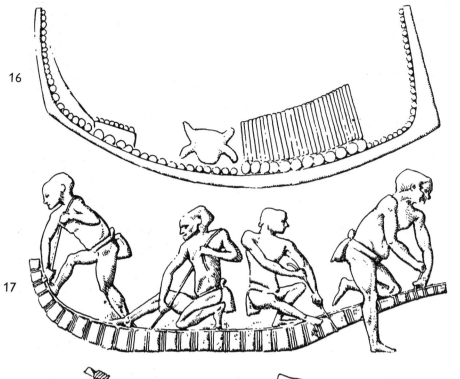

16

17

Egypt, 3400-3000 B.C.

Pharaoh Menes, according to tradition the first king of Egypt, began to reign about 3400 B.C. A palette belonging to this time has a finely carved picture of a high-prowed boat (16) with a hull of roughly the same type as that of the previous sailing craft (11). Reliefs from some six hundred years later partly show the binding of a papyrus boat (17) and partly the building of a wooden boat (18).

Even in those days there were no trees that provided good ship's timber, and although wood for the larger vessels began to be imported later, the Egyptians had for the most part to make do with homeland acacia and sycamore which could only be obtained in short pieces. The relief and a boat find from about 2000 B.C. (19) show how these boats

18

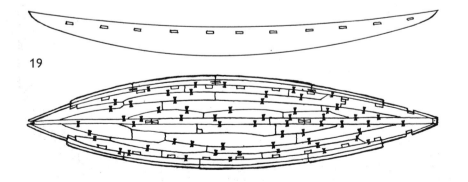

19

14

were built: without ribs and with a planking of thick wooden blocks joined together partly with wooden pegs and partly with hourglass-shaped pieces of wood, the ends of which fitted into adjacent blocks. The pressure of the water helped to hold together the submerged part of the hull, and the beams, pegged to the planking, gave support athwartships.

A relief in a stone wall shows a boat with binding very like that of the papyrus boat (20) and another boat which gives the impression of being built of wood (21). The former is propelled by paddlers. The latter shows us oarsmen for the first time. Perhaps the difference does not seem so very remarkable, it was just a matter of giving the oar some form of attachment at the gunnel but the discovery gradually made it possible to build considerably larger boats which could not have been propelled by paddlers.

The sailing vessel (22) displays quite an advanced construction with a presumably broadened platform for the men at the rudder oars. The *bipod mast* has many aft and one single forestay; there are no shrouds. The sail is *braced* by a man furthest aft and it is possible that it was even sheeted, but it is more probable that the sail was used only when the wind was aft.

Pharaoh Sahure's sea-going ships

Is is believed that the Egyptians sailed out over the Mediterranean to Syria and Crete before 3000 B.C. and hieroglyphs relate that Pharaoh Snofru sent forty ships to Byblos in Phoenicia about the year 2900 to buy cedar for shipbuilding. Two hundred years later Pharaoh Sahure sent an armed flotilla of eight ships to harry the coast of Syria and it returned safely with Phoenician prisoners. Fragments of a very detailed relief of that date (24) portrays the expedition and shows some of the vessels so clearly that it is possible to form a good idea of their appearance and construction.

Apart from reinforcements necessary for sea-going voyages they do not differ much from the boats that sailed on the Nile. Presumably the hulls, as earlier, were built without a keel or frames with the thick blocks pegged to each other, and for further support fore-and-

aft a strong rope had been stretched over a series of props from bow to stern and made taut with the aid of a stick thrust between the cords of the rope and twisted (25—26). The relief shows no signs of through deck-beams and it is probable that these first came into use some hundreds of years later (cf. 19). Satisfactory support athwartships was given by two ropes running round the upper planking of the vessel which were kept taut and together by another rope running zig-zag between them. The bipod mast was collapsible and no doubt lowered when the ship was under the oars. It is probable that it functioned as shown in the reconstruction (25) with large stones as counter-weights. The method of support and positioning of the mast had as yet not undergone much change and when the wind was unfavourable the oars had to be used. It is uncertain whether the upright stem and stern posts had any function other than bearing significant symbols. The stern-post bore the sign of general protection and the fore-post the all-seeing eye which we shall later find on different ships round the world to this day.

25

26

17

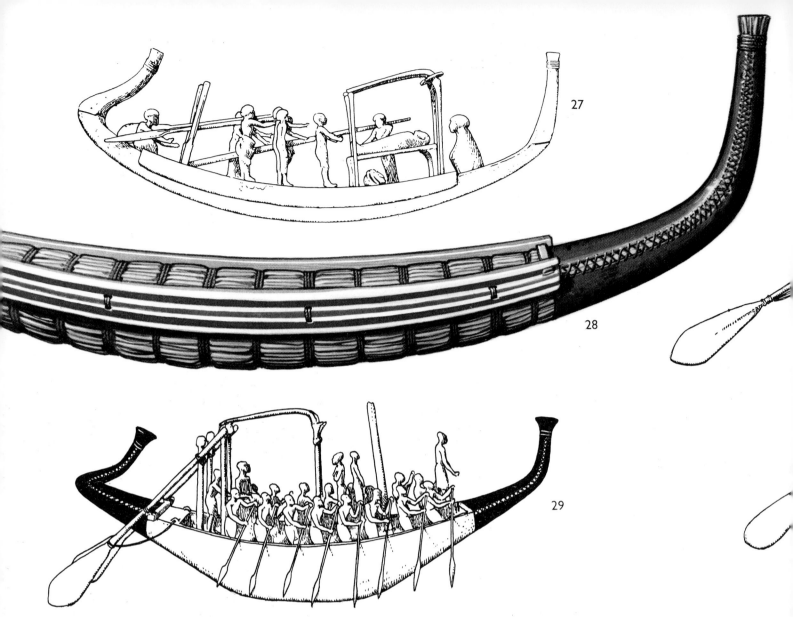

27

28

29

Nile boats, 2000 B.C.

Pharaoh Mentuhotep who reigned about the year 2000 had as his chancellor and vizier the remarkable Mehenkvetre who has chiefly gone down in history for the number of models filling his tomb. They represent the palace and houses of the deceased, outhouses with people and animals and implements, and furthermore, to our great fortune, a large number of boats clearly intended for use on the Nile.

Perhaps the most interesting is a little craft with paddles (29) strangely decorated with a zig-zag pattern running along the sides of the brown fore and sternposts. If we compare this with an even more elegantly shaped model from another tomb (27) we will see that the bow and stern have almost exactly the same form

and as the latter model is so similar to a papyrus boat we may presume that the former is also. Papyrus is a soft and unsubstantial material and it obviously can have been no easy thing to shape such elegant fore and sternposts without special means. This is why I believe that the dark posts on model 29 was a sort of ready-made cover of cloth or leather which was later stitched around the pointed ends of the papyrus boat to give it this graceful form (28). After a few months the boat would be waterlogged and condemned, but the post casings were more durable and would be used again for the next boat and the next. One of the models (27) shows a long plank attached to the outside of the hull, and such a board would provide excellent support to the papyrus boat athwartships as well as fore-and-aft. Both models indicate that the numerous steering oars have been replaced by a single large one on each side bound to a cross-piece and two sturdy poles.

18

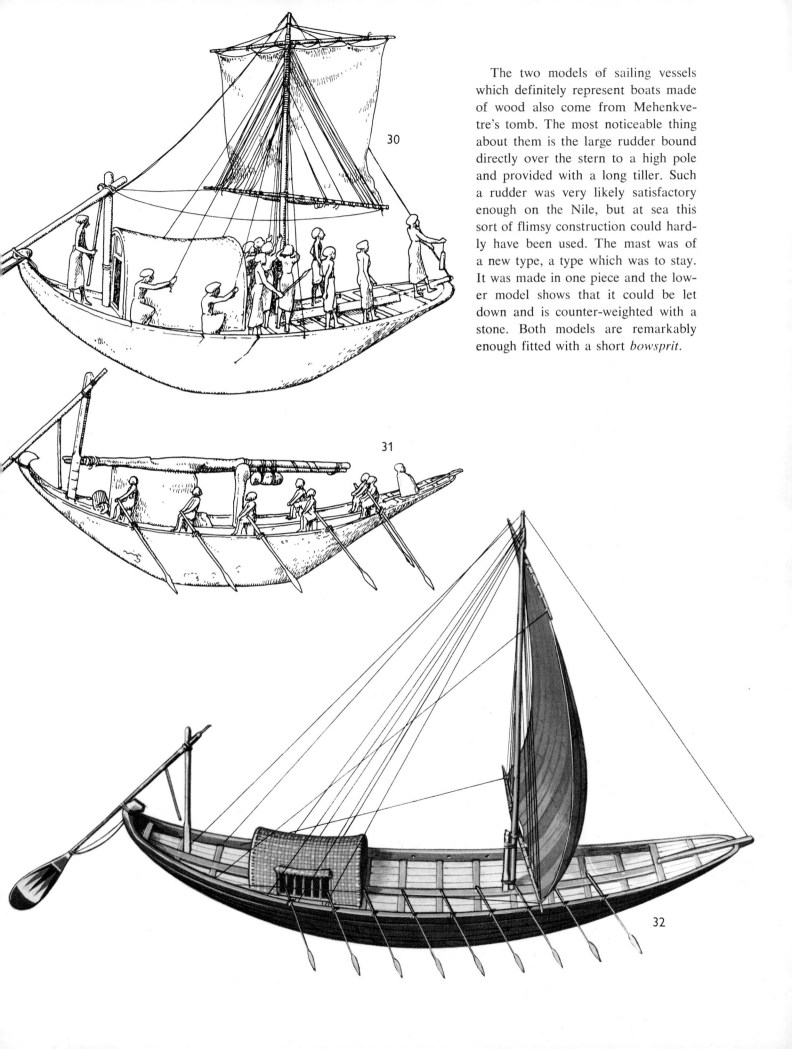

The two models of sailing vessels which definitely represent boats made of wood also come from Mehenkvetre's tomb. The most noticeable thing about them is the large rudder bound directly over the stern to a high pole and provided with a long tiller. Such a rudder was very likely satisfactory enough on the Nile, but at sea this sort of flimsy construction could hardly have been used. The mast was of a new type, a type which was to stay. It was made in one piece and the lower model shows that it could be let down and is counter-weighted with a stone. Both models are remarkably enough fitted with a short *bowsprit*.

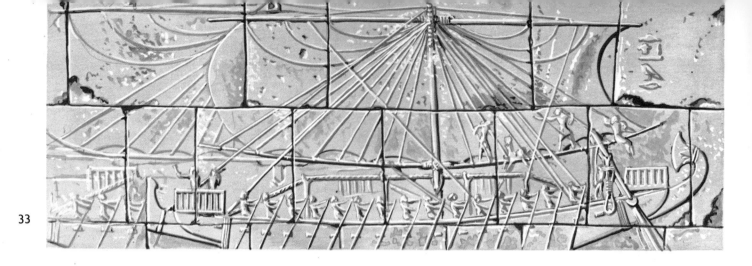

33

Queen Hatshepsut's ships

In the valley of Deir el-Bahari there is a temple with a long row of reliefs showing the expedition Thotmes II's co-regent and sister Queen Hatshepsut sent to the land of Punt about 1500 B.C. to buy such sought-after goods as myrrh and ivory, ebony, monkeys and greyhounds. No one knows today where this land of Punt lay, but most people guess at Somaliland which would be a long voyage from Egypt.

The pictures are both detailed and full of variety, and the sea-going ships are portrayed with the sails hoisted (33) and lowered, under the oars and in port. It seems as if the hulls are now constructed around a high and strong keel-plank which projecting forward is formed into a vertical prow and projecting aft curves upwards

34

and forwards, ending in a large lotus flower. There is nothing to suggest that ribs have come into use, but the deck beams project in a long row through the side of the vessel and are undoubtedly so fitted between the boards that they give support athwart-ships. In spite of the keel (if it really is such), the hull is still supported fore-and-aft by a rope bound round the fore and after parts of the hull.

The mast is situated amidships and presumably rests directly on the keel. There are no shrouds but two stays run forward and one aft, the latter being complemented by the double halyard running through the movable block on the top of the mast. The block rests on two ridges with holes for the lifts holding the lower yard to the upper yard when the sail is lowered. The sheets are attached halfway along the lower yard and it seems as if the braces began at the top of the mast, running down to the after-deck through small pulleys on the upper yard. The position of the mast and the arrangement of the rigging indicate that the ship could be sailed even in half-wind. Judging from the number of oarsmen the ship would have been about 80—90 feet long.

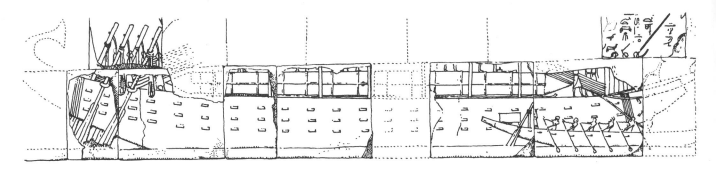

Queen Hatshepsut's obelisk barge

The obelisks that today stand in Paris and London and New York once stood before temples at Luxor and Heliopolis. They were originally carved in a single piece from the rock at Assuan far up by the first cataract of the Nile. The barges that transported these stone monsters down the river were, because of their size, the most remarkable vessels ever built in Egypt. The official Ineri, who lived about 1550 B.C., relates in his epitaph that for his master Thotmes I he had a vessel built for the transport of two obelisks and that it was 120 cubits long and 40 cubits broad — in other words about 195×70 feet.

The only contemporary picture we have of such a

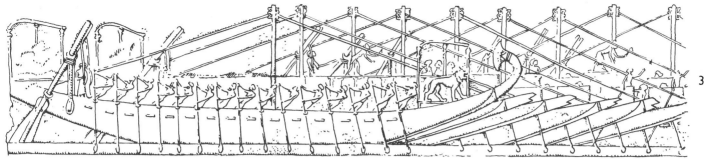

vessel (35) is in the rock temple at Deir el-Bahari together with the ships from the expedition to Punt. Queen Hatshepsut had two obelisks hewn at Assuan to the memory of herself and her father and a long relief shows how they were transported down the Nile to Karnak. One of them still stands intact before the temple of Amon Ra. It is nearly a hundred feet high and weighs 350 tons. The two obelisks together thus weighed 700 tons, whereas Thotmes I's obelisks were only half as heavy. There are no contemporary details of the size of Queen Hatshepsut's giant vessel.

The relief shows both obelisks on board lying behind each other, but if they had been placed in this fashion in reality it would have meant that the ship was over 280 feet long and this we do not believe. The Egyptians never made perspective drawings, and if they wanted to show that there were two obelisks on board it would have been most natural for them to portray this as they have done. This is why it is understood that the colossi in fact lay side by side, and from their length and weight the dimensions of the ship would have been: length 200 feet, beam 80 feet, draught 7 feet, weight without load 800 tons and with load 1,500 tons. It was presumably built in the traditional manner of small, perhaps 12-inch thick blocks of wood pegged together. Water pressure held the bottom portions tight, three layers of beams supported the high freeboards and a whole system of stretched ropes strengthened the hull from fore to aft. The great barge was towed by 27 smaller craft (36) in three lines and each of these smaller craft had 30 oarsmen apart from helmsmen and drivers. This took place about 1500 B.C.

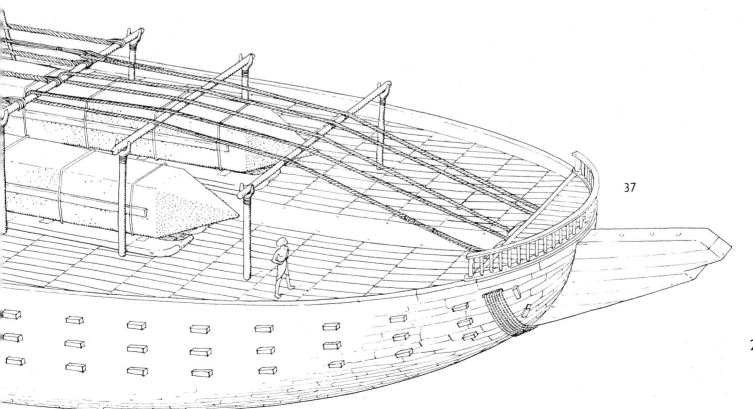

37

38

39

Ramses III's warships

About 1200 B.C. Egypt was threatened by a large invasion force. The inscriptions call the enemy "the people from the sea" and it is believed that they were tribes who had been driven from Crete to the mainland, the Philistines of the Bible among them, who were now forcing their way into Egypt by land and by sea. Ramses III, who has been called the last great Pharaoh, made decisive counter-attacks and defeated the enemy on land and at sea. In his tomb at Medinet Habu the battle is portrayed — the first picture of a naval action (38).

The pictures of the boats are more conventional than at Deir el-Bahari, but we see anyway that a clear advance has been made during the three hundred years. The fact that the Egyptian ships had many details in common with the invasion craft intimates that the Egyptians, as far as their sea-going vessels were concerned anyway, had learned from the seafaring peoples in the north and north-east. Although the fore and aft parts

of the hull are of a different construction (cf. 39 and 41) all of the vessels in the engagement have a high *washboard* to protect the oarsmen. It is uncertain whether the Egyptians had gone so far as to use ribs, and the reconstruction of the details of the hull (39—40) is mostly based on guesswork.

The rigging is surprisingly novel and presents many innovations. This is the first time we see *"tops"* portrayed and also for the first time a sail that has been furled by means of *brails* without the yard being lowered, all of course of much importance for fighting vessels. The boats of the people from the sea have exactly the same rig, and we believe that all of these innovations came from the northern shores of the Mediterranean.

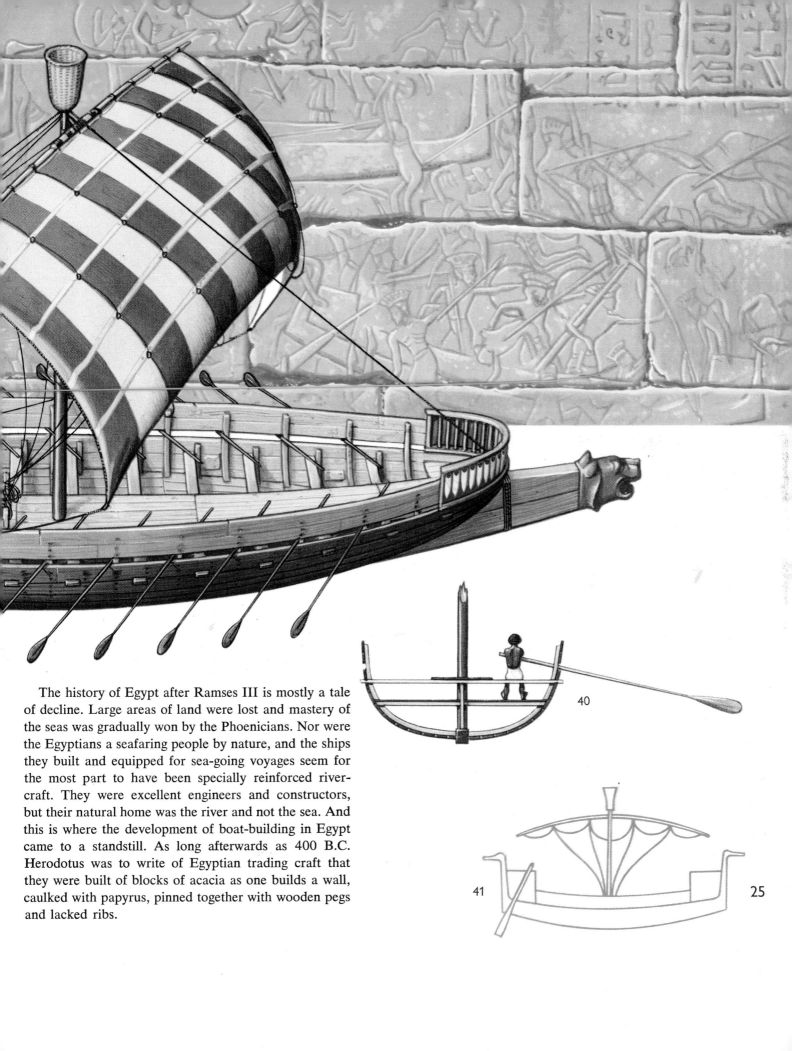

The history of Egypt after Ramses III is mostly a tale of decline. Large areas of land were lost and mastery of the seas was gradually won by the Phoenicians. Nor were the Egyptians a seafaring people by nature, and the ships they built and equipped for sea-going voyages seem for the most part to have been specially reinforced river-craft. They were excellent engineers and constructors, but their natural home was the river and not the sea. And this is where the development of boat-building in Egypt came to a standstill. As long afterwards as 400 B.C. Herodotus was to write of Egyptian trading craft that they were built of blocks of acacia as one builds a wall, caulked with papyrus, pinned together with wooden pegs and lacked ribs.

40

41

25

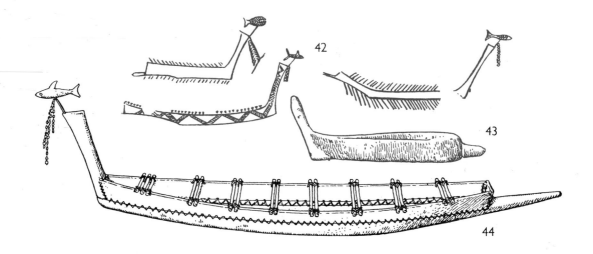

42

43

44

Aegean Bronze Age vessels

It is understandable that seafaring developed early among the people living on the islands and in the bays of the Aegean Sea, and it is believed that cultural connections between the mainland and Crete can be traced as far back as 3400 B.C. There are no pictures of the vessels that bore men and merchandise between the island and the mainland, but they can hardly have been much different from the type of boat discernible in the pictures on the vase fragments found on the island of Syra, one of the Cyclades (42), and dated to about 2800 B.C. The model of a ship of the same type found on Crete (43) gives further information for a reconstruction (44), and with a little guesswork we arrive at an oak dug-out, the

sides stitched on, with a high, almost vertical stern-post decorated with the image of a fish (cf. 11). Perhaps it is also possible to discern a little historical development in the three pictures from Syra (42). The boat with the flat waterline would be the oldest type. Later it was attempted to lift the bow out of the water by choosing a curved trunk, and in the third phase a fore-post might have been attached to the dug-out.

On Cretan gems and seals of a somewhat later date, perhaps 2200—2000 B.C., we find pictures of sailing craft (45) with a sharply rising fore-post, sometimes as if it were a ram, and a less-curved stern-post. In those days when it blew too freshly, the ships were sailed or rowed down the wind and a slightly raised and rounded stern would have made the hull more buoyant and given

45

46

47

48

26

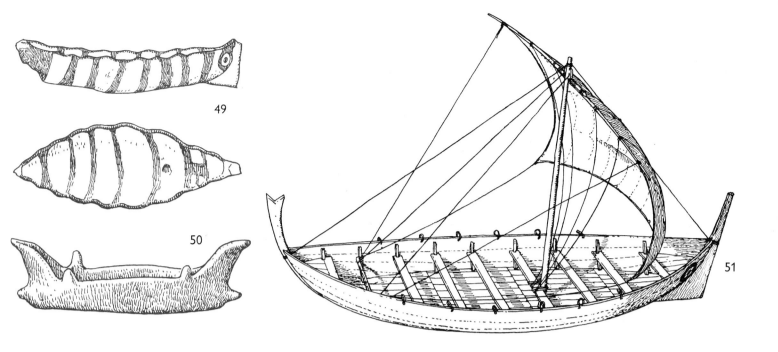

49

50

51

shelter to the helmsman. The curiously shaped fore-post has given many reason for believing that the pictures are of fighting-craft fitted with rams, but I prefer to think of the "cutwater" as a relic from earlier boats. When it was definitely found that this extension of the keel made it easier to keep the boat on course and furthermore lessened drift when sailing closer to the wind, many places continued to build merchant vessels with such a cutwater. — A small clay model with a cutwater, painted with stripes (ribs) and eyes in the bow support this theory, and I believe that a trader from the days of Cretan power might well have appeared as in the reconstruction.

But after 2000 B.C. we find pictures of boats with both fore and stern-posts gracefully curved (47), and even if it is difficult to make out anything of the hull,

the rig shows clear Egyptian influence (48). Perhaps the influence was from the opposite quarter? Perhaps the Egyptians were learning from the Cretans as early as that? It is generally agreed that the peoples around the Aegean Sea, having access to excellent ship's timber, began to build their boats with keel and ribs at an early date.

About 1400 B.C. Crete was invaded by people from the mainland and their civilization was destroyed. Remnants of the original population managed to flee to Cyprus and other eastern Mediterranean lands. A symmetrical boat model in clay is very reminiscent of the boat belonging to "the people from the sea" from the tomb at Medinet Habu (38, 41, 53), and, without comments, we can look at a rock-carving from Brandskog in Sweden of Nordic Bronze Age.

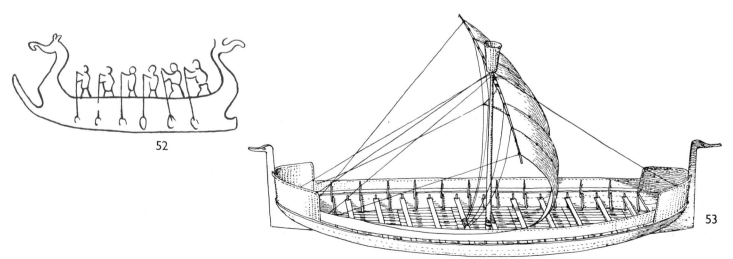

52

53

54

55

Greek warships

About 3300 B.C. the Dorians drove down to the shores of the Aegean from the north and with them began the Iron Age in Greece. There are no descriptions of the seafaring of those times but we know what the Dorian warships looked like from carvings and paintings on vase fragments (54, 55, 58).

They seem to have been light vessels of shallow draught but certain authors have come to the most fantastic conclusions as to their size and appearance as they presumed that the oarsmen sat in tiers above one another. At that time it was not known how to create perspective, and when the artists wanted to show that the boats were propelled by two rows of oarsmen the rows were drawn one above the other. The shape of the ram and the shield for the soldiers in the bow seem to be almost identical with the corresponding details on canoes from the Bismarck archipelago which are still in existence today (59).

We therefore believe that the early Greek warships were really large dug-outs. In this way the sharp yet strong ram would have been an integral part of a sturdy, relatively light, easily propelled hull. If we presume that such a boat was driven along by 24 oarsmen, 12 on each side (56, 57), it can have had the following dimensions: length 65 feet, beam 4 feet. The trunk was far too narrow for the sides to be of any support for the oars and so the vessels were fitted with *outriggers*.

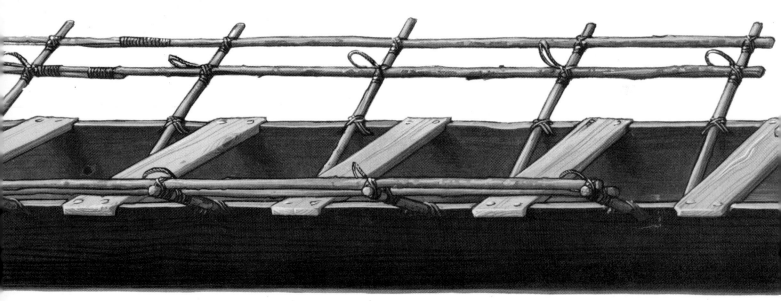

56

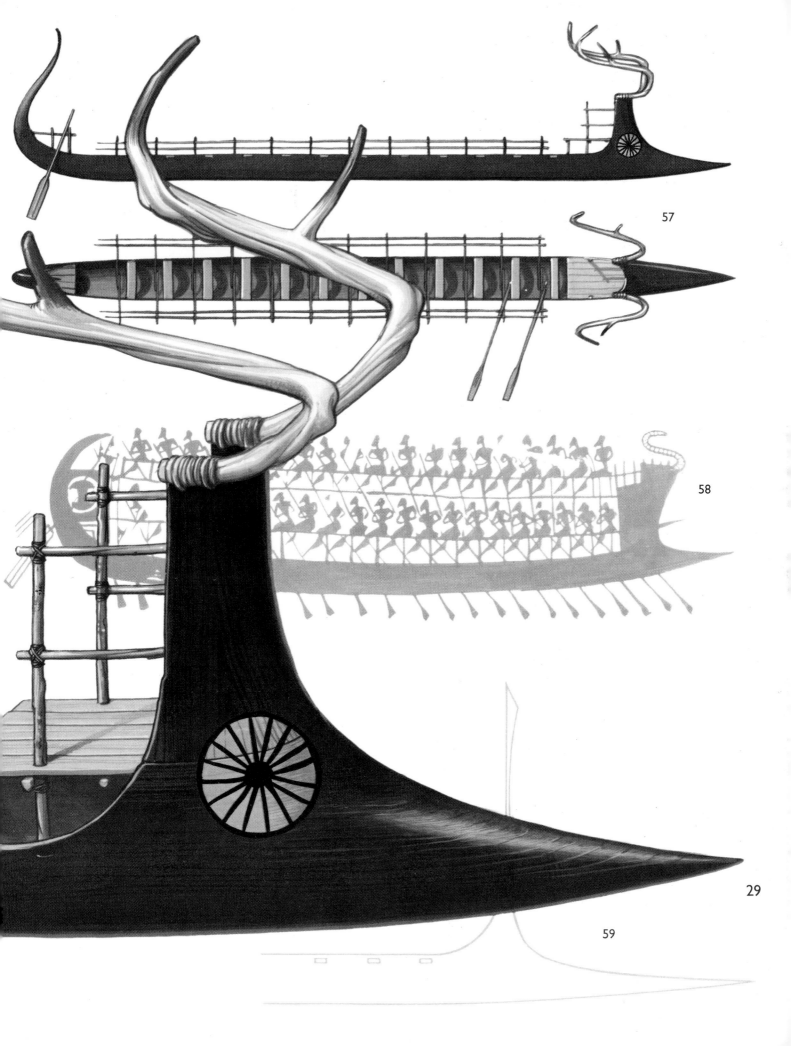

57

58

29

59

60

Phoenician merchant ships

The Phoenicians have left a firm reputation of having been the most prominent trading and seafaring people of their times, but there is not much we know of their ships, and the little we do know comes from Egyptian, Assyrian and Greek portrayals. As art in these ancient civilizations was very stereotyped and traditional, and as the artists would most naturally have been occupied with ships of their own country, the pictures are not considered to be wholly reliable.

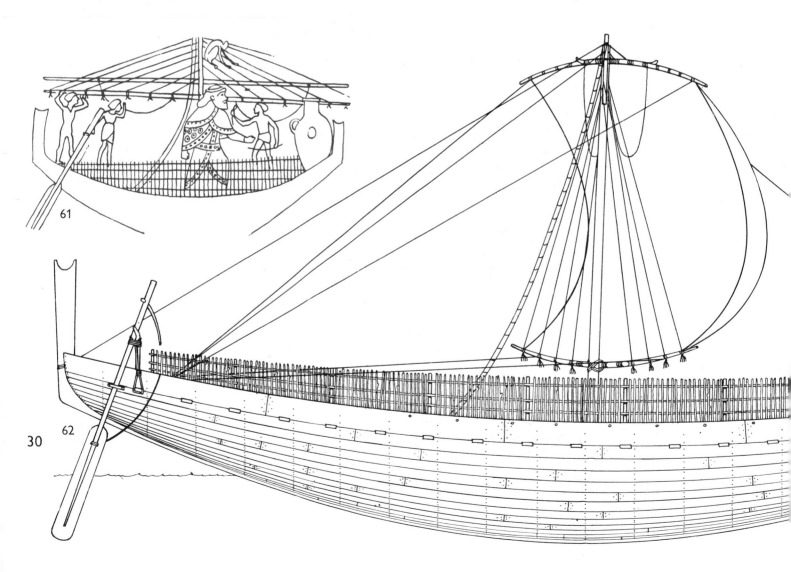

61

62

30

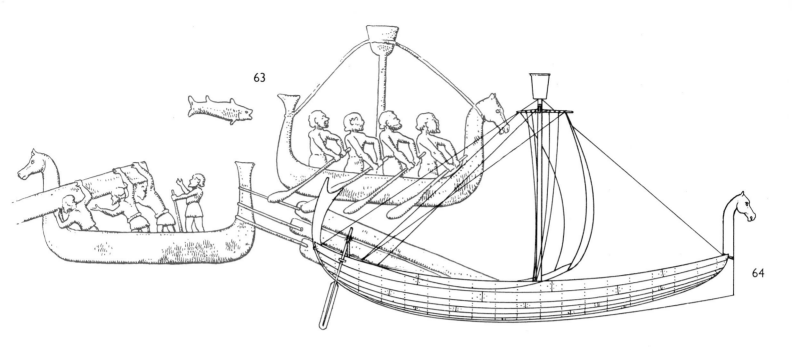

63

64

In an Egyptian tomb at Drah Abou'l Neggah from about 1500 B.C. a number of murals were found — now unfortunately destroyed by damp — portraying Phoenician trading ships (60, 61). In many ways they are reminiscent of Queen Hatshepsut's ships of roughly the same period, but there are dissimilarities: a rope-ladder leading up to the masthead, the jar bound to the fore-post, the fence running from fore to aft. The paintings show no sign of any rope support for the hull, perhaps indicating that the ships were sturdy enough without being built on keel and ribs. As I see it the fence can be explained as a partition for deck cargo, so that the sides of the deck would be left free for the oarsmen (62).

The Bible tells of the Phoenician king Hiram that in a message to king Solomon he was to have included: "My servants shall bring them [timber of cedar and timber of fir] down from Lebanon unto the sea: and I will convey them by sea in floats unto the place that thou shalt appoint me . . .". In an Assyrian relief from 700 B.C. (63) we see ships loading and towing timber. The fore-posts are shaped like horses' heads and the stern-posts like fishtails, and one ship has a mast with a "top". On an archaic vase there is a picture which is supposed to be of a Phoenician ship, and we can make out the fishtail, "top", fence (or fighting bridge?) and a fore-post with cutwater. Thus we have an idea of how Phoenician trading ships might have appeared (62, 64), but this is based on fifty percent guesswork.

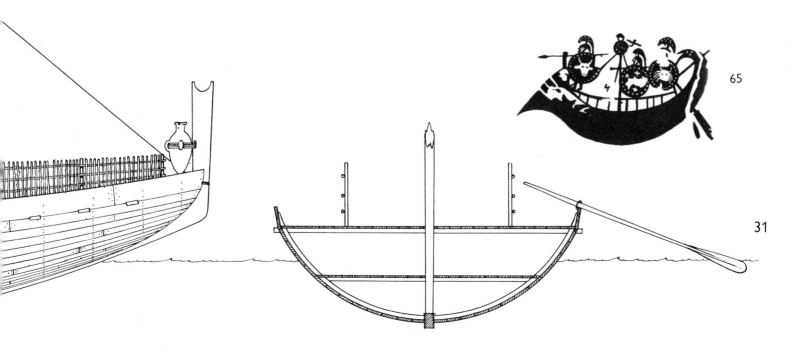

65

31

66

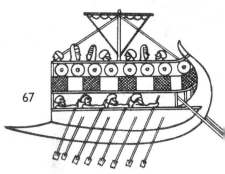

67

Phoenician biremes

The first known picture of *biremes* (a galley with the oars situated on two levels, in two banks) are found on two Assyrian reliefs from 70 B.C. They are believed to represent Phoenician warships (66, 67).

In the first picture (66) we can clearly see how the arms of the outer oarsmen are in a plane outside the upper-deck supports and both pictures show that the hull itself has been given an extension to bear the oars. Here too it is probable that the hull is made in one piece from a very thick trunk, and from this it is not difficult to imagine that the outriggers, the supports for the oars, were fitted with planking. The outer oarsmen are thus sitting on thwarts projecting from the hull into the outriggers (68). In this way it was possible to retain the narrow, easily propelled hull, a narrow fighting deck where the soldiers could move without upsetting the balance of the vessel; it was possible to attain greater speed and power for ramming by the increase in the number of oarsmen, and by planking the outriggers to achieve a reserve displacement which would hinder capsizing when heeling over sharply.

Both the Phoenicians and the Greeks were seamen of a practical nature and it is impossible for us to believe that they allowed their warships to become mastodonts of slower speed and less manoeuvrability. The further development of the warship was surely aimed at retaining manoeuvrability at the same time as strength and speed was increased.

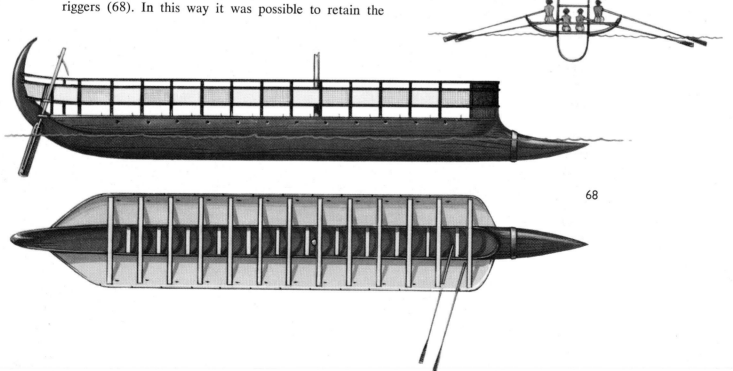

68

70

71

Greek trading ships

During the eighth century B.C. the Greeks began to devote themselves to sea trade on a larger scale and they were soon to offer much competition to the Phoenicians, founding colonies in southern Italy and Sicily, in North Africa and on the shores of the Black Sea. The country prospered, the population grew so that grain had to be imported both from the countries around the Black Sea and from Italy, and trade increased the more. It was a bustling time for both Greek and Phoenician shipbuilders and we may suppose that vessels of many different types and sizes sailed the Mediterranean. Artists, however, seldom wish to portray such prosaic objects as these and although hundreds of pictures of Greek warships have come down to us there are only a few that portray trading vessels.

A vase, now in the British Museum (70), shows Ulysses' ship as a combination of warship and trading vessel, and a boat on another vase has a similar appearance although more rustic. It is possible, probable even, that when longer voyages were made where there

was a risk for attack by pirates or other antagonists such a combination of trader and warship was used which was fitted with rams and had a relatively large crew capable of rowing and fighting. Perhaps what looks like a ram was just a cutwater which improved the sailing ability of the ship, perhaps it was a combination of both? A carving has been found on the quay at Utica near Carthage which is believed to be of a Phoenician trading vessel from 300 B.C. It has the same combination of ram and cutwater, it has eyes in the bow like the Greek ships, but it seems to have at least two masts (72).

Trade was also plied in sheltered waters, in home water between the islands, and here it was simpler and easier to sail with a small crew. The best picture we have of a Greek trader (74) shows it at sea with sail furled. No oars are to be seen and it may therefore be presumed that it was only rowed when there was no

wind. It has a curious bow, almost like the bow of a clipper, and if there was not almost exactly the same bow to be found today on Sicilian and Maltese fishing-boats (73) it would have been nearly impossible to interpret the picture. The projecting part of the bow is a separate piece which has been nailed on, its purpose having perhaps been to carry the all-seeing eyes further out over the water. The boat, like Greek coastal craft of today, has a raised *bulwark*. It appears as if the deck was loaded right out to the bulwarks, but a bridge from the helmsman to the bow affords free passage over the deck cargo.

72

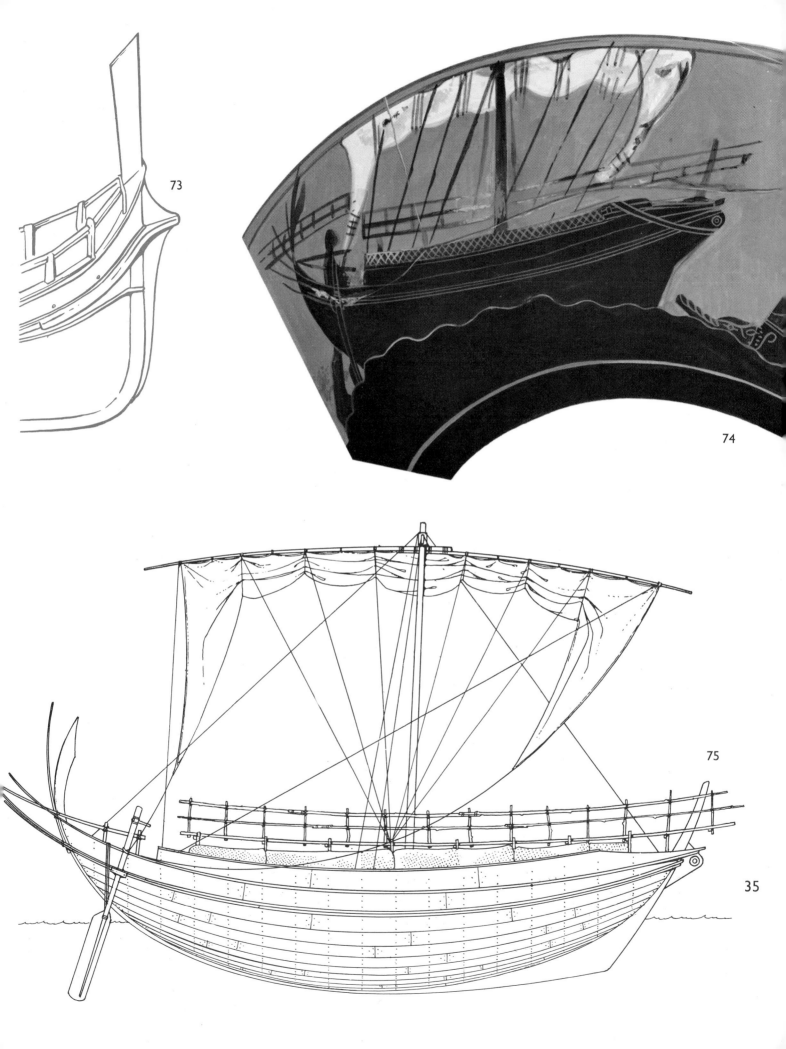

73

74

75

35

Greek biremes, 500 B.C.

The pictures of Greek warships found on vases and dishes from the sixth century B.C. are the lightest and most elegant craft we know of from classical times (76, 78, 79). They are decidedly built on ribs, and when Thucydides in his History of the Peloponnesian War says that the Corinthians were the first to make changes in the art of shipbuilding so that it conformed with what is usual today, we understand that it was the Corinthians who were the first to replace the dug-out warships with those built on ribs. We know that the vessels were so light that the crew, if necessary, could haul them onto the shore for the night, aft first of course.

For the shipbuilders it was a question of combining this lightness with great strength fore-and-aft so that the vessel could stand up to the shocks of ramming. The keel was the backbone of the vessel and it was further reinforced by the *storming bridge* which ran amidships from fore to aft (77). It seems as if the fore-post rose at the forward edge of the fighting bridge (78, 79) and it is possible that the ram itself was not an integral part of the construction of the keel but only nailed on so that it could be torn loose after a powerful ramming without too much harm being done to the hull. — This is speculation of course, but there is a great deal of speculating to be done when interpreting ancient pictures.

The end of the keel and wales, railing and outrigger lists and the rail of the helmsman's barrier were drawn

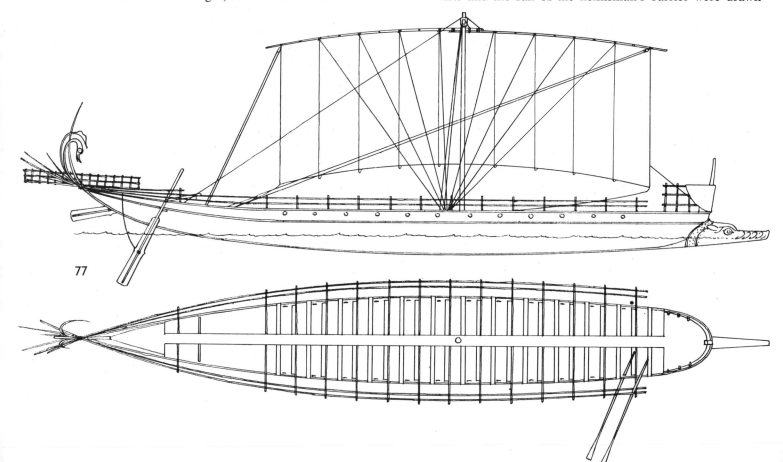

77

78

79

together in the stern like a spray of flowers. What looks like a ladder (74, 77, 78) is the brow. One picture (76) shows the oars resting directly on the railing. The outrigger indicates that the boat is a bireme, but for the moment only one bank of oars is in use. Another (79) shows oars passing through round holes in the side of the vessel and others resting on the outrigger.

The length of the hull in the reconstruction (77, 80) has been decided by the number of oarsmen, twenty-five on each side, and the space they would need. As they sat at different levels and at different distances from the sides of the vessel the seats could be placed closely together. The narrow stern could not have held oarsmen for the sake of balance. In this way the length, ram included, would have been about 80 feet and the beam a little over 10.

All pictures I know of biremes of those times have a mast, sometimes lowered (76). The broader beam permitted sailing; the sail was carried on a very slender yard and could be reefed and furled with brails. It is likely that the mast was always lowered when rowing into the wind.

80

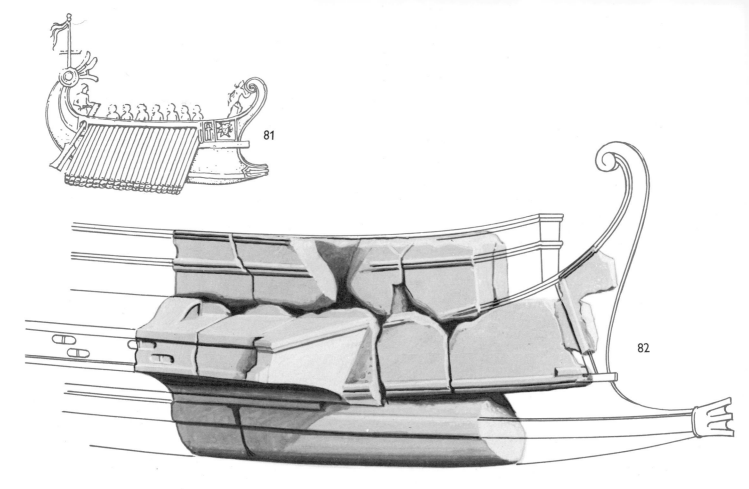

81

82

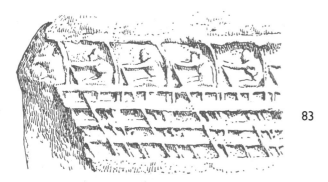

83

Greek triremes

During the thousands of years that different vessels have sailed the oceans of the world none has raised so many problems and caused so much disagreement as the *trireme*, the Greek galley with three banks of oars. Thucydides relates that the first triremes were built by the Corinthians about 260 years before his own time, in other words about the middle of the seventh century B.C., and he goes on to say: "But a little before the wars with the Persians and the death of Darius, the Sicilian tyrants and Corcyrans had many triremes. These

were the last of the great sea powers in Hellas before Xerxes' expedition. The Aeginians, Athenians and others had few ships, and most of these were of 50 oars. Only when Themistocles had persuaded the Athenians, while they were warring with Aegina and also expecting attack from the Persians, did they build warships with which they gave battle at sea. These ships were still only partially decked." — The combined Greek naval forces were victorious over the Persians at the Battle of Salamis in 480 B.C.

Before we approach the difficult problem of trying to form an idea of the appearance and functioning of a Greek trireme we must first study the little pictorial material at our disposal. A fragment of a relief in the Acropolis at Athens from the fifth century B.C. (83) shows — unfortunately with many different possibilities of interpretation — a section of a trireme directly from the side. As it is in a single plane it does not clearly show which of the horizontal lines represent the outrigger (all of them perhaps?) and which represent the hull itself. Between the oarsmen in the outermost row there are curved supports holding up a bridge. — In the Louvre the winged "Victory of Samothrace" stands on a marble pedestal shaped like the bow of a galley with manifest outriggers (82). The sculpture, however, is from the fourth century and probably represents a bireme.

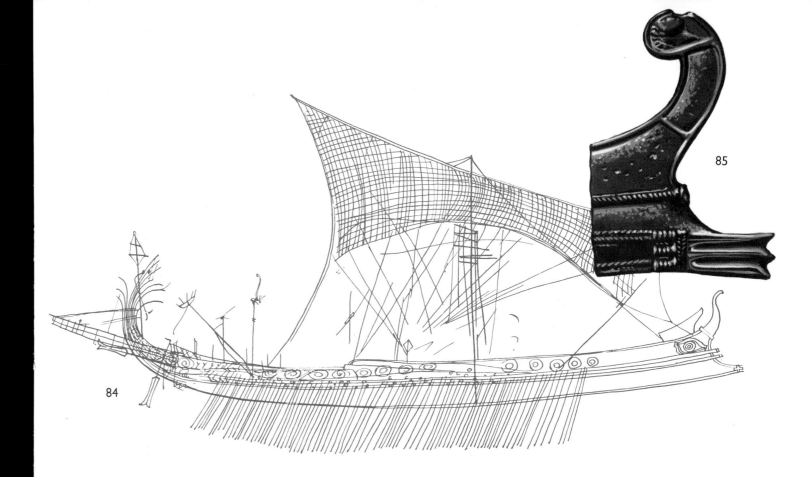

85

84

Two large carvings of classical warships have been found in the wall of a house on the island of Delos. In the one (84) it is easy to discern three banks of oars and above them a row of shields. A rock relief from Lindos on the island of Rhodes (86) shows the stern of a bireme or trireme with lifted rudder and seat for the commander, and a vase of Greek origin (90) found in southern Italy and dated to the fifth century shows curved supports which lead us to believe that there is an outrigger. — Two reliefs (81, 88) and the bronze model of a prow (85) are Roman, but as they seem so similar to their Greek prototypes they may help us further.

If we were to ask ourselves what the object of the trireme was, what reason there was to squeeze in a further bank of oarsmen on both sides, there can be but one answer: the constructors wanted to increase the speed, the forward thrust, the effect — preferably with as little loss in manoeuvrability as possible.

It is probable that the elegant and easily propelled biremes were found to be too light and fragile. Attempts had very likely been made to build heavy, powerful biremes but these can have proved themselves to be too slow just as the oarsmen had probably been increased to thirty or more on each side only to make the hull too long and difficult to manoeuvre. The idea of building a trireme, a vessel with the oars in three banks, and in

this way of increasing the forward thrust without making the ship particularly longer or so heavy that the extra oarsmen were a loss, was certainly not new when a man in Corinth finally solved the problem.

The Corinthian shipbuilder — as far as I see it — placed the thwarts at an angle, each running obliquely

86

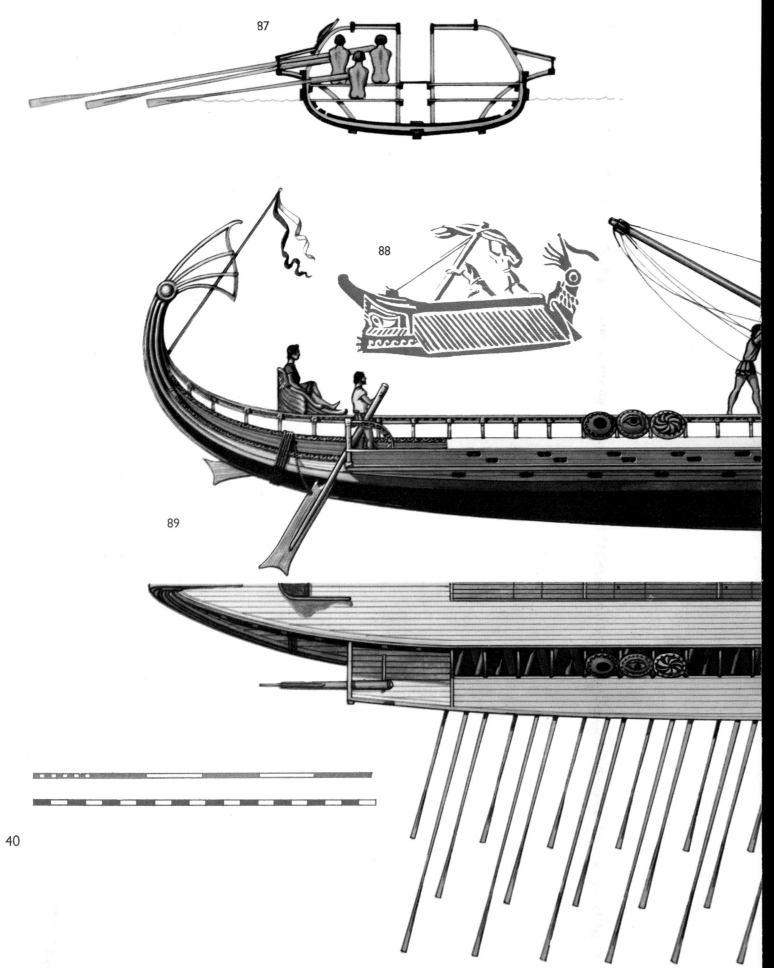

87

88

89

forwards and outwards from the centre-line of the vessel (89). Two oarsmen sat side by side on the upper bank of thwarts and only one on the lower, sitting in such a position that he could stretch his arms forward between both oarsmen in front of him (87). His oar rested in a hole in the side of the vessel itself while the upper bank of oars rested on the outrigger, the inner oarsman's somewhat higher up than the outer oarsman's. The outrigger itself, probably towards the beginning of the third century anyway, was planked both below and above (82).

The curved supports (82, 83, 87, 90) held up the fighting bridge, perhaps leaving a sunken passage in the centre. — Thucydides does say that the vessels were not completely decked in those days. — When an attack was being put in, the soldiers would be under shelter in the passage, and the oarsmen, hardly sufficiently though, would have been protected by the soldiers' shields which were hung over the openings between the supports.

The ram was an integral part of the hull, really consisting of the forward part of the keel and sturdy wales which ran together to a point (82, 97). The fore-post began at the point of the ram and swept backwards and upwards until it finally pointed forwards again. We are able to see the construction clearly in the remains of the Roman ships which lay at the bottom of Lake Nemi (97, 98). The stern was in the main as before, and keel, wales and all lists of the hull were joined together into something like a fishtail.

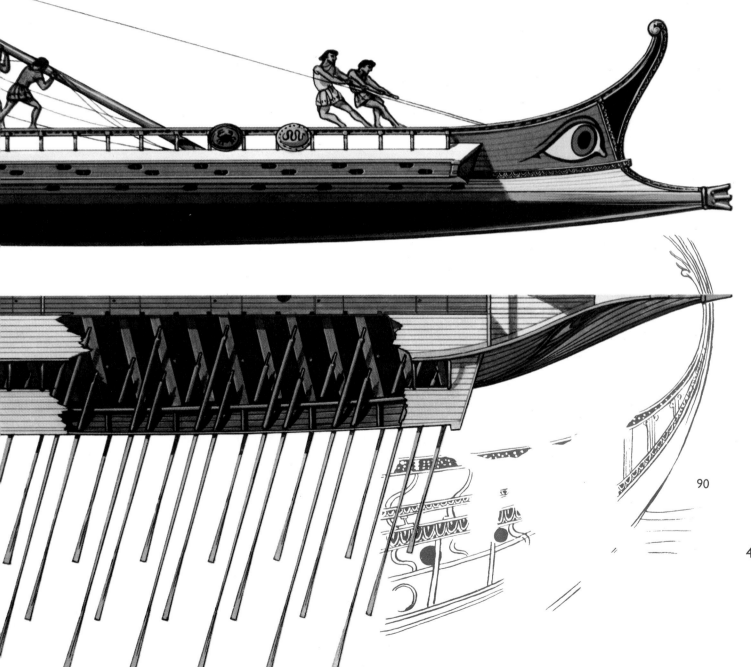

90

41

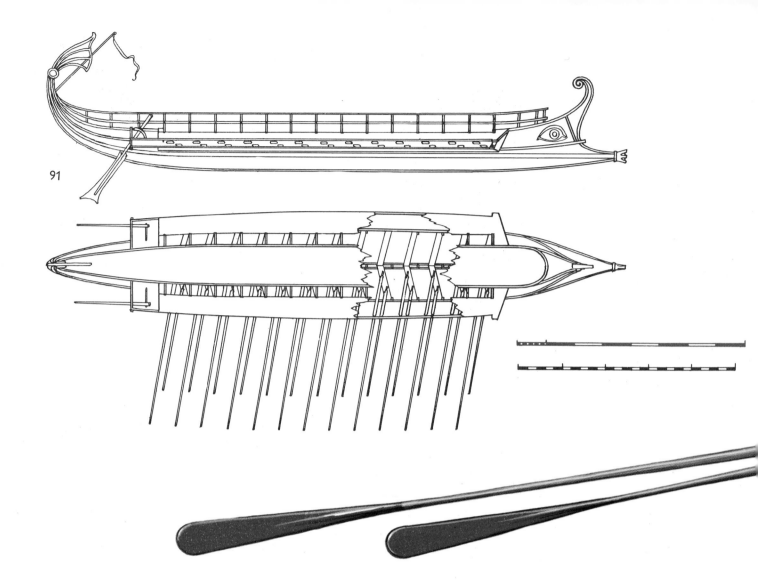

91

Greek bireme, fourth century

It is generally agreed that the pedestal to the "Victory of Samothrace" in the Louvre (82) represents the bow of a bireme and that the sculpture celebrates a victory at sea won by Demetrius Poliorcetes over Ptolemy in 306 B.C. This would mean that the trireme had not completely superseded the bireme. The situation of the oval openings for the oars in the outrigger indicate, however, that the bireme had undergone revolutionary change since the sixth century.

I believe that the seating arrangement of the trireme suggested a new form of construction in the old bireme. The triremes were expensive both to build and to man, and it would have required much training and art to row with the many, closely-set oars and to manoeuvre the long vessel. Now if the lower bank of oars, the one which had only one row of oarsmen, was done away with and

the remaining thwarts still be pointed forwards and outwards, the vessel could be shortened considerably and this would mean much improvement in manoeuvrability. The two oarsmen on the same seat would now be able to move closer together as no oarsman behind would need room for his arms. In this way the hull could be narrowed and thus made lighter without losing its strength. Furthermore when the passage between the fighting bridges was done away with the vessel would become completely decked — just as Thucydides writes that the ships of his time were.

According to the reconstruction (91, 92, 93) the fourth-century bireme with its fifty-two oarsmen was about 65 feet long and over 8 feet broad whereas the sixth-century biremes with fifty oarsmen were about 80 feet long and 10 feet broad. It is possible that the new type had become somewhat heavier in spite of this, but they were superior in strength and manoeuvrability.

42

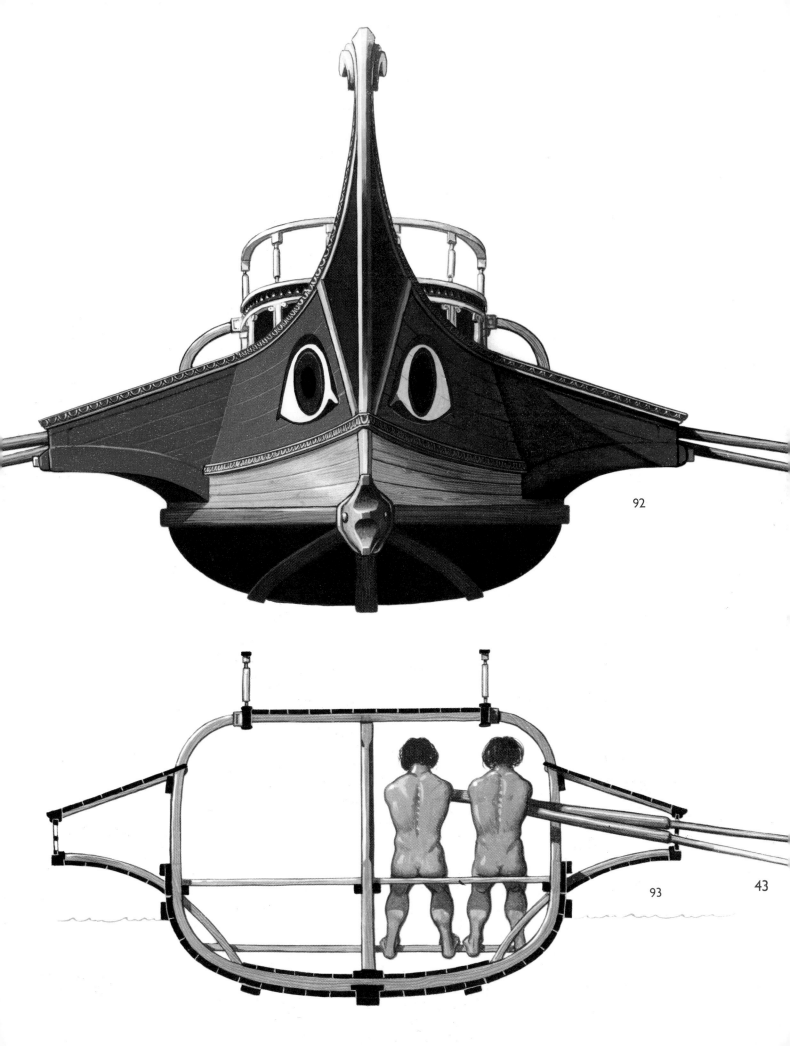

92

93

43

Quadriremes and quinqueremes

It is narrated that the Greeks at Syracuse in Sicily are to have built *quadriremes* and *quinqueremes,* in other words galleys with four or five banks of oars, as early as the beginning of the fourth century B.C., and not long after this we hear of a *fifteen-"banked" vessel.*

Now it is not necessary for us to understand that the oars of these vessels were situated in four or five or as many as fifteen different planes. It is probabie that the oars were never on more than three levels, but on the other hand it was not impossible to have more than one oarsman at each oar if only the vessels were made broad enough. If one was now to count all oarsmen in the same group it would be easy to come up to five or even fifteen-"banked" vessels. But the outermost oarsmen on the longest oar was of course — for each stroke — bound to run forwards and then backwards along the deck.

94

95

44

Roman warships

There are many pictures of Roman warships which are presumably meant to be triremes but few of them are so clear that we can decide to what extent they differ from the Greek ships. At the Vatican Museum in Rome there is a relief from the temple of Fortune at Praeneste (97) dated to 30 B.C. The relief contains a picture of what has usually been referred to as a *bireme* but which is now considered to be a trireme with the upper bank of oars shipped so that only the blades can be seen. It has also been suggested that the tower in the forebody is a part of the background, not belonging to the vessel at all, but another Roman relief at Madrid shows seven galleys of which all have a similar tower amidships or in the stern (96).

We do not need to assume that the vessel is a trireme however. It gives the appearance of being large and heavy, and it is possible that the artist's model was a ship broad across the beam with space for many men at each oar, that is was in fact a *quinquereme* or *septireme*, a five or seven-"banked" vessel or something even more imposing.

We may presume that the vessel was completely decked. The bow would have been open to give the oarsmen enough air, and it seems as if several planks immediately below the deck had simply been left out. The tower which would have afforded a good fighting bridge was most likely built of wood but painted so that it would give the impression of solid stone. The relief shows a spar jutting out obliquely over the bow. Other Roman portrayals enable us to understand that is is the mast for a small foresail called the *artemon*.

96

45

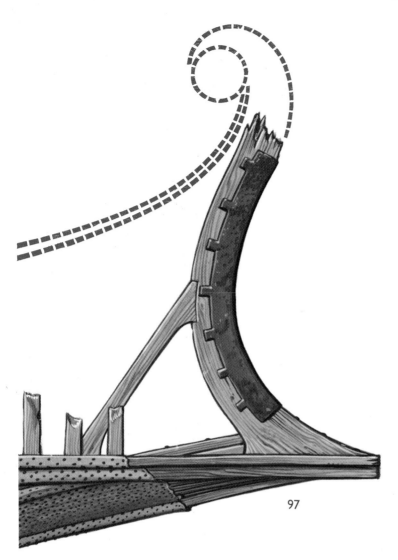

97

The mysterious Nemi ships

Some twelve miles south-east of Rome, high among the Albano mountains, is the Lago di Nemi. A rumour that two large ships were to lie at the bottom of this lake had been passed on from Roman times right through the Middle Ages, and historians relate that Cardinal Don Prospero Colonna made an unsuccessful attempt at salvaging the vessels from the depths in 1446. Many other efforts, just as unsuccessful, were made later until a full-scale operation was begun in 1927 to drain the lake in order to reach the ships. During the course of the work a long-forgotten Roman underground canal was rediscovered and the water led out through it. In 1932 the remains of two enormous hulls were hauled onto the shore from the mud.

The rumour ran that Caligula had ordered the ships built, but a large number of coins minted by many different emperors were found in and around them —

the most recent from 164 A.D. Nothing could be proved about the origin of the mysterious vessels. They were of about the same size, the one measuring nearly 235 feet long and 110 feet broad, the other 240 by 47.

The first ship, the broader one, had the appearance of a warship with ram and bow (97) shaped exactly as we see them in the old pictures. Nearly the whole of the submerged hull, a portion of the stern-post, the after-part of the starboard outrigger with the starboard rudder were also intact. The hull was extremely well built with closely set frames (100), and the planking — where the planks were partly pinned to each other and partly nailed to the frame — was completely sheathed in lead.

It is very likely that the ship had at least two decks. The lower, where the oarsmen worked, was at roughly the same level as the waterline and carried by beams which rested on supports from the *keelson* and the double *bilge-stringers* (102). Of the upper deck — or decks — there was no trace, but the broken frames ran so high up the sides that a further deck at this level would seem necessary. A reconstruction (98) shows what the shape of the hull was probably like.

The second ship, not so well preserved, seems to have had the classical shape (99) which we have already met with in Egypt and was still to be typical of Mediterranean traders for many hundreds of years to come. The most remarkable of the other finds made in connection with the ships were two anchors, one of which (101) had a shank and arms of wood while the stock was made of lead. Many such lead stocks had been found before, but they had not been understood until the finds at Nemi.

No one has been able to give a satisfactory explanation as to why these vast ships were built to voyage on the small lake high up in the mountains. It has been suggested that they were the result of imperial whim, that they were sorts of floating amusement parks for the court. It has been suggested that minor engagements were to have taken place between the vessels for entertainment of the great. And it has also been suggested that there was a connection between them and the temple situated on the shores in honour of the Tauric Diana.

Even if the secret of the ships lies hidden for ever, the remains brought up onto the shore have given us valuable information about classical shipbuilding, and we need not doubt the ability of the Romans to build the ships which the writings call fifteen-banked. — The Nemi Ships no longer exist. In the fighting which took place in Italy during the Second World War a fire, mysterious in itself, occurred in the museum where the ships were kept and they burned to ashes.

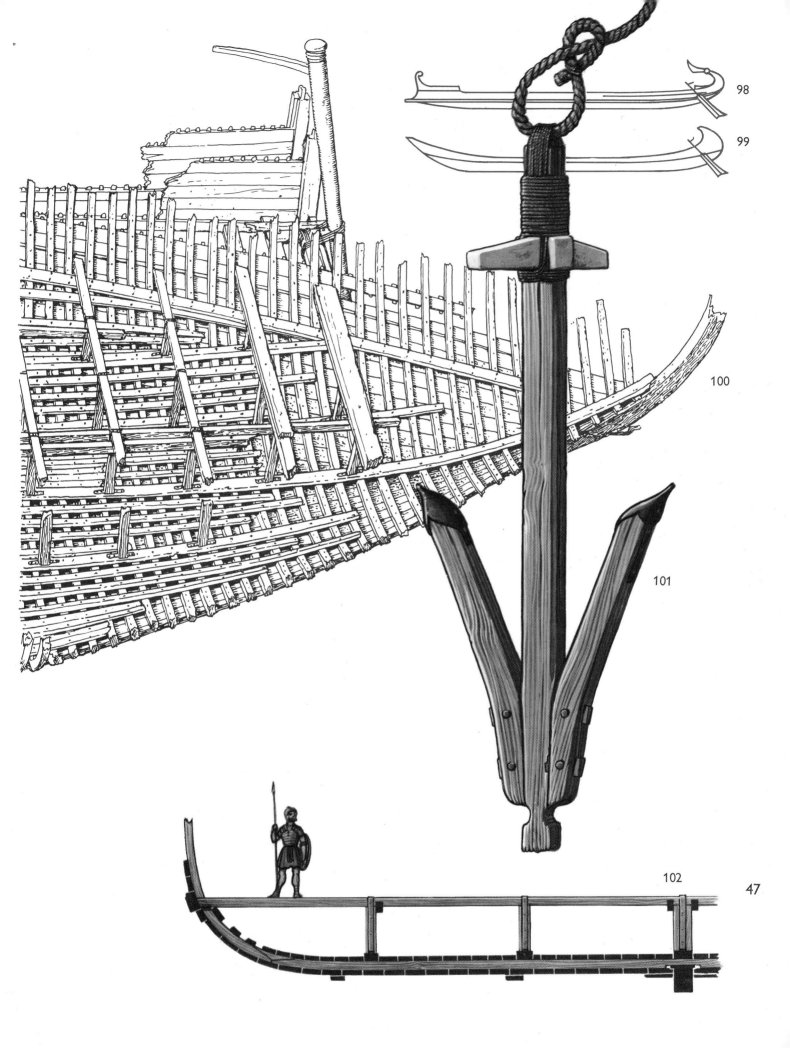

98

99

100

101

102

47

103

104

48

Roman merchantmen

There are numerous portrayals of merchantmen from the period when Rome ruled over land and sea, and with few exceptions they seem to be of the same basic type. They are broad round vessels with a forward-leaning fore-post and a high stern where the stern-post is bent inwards and often has the shape of a swan's neck.

The most detailed of the pictures was found at Ostia and is considered to be from the third century A.D. (103). We see two sturdy hulls with through deck-beams. The deck is extended in the stern to give room and support for the rudders. A thick forestay is stretched with *dead-eyes* and *lanyards* and the many shrouds also seem to be tightened with some system of lanyards. The brails run through rings sewn to the front of the mainsail, and two (or four?) triangle-shaped *topsails* are situated above the yard. The halyard-block for the foresail can be seen on the sloping foremast, and on the smaller vessel we can see two large blocks for the main halyard nailed to the mast.

Thus it is not difficult to imagine what a medium-sized trader (104) from the time of Septimus Severus of Caracalla looked like, and the pictures we have of vessels one hundred and fifty years older do not differ very much from these.

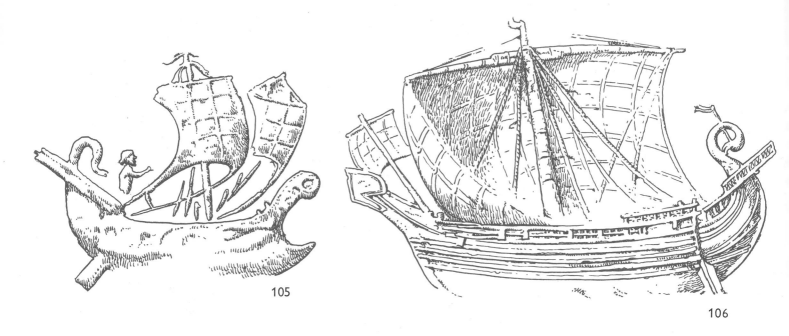

105

106

Roman merchantmen

Certain representations of Roman merchantmen, among them the small bronze relief (105) in the coin collection at Paris, still shows the remarkable ram or cutwater bow we saw on Cretan, Phoenician and Greek vessels, but which we have seen no trace of in the Mediterranean since. This relief — and others — also shows a foresail almost as large as the mainsail, but most predominating in the portrayals is the small foresail (artemon) the main purpose of which was to assist in steering. A sarcophagus from Sidon shows a vessel (106) very like the ships in Ostia (103). It is only the bow which is of a different shape, and we can imagine there being a platform farthest forward. A representation (107) from the second century A.D. shows a deckhouse on the foredeck, topsails — and a swan's head forward of the stern-post.

Roman grain ships

A ship which in its lifetime must have been of imposing dimensions is portrayed on a tombstone at Pompeii and is dated to 50 A.D. (108). Perhaps it was a similar vessel to the one that appeared one day about the middle of the second century in Pireus, the port of Athens, and created a sensation. The satirist Lucian saw the ship, interviewed its crew and wrote about it later with much enthusiasm: "What a tremendous vessel it was! 180 feet long, as the ship's carpenter told me, and more than a quarter of this across the beam, and over 44 feet from the deck to the deepest part of the hold. And the height of the mast, and the yard it bore, and the forestays that were necessary to keep it upright! And how the stern rose in a graceful curve ending in a gilt goose-head, in harmony with the equal curve of the bow and the fore-post with its picture of Isis, the goddess who had given the ship her name! All was unbelievable: the decoration, paintings, red topsail, the anchors with their windlasses, and the cabins in the stern. The crew was like an army. They told me she could carry enough grain to satisfy every mouth in Athens for a whole year. And the whole fortune of the ship is in the hands of a little old man who moves the great rudders with a tiller no thicker than a stick. They pointed him out to me, a little white-haired,

50

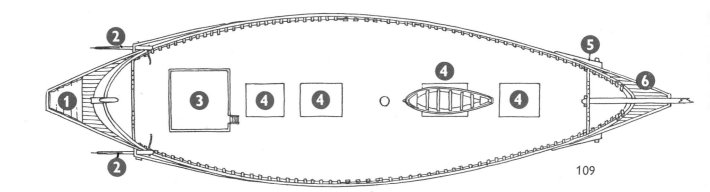

109

107

108

almost bald fellow — I think they called him Heron."
— Starting from the relief at Pompeii (108) and Lucian's description we can attempt to reconstruct such a grain ship (109, 110) over 175 feet long, perhaps 45 to 50 feet across the beam and over 42 feet deep from deck to keel.

1. A balcony jutting over the stern is covered with an awning for the comfort of the captain and the most prominent passengers. 2. The long rudders can be hoisted out of the water with tackles. 3. Deckhouse with cabins for the officers and important passengers. 4. Hatches to the holds. 5. Cat-head. 6. Gallery round the bow. 7. Mainsail with brails. 8. Topsail in front of the topping lifts. 9. Artemon with brails.

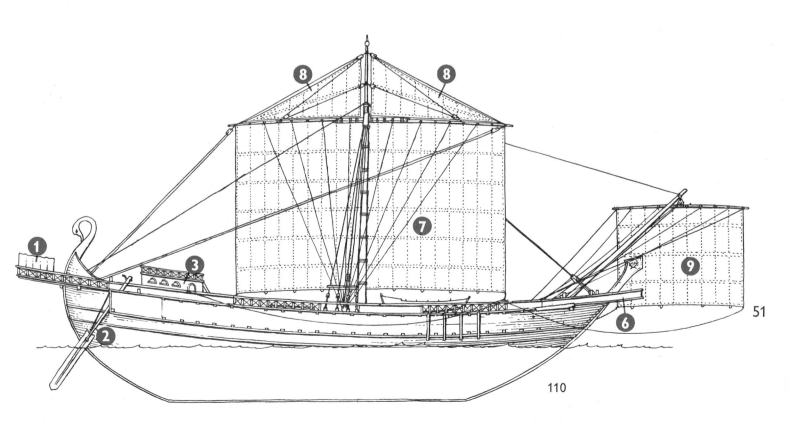

51

110

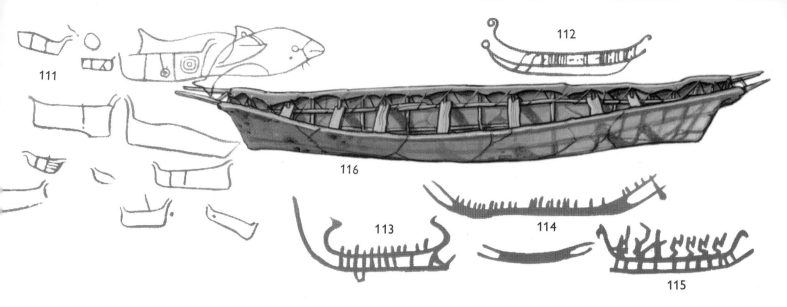

Scandinavia

Naturally it was not only around the Mediterranean that men built ships and devoted themselves to seafaring in the dim and distant past. Water craft of different sorts must have been built in all parts of the world where people lived near water even if we have no concrete evidence of this in the form of pictures and remains.

The Scandinavian rock-carvings, however, which are spread all over Norway and Sweden and a part of Denmark form a unique archive of boat pictures from the Stone, Bronze and Iron Ages, from 2000 to about 200 B.C. They are usually divided into two groups, the N. Scandinavian which were probably done during the Stone Age, and the S. Scandinavian, the majority of which are from the Bronze Age. Generally speaking it may be said that the S. Scandinavian boat-carvings all present similar features: curved ends often finishing in animal heads, curved rams or runners, and frequently transverse stripes.

These pictures have been interpreted as rafts with platforms, as canoes with outriggers. Similarities with the oldest Greek rowing craft have been remarked and early connections with Mediterranen peoples suggested. Finally some have explained that they are not boats at all but sledges! I do not believe in any of these explanations.

It was suggested early on that the pictures at Evenhus in N. Trøndelag in Norway (111) and other of the N. Scandinavian carvings portray hide boats, roughly similar to the Greenland *umiak* (116) and the Siberian *baidarka*. In these craft the railings run out beyond the ends to form "handles" — poles to grasp when the light boat was borne up on land.

The *Hjortspring boat* (124), called after the farm on the Danish island of Als where it was found, is a wooden craft somewhat over 43 feet long and over 6 feet wide, built about 200 B.C. It is very reminiscent of some of the rock-carving boats (114). The construction has caused much surprise, especially the shapes of the ends which do not appear at all natural for a boat of wood. It is the oldest find made in Scandinavia of a boat built of wood, and I believe that it was made with a hide boat as a model.

But let us return to the type represented by the oldest carvings, the umiak. When it was found necessary to build such a boat larger, for longer journeys, to take more cargo, the problem of its becoming too heavy immediately arose. It was no longer possible to carry it on shore, and had it been dragged the hide would have been damaged. What then could have been more natural than for the bottom to be protected by a runner of wood, a branch reaching from bow to stern? A runner curved anyway in the bow would have been chosen to make it easier to haul the boat on shore. And when it

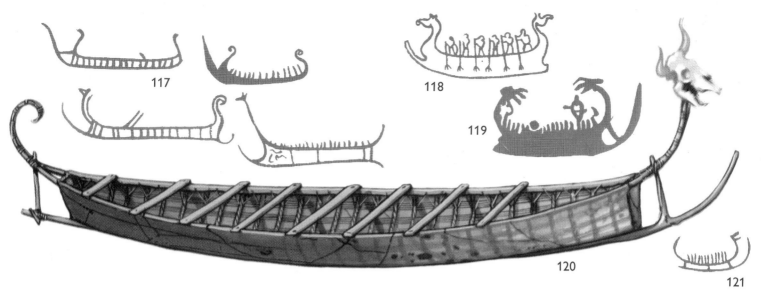

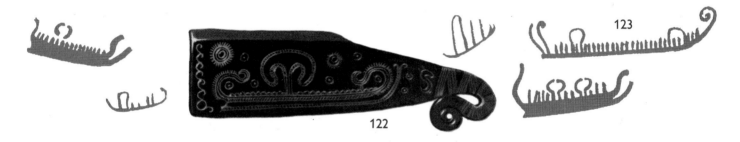

was no longer possible to lift the craft it would have been natural for the railings to be joined fore and aft, these junctions at the same time affording a better point of fixture for the runner (120).

The boat which we have allowed to take shape in this way is in complete accord with most of the different rock-carvings. What were earlier considered to be supports for a platform are quite simply the frames of the hide boat. Anyone who has seen a umiak with the

unknown reason have been passed on through the centuries. There can be no doubt that hide boats were the sea-going vessels of the North during the Stone and Bronze Ages. Umiaks and Irish *curraghs* have proved the capabilities of the hide boat in rough sea and breakers.

Some of the rock-carving boats (123) and perhaps even more clearly a picture on a bronze razor (122) found at Honum in Denmark present features which

sun behind knows how the ribs appear as dark stripes along the side of the boat. And no boatbuilder in the world would hit on the idea of building a wooden craft like the *Hjortspring boat* if he had not had a similar hide boat as a model. Development proceeded at a snail's pace, and the *Hjortspring boat* is only a single example of many thousands where details for some seemingly

have sometimes been interpreted as sails. The way I see it the "sail" on the razor boat most approximates a tree, and in my childhood it was usual, on longer trips in a rowing-boat on the Finnish lakes, to take along leafy branches which could be stood upright in the boat and used as sails if and when the wind blew from the right direction.

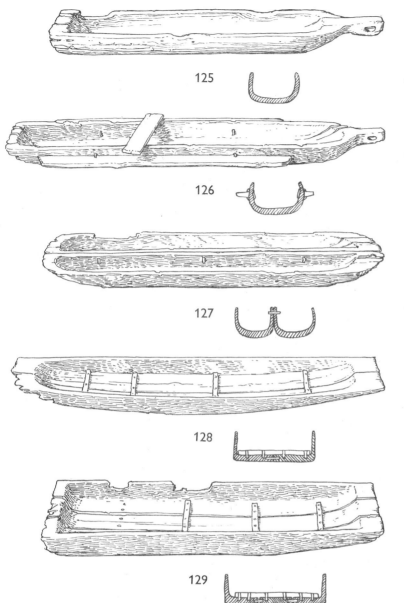

Dug-outs

The hollowed-out tree-trunk, the dug-out in its various forms, is perhaps an older type of craft in Scandinavia than the hide boat, but its use would have been restricted to lakes, rivers and sheltered bays. It may be objected that dug-outs in the South cross large stretches of water, but no dug-outs light enough to ride the large waves met with at sea have been found in the North — and outriggers proper are unknown in Europe.

Thousands of dug-outs have been found in marshes and lakes all over Scandinavia, the oldest from the Stone Age and the most recent from our own times, varying in shape and appearance, but of the same basic type. When there were not enough massive trunks the simple dug-out (125) was often too unstable, and different methods of making the boats broader and thus stronger were gradually developed. The hull was broadened by stitching on an "outrigger" (126), two separate hulls were joined together (127), the boat was built in two halves which were joined together with pins and stretchers (128), and finally boats were made with three, four or five boards side by side (129). A more advanced form of the dug-out was still being made at the beginning of this century in Finland. It was made of an aspen log and to give it a suitably broad beam the hollowed-out hull was steamed over a fire until it became soft, after which the sides were pressed outwards. Several sturdy naturally-formed ribs were attached to retain the shape and a plank was stitched to either side to raise the freeboard (130).

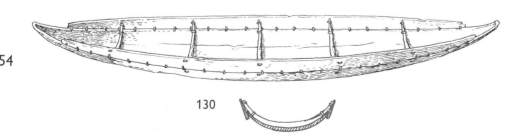

130

Wooden constructions

The *Hjortspring boat* (124, 133) with its peculiarities was the result of a very skilful builder's work. It is a round-bottomed boat made of five overlapping planks stitched together, midships 20 ins broad and ⅝ ins thick, which are joined to two end-pieces each hewn from a solid block. The bottom plank projects like the end of a runner outside the boat proper, and between this runner and the elongated "noses" of the end-pieces these remarkable vertical end-posts are fitted. When hewing the planks cleats were left into which thin ribs were attached with bass binding (133). Ten thwarts in the narrow boat gave room for twenty paddlers, and it is believed that the craft was used for warlike purposes.

The remains of two boats which were uncovered at North Ferriby on the Humber in 1937 are believed to be of a somewhat later date. The more intact of the *Ferriby boats* (131) seems to have been a flat-bottomed craft roughly 45 feet long and 7½ feet across. The bottom consisted of three oak planks set edge to edge and the sides were three planks high. The planks fitted each other well and were stitched together with yew withes. Battens were placed over the seams which had been caulked with moss. The bottom was reinforced by cross-pieces which passed through cleats left for the purpose. We do not know of such a method of building either from Mediterranean countries or Scandinavia, but after all, there is little we do know of the boatbuilding of northern Europe in those times.

One boat, more than 23½ feet long, found at Björke in Sweden shows a stage in the development of the Scandinavian boat type (132, 134). It is more primitively

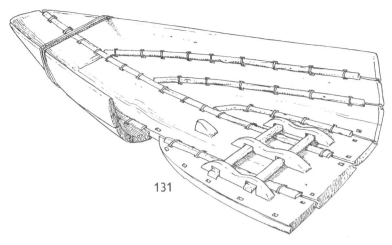

131

built than the boat from Hjortspring, but as a type it is more advanced, the find, moreover, being dated to 100 A.D. The bottom board is a hollowed-out log, 2 feet 4 ins wide in the middle and slowly tapering off towards the ends. The sides are fastened to the bottom and its extensions at the ends with iron rivets. When this had been done a further end-piece was riveted to the extension. Cleats had also been left in the planks of this boat and the six sturdy naturally-formed ribs are stitched to the cleats with withes, but up by the railing the ribs are fastened with rivets.

Both the *Hjortspring* and *Björke boats* are *clinker-built*, the edges of the upper planks projecting over the lower, as opposed to all the vessels we know from the Mediterranean which are *carvel-built* — with the planks edge to edge. Clinker-built craft have certainly been found in certain other parts of the world, on the Ganges in India for instance, but clinker-building was still to be a characteristic of Scandinavian shipbuilding for nearly the whole of the Middle Ages.

132

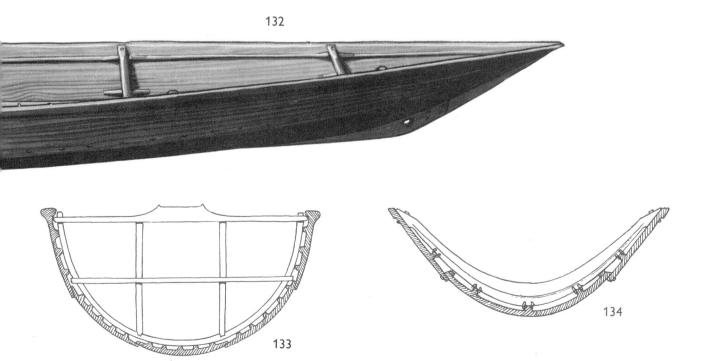

133

134

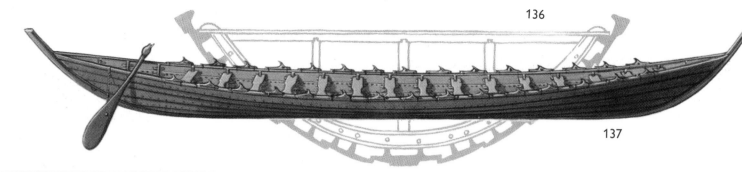

136

137

135

The Nydam and Kvalsund boats

The Roman historian Tacitus writes about 100 A.D. that the vessels of the Sviones or Scandinavians, as opposed to the Roman, are alike at the ends. Unfortunately there are no finds of any larger Scandinavian ships from that period, but the large boat which was excavated in 1863 from Nydam peat bog in Schleswig and dated to about 300 A.D. presents the characteristics mentioned by Tacitus. It is clinker-built of oak timbers and was meant to be rowed (136, 137), 75 feet between the ends and 10 feet 8 ins across the beam. It has no keel in the modern sense, only a bottom board, somewhat wider and thicker than the other planks which were five on each side. As the boat is built acutely V-shaped the riveted planks give satisfactory strength fore-and-aft, but the boat must have been unstable for when it was found it had a ballast of a ton of stones. The frames are bound to cleats with bass as in the earlier finds.

There are two boat finds from the seventh century which were made at Kvalsund in Norway in 1920 of which the larger (138, 139, 140) was about 60 feet long and 10½ feet wide. The method of building this vessel is close to that of the Viking ships and the bottom board is so formed that it may be designated keel. The builder was able to make the hull more U-shaped amidships

138

139

and in this way, even without ballast, obtained a sturdier craft. A picture on a stone in Bro on Gotland from the fifth century (135) has a great deal in common with the Kvalsund boat. There are portrayals of Scandinavian sailing vessels from as early as the sixth century. The Kvalsund boat would also have been well able to carry mast and sail.

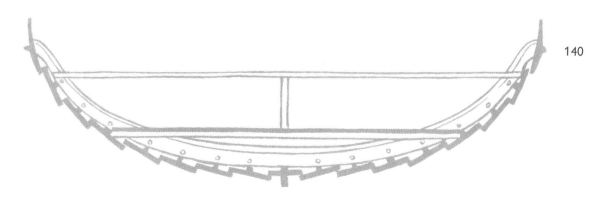

140

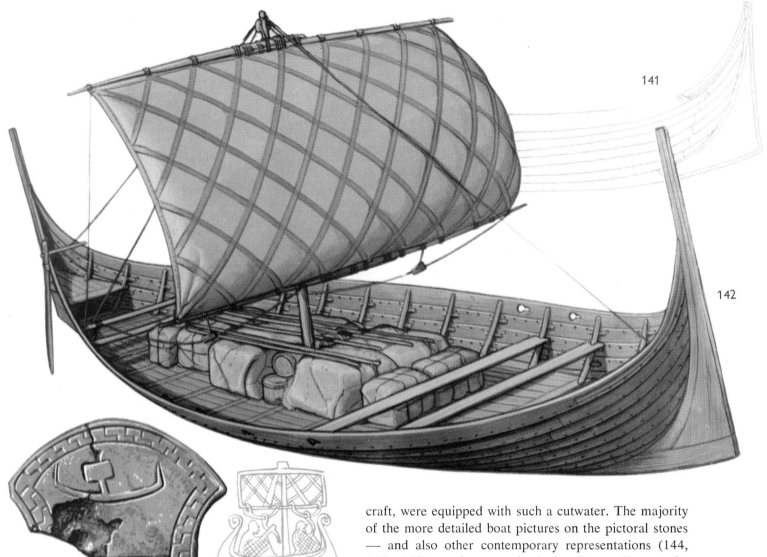

141

142

143

144

Eighth century merchantmen

The early Gotland pictorial stones — from the seventh and eighth centuries — already seem to show two different types of boat: those where the sterns form a sharp angle with the keel (143, 145), and those where the sterns curve gracefully up from the keel (144). It might have been thought that certain pictures (143, 145) were only badly drawn were it not for a carving found on the under side of a deck plank on the *Oseberg ship* which gives an almost naturalistic view of the bow of a vessel (141). And there we find almost the same broad cutwater that we have seen earlier in the Mediterranean.

It is therefore believed that many vessels which sailed Scandinavian waters, especially the traders which were more dependant on good sailing ability than fighting-

craft, were equipped with such a cutwater. The majority of the more detailed boat pictures on the pictoral stones — and also other contemporary representations (144, 147, 159) — have a checked sail, usually on the diagonal. It is known that the Scandinavians commonly made their sails of homespun which, especially when wet, became weak and stretchable. This is why it is believed that the diagonal lines represent reinforcements of double-thickness homespun, of linen or of leather. It also seems fairly clear from the pictures that a yard at the foot of the sail was used, at an early stage anyway, and that the sheets were attached to *bridles* on it (144).

Proceeding from these pictures and from earlier and later boat-finds we are able to form an approximate idea of what a small merchantman from the seventh or eighth century looked like (142). An open hull where the cargo rested on the floor amidships. Room for eight oarsmen — and it was seldom that a trader had such a large crew. Homespun sail with leather reinforcements. And the Scandinavian rudder, a long oar on the right side of the vessel, the side to which the oar gave the name "steer-board", i.e. *starboard*.

145

146

147

58

148

149

The Oseberg ship

The two important finds which, better than any others or any pictures, have given us an idea of the ships of Viking times were made in 1880 on Gokstad farm near Sandefjord and in 1904 on Oseberg farm near Tønsberg in Norway. Both ships were very well preserved and now stand fully restored in their own large museum outside Oslo. The *Gokstad ship* is dated to the tenth century and the *Oseberg ship* is considered to be a hundred years older.

The *Oseberg ship* is 70 feet long and nearly 17 feet across the beam. It is built of oak throughout on a robust keel and planked with twelve planks on each side (148, 150). The tenth plank is stouter than the others and L-shaped. The upper ends of the ribs are riveted to the ninth and tenth plank but are otherwise bound in the old manner to the other planks and rest loose on the keel. The rudder has the same construction as that of the *Kvalsund boats*. A withe passes through the blade of the oar and a rounded block and is fastened on the inside to an extra strong rib while the fixture at the railing is a plaited leather thong. The deep and very effective rudder is easily managed with the short tiller.

The ship could be rowed with fifteen pairs of oars and could also be sailed. The mast is situated a little forward of amidships on a stock lying directly on the keel with grooves cut in it for two ribs. The *mast partners*, open aft to facilitate raising the mast, lie across four deck planks, and the deck-beam which runs across just forward of the mast is bent upwards to give support to the partners. The deck is laid between the beams and is raised both fore and aft to a platform, the so-called *lyfting*.

The ends of the ship and a large number of the household utensils and other objects are very richly decorated (145, 148, 149), and it is from these decorations that it has been possible to date the find. The head of a beast (146) decorating a bedpost gives us an idea of what the dragon's heads that were placed in the bows of the fighting-ships when the Vikings closed for battle might have looked like. The *Oseberg ship* was no fighting vessel, however, more a pleasure vessel, and in shape a small coastal vessel of the sort that was called a *karv*.

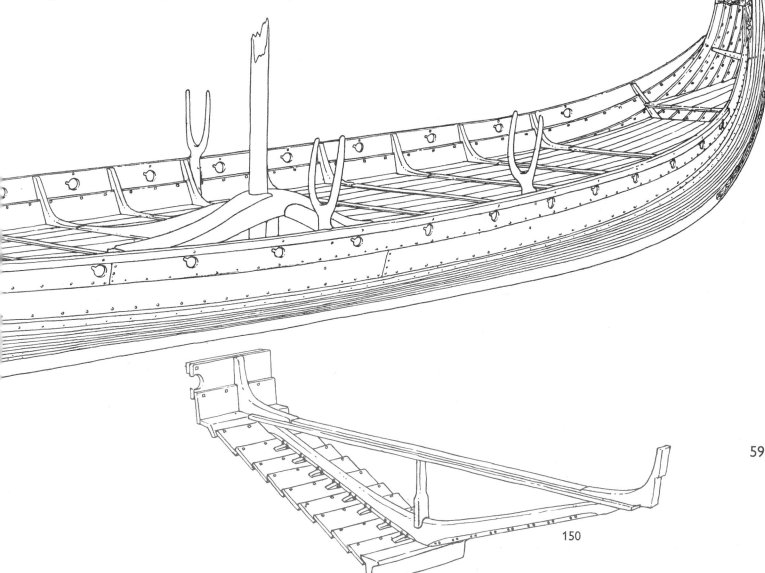

150

59

The Gokstad ship

The ship from Gokstad is larger, sturdier and more intended for sailing in open waters. It measures 76½ feet from stem to stern, and is over 17 feet broad at its widest point, yet regarding size and type is still no more than a coastal vessel, a *karv*. It has been calculated that it would have weighed some 20 tons fully equipped, and like the *Oseberg ship* is built of oak with sixteen planks on each side (151, 152, 153).

Neither of the ships shows any trace of thwarts for the oarsmen and it is unthinkable that they stood to row as the holes for the oars are situated so low down. It is possible that they sat on loose benches or chests (153), it is also possible that the benches were removed when the ships were placed in the burial mounds

and loaded with household utensils which were presumably considered to be of more importance than benches for the final voyage.

We can see that the holes for the oars, sixteen on each side, may be covered by small wooden discs so that the water would not gush in when the ship heeled under sail. — Underneath the railing there is a narrow strip of planking with square holes. This is where the shields were hung as a decoration on the outside of the vessel. When the ship was excavated in the burial mound 32 shields were hanging on each side, and since that time they have dogged nearly every picture of a Viking ship under sail. But we can be certain that they only hung there when the vessel was shown off and only in calm weather otherwise the waves would have washed them away. For the *Gokstad ship* could sail

151

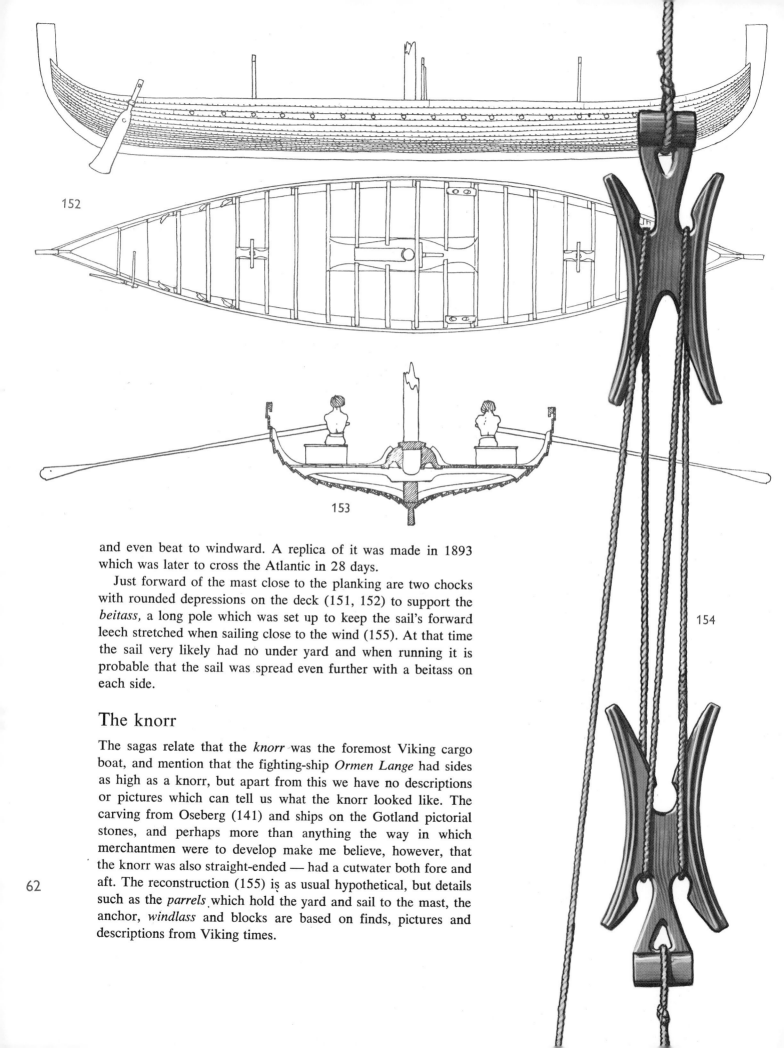

152

153

and even beat to windward. A replica of it was made in 1893 which was later to cross the Atlantic in 28 days.

Just forward of the mast close to the planking are two chocks with rounded depressions on the deck (151, 152) to support the *beitass,* a long pole which was set up to keep the sail's forward leech stretched when sailing close to the wind (155). At that time the sail very likely had no under yard and when running it is probable that the sail was spread even further with a beitass on each side.

The knorr

The sagas relate that the *knorr* was the foremost Viking cargo boat, and mention that the fighting-ship *Ormen Lange* had sides as high as a knorr, but apart from this we have no descriptions or pictures which can tell us what the knorr looked like. The carving from Oseberg (141) and ships on the Gotland pictorial stones, and perhaps more than anything the way in which merchantmen were to develop make me believe, however, that the knorr was also straight-ended — had a cutwater both fore and aft. The reconstruction (155) is as usual hypothetical, but details such as the *parrels* which hold the yard and sail to the mast, the anchor, *windlass* and blocks are based on finds, pictures and descriptions from Viking times.

154

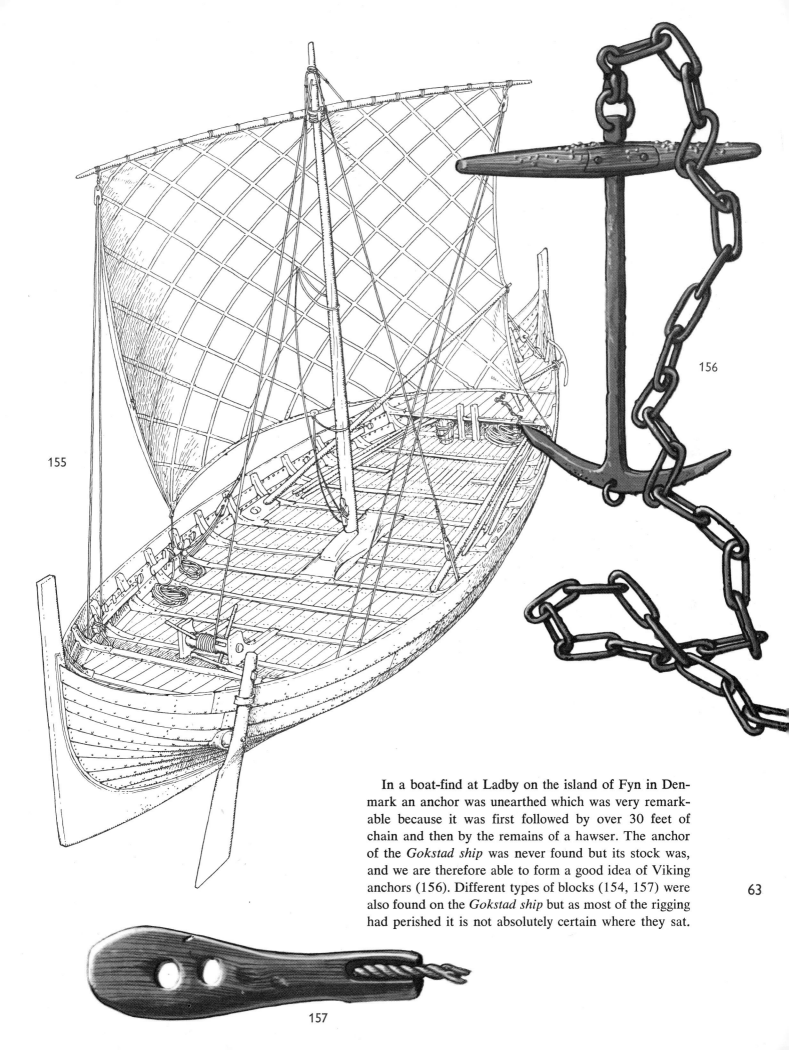

155

156

In a boat-find at Ladby on the island of Fyn in Denmark an anchor was unearthed which was very remarkable because it was first followed by over 30 feet of chain and then by the remains of a hawser. The anchor of the *Gokstad ship* was never found but its stock was, and we are therefore able to form a good idea of Viking anchors (156). Different types of blocks (154, 157) were also found on the *Gokstad ship* but as most of the rigging had perished it is not absolutely certain where they sat.

63

157

158

159

Drakkars and long ships

During the Viking period, and perhaps even earlier, the size of a ship was measured by the number of *rooms* as they called them — the number of spaces between each deck beam. Each of these rooms on a fighting-ship meant a pair of oars, and for each pair of oars there was a thwart. — *Ledung* is an old Norse word which partly meant war service and partly the manned naval force the various provinces had to put at the disposal of the king. It appears from the old law books that these ledung ships were usually *twenty-roomed,* thus being propelled by forty oars. But they also mention twenty-five and thirty-roomed vessels for fifty and sixty oarsmen. All of these were designated *long ships* as opposed to the merchantmen which were shorter and rounder.

The ship which in Norway was called *skeid* often seems to have been 32-roomed or even larger, and is sometimes referred to as a *drakkar,* the very largest fighting-vessel. *Ormen Lange,* Olav Tryggvason's famous drakkar, was 34-roomed and Earl Håkon's ship is stated as being 40-roomed, an eighty-oared vessel. The largest ship mentioned in the sagas is Canute's drakkar of 60 rooms. But it occasionally happens that the sagas exaggerate. The distance between the holes for the oars on the *Gokstad ship* is 38½ ins. If we try to calculate the length of the long ships from this we find that a 20-roomed vessel would have been about 100 feet long and *Ormen Lange* 150 feet long. But King Canute's phantom drakkar would have measured over 260 feet from stem to stern.

All we know of the long ships comes from pictures, from Gotland pictorial stones (159) and from the Bayeux tapestry (160). A terrifying dragon's head has been found in the estuary of the Scheldt and is most certainly from a Viking ship. Arnold Jarlaskald in his verse eulogy on the expedition of Magnus the Good to Denmark says that the ships were decorated with gilt heads, and that from the mast tops "the gold shone like fire in the sun". Gilt weather-vanes from Viking times have in actual fact been found (162).

We have to imagine the long ships as an enlarged type of Gokstad ship, the largest perhaps somewhat narrower in proportion. The dragon heads were detachable and it was forbidden to carry them by law when a ship neared the shores of home. It is possible that other, less terrifying decorations were set up. The Bayeux tapestry shows ships with painted sides and coloured sails, and we know that kings' ships often had linen sails of different colours, sometimes embroidered, sometimes with applications of silk. William the Conqueror's ship *Mora* (161) carried at the masthead something that has been said to be a lantern.

There are pictures from as early as the eighth century showing *bowlines* running from the leeches to the fore-post which replace the beitass in keeping the sail from sagging on the tack. We also see a raised platform in the forepeak, which was later to develop into a "castle", and there is also a strange system of sheets in bridle after bridle that was soon to disappear (159, 163), presumably intended to stretch the weak homespun sail evenly.

SÆ:-

HIC EXEVNT: CABA

160

161

162

65

163

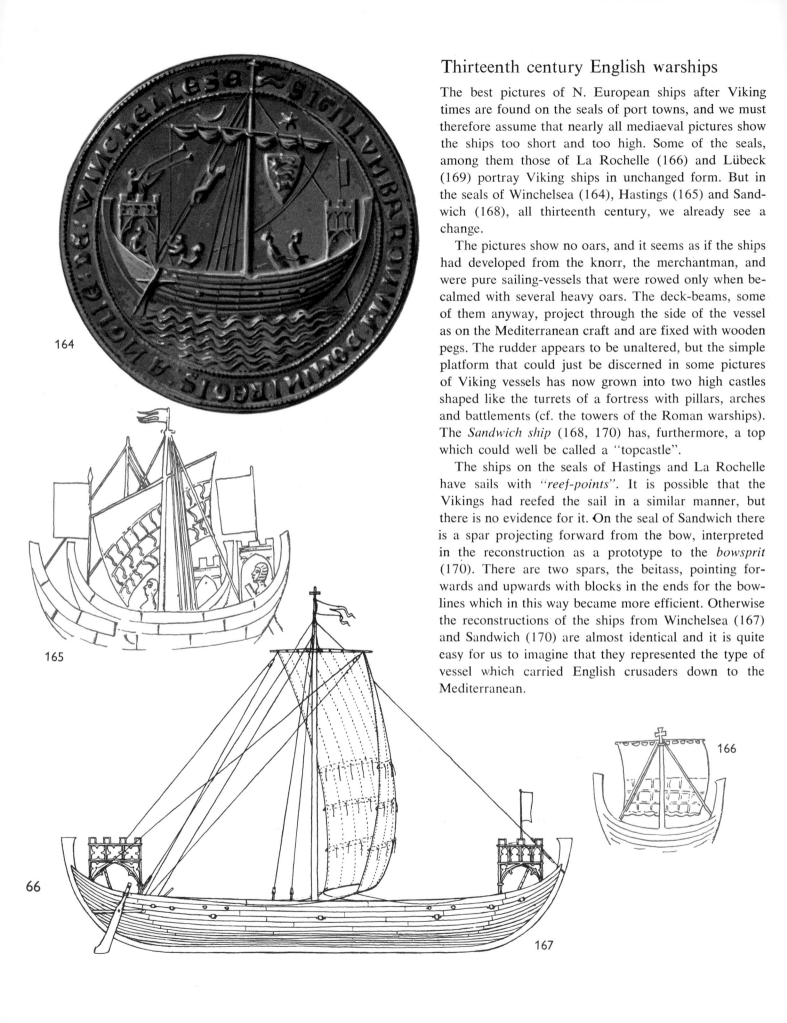

Thirteenth century English warships

The best pictures of N. European ships after Viking times are found on the seals of port towns, and we must therefore assume that nearly all mediaeval pictures show the ships too short and too high. Some of the seals, among them those of La Rochelle (166) and Lübeck (169) portray Viking ships in unchanged form. But in the seals of Winchelsea (164), Hastings (165) and Sandwich (168), all thirteenth century, we already see a change.

The pictures show no oars, and it seems as if the ships had developed from the knorr, the merchantman, and were pure sailing-vessels that were rowed only when becalmed with several heavy oars. The deck-beams, some of them anyway, project through the side of the vessel as on the Mediterranean craft and are fixed with wooden pegs. The rudder appears to be unaltered, but the simple platform that could just be discerned in some pictures of Viking vessels has now grown into two high castles shaped like the turrets of a fortress with pillars, arches and battlements (cf. the towers of the Roman warships). The *Sandwich ship* (168, 170) has, furthermore, a top which could well be called a "topcastle".

The ships on the seals of Hastings and La Rochelle have sails with *"reef-points"*. It is possible that the Vikings had reefed the sail in a similar manner, but there is no evidence for it. On the seal of Sandwich there is a spar projecting forward from the bow, interpreted in the reconstruction as a prototype to the *bowsprit* (170). There are two spars, the beitass, pointing forwards and upwards with blocks in the ends for the bowlines which in this way became more efficient. Otherwise the reconstructions of the ships from Winchelsea (167) and Sandwich (170) are almost identical and it is quite easy for us to imagine that they represented the type of vessel which carried English crusaders down to the Mediterranean.

164

165

166

66

167

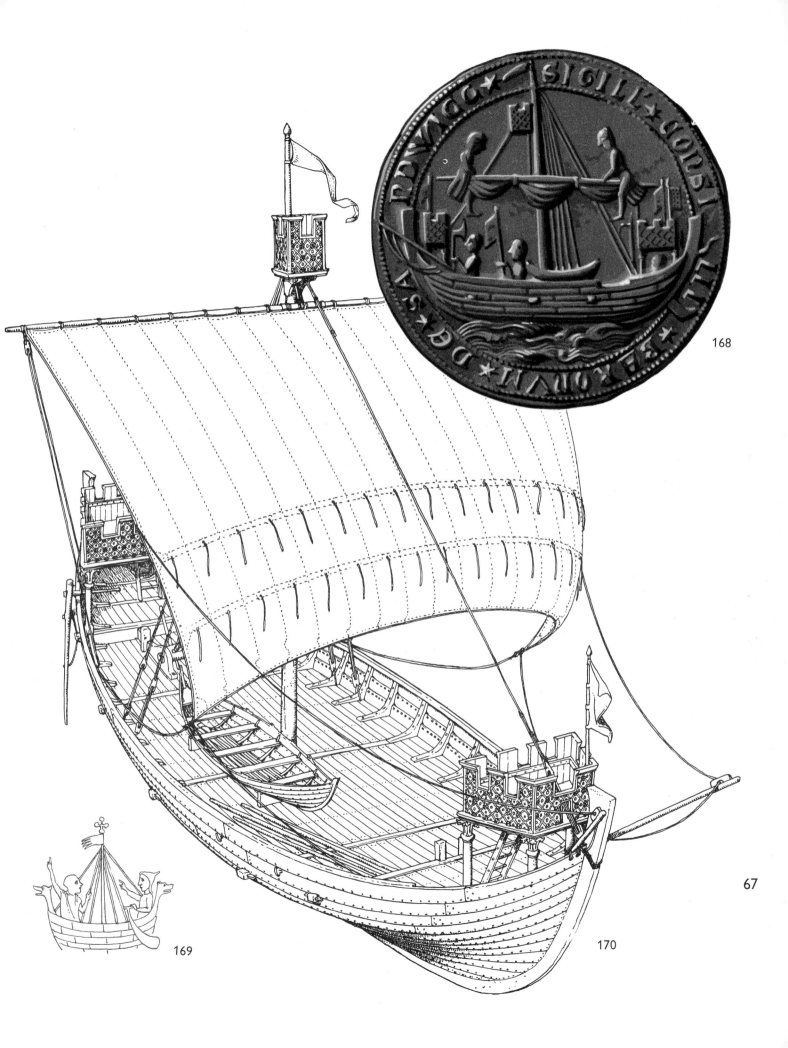

168

169

170

171

173

Ships from the Cinque Ports, 1284

A miniature in a manuscript which is said to have been made in the crusader port of Acre in Palestine in 1279 for Queen Eleonora of Castile shows a northern ship with the castles extending to the end-posts and with a large "topcastle" (171). In this picture we are already able to discern a certain development which we are later to see so much more clearly in the picture of the ship on the seal of Dover, dated to 1284 (172). Dover was one of the strongly defended port towns that together with Sandwich, Hythe, Romney and Hastings formed the five Cinque Ports. These towns — and later Winchelsea and Rye — had been given certain rights on condition that they equipped a number of ships, and these ships sailed under a mutual flag.

The ship on the seal of Dover shows us this flag, but other details are of more interest. The fore and after castles have now been extended right over the ends, perhaps now blending more harmoniously with the hull. It also seems as if there is a fully developed bowsprit, as in the reconstruction (173), and we can imagine the bowlines running through a block at its end. The bowsprit carries a leafy branch, perhaps as a sign that the ship is on peaceful business. But it is nevertheless a ship from the dim past with a Viking rudder. The engraver who made the matrix of the seal perhaps did not consider that the impression would show the rudder on the wrong side — it may be presumed that the rudder was always situated to starboard. The word *port* for the other side was so called because it was this less fragile side that was turned to the quay in port.

174

175

176

The stern-rudder

The oldest-known picture of a vessel with a *stern-rudder* is to be found in a relief on the font in Winchester Cathedral (176), and is considered to be Belgian work from about 1180. Scholars, however, are not quite agreed about the date nor that the picture in actual fact represents a vessel with a stern-rudder. Especially those who believe that the stern-rudder first came into use on the *Hansa cogs* assert that the rudder of the Winchester ship is merely a broad side-rudder. It cannot be denied that its leading edge projects in front of the stern-post.

At Fide Church on Gotland there is a picture carved in the plaster of the wall (174) which on good authority is considered to date from the early thirteenth century showing quite undisputably a vessel with a stern-rudder. The tiller is drawn at an angle over the upper part of the stern-post, and this detail was at first believed to have been a mistake of the artist. But as a thirteenth century relief on a triptych in a church in the S. Swedish province of Skåne shows how the tiller could be led around the high stern-post inherited from Viking times by making it curved, the picture at Fide must be taken as correct. The reconstruction (175) shows the end-post decorations detachable as on the Viking ships. The mast can be lowered and is supported in the raised position by a pole. In the line cutting the upper planks in the carving one can see a cleat with a hole for the *tack tackle* and possible belaying.

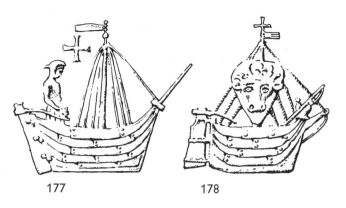
177

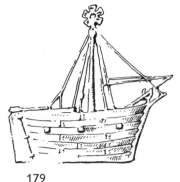
178

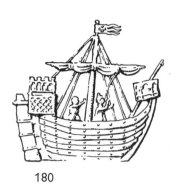
179

180

The Hansa cog

Towards the end of the twelfth century many of the German trading towns began to join together into groups in order to ply their trade and defend themselves the better. The most important of these groups was the Hansa League which was soon to control the trade of northern Europe. The League quite naturally made use of all types of contemporary merchantmen, but the most well-known of them all and primarily connected with the name of Hansa was the *cog*. There is much disagree-

(179) and many others from the area controlled by the Hansa League show ships of the same type. But the town of Ipswich, lying outside the League's sphere of influence, has on its seal a ship (180) with a rounded bow like those of other English towns of the times.

If we presume that the ships on the German seals are cogs we may conclude that the cog had a high freeboard and was straight-ended. What is meant by this is most clearly shown in the seal of Elbing (181) from the year 1350. As the end-posts ran straight down to the keel, the roomy, deep-draught cog would have sharp ends and a long lateral plane and because of this would

181

ment regarding the origin and the appearance of this vessel, but I believe that the pictures on the thirteenth and fourteenth-century seals give a clear indication.

The seal of Elbing from 1242 portrays a straight-ended vessel of indefinite size (177). We see that the ship has a high freeboard, is clinker-built and fitted with a bowsprit. The seals of Wismar (178) and Harderwijk

have been a far better sailing-craft than the round-ended, shallow-draught vessels. The importance and predominance of the cog may in part be understood by the fact that towns lying far from estuaries which therefore could not be reached by deep-draught ships were moved closer to the sea so that their ports might accommodate them.

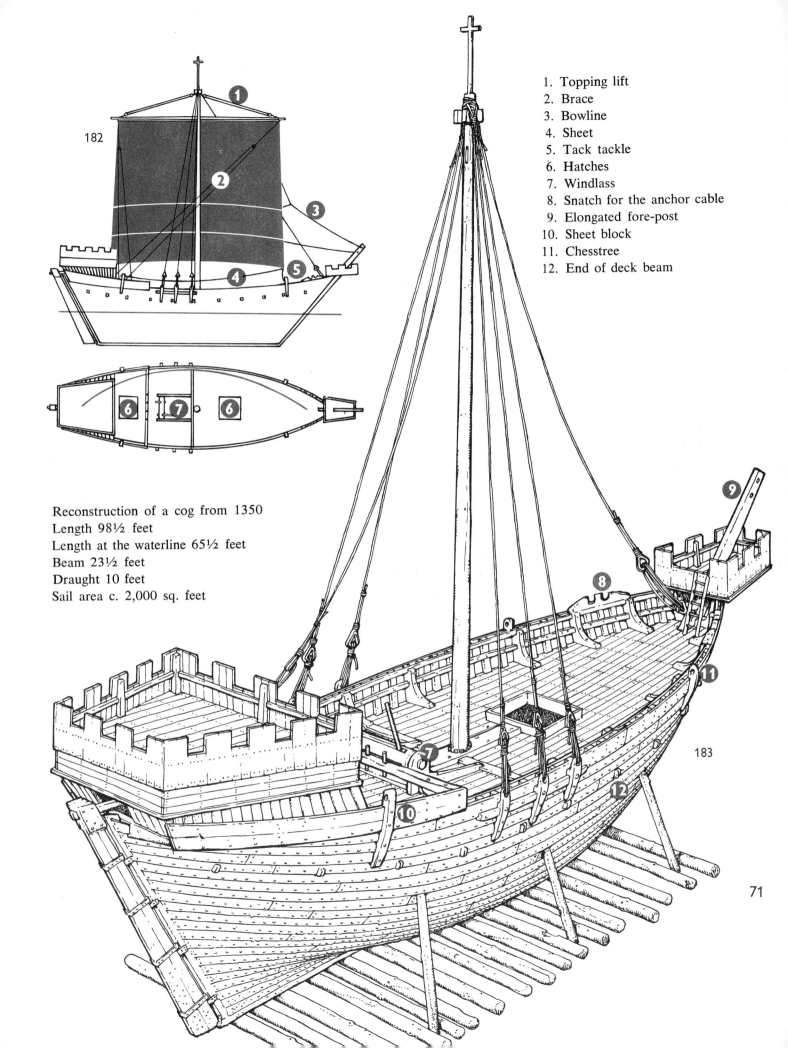

182

1. Topping lift
2. Brace
3. Bowline
4. Sheet
5. Tack tackle
6. Hatches
7. Windlass
8. Snatch for the anchor cable
9. Elongated fore-post
10. Sheet block
11. Chesstree
12. End of deck beam

Reconstruction of a cog from 1350
Length 98½ feet
Length at the waterline 65½ feet
Beam 23½ feet
Draught 10 feet
Sail area c. 2,000 sq. feet

183

71

The Hansa cog

The cog did not suddenly come into being of itself, of course, but was the result of a development which we unfortunately can only guess at. But if we presume that many merchantmen from Viking times had a cutwater, were straight-ended roughly speaking, a certain line of development is possible. A vessel that was planked right out to the sharp angle between keel and end-post would naturally have been stronger. And it is easy to understand of what importance it was that a long-keeled vessel was able to cruise in the seas around the coasts of northern Europe in ever-changing winds.

The seal of Stralsund from the fourteenth century shows a cog (184) which is perhaps slightly more modern than the Elbing cog (181), but otherwise the ships are quite alike (cf. reconstructions 182, 183, 185). The projections through the fourth plank are deck-beams whose ends are locked between the planks. The aftercastle has already begun to harmonise with the hull although it still gives the impression of being an addition. The forecastle has become a great deal smaller. The long heavy yard is hoisted with a windlass which also serves for the anchor. None of the seals show bowlines, but we know that such were to be found as early as the Vikings, and without bowlines it is impossible to understand the meaning of the bowsprit or the forward extension of the stem. The *topping lifts* supporting the yard are pure guesswork, but it is a known fact that northern

186

187

Europe of those times was in close connection with the Mediterranean, and Roman merchantmen had had topping lifts a thousand years before.

Bonnets, long strips which were latched to the foot of the sail when the wind was slight and removed when it became too strong, were in use at that time, but we more often see pictures of sails with *reef-points.* The sails were often treated with red bark dye so that they would not moulder and rot, but in old manuscripts we can read of sails which had red and white or green and white stripes and even of completely black sails. The cordage of earlier times was generally made of bast or cut from walrus skin, but the ships of Hansa times were already using cordage of hemp.

In the British Museum there is a fourteenth-century manuscript showing an animated drawing of a fight between two cogs (186). Here for the first time we see how both the fore and after castles have become an integral part of the hull. One of the cogs has its rudder secured with lines, and on the forward part of the top planks of both vessels there is a knee which in the reconstruction (187) I have interpreted as a *snatch* for the anchor cable. The dark, triangular areas on the sides of the ships may, with a certain amount of reservation, be looked upon as types of fender cleat.

Towards the end of the fourteenth century the cog began to be superseded by the more roomy *hulk* and that the originality of the cog was soon to be forgotten is exemplified by the fact that the same vessel was called both cog and hulk by one and the same chronicler.

73

188

Coasters, thirteenth century

When restoring Kalmar Castle in Sweden, the old castle bay was drained during the years 1932—1934 and in its mud a large number of vessels of mediaeval to seventeenth-century date were found. The most well-preserved were the finds which lay deepest i.e. the oldest, and on the sand bottom beneath the mud was a vessel whose parts it has been possible to restore almost completely. In this way we have a reconstruction of a small coastal vessel dating from the middle of the thirteenth century which need only be based on very little guesswork (188—191). The rigging and sail are wholly supposition, and as several of the upper planks in the uppermost parts of the bow and stern had been destroyed some small details in the hull are also uncertain.

The hull is of course clinker-built and almost entirely made of oak. It is decked only in the bow and stern. As we have already seen in the thirteenth and fourteenth-century seals (164, 168, 179, 181) it was usual to allow several through-beams to project through the sides of the ship and be locked between the planks to give greater strength athwartships. We find this actually done for the first time in the *Kalmar boat* (189), and the beams are further joined to the planking with knees. On the seal of Winchelsea (164) two men aft are seen raising the anchor with a windlass and two others forward hauling directly on the cable. Here we see such a windlass (191). In the carving at Fide Church (174) it seemed as if there was a support for a lowerable mast. The mast of the *Kalmar boat* can also be lowered between two *side supports* and when in the upright position is locked with a short cross-piece fixed to the side supports with wooden pins. The ribs are now riveted to the planking and are no longer bound to cleats. It might not be so far-fetched to assume that even the heavier Viking merchantmen were built in this labour-saving manner without the resilient construction that was necessary or anyway desirable for long, light vessels in heavy sea. A short, powerfully-built vessel with sufficient reinforcement athwartships is strong enough to withstand much strain without possessing appreciable elasticity.

189

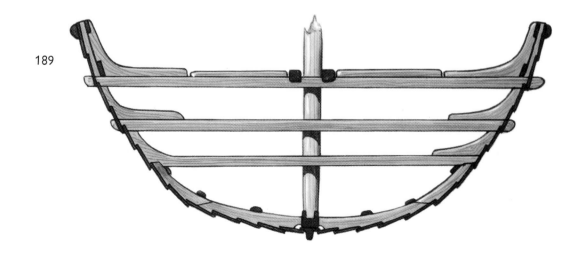

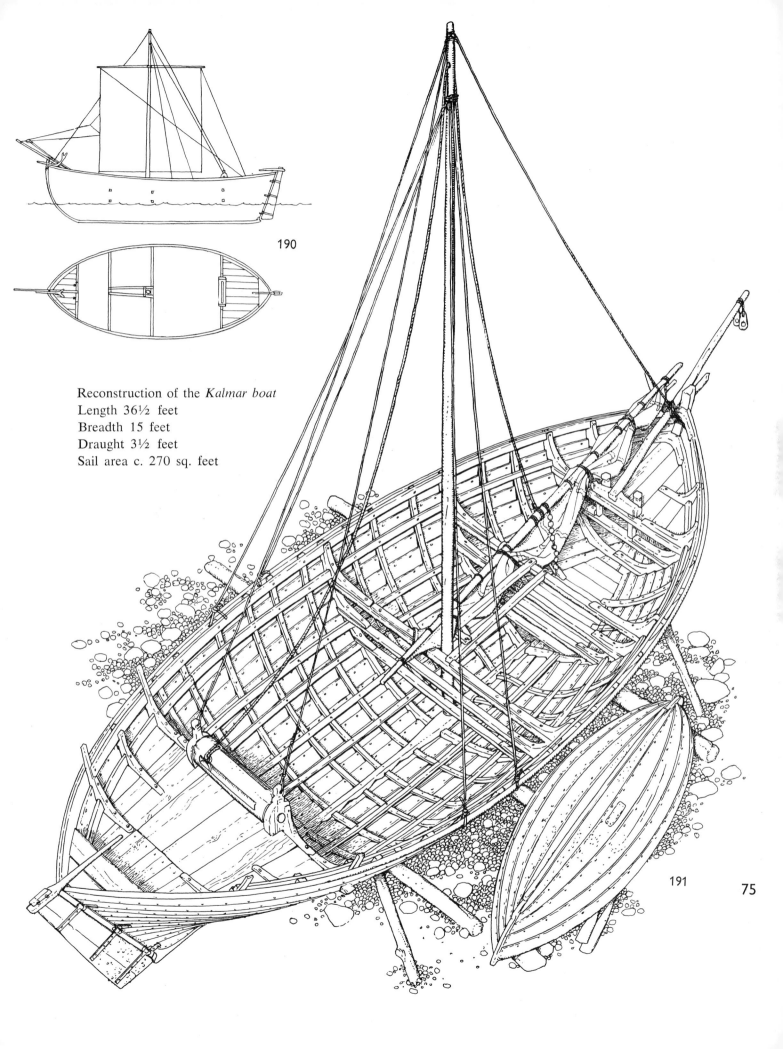

Reconstruction of the *Kalmar boat*
Length 36½ feet
Breadth 15 feet
Draught 3½ feet
Sail area c. 270 sq. feet

190

191

75

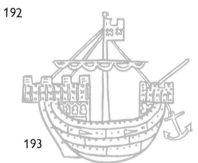

The Skamstrup ship

The seal of Poole from 1325 shows a ship with such a large aftercastle that it may be said the ship has a *quarter-deck* (193), but even more remarkable is the ship painted on a ceiling at Skamstrup Church in Denmark. There are two representations of ships in the church and the paintings are believed to be from the end of the fourteenth century. The smaller of them (195) is of the same type as the Fide ship with the tiller curved round the stern-post, but we can see that the yard is held to the mast with a *parrel truck,* and a poised weathervane (just discernible on the Fide ship) is clearly presented here. The hull of the larger vessel is similar to a Viking ship (196) which the conservative builder has taken great pains to alter according to the demands of the times with a stern-rudder and castles. Here the aftercastle takes up the whole room aft of the mast. No attempt has been made to make it fit snugly to the hull. It seems as if the descendants of the Vikings had difficulty in accommodating themselves to the changes of the times. The reconstruction (192), like the original, shows a sail with horizontal as well as vertical reinforcements. The multi-coloured planking indicate that it is a vessel intended for warfare.

194

The Danzig ship

The maritime trade routes between the countries of northern Europe and those around the Mediterranean became much livelier, and it is difficult to decide whether the shipbuilders of the North or the South had the more to learn. In any case the picture decorating the seal of the Hansa town of Danzig from 1400 ought to represent the most advanced of contemporary ships (197).

The castles are now quite a part of the hull (194). The anchor cable runs through a *hawse*. Such a hawse has been found on a Mediterranean relief from 1340 (232) and something which may be interpreted as a hawse on a miniature from 1219. We see *ratlines* in the shrouds of the Danzig ship for the first time — a hundred years were to pass before they were to become a common feature on southern ships. The top is of a new type, round with the sides turned out and resting on *trestle* and *cross-trees* around the masthead. We have of course already seen round tops on Egyptian and Phoenician vessels (38, 63) but since then they have been absent from the representations.

195

196

197

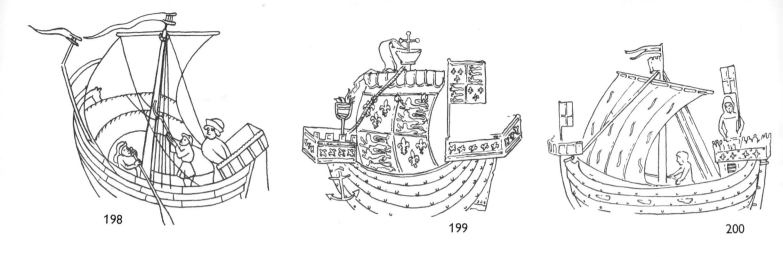

198   199   200

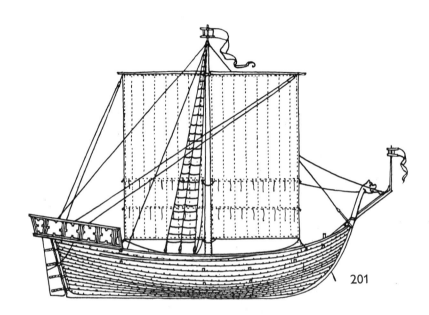

201

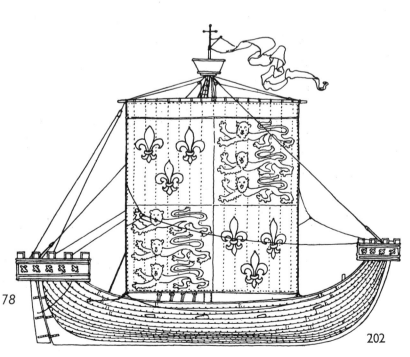

202

Single-masted ships, fifteenth century

The great revolution of the three-masted ship came towards the end of the fifteenth century. The pictures we know of N. European vessels in church decorations, seals and miniatures from the period just before this revolution constitute a sample of types in different stages of development. A mural at Højby Church in Denmark (198) includes a ship whose bow is still decorated with a dragon's head. In this picture the bowlines are clearly seen for once, and we notice a parrel truck on the yard and also a parrel in the sail at the bottom reef, yet the only innovation seems to be the flagstaff at the end of the bowsprit. (Reconstruction 201). The remarkable thing is that it was not for another hundred years that a flagstaff appeared on the bowsprit (293).

The seal used by Richard Cruikshank (later Richard III) while Duke of Gloucester (199) and the seal of Rye (200) are both decorated with ships which except for the stern-rudder hardly show any development from the thirteenth-century stage. The round top, however, is to be seen on Richard's ship. (Reconstruction 202). At Kirkehyllinge Church in Denmark a ship is portrayed with a hatch in its side (203), perhaps for loading timber or horses.

The ship in Froissart's Chronicle (206) and on the two French miniatures (204, 205) are of roughly the same type as the Danzig ship from 1400. On the first we can see sharp hooks on the yard-arms for incapacitating enemy rigging at close quarters. The masts consist of many spars lashed together, indicating that the ships were uncommonly large. They have many features in common with contemporary Mediterranean vessels, but nevertheless give away their northern origin by being clinker-built and having ratlines in the shrouds.

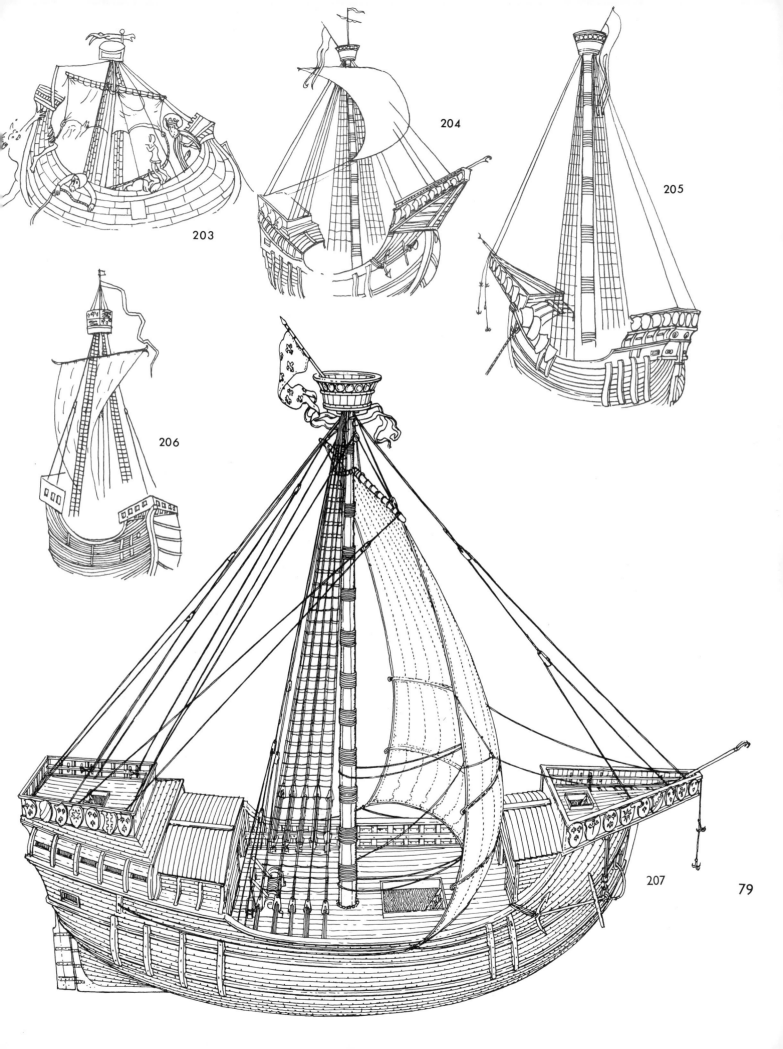

203

204

205

206

207

79

208

The lateen sail in the Mediterranean

Six hundred years of Mediterranean shipbuilding are an unknown chapter for us, and it is in two Greek manuscripts from the end of the ninth century, now at Paris and Moscow, that we have our first glimpse of mediaeval Mediterranean vessels (209). They are seemingly small craft shaped like the merchantmen of classical times with two rudders, but they do show something quite new in the history of the ship — the *lateen sail*.

It was called lateen because it was the type of sail seen by N. Europeans in the Latin countries when they began to sail down to the Mediterranean during the Middle Ages. Yet no one knows where the three-cornered sail originally came from. We can still find it today in Portugal, in the Mediterranean countries and in the Black Sea, the Red Sea and the Persian Gulf, on the W. coast of India and on the E. coast of Africa, on all the seas once under the power of the ships of the Arabian Empire. It is because of this that many believe the sail to be of Arabian origin or that it anyway came to the Mediterranean via them. No one can prove otherwise nor does anyone know how the square sail disappeared from these regions. We do not see it reappear in pictures of Mediterranean vessels before the fourteenth century, and it is assumed that it was the N. Europeans who reintroduced it.

The uppermost of the Greek manuscript pictures (209)

209

210

gives nearly all details characteristic of a lateen rig. The strange hook at the masthead which is also to be seen in a mosaic at San Marco in Venice was presumably to hold the halyard as far forward of the mast as possible. In lateen rigs the halyard always ran in a block *above* the shroud attachments. The mast was leant slightly forwards as forestays could not be used. The shrouds were permanently set as on northern craft but were made taut with tackles and could easily be loosened when sailing on different tacks. The main halyard also served as a backstay (208, 209). The long yard consisted of two or more sections bound together and was held to the mast by a parrel in the form of a slip-knot which could easily be loosened from the deck. The position of the sail was controlled by two *tackles* running from the lower yard-arm and one or two *braces* which usually ran from a point somewhat further in on the upper yard-arm.

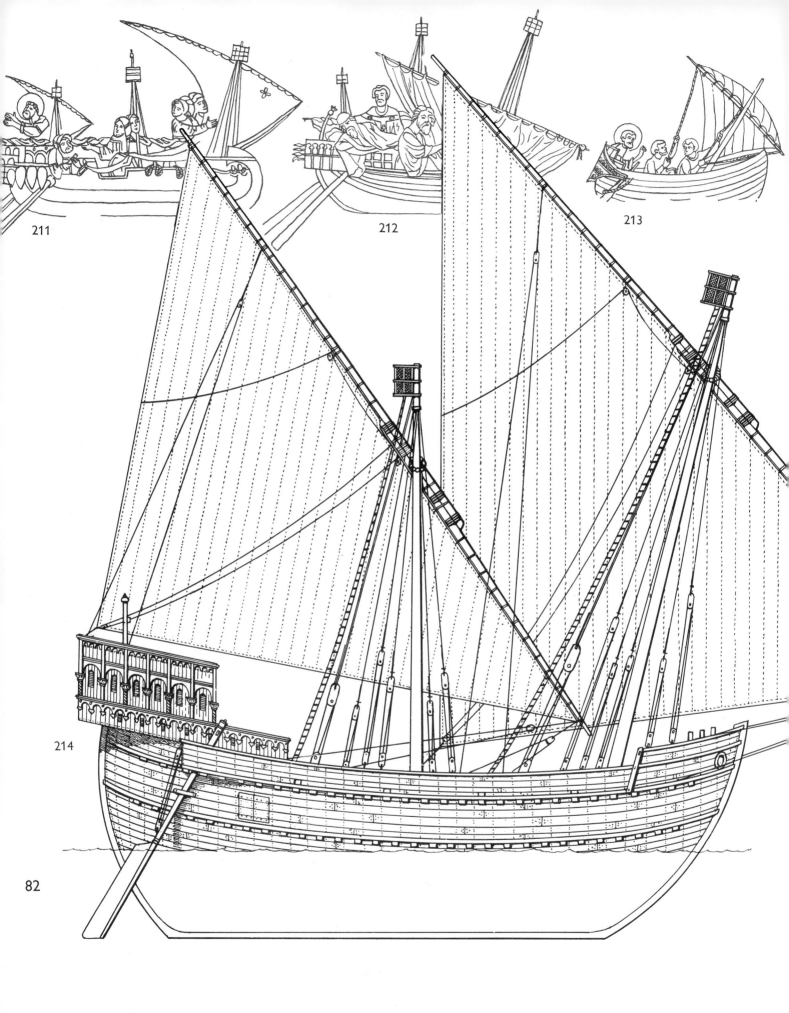

211

212

213

214

82

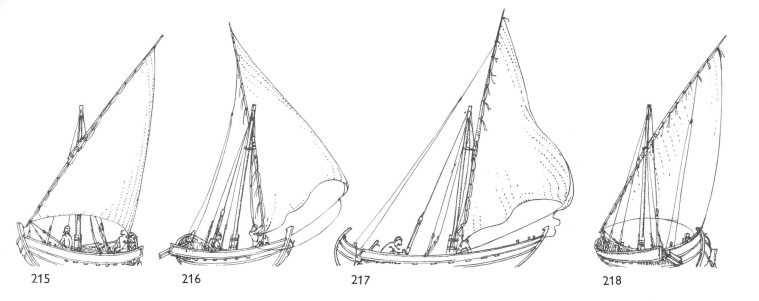

215   216   217   218

Venetian ships, 1268

When Louis IX was preparing for his crusade in 1268 he ordered ships from Venice and Genoa, and details of the size of the vessels built have fortunately been preserved. The Venetian ships were: length 84½ feet from stem to stern, length of keel 57 feet, beam 21 feet, depth from railing to keel 21½ feet. They had two complete decks, and two short decks in the stern provided room for cabins. The Genoese ships were somewhat smaller, and the sizes of the yards given show that they were longer than the ships themselves.

Contemporary portrayals of Venetian ships have been found in the mosaics at San Marco (211, 212). The representations are extremely stereotyped, but we do see that it is a question of a three-masted vessel with double rudders. Another mosaic from the twelfth century shows a smaller craft with a strangely shaped aftercastle (213). A similar aftercastle is found on a Spanish miniature from 1280 which also shows projecting deck-beams and — remarkably enough — a hull which seems to be clinker-built.

If we had had only these representations it would have been hopeless trying to form any idea of crusader ships from 1268, but aided by the above measurements I have made an attempt at a reconstruction (214) in which a good deal of guesswork has been done. It may be presumed that the large sails were furled with some form of *brails*. Contemporary and later pictures show that the top was usually situated on the after side of the mast.

The lateen sail was hoisted outside the shrouds, and the leeward shrouds were slackened so that the yard could be trussed to the mast. If it was desired to tack when going to windward (215) it was necessary to fall off the wind. The brace and sheet were made loose (216), the parrel was slackened somewhat so that the yard was freed slightly from the mast, and then one of the crew hauled on the yard until it was vertical. The sheet was then transferred to the other side (when there was only one sheet) and the sail was allowed to blow forward (217) while the shrouds now to windward were made taut and those now to leeward were slackened. When the vessel began to turn into the wind the sail was sheeted home on the leeward side, the yard retrussed to the mast and trimmed with the tacks and braces for the new tack (218). On ships as large as the crusader vessels (214) it must be assumed that the yard was forced over with the aid of the *tack tackles*.

219

83

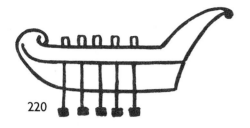

220

Warships, twelfth century

Culture does not usually flourish in times of great change, and records of ships and seafaring after the fall of the W. Roman Empire are few or non-existent. We do not know when and how — and if? — the square sail disappeared from the Mediterranean. We do not know when the trireme became out of date. We know very little about the ship — or ships? — that replaced it, the *dromon* and the *selander*.

The Greek word *dromon* means "runner". The warships of the E. Roman Empire were also called dromons. They were very likely biremes with fifty oars on each side, and it is stated that they were rowed by 100—230 men. It has been asserted that the oars projected directly out from the sides of the vessel, that outriggers were no longer in use, but there are no specific representations of dromons. The oldest portrayal I know of a mediaeval Mediterranean warship is a miniature from 1047 preserved at Madrid (220). It gives us little to go on. There is a manuscript in the National Library at Paris whose illustrations probably belong to the period 1154—1235, and in it are representations of both warships and merchantmen (221, 222, 223, 229).

All of these drawings have one detail in common: two "wings" curving upwards in the stern. Something similar can be discerned in the mosaics at San Marco (212, 213) and in the Spanish miniature (219). It appears as if they were curved extensions of the bulwark which ran outside the planking of Roman vessels to leave room for the rudder-stock (103—110). Some pictures have a cross-piece between the "wings", and if we bear in mind that the yard of the lateen sail could often be longer than the ship itself it is understandable that the "wings" and cross-piece could be both support and lock for the yard when lowered.

Another remarkable detail on the warships is that the ram no longer appears to lie at the waterline but well above it. The uppermost picture (221) shows the lower bank of oars projecting through round oar-ports in the planking whereas the upper bank seems to be resting on an outrigger. It is possible that none of the pictures represent a dromon if the dromon is in actual fact something quite special regarding type and size and not merely a "runner", a fast-going craft, as its name suggests. Later anyway the name dromon seems to have been used of warships in general.

When Richard Cœur de Lion was approaching Palestine on the Third Crusade in 1191 he was forced to give battle with a large Saracen "dromon" described as a three-masted vessel much larger than the usual ships of the times. There appears to be much disagreement as to whether the *selander* was a large or small dromon. Because of this it is not possible to say more than that the reconstruction (224) shows a warship, a two-banked galley, from the end of the twelfth or beginning of the thirteenth century.

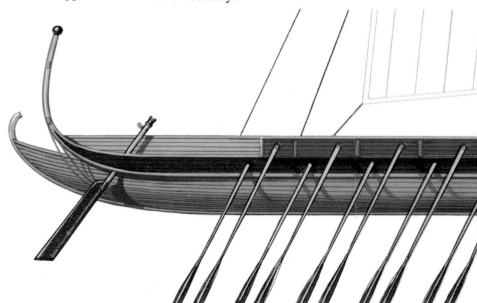

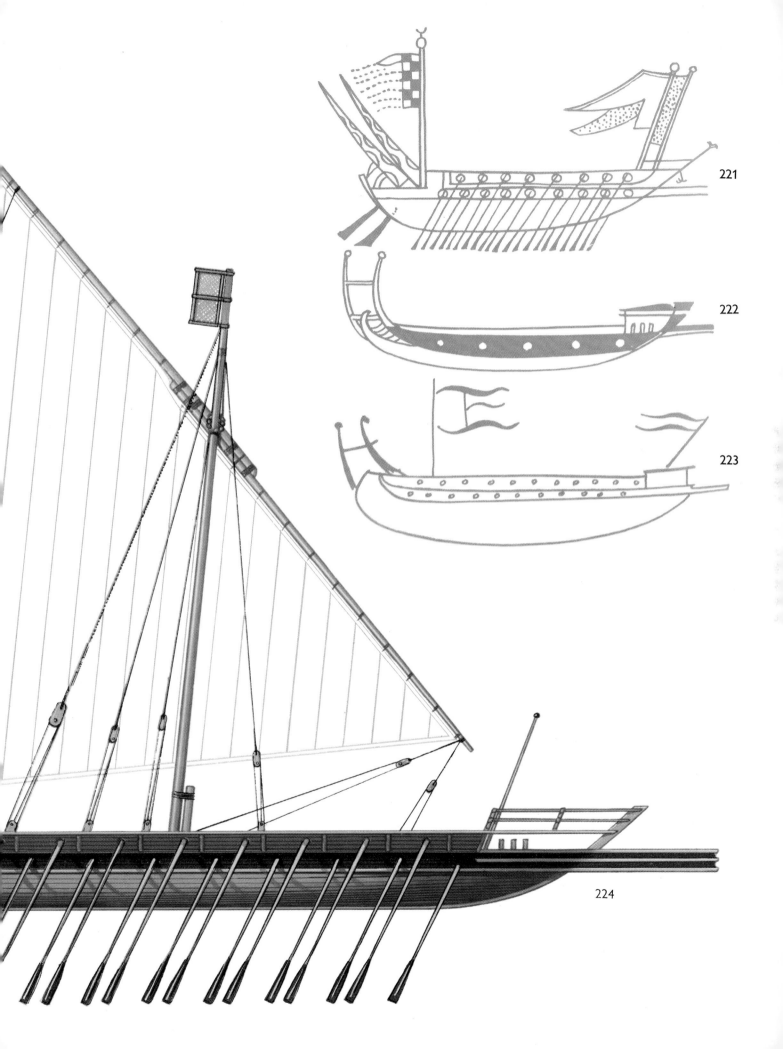

221

222

223

224

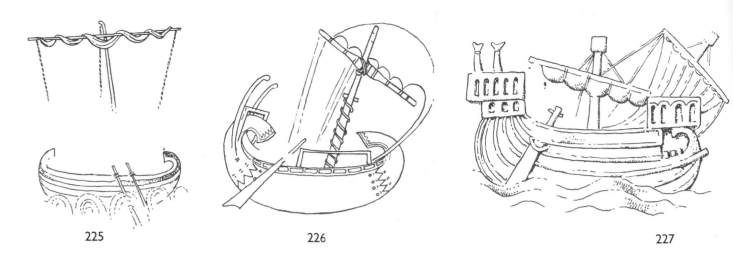

225   226   227

Merchantmen, thirteenth century

The three Italian republics of Genoa, Pisa and Venice, together with Marseilles and Barcelona, were in control of the naval movements of Christian powers in the Mediterranean during the crusades. We are able to form an idea of their merchantmen from some twelfth and thirteenth-century illustrations, miniatures, mosaics and reliefs, nearly all of which portray vessels with ends curving, remarkably, inwards. A relief on the Leaning Tower of Pisa (227) and the miniature in the National Library at Paris (229) show two almost identical ships which have similarities with a ship in a mosaic at the San Giovanni Evangelista in Ravenna (230). The reconstruction (228, 231) is of a ship with a hull not unlike that of the Roman merchantmen. The "wings" — the supports for the yard — are an addition. A castle sits over the curved stern and a forecastle is situated over the bow and railings like a roof above the foredeck. The rig is the same as on the Venetian crusader ship (214).

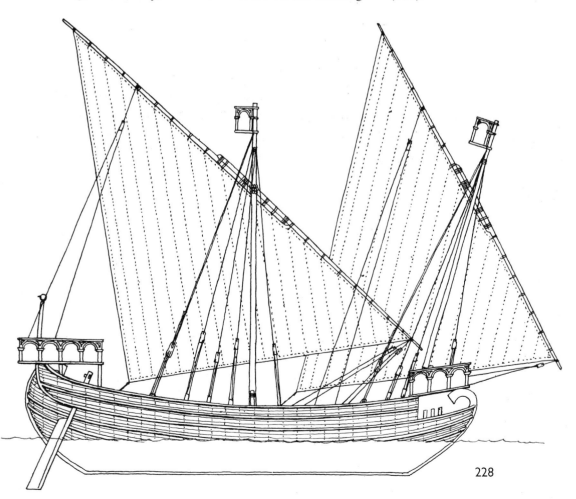

228

229

230

231

87

232

Merchantmen, fourteenth century

The most well-known representation of a fourteenth-century ship is to be found on the tomb of St. Peter the Martyr in the Church of St. Eustorgio at Milan (232). The Roman hull wiht its through-beams is still present, and even the rudder does not seem to have changed since classical times. The aftercastle contains a cabin with an oriel window (cf. reconstruction 238) and here for the first time is a clear and unmistakable *hawse* in the planking for the anchor cable. We also see the tackles for tightening the shrouds, exactly like those of today

233

234

88

235

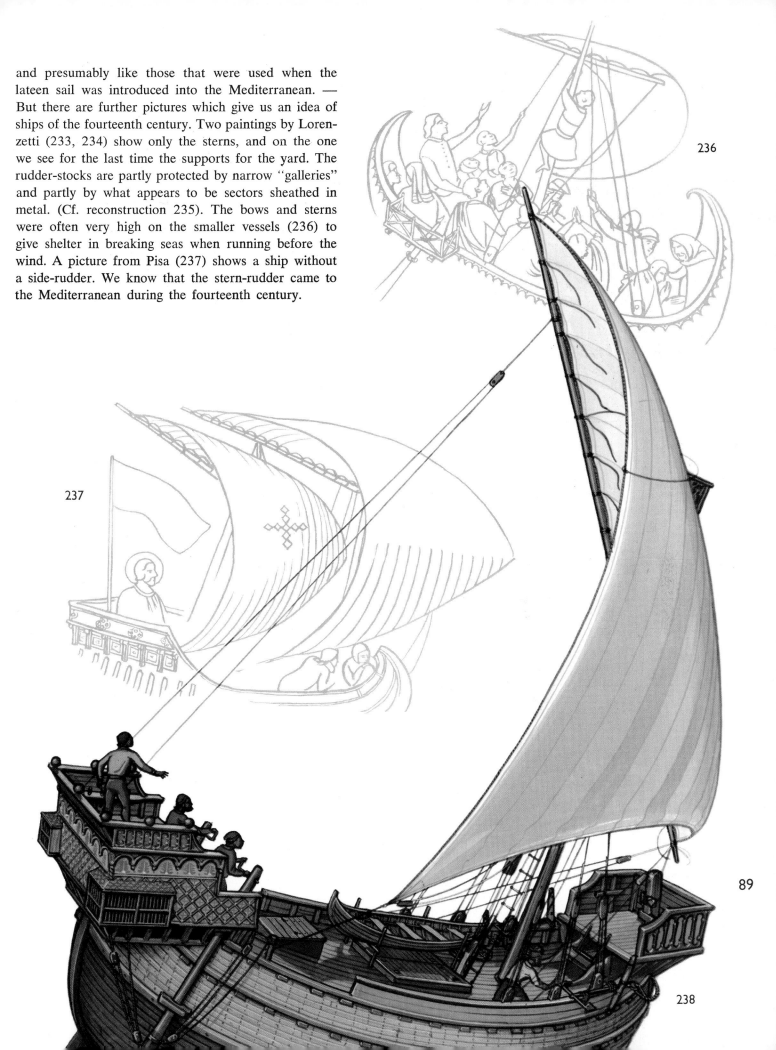

and presumably like those that were used when the lateen sail was introduced into the Mediterranean. — But there are further pictures which give us an idea of ships of the fourteenth century. Two paintings by Lorenzetti (233, 234) show only the sterns, and on the one we see for the last time the supports for the yard. The rudder-stocks are partly protected by narrow "galleries" and partly by what appears to be sectors sheathed in metal. (Cf. reconstruction 235). The bows and sterns were often very high on the smaller vessels (236) to give shelter in breaking seas when running before the wind. A picture from Pisa (237) shows a ship without a side-rudder. We know that the stern-rudder came to the Mediterranean during the fourteenth century.

236

237

89

238

239

Stern-rudder and square sail in the Mediterranean

It is possible that the square sail never completely disappeared from the Mediterranean even if it appears that the lateen sail dominated for nearly a thousand years. Viking ships and northern crusader vessels had sailed there, and the pictures, which are always our most reliable source of information, show that the square sail again came into general use about the middle of the fourteenth century. The stern-rudder was also introduced at the same time.

A Florentine manuscript relates that in 1304 pirates from Bayonne came to the Mediterranean in *cogs,* and that the merchants of Genoa, Venice and Barcelona immediately began to build similar ships. A picture of a ship with a square sail (240) is probably from the beginning of the fourteenth century, but the ship has no rudder. A Spanish miniature from 1350, on the other hand, shows many ships (239) all fitted with square sails, stern-rudders and cog ends, and it seems by this as if there had been definite influence from the North. A painting of the same date by Giovanni di Milano portrays a ship (241) which in many details is reminiscent of both fighting cogs (186) on the thirteenth-century manuscript in the British Museum. But other contemporary pictures (242) have details which indicate side-rudders, and we may not imagine that the stern-rudder was to dominate immediately. In the year 1500 we still find vessels with the old side-rudders in the cosmopolitan harbour of Venice.

90

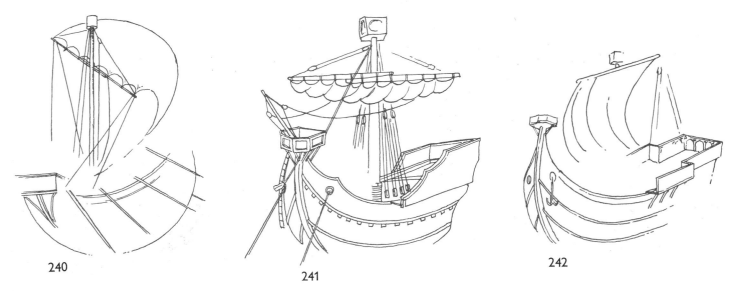

240

241

242

243

Warships, fourteenth century

A relief on a bronze door of St. Peter's in Rome portraying the departure of the Emperor Johannes VI Cantacuzene from Constantinople shows a warship (243) that may well be considered typical of the times, the middle of the fourteenth century. The upper bank of oars rests on the outrigger, the lower seems to pass out through the side of the vessel. The ram sits high above water-level. The anchor is a large grapnel of the type that was still in use on galleys in the seventeenth and eighteenth centuries.

The Byzantine warships, the dromons if we so wish to call them, had already been fitted with a dangerous weapon during the seventh century — "Greek fire" as it was called, and said to be the invention of the Syrian engineer Callinicus. The combustible was a mixture of naphtha, sulphur and saltpetre, and this was packed into a long tube the other end of which was fitted with a powerful bellows. This blazing material was then squirted at the enemy when at close quarters, and it is believed that it was thanks to this "Greek fire" that the E. Romans held out against the Arabs for so long.

On the Catalan Atlas of 1370 there is a picture of a smaller warship (244), and on Pizigani's map of 1367 a two-masted vessel of wholly new type (245) with both a square and a lateen sail.

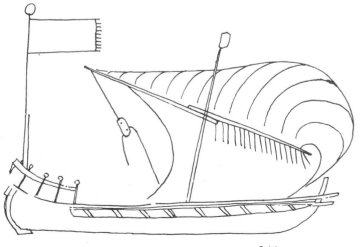

244

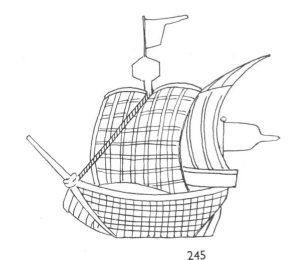

91

245

The carrack

The large ships, those that traded beyond the Pillars of Hercules, went over almost without exception to the modern square sail. But Mediterranean seamen were used to sailing with two or three-masted ships, and as they very likely often found it difficult to keep the square-sailed vessels on course it is understandable that they might well have rigged a small mast aft of the mainmast with a lateen sail to help steering. The first evidence we have of this is from 1367 (245), and the rig seems to have been common by the beginning of the fifteenth century.

At about the same period we hear of the *carrack*. All we really know is that it was a merchantman of Mediterranean type, round-sterned like all ships of those days. Perhaps the name indicated that the ship had a stern-rudder, square sail and a small *mizzen* exactly like the ship on the painting from the beginning of the fifteenth century by Gentile da Fabriano in the Vatican Museum (247). Perhaps the carrack was identical with the *hulk* which had superceded the cog in the North. The hulk, however, was clinker-built, and the carrack, like all Mediterranean vessels proper, was carvel-built.

The ship on Gentile's painting has the same long row of projecting deck-beams as Queen Hatshepsut's ships. The raised quarter-deck is also supported by through-beams, and the iron bands reinforcing the aftercastle indicate that it was no sturdy construction. (Cf. reconstruction 248). A hull of the same type — curiously enough sailing backwards — is to be found on a painting by Fiesole which is also in the Vatican Museum (246). Under the forecastle there is a long, curved beam, the *riding bitts,* whose ends presumably project through the planking. It was around this that the anchor cable was made fast. Both pictures show a six-sided forecastle.

The shrouds of the carrack, like those of the lateen-rigged ship, are fitted with blocks and long tackles, and a ladder leads up to the round top. The square yard consists of two lashed spars and is supported by topping lifts. It is possible that topping lifts first began to be used when the square sail reached the Mediterranean. We can see them in Italian pictures from the beginning of the fourteenth century (240, 241) but never in northern pictures before the end of the fifteenth century. Roman ships did have topping lifts. Perhaps the square rig and its details never disappeared from the Mediterranean after all?

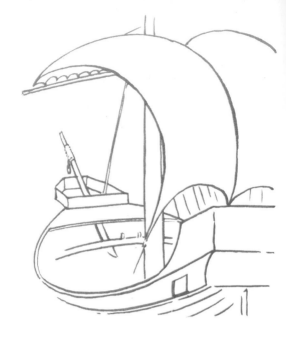

246

247

248

249

clamp on either side of the forecastle — what was later to develop into the *cathead*. And we can see the strange construction or rather covering of the forecastle which has such a curious appearance on many pictures (204, 255, 257), the curved, clinker-fitted planks under the forecastle.

Today the model has only one mast. Earlier it had three, but experts are agreed that at any rate the mast situated on the forecastle was a later addition. A picture in a treatise on shipbuilding in the British Museum shows a similar vessel with only one mast (251), but many other contemporary pictures illustrate ships of the same type with both mainsail and mizzen (252). Now the mast on the forecastle of the model had been forced through the forecastle deck while the mizzenmast sat in a round hole on the quarter-deck. This has led to a belief that the Mataró model represents a two-masted carrack (cf. reconstruction 253). Officially the model is called a Spanish *nao*, but this word means nothing more than "ship". To indicate that Columbus' flagship *Santa Maria* was not a caravel it was called nao. There is reason to presume that all larger, round-sterned and square-rigged vessels of those times were called nao in Spain, and elsewhere were designated by different forms of the word carrack, in the North both carrack and hulk. It is nearly impossible to tell if the different words were intended for the same object or if they actually described different types of craft.

The Mataró ship, 1450

In a church at Mataró not far from Barcelona there hung for many hundreds of years the model of a ship which had been made some time about the middle of the fifteenth century (249, 250). How it was later to leave Spain and via many hands reach America and England, finally to come to port in a glass case in the Maritiem Museum Prins Hendrik in Rotterdam, is a long and on many points unclear story which I shall not go into here. It is the only model we know of a ship from the time when the history of the great voyages of discovery began — the next known model is dated to a hundred years afterwards.

With the aid of the model we are able to interpret pictures which before had been difficult to explain, and on it are details which we could previously only guess had been present. We can see the much-debated through-beams, the riding bitt, the cross and trestle-trees under the top, the triple parrel truck and a sheave hole in a

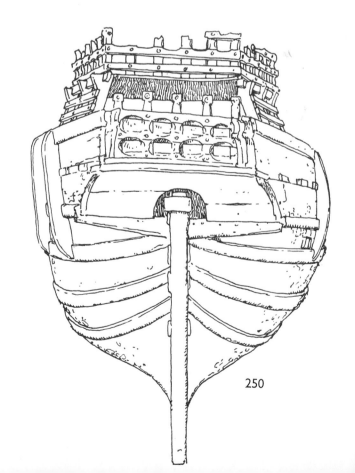

250

251

252

253

95

The three-masted ship

The step from the two-masted to the three-masted vessel was a natural one and it was not long before it was taken. The men who understood the need for a poised sail aft of the mainmast ought to have understood almost straightaway the advantages of a similar sail on the forecastle. It is possible that there were three-masted carracks as early as at the beginning of the fifteenth century or even earlier, but the earliest-known dated representation is on the seal of Louis de Bourbon attached to a document from 1466 (254).

A large Spanish-Moorish bowl believed to have been made in Malaga at the beginning of the fifteenth century and now exhibited at the Victoria and Albert Museum has a very fine, clear picture of a three-masted Portugese ship (255). The hull is of the same type as on the Mataró model, the bulwark around the quarter-deck, only, appears to have been of a lighter construction, a wooden trellis-work open to cooling breezes.

The yard of the new mast has been lowered, but we see that the foresail must have been small, even smaller than the mizzen. These end-sails were still not intended to propel the vessel, they were only steering auxiliaries. The mainmast appears to be very thick, and we can assume that on a ship of this size it would have consisted of many spars bound together. The shrouds are of southern type without ratlines, but the yard is of one piece according to northern fashion. It is also possible that the artist has simplified it as we are to see pictures of southern vessels with a bipartite yard for quite some time to come. A bonnet is latched to the foot of the sail. The ship's boat is on the deck and it may be guessed that it has a flat stern.

The reconstruction (256) shows the numerous *fender cleats* which were partly to protect the vessel from damage against a quay and partly to reinforce the upper, weaker part of the planking and bulwarks. The anchor is catted with a purchase attached to the anchor ring running through the sheave hole to the clamp on the side of the forecastle. The end of the riding bitt can be seen projecting through the planking under the anchor. Yet another deck has been constructed above the quarter-deck aft of the mizzen-mast, a deck that was later to be called the *half deck*. The main yard is at half mast. A long lanyard runs between the block of the main halyard and its double sheave holes which are situated in a pole, the *knight*, firmly fixed right down into the keel.

256

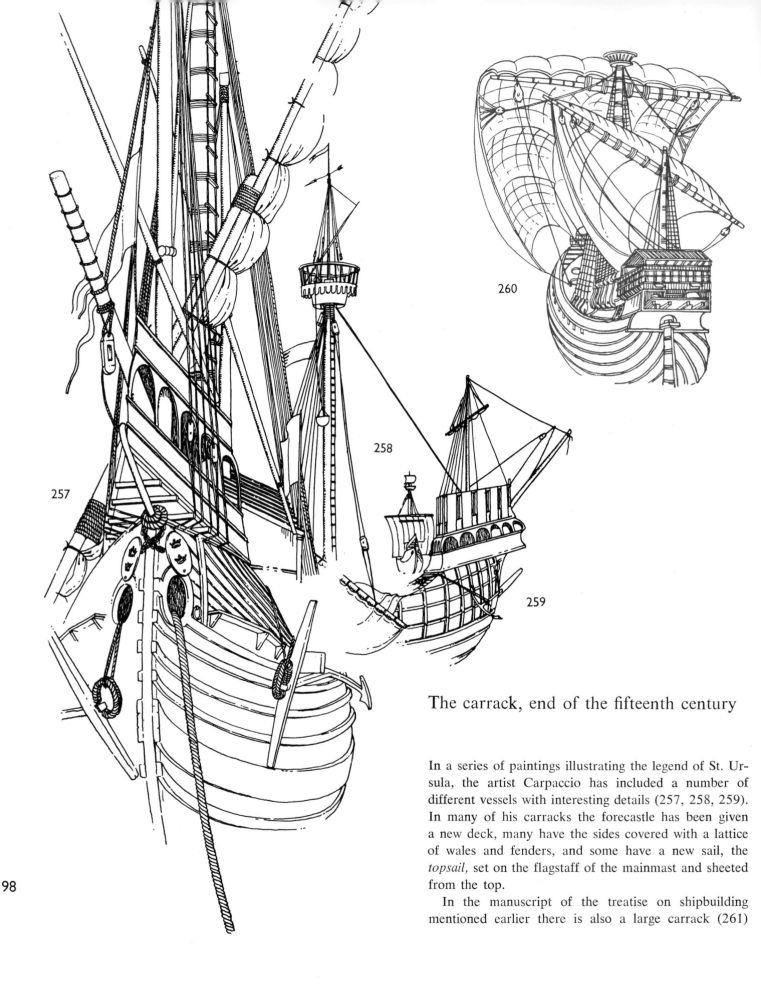

The carrack, end of the fifteenth century

In a series of paintings illustrating the legend of St. Ursula, the artist Carpaccio has included a number of different vessels with interesting details (257, 258, 259). In many of his carracks the forecastle has been given a new deck, many have the sides covered with a lattice of wales and fenders, and some have a new sail, the *topsail,* set on the flagstaff of the mainmast and sheeted from the top.

In the manuscript of the treatise on shipbuilding mentioned earlier there is also a large carrack (261)

261

262

whose upper rows of projecting beams show that the upper deck did not always lie in one plane. The dimensions of the ship are also given: length from stem to stern about 125 feet, length of the keel 85 feet, beam 34 feet.

More instructive than any of the old pictures is the Flemish master W.A.'s "kraeck" from circa 1470 (262). His carrack has two forecastle decks with an awning above them. A long, new deck is also to be seen above the quarter-deck, and aft of the mizzenmast another awning. An open *gallery* runs between the two conveniences. Both the foresail and the mizzen are now propelling sails. The main shrouds are attached in northern fashion to the *channels* with deadeyes and lanyards, but

they still lack ratlines. The square yard has double topping lifts and the mizzenmast has been given a lift to the maintop. Both this picture and a woodcut illustrating Breydenbach's Pilgrimage of 1486 (260) have *martnets* for furling the mainsail. There is a strange system of *buntlines* which proceed from the maintop and often continue as a bridle on the front and rear sides of the sail finally ending in a crowfoot round the leeches. When the yard was hoisted the martnets were tightened, drawing the sail together. The woodcut (260) also shows *clewlines* which drew up the clews under the yard when the sail was furled. On W.A.'s "kraeck" we can see a bowline running from the mainsail, past the foremast, through a block on the bowsprit.

99

Carrack, 1470

This is a reconstruction of the Flemish artist W.A.'s "kraeck" (262). It differs from all previous portrayals of sailing ships proper in that it carries guns, and we must consider it to have been a strongly-armed merchant-man. On the quarter-deck, from the mizzenmast aft, five guns have been mounted on each side (cf. 262). All masts have tops, and spears can be seen in those of the main and foremast. The mizzentop has a small moveable gun. Ammunition-hoists lead up to the main and foretop, and at the end of the bowsprit there is a grapnel which was dropped across into an enemy ship to keep it at close quarters.

263

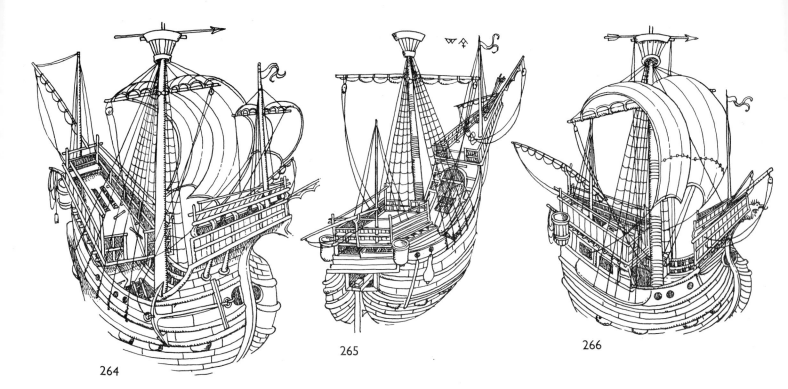

264

265

266

The Santa Maria, 1492

With the exception of Noah's Ark, Columbus' flagship is surely the most well-known ship in the world, and there are many, many thousands of models to be found today which are supposed to represent the *Santa Maria*. There are well-made and well-equipped models monstrosities sold as souvenirs. Yet they all have one thing in common: they are inaccurate. There is no absolutely correct model of the *Santa Maria* because no man alive knows exactly what the famous ship was like. We know at least that she was not a caravel. (That we do not know with certainty what a caravel really looked like is another matter.) Columbus often speaks of her as *La nao*, the ship, as opposed to *Las carabelas*, the caravels *Pinta* and *Niña*. The experts of today are almost agreed that she was a carrack. She would have been a small carrack as Columbus' contemporary biographer, the priest Las Casas, says that she was "somewhat" larger than the two others. And we know exactly what sails she had; Columbus tells us himself in his logbook under 24th October 1492: "I let them set all sails, the main course with two bonnets, the fore course, the spritsail, the mizzen, the topsail and the boat's sail on the half deck".

Columbus was not pleased with *Santa Maria*. She was slower and more difficult to manoeuvre than the caravels. She had too great a draught, she was "not suited for voyages of discovery" as her captain himself says. Her draught is not known. All we do know is that the caravel *Niña* cannot have drawn more than a fathom or so otherwise she would never have been able to negotiate the shallows off the S. coast of Cuba. On his third voyage to the West Indies Columbus notes that two of his ships were too large, the one over 100 toneladas and the other over 70 "and only smaller ships are desirable for voyages of discovery, for the ship I took with me on my first voyage was cumbersome and, because of this, was lost in the harbour at Navidad". The size of the ships was thus recorded in toneladas, tuns, and a ship of 70 toneladas was considered large enough to carry 70 tuns of wine. It is known that *Niña* was reckoned to be of 60 toneladas, and we may then guess that *Santa Maria* was at the most of 80 — as Las Casas says, she was only "somewhat" larger. Following on this we may guess that *Santa Maria*, in consideration of the fathom drawn by *Niña*, might have had a draught of about 6½ feet.

But what did she look like? There are not many pictures of small carracks and caravels from the end of the fifteenth century in existence. We are once more indebted to the painter W.A. for pictures of small Flemish merchantmen from 1470 (264, 265, 266) which give a certain number of clues. Columbus mentioned the *spritsail*, a small innovation set on a yard below the bowsprit. None of W.A.'s ships carries it but on the first (264) there is a furled sail under the foresail, and it was quite common, at least to begin with, to stow the small sail in the *forecastle* when not in use. In all three pictures we can see that the quarter-deck rests on beams above the bulwarks so that light and air could reach the cabins that were presumably under it. — At St. Mary's Church

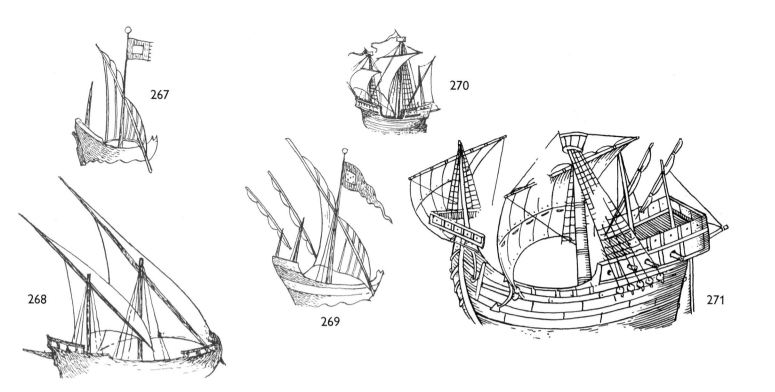

267

270

268

269

271

in Lübeck there is a painting from 1489 which includes a small three-masted vessel (270) and in a book printed at Lisbon in 1496 a woodcut of a ship (271) having four masts but which we are able to understand thanks to Columbus' description: the lateen sail of the ship's boat was rigged up on the half deck. — Finally, for the sake of comparison, I have included some pictures of caravels from the beginning of the sixteenth century. Two of them (267, 269) are to be found on the atlas drawn by Columbus' fellow-traveller Juan de la Cosa in 1500, but a painting of a somewhat later date by Simao Bening gives us a better idea of the appearance of the caravel (268).

An old rule of thumb for shipbuilders was that a vessel's measurements athwartships, length of keel and length from stem to stern ought roughly to be in the proportions 1:2:3. If we had one of these measurements it would have been easy to work out the approximate proportions of the *Santa Maria,* but we have only been able to guess at her draught and the number of tuns of wine she could carry. In order to reconstruct a vessel of roughly the correct size it has been necessary to guess what remains:

Length from stem to stern 78½ feet, length of keel 55½ feet, breadth 26 feet. Total sail area about 3,500 sq. feet, of which the mainsail plus its two bonnets would have been about 2,200 sq. feet.

The numbers in the reconstruction (272, 273) indicate: 1. Spritsail. 2. Foresail. 3. Mainsail with bonnets. 4. Topsail. 5. Mizzen. 6. Martnet. 7. Clewline. 8. Clewline. 9. Windlass. 10. Hatch. 11. Pump. 12. Ladder from quarter-deck to main deck. 13. Half deck.

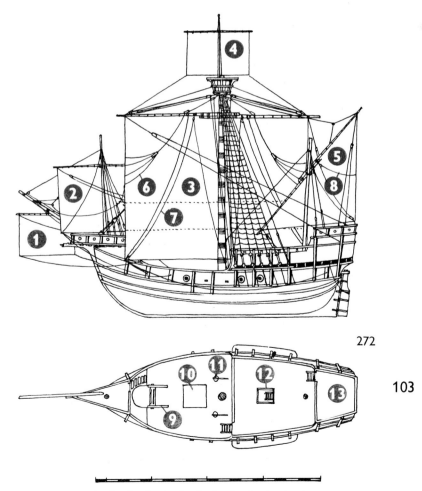

272

103

The Santa Maria, 1492

This then is roughly what a small Spanish ship from Galicia might have looked like at the end of the last century of the Middle Ages. This is how Columbus' flagship the *Santa Maria* might have appeared when she set sail from Palos on 3rd August 1492. It is in fact believed that she was on the whole like this even if nearly all details may have been otherwise. The number of sails is correct, but their actual size has had to be guessed. The small square topsail was perhaps sheeted directly to the top. Here the system of sheets is based on a relief at Padua, but it might be that the sheets from the main yard were led down to the poop deck as we can see on a picture from the beginning of the next century (283).

105

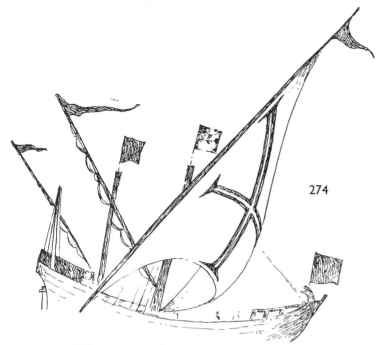

274

The caravel

The age of discovery was begun by the Portuguese prince Dom Henrique, usually referred to as Henry the Navigator, who systematically sent expeditions southwards along the coast of Africa at the beginning of the fifteenth century in the hope of eventually finding a sea route to rich and coveted India. The majority of ships on these expeditions were almost certainly caravels.

In a Portuguese manuscript from 1255 the word *caravela* occurs as describing fishing vessels. Several of the hulls on the early pictures of caravels that do exist (267, 268, 269, 274) look more like large boats than ships, yet it seems quite plausible that a well-tried, national type be developed for voyages longer than anyone had previously dreamed of. Scouting the dangerous route would first have been done in short hops along the coastline, and for the homeward journey against the N.E. trade-winds Henry's captains would above all have needed ships able to go to windward. And we do see on all the old pictures that the caravels were rigged with two or three lateen sails.

If these pictures had been the only ones at our disposal it would have been difficult to visualise the vessel that Columbus commended as being seaworthy, swift and of shallow draught. The indifferent drawings on Juan de la Cosa's atlas portray vessels with a cloven forepost and some sort of quarter-deck or castle in the stern. The other pictures, especially the one on the Portuguese map of 1520 by Lopo Homen (274) show us long, and for the times unusually low hulls with an arched stern, and on the stern something which may be interpreted as a fork, a holder for the longest lateen yard

106

when lowered. On the River Tagus and the waters just outside Lisbon we can still see today a small, often multi-coloured vessel, a *frigata,* which is so like the pictures on the old maps that it is believed they are a relic of the caravel. (See page 210, fig. 494.)

Working from this material, it has been possible to reconstruct Columbus' most loved vessel the *Niña* which on departure from Palos was still a *caravela latina,* i.e. carried a lateen sail on all three masts (276, 277). She was flat-sterned as we imagine the caravels on the maps to have been, as we later know the caravels always to have been, like the frigata on the Tagus. She had a sharp bow with concave waterlines and like the frigata she was neither deep-draughted nor broad across the beam, and to be sturdy enough for windward work she had flaring sides.

But when she was sailing out to sea where Columbus had no intention of going to windward it was found that the high lateen rig was no longer suitable. The *Pinta* was already rigged at Palos as a *caravela redonda,* a square-sailed caravel, and when they reached the Canary Islands the *Niña* was also rerigged. The centre mast was moved far forward in the bow to become the foremast, a bowsprit was rigged up for attaching the bowline blocks, the mainmast was restayed so that it was not vertical and was fitted with a forestay, the yards were shortened and the sails recut. In this way the *Niña* also became a caravela redonda (275).

This is roughly what must have happened and this is roughly what Columbus' and Portuguese caravels must have looked like. Long, relatively light so that they could ride the waves of the Altantic, of shallow draught so that they could be used for coastal reconnaissance, swifter than carracks and other round-bellied vessels. It is conceivable that the word caravel gradually came to mean something different. In the North, in Scandinavia, it is possible that the foreign method of carvel building gave its name to the *kravell,* a vessel which appears to have very little in common with Columbus' caravels the *Pinta* and the *Niña.*

276

275

107

277

278

Venetian carrack, 1500

On Jacopo de Barbari's large picture of Venice from the year 1500 we can see among many other different vessels a large carrack (278) which shows a development of thirty years on the Flemish master W.A's carrack. It has a topsail, spritsail and — like the Portuguese ship from 1496 (271) — an extra mizzen, the *bonaventure mizzen,* the bonaventure for short. Contrary to all other ships in the Port of Venice the carrack has ratlines in the shrouds and it must be considered that she represents the most modern type of the times.

Turkish pirates were a constant danger to the Italian merchantmen and because of this the latter were strongly manned and gunned, so strongly in fact that they may almost be looked upon as warships. On the Venetian carrack we can count on the side towards us 28 guns, indicating that she probably mounted at least 56. Ships' guns, however, were still quite small and light. The larger ones lay bound to stock-carriages (281) and the smaller were mounted in mikes (forks) on the railings.

The closely-lying spars for the awning must have hindered the enemy boarding, and it is possible that a *boarding net* was set up over them at this early stage to make it even more difficult.

When reconstructing the carrack the following dimensions were reached: length from stem to stern 98½ feet, length of keel 69 feet, breadth 33 feet, depth from the railing amidships to the underside of the keel 21½ feet.

In the section (279) the numbers indicate: 1. Outrigger for the bonaventure stay. 2. Bonaventure mast. 3. Mizzenmast. 4. Mainmast. 5. Foremast. 6. Bowsprit. 7. Half deck with awning. 8. Quarter-deck where the guns were positioned on their carriages. 9. Knight with sheave holes for hoisting the main yard. (It is possible that there were two knights abreast.) 10. Hatch. 11. Main deck. 12. Lower deck. 13. Mast foot. 14. Hold.

In the perspective reconstruction (280) the numbers indicate: 1. Bonaventure outligger with guys. 2. Bonaventure sheet. 3. Bonaventure brace. 4. Bonaventure yard. 5. Bonaventure stay. 6. Mizzen brace. 7. Mizzen shrouds. 8. Mizzen yard. 9. Mizzen stay. 10. Mizzen topping lift. 11. Main topping lifts. 12. Martnets. 13. Main halyards. 14. Main shrouds with ratlines. 15. Main bowline. 16. Mainbrace. 17. Mainstay. 18. Topmast. 19. Topsail topping lift. 20. Topsail bowlines. 21. Foresail topping lift. 22. Forestay. 23. Foresail bowline. 24. Forebrace. 25. Spritsail.

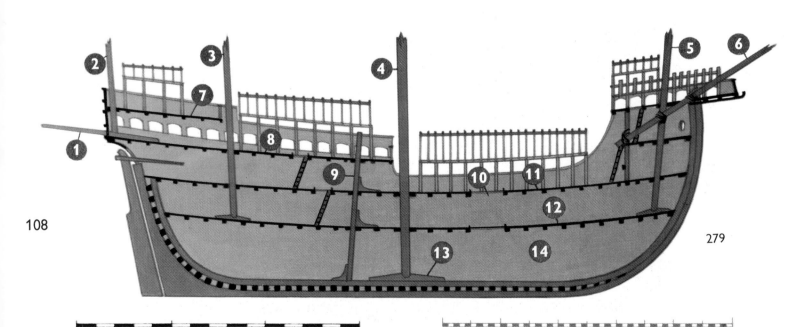

279

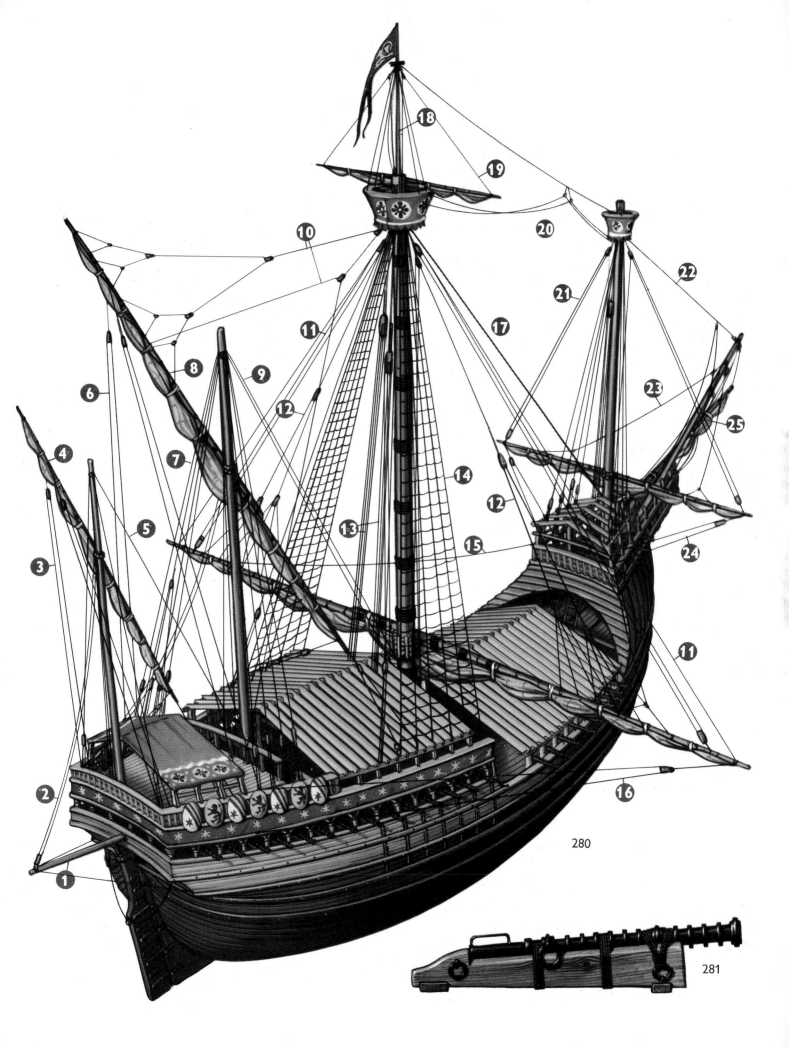

280

281

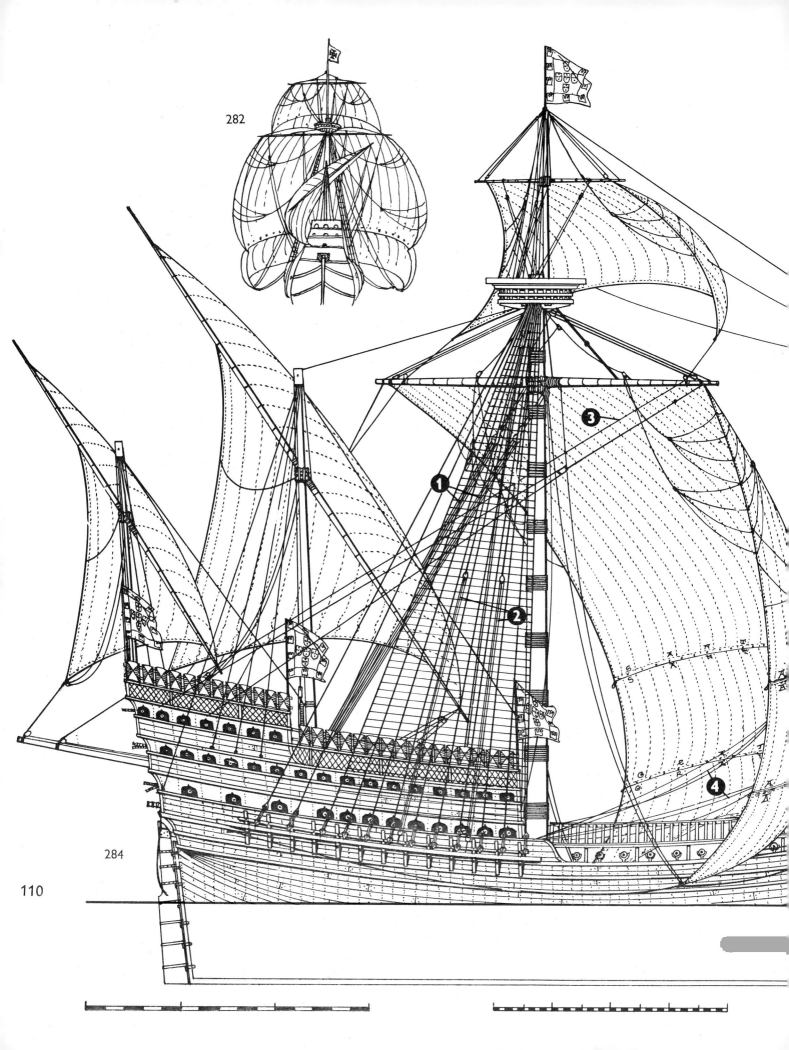

282

284

110

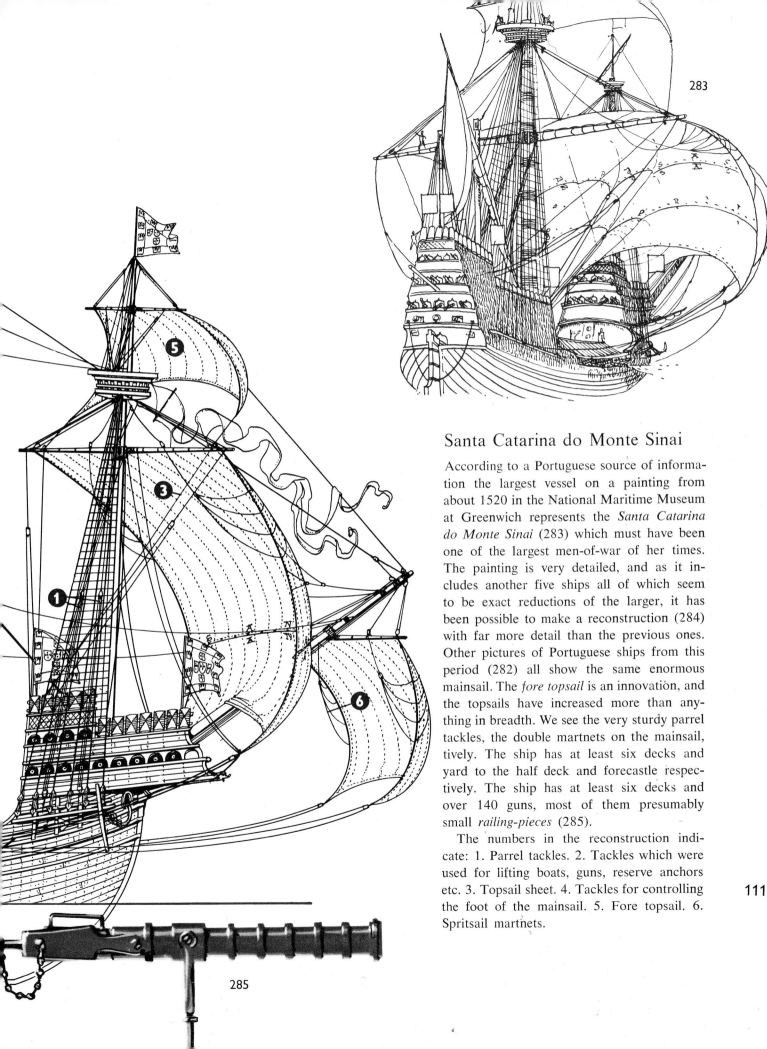

Santa Catarina do Monte Sinai

According to a Portuguese source of information the largest vessel on a painting from about 1520 in the National Maritime Museum at Greenwich represents the *Santa Catarina do Monte Sinai* (283) which must have been one of the largest men-of-war of her times. The painting is very detailed, and as it includes another five ships all of which seem to be exact reductions of the larger, it has been possible to make a reconstruction (284) with far more detail than the previous ones. Other pictures of Portuguese ships from this period (282) all show the same enormous mainsail. The *fore topsail* is an innovation, and the topsails have increased more than anything in breadth. We see the very sturdy parrel tackles, the double martnets on the mainsail, tively. The ship has at least six decks and yard to the half deck and forecastle respectively. The ship has at least six decks and over 140 guns, most of them presumably small *railing-pieces* (285).

The numbers in the reconstruction indicate: 1. Parrel tackles. 2. Tackles which were used for lifting boats, guns, reserve anchors etc. 3. Topsail sheet. 4. Tackles for controlling the foot of the mainsail. 5. Fore topsail. 6. Spritsail martnets.

285

Spanish galleon, 1540

already find it both in Italy and England by the middle of the sixteenth century. People usually think of the galleon as being a very richly decorated vessel riding high out of the water, yet the type of ship represented by the early galleons seems to have made its appearance as a protest against the broad and ever-growing naos or carracks, or whatever we wish to call these ships of the early sixteenth century (283).

The word *galleon* seems to be related to *galley,* and a Venetian manuscript from 1550 describes "un galion che voga a remi" — a galleon propelled by oars, but it is believed that this was a question of a *galeass.* The early, unfortunately not so very clear pictures existing of Portuguese galleons from 1535, and above all the 1540 model which is in the Museo Naval at Madrid (286) represent pure sailing-ships with no trace of oars.

Of perhaps even more obscure origin than the caravel is the *galleon.* We usually connect it with Spain, and it is possible that it did come from that country, but in which case it must have spread very quickly because we

286

The Venetian manuscript also gives the dimensions of a large *sailing* galleon; length from stem to stern 135½ feet, length of keel 100 feet, beam 33 feet, giving the rough proportions 4:3:1. As a rule the carracks had 3:2:1.

But slimness was not the only characteristic of the new type. On the carracks the superstructure of the forecastle projected far out over the bow (284). On the galleons the castle was within the bows, and proceeding from the hull itself — as a sort of continuation of the deck and bulwarks — there was a projecting part later to be called the *beak-head*. In its early stages this projection most approximated the ram of the galleys — or the relic of a ram — and it is possible that this detail caused the new ship to be called galleon. It has this shape in the Portuguese picture from 1541 (288), but the model (286) has the form of beak-head which was developed later.

The reconstruction (287) shows a Spanish galleon from the same period as the model. Gun-ports have come into use. Running over the boarding net is a *gangway* from the quarter-deck directly to the forecastle deck. The projection over the bows, the beak-head, facilitates manipulating the spritsail. The insignia of Emperor Charles V are painted on the mainsail. As on all larger ships of those times the galleon has four masts.

113

288

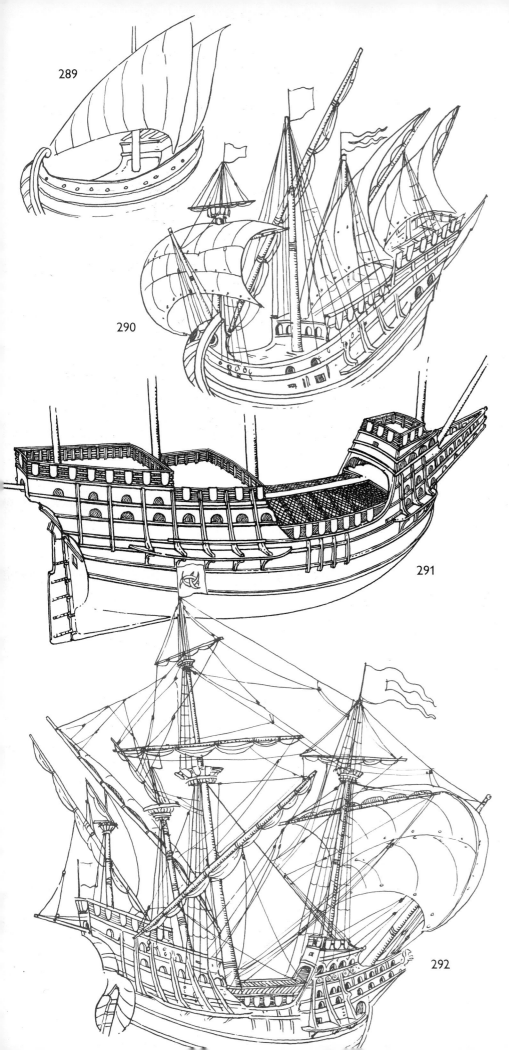

289

290

291

292

French men-of-war, 1545

In 1545 Francis I of France equipped a naval force for the invasion of England, and on a corner of a map of Normandy from the same year a part of the force is to be seen. It is a variegated collection of carracks, galleys, galeasses, galleons and caravels — three of the ships are reproduced here: two caravels (289, 290) and a galleon (292). The smaller caravel hardly shows any difference at all from the Portuguese caravels we saw earlier, but the larger of them has a rig which is to be found on many fifteenth-century caravels. Forward of the three lateen sails there is a foremast with square foresail and fore topsail.

The long top yards on the galleon indicate that the topsails have become larger, and above the main topsail there is now a *topgallant*. Both the mizzen and bonaventure masts have been given topmasts where small lateen sails can be seen. As on the Spanish galleon a gangway runs from the quarter-deck to the forecastle (reconstruction 291), and a boarding net has been set up over the spars of the awning. (It may be questioned whether the spars above the deck between the castles were not always intended to support the boarding net).

Henry Grâce à Dieu, 1545

Topgallants were nothing new for 1545 even if we have not seen them before. It is stated in manuscripts of the times that the English ship *Regent* was to have carried topgallants on the mainmast and topsails on the three other masts as early as 1509, exactly as on the French galleon (292). And the large and well-known ship *Henry Grâce à Dieu,* colloquially referred to as *Great Harry,* was already rigged when it was built in 1514 with topmasts and topgallant masts on the forward three and a topmast on the bonaventure. She was at the time fitted with 184 guns, presumably quite light. Unfortunately there is no contemporary picture of her.

She was almost wholly rebuilt during the years 1536—39 and in 1545 was depicted in her new form together with the whole of Henry VIII's navy by an artillery officer, Anthony Anthony. The picture is still in ex-

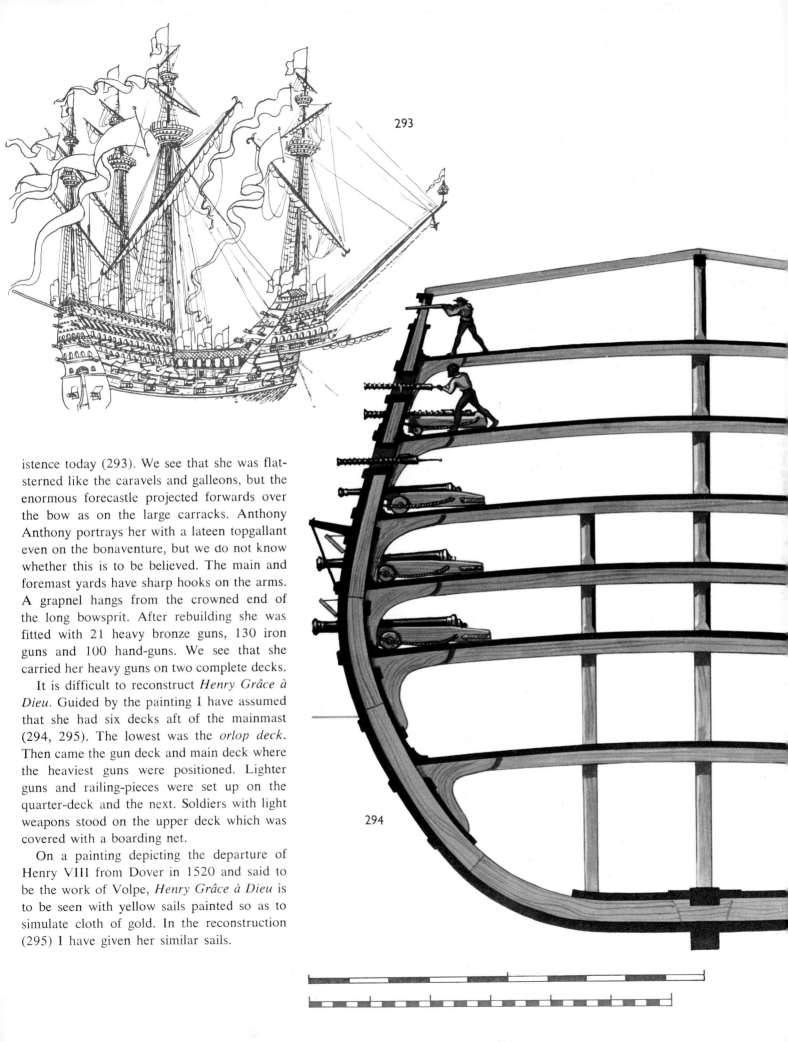

293

istence today (293). We see that she was flat-sterned like the caravels and galleons, but the enormous forecastle projected forwards over the bow as on the large carracks. Anthony Anthony portrays her with a lateen topgallant even on the bonaventure, but we do not know whether this is to be believed. The main and foremast yards have sharp hooks on the arms. A grapnel hangs from the crowned end of the long bowsprit. After rebuilding she was fitted with 21 heavy bronze guns, 130 iron guns and 100 hand-guns. We see that she carried her heavy guns on two complete decks.

It is difficult to reconstruct *Henry Grâce à Dieu.* Guided by the painting I have assumed that she had six decks aft of the mainmast (294, 295). The lowest was the *orlop deck.* Then came the gun deck and main deck where the heaviest guns were positioned. Lighter guns and railing-pieces were set up on the quarter-deck and the next. Soldiers with light weapons stood on the upper deck which was covered with a boarding net.

On a painting depicting the departure of Henry VIII from Dover in 1520 and said to be the work of Volpe, *Henry Grâce à Dieu* is to be seen with yellow sails painted so as to simulate cloth of gold. In the reconstruction (295) I have given her similar sails.

294

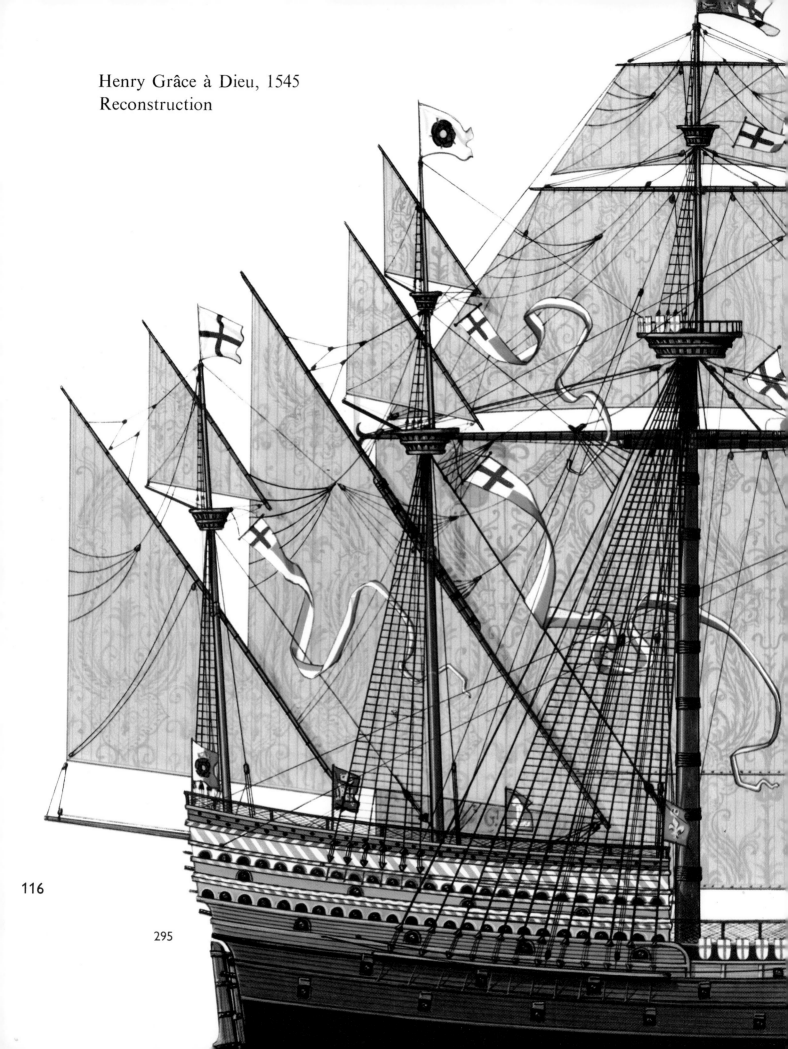

Henry Grâce à Dieu, 1545
Reconstruction

295

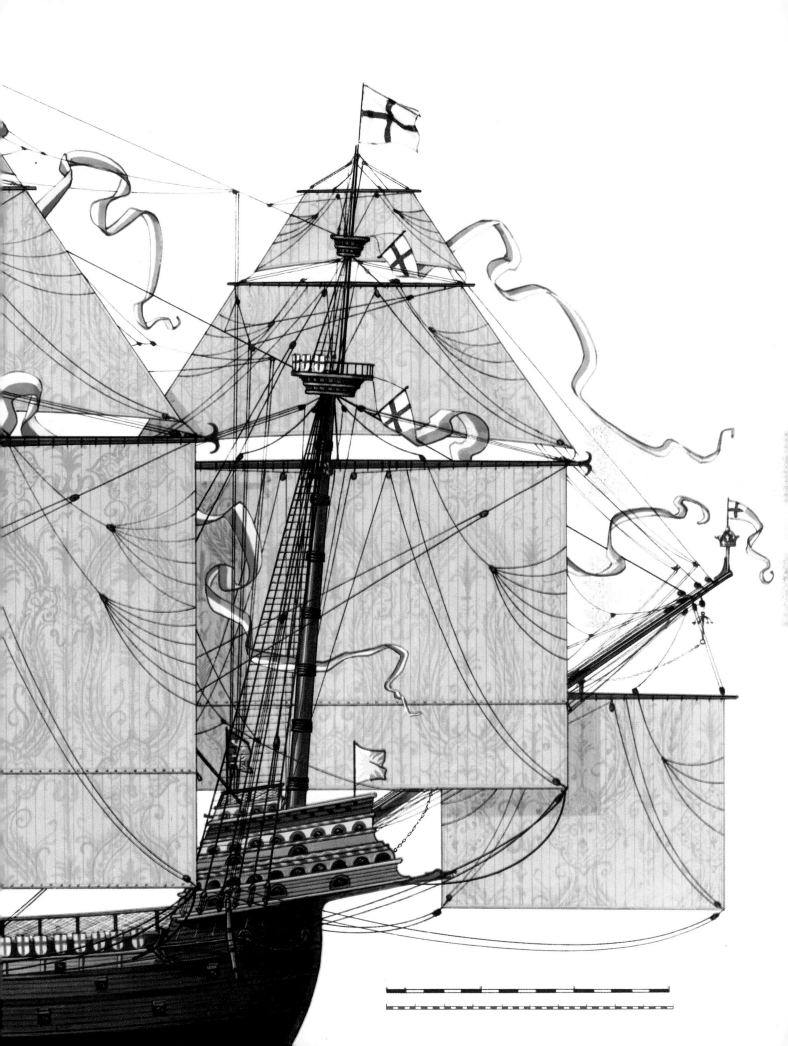

296

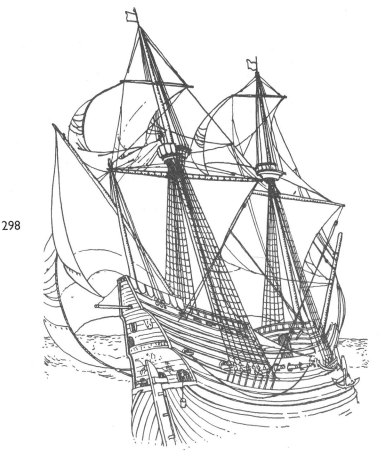

297

298

Vessel types, 1565

About 1565 the Flemish artist Pieter Brueghel the Elder painted a number of ships in great detail. The small galleon decorated with shields (296) with two gun decks may with certainty be considered a pure man-of-war, while the vessel with the curious forecastle (297) is more of a merchant caravel. It has the usual rounded bow of the Portuguese caravels, but is also fitted with a projecting platform under it, almost like a ram, and it is probably because of this that she has been described as a galleon. As Brueghel's paintings all seem to be well-drawn we have to accept the enormous aftercastle. The construction of the forecastle is different from anything we have seen so far, but we have no evidence that this type was to remain on the seas for long.

The third ship, on the other hand (298) with its round stern and narrow poop seems to have been a prototype of the Dutch *fluyt* which was to be perhaps the most prominent type of merchantman in the seventeenth century. We can see that the mizzen has now been fitted with a bonnet — something which we may already have guessed at on Francis I's caravel (290).

The art of shipbuilding, 1400-1514

Within the period of a hundred years the sailing-ship had undergone more profound development than during the 5,500 years of its history that had passed and more than was to occur during 400 years to come. The one-masted ship of the beginning of the fifteenth century had step by step, yet swiftly, become two and three-masted, had been given spritsail and topsails, was fitted with a fourth mast and later topgallants also. What was to occur after this was really only polishing and completion.

The art of shipbuilding was still no science; pure science it has never become. Building was carried out according to inherited experience, and certain methods were kept as top secrets within the families of shipbuilders. Attempts were made to copy the vessels that had proved to be good sailers, and there was a certain amount of understanding for the importance of the shape and dimensions of the hull for seaworthiness. Yet the many catastrophes which occurred with vessels that were extreme for their times show that the deepest misjudgements were to be made both then and later. Ships were not built to drawings but with regard to certain basic dimensions and norms when forming the keel and frames. Some shipbuilders who were more gifted in such matters recorded their rules and norms and illustrated their manuals with explanatory drawings (251, 261).

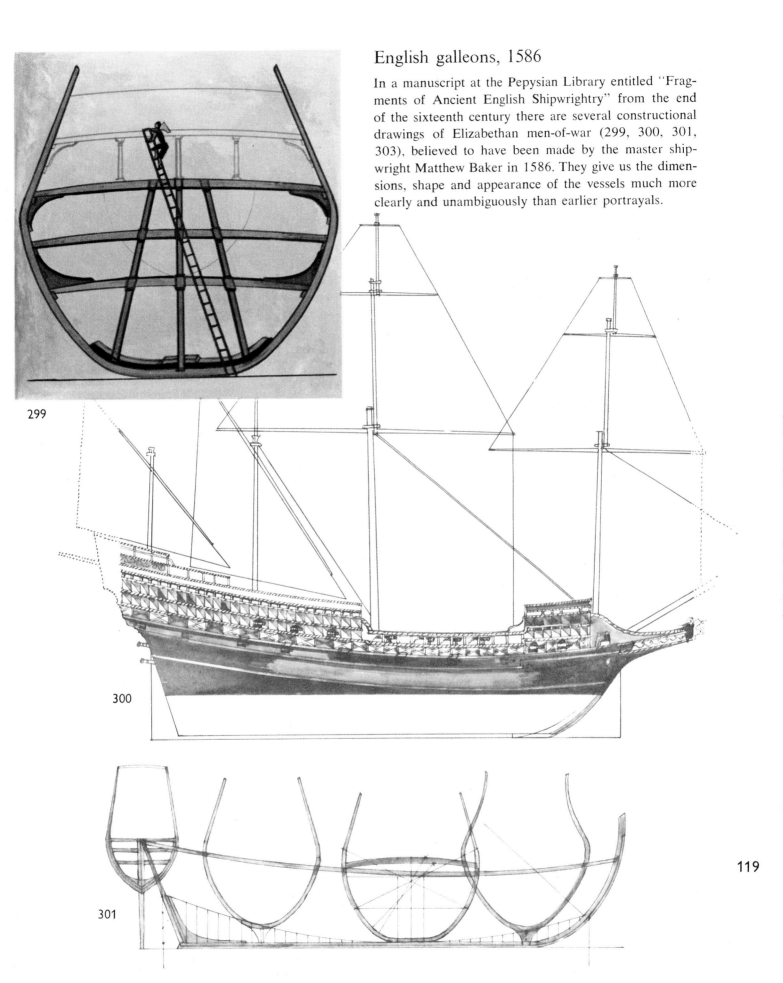

English galleons, 1586

In a manuscript at the Pepysian Library entitled "Fragments of Ancient English Shipwrightry" from the end of the sixteenth century there are several constructional drawings of Elizabethan men-of-war (299, 300, 301, 303), believed to have been made by the master shipwright Matthew Baker in 1586. They give us the dimensions, shape and appearance of the vessels much more clearly and unambiguously than earlier portrayals.

299

300

301

119

English galleons, 1588

Queen Elizabeth's foremost ships in the navy that defeated the Spanish Armada in 1588 may well have had the appearance of the galleons in Matthew Baker's manuscript. Other contemporary, or roughly contemporary, representations of the notable English vessels show clumsier ships, but this may be due to their having been drawn by inferior artists. A picture which is stated to represent the flagship *Ark Royal* (304) built in 1587 shows a galleon with two gun decks, double forecastle deck, quarter-deck, half deck — and above the half deck furthest aft a *poop deck*. An innovation is the balcony, the *gallery* which ran forward from the stern a certain distance on either side of the half deck.

The rig is still inefficiently overburdened with lateen top and topgallant on the mizzenmast and topsail on the bonaventure, in contrast to the simple and effective rig shown by Matthew Baker (300 and reconstruction 302). But it may be that the remarkable lateen sails on the top and topgallant masts of *Henry Grâce à Dieu*, the *Ark Royal* and other larger ships were merely decorative, seldom if ever being used, to be hoisted when the new ships were paraded but soon to be removed, masts and all, by the practical commanders. An experienced shipbuilder like Matthew Baker was unwilling to include such masts and sails, but the artists who portrayed the ships to record the victory were less finicky.

Baker's galleons are low and elegant for the time. The long beak-head is supported by a knee, divided above, on the leading edge of the fore-post, a *cutwater*. The *figurehead* is a dragon. The forecastle is composed of a single deck, but like the *Ark Royal*, the reconstruction (302) has both quarter-deck, half deck and poop deck. On the diagram of sails (300) both mizzens extend a

120

302

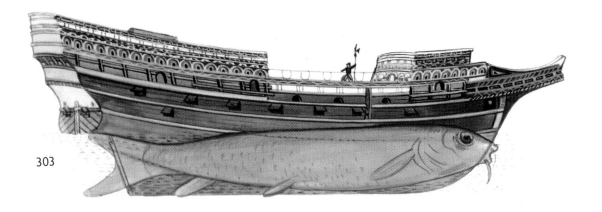

303

304

little beyond the yard-arms, causing us to believe that they were fitted with bonnets.

The English men-of-war must be considered as the foremost of the times. The high castles — which had been of much use when sea fighting nearly always meant boarding — had been reduced as the seaworthy and easily manoeuvred vessels were now intended to meet the enemy with gunfire. The Spaniards themselves have said that the English guns were more effective than their own.

Dutch ships, 1590's

Portugal and Spain were the great colonial powers during the sixteenth century, and to gain advantage of their colonies they were dependent on defence of the long transport routes. When Henry, King of Portugal, died in 1580 Philip II seized the crown. Holland, then a province of Spain, had not previously sent their merchantmen further than Lisbon but when the Dutch revolted as a result of Philip's relentless policy, the port of Lisbon was closed to them, leading them to send their own ships to the East Indies.

Four ships set sail in April 1595. Three of them returned in August 1597, and their voyage laid the foundations of Dutch imperial ascendency. A reproduction of them is to be found on the covers of a description of the voyage which was printed that same year. The picture does not give many details (306), but an engraving of Amsterdam harbour from about the same time contains a clearer representation of a similar vessel (307, reconstruction 308, 310).

It is a small galleon — from this time right up to the days of Nelson it must be considered that most larger sailing-ships, men-of-war in particular, were galleons. It has a gallery, a single forecastle deck, quarter-deck and half deck. The arched opening in front of the mizzenmast (307) is presumably the helmsman's "window". Earlier the helmsman or helmsmen of larger vessels had stood way in under the half deck, steered by compass and command and managed the long tiller with tackles. The *whipstaff* probably came into use about the end of the sixteenth century making it possible for the helmsmen of larger vessels to observe the sails when steering (309)

An engraving by W. Barentsoen from 1594 shows a large Dutch man-of-war with two galleries (305). The boatswains of those times excelled in complicated details of the rigging with many crowfeet ends at spars, stays and leeches. Their real purpose was to even the pull, but they were finally to become merely decorative ends in themselves. We see how complicated the arrangements were for the foretop and fore topgallant halyards, and the same is true for the ties for the mizzens and top-mizzens.

122

305

306

307

308

309

With the aid of the whipstaff the helmsmen of the even larger vessels were able to observe the sails when steering, and this was of great importance when going to windward. The lock of the rudder was not extensive and on greater alterations of course the ship had to be trimmed with the sails.

310

311

312

Flemish galleon, 1593

The most beautiful model of a sixteenth-century ship is to be found at the Museo Naval in Madrid (311). It was presented to Philip II in 1593 by faithful Flemish subjects and we may therefore be fairly safe in assuming that it represents the foremost type of ship known to them at the time.

The long carved gallery begins at the aftermost channel and curves right around the stern. The whole space between the gun decks is carved and gilded, and the remaining ornamentation painted. The model is not made to scale. The underwater hull is too small and the rig out of proportion. It is clear that the model has suffered damage, and the ignorant repairer has cheated with the rigging so that anachronistic details have been added.

With proportions according to Matthew Baker I have made a reconstruction (312) with exactly the same ornamentation as on the model. Only the lower masts are raised. We notice that the foremast, as on most sixteenth century galleons, is situated forward of the forecastle. The shrouds are fixed with lanyards through heart-shaped deadeyes. A boarding net is set up over the main deck, and at the level of the bulwark a gangway with rail runs on each side.

The gun with the curious carriage is Danish (313) and is portrayed in an ordnance manuscript from 1585.

313

125

314

315

316

Fore-and-aft spritsail and forestay sail

We have a picture of a small vessel with *fore-and-aft spritsail* and *forestay sail* from as early as the end of the fifteenth century, and as pictures of small craft from those times are very rare it is believed that both the sails are even older. When the Dutch began to fight for independence from the Spanish Empire they had no navy to speak of, and many small coastal vessels were rebuilt in an improvised way so that they could carry some guns (317). The Spanish ships were handicapped in the shallow Dutch waters and we are later to see how the Dutch managed to build vessels that were both ocean-going and suited to shallow harbours.

An engraving from 1599 shows one of the ship's boats (316) from Willem Barentz' polar expedition 1596—

1597 where all the details of the fore-and-aft spritsail rig are clearly illustrated, and on a picture of the same date there are small coastal vessels (314) partly riding at anchor and partly sailing on different tacks. But we find the fore-and-aft spritsail on relatively large vessels as well. In Aurigarius' "Speculum Marini" from 1586 there is an engraving showing a Norwegian *bojort* (315). It was a clinker-built merchantman, also quite common in the Baltic, but probably originating in Holland where it was called *boejer*. The original Dutch boejer disappeared during the seventeenth century, but the name was transferred to a small, round-sterned vessel which was often used for pleasure trips. The Norwegian bojort in the illustration (315) carries a topsail, a square topsail above the spritsail. It also has a lateen mizzen and spritsail under the bowsprit, and, like the bojorts in the Baltic, a forestay sail presumably.

317

Galleys, end of the fourteenth century

In the Mediterranean the wind is usually either too fresh or too light for heavy sailing-ships. It is because of this that heavy-going cargo vessels without an escort had always been easy prey for the pirate galleys which could manoeuvre regardless of the wind, and ever since classical times the large, oar-propelled vessels, the triremes, the dromons and selanders, had been the dominating warships. Sea-fights were hardly ever contracted in the Mediterranean in heavy seas; for this the galleys were not at all suitable.

As their names tell us, and as we have seen them portrayed, the warships of classical times were rowed with oars in two or three banks, and with one or more oarsmen to each oar. Still during the early Middle Ages, even to the middle of the fourteenth century — as we can see on the bronze door at St. Peter's (234) — ships were rowed with the oars in two banks. A change seems

to have occurred about the end of the fourteenth century.

At the Palazzo della Signoria in Siena there is a painting which portrays a sea-fight between the Venetians and Frederick Barbarossa's son Otto (318). It was painted by Spinello Aretino probably about the end of the fourteenth century. The warships portrayed, the *galleys*, are of a type which might be called biremes, yet the oars are no longer in two banks but lie in close pairs on a long beam, the *apostis*. Lowest in the picture we can see how they hang in strap-like fixtures. It may be said that these galleys differ very little in principle from the late Greek bireme as it is found on the pedestal to the "Victory of Samothrace" (82).

As on the dromons the ram lies above the waterline and it had very likely lost its old function, serving no more as a boarding bridge. The sloping flagstaff (can this have been a relic of the artemon mast?) was already seen on the dromons. On one of the ships a broken rudder seems to be lying under a platform for the soldiers. In Italy such a galley with the oars in close pairs was called a *fusta*. Not so very much later, about the middle of the fifteenth century, we come across galleys with the oars in groups of three, all in the same plane. These triremes were called *galia sottil*.

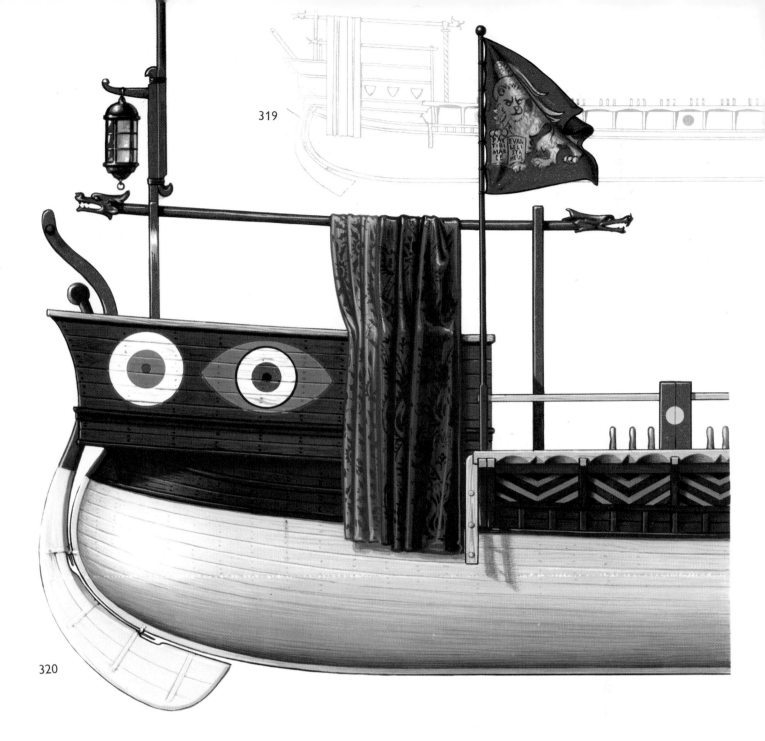

319

320

Galleys, fifteenth century

Galleys were not only built for fighting. In "Jacobi Aurie Annales ad annum 1291" we can read of the first attempt at finding a sea-route to India along the coast of Africa. The brothers Ugolino and Guido Vivaldi sailed that year from Genoa in two galleys in the direction of Ceuta, but after they had rounded Cape Gozora nothing more was heard of them. We do not know what their galleys looked like, but in the twice-mentioned treatise on the art of shipbuilding from the middle of the fifteenth century there is a picture of a transport galley (323). It is a large *galia sottil* with nineteen groups of oars on each side, i.e. 114 oars in all. It is rigged like the Portuguese caravels, and the flagstaff in the stern rests on the large fork in the bow. If we disregard the oars and the shape of the stern the picture could very well be of a caravel — and little it is we know of the

321

origin of the caravel. But we do know that Mediterranean transport galleys journeyed each year as far as England.

On Gratiosus Benincasa's atlas of 1482 there is, among other vessels, a picture of a fusta with 23 pairs of oars on each side, making a total of 92 oars and oarsmen. It has a mast with a large lateen sail, having been usual, it seems, on galleys right up to the seventeenth century. Of roughly the same period are the paintings by Carpaccio on which the reconstruction of a large *galia sottil* and its stern (319, 320) has been based. There is perhaps reason to point out that the "modern" decoration on the stern is directly copied from a painting at the Doge's Palace in Venice.

On Carpaccio's large galley from one of the paintings treating the Legend of Ursula it is just possible to count 84 rowlocks, making 84 oars on each side manned by a total of 168 oarsmen. It is not quite clear how these oarsmen sat, but in 1881 Admiral Fincati of Venice had a model of a *galia sottil* built in which the placing of the oarsmen appears to be acceptable (322). On the fore-deck (319, 322) are the two curved cat-heads typical of the galleys. Midships, as on the earliest Greek galleys, there is a long bridge between the oarsmen, the *corsia*, really a raised part of the hull whose sturdy side planks give much strength to the vessel fore-and-aft. The after-castle with its poles for the awning is for the officers. Furthest aft there is a gallows for the long yard, a development of the "wings" we saw on the early mediaeval vessels of the Mediterranean (221—223). Carpaccio's galley shows the sloping flagstaff for the last time.

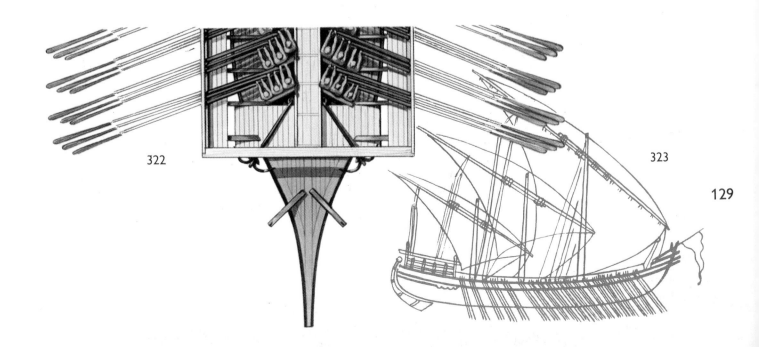

322

323

129

325

324

Galleys, sixteenth century

It is likely that the galleys introduced a new system of
propulsion as early as at the beginning of the sixteenth
century. It had been experienced that propulsion became
boht simpler and more efficient if the number of oars
was reduced and several men, usually five, placed on
each oar. The painter Pinturicchio who died in 1513
includes in a painting which now hangs in the cathedral
at Siena a large *galeass*, a cross between a galley and a
large sailing-vessel (327), where the oars now rest evenly
spaced on the apostis, indicating that the new system
had come into use.

It is possible that this new method of rowing soon
became general. In a painting by Tintoretto from the end
of the century and now at the Doge's Palace we do in
fact still see the oars in groups of three (329), but it portrays a sea-fight which took place in 1176, and Tintoretto has presumably wished to show old-fashioned
galleys.

Two watercolours by Raphael (324, 326) seem to illustrate the new system and the one clearly shows what
happened when a lateener wore round before the wind
and was to transfer the yard over to the other side of the
mast (Cf. 215—218). The drawings show rough, simplified details, which might suggest that Raphael did them
from a small model.

326

327

329

328

330

The only existing model of a sixteenth-century galley is to be found at the Museo Storico Navale in Venice (330). It is unfortunately damaged, and nothing remains of the aftercastle or poop as it properly should be called on a galley. The ram, corsia and all thwarts are absent, yet what does remain gives us a good idea of the Venetian galley, especially as we are able to complement it with the picture of an almost exactly similar galley (328) on a fresco by Andrea Vicentino in the Palazzo Barbarigo in Venice. The latter is quite definitely three-masted while the model shows no evidence of more than one mast, but we do see the same arched holes in the bulwarks above the apostis and the same windows in the quarter.

The galley's use of guns also seems to have begun during the sixteenth century, and on an engraving by Pieter Brueghel the Elder, all of seven forward guns may be counted (325). The picture is supposed to represent a Portuguese galley of 1565. In the portrayal of Francis I's invasion force of 1545 there are also several galleys but it cannot be seen whether they have guns and they still seem to be propelled with oars arranged in the old fashion (331). The English also made attempts to use galleys, and in the seventeenth and beginning of the eighteenth centuries the Swedes and the Russians used them in the Baltic, but they were never to become a success in northern waters.

131

331

332

132

333

Venetian galleys, sixteenth century

The tomb of the Venetian Admiral Alexander Contareni at St. Antonio Cathedral in Padua is decorated with reliefs of ships, among them a sailing galley (332). The reliefs were carved in the middle of the sixteenth century, at roughly the same time as the Venetian galley-builder Pre Theodoro de Nicoló wrote his instructions to succeeding galley-builders in a manuscript which is still in existence at the Biblioteca Nazionale in Venice.

Among other things he gives us the dimensions of galleys of different sorts and sizes and we are told that: a fusta was 88½ feet long from stem to stern-post, 13 feet wide and 4½ feet deep from freeboard to keel. The measurements for a light galley were 131 feet, 16½ feet and 5½ feet, and for a large galley 151 feet, 24½ feet and 10 feet. The corsia, the raised bridge between the thwarts, was on the large galley 2 feet 9 ins wide and the planks forming its sides were 8 ins thick. The distance between the corsia and the apostis, the long beam on which the oars rested, was 14½ feet.

With regard to all this, the relief, Pre Theodoro's measurements, Andrea Vicentino's fresco, and above all the model in the Museo Storico Navale, I have drawn a reconstruction of a Venetian galley from the latter half of the sixteenth century (333).

133

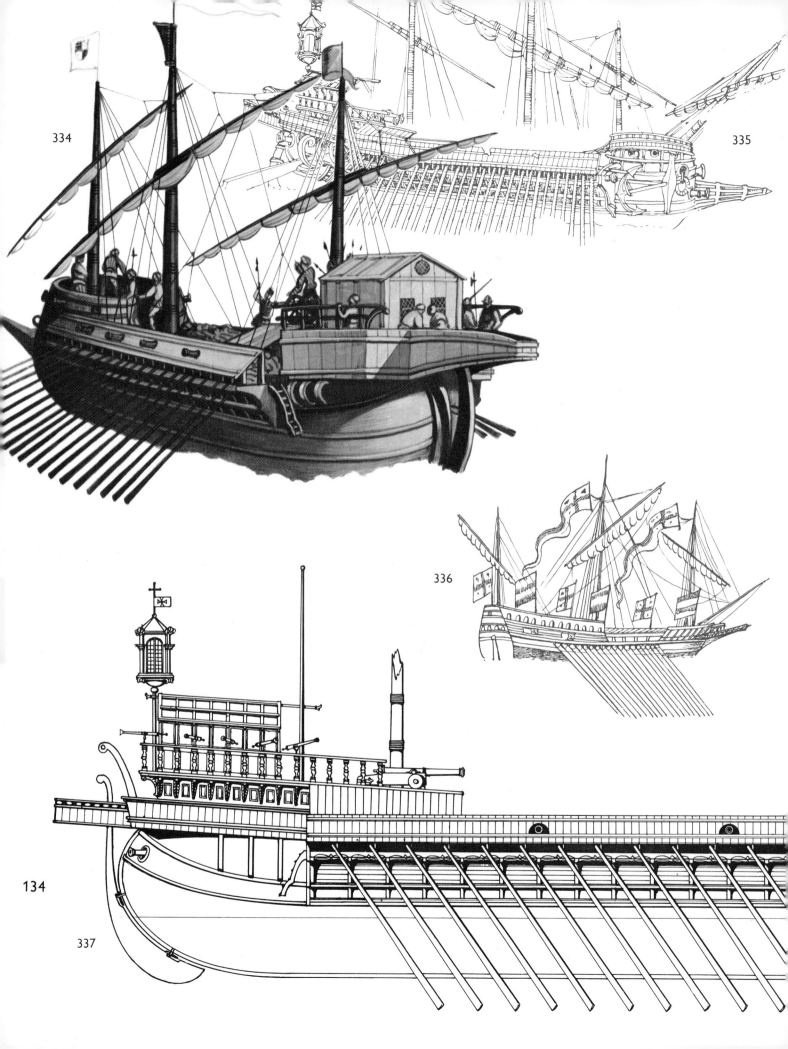

334

335

336

134

337

Galeasses, sixteenth century

The greatest galley-fight known to history was foght on 7th October 1571 at Lepanto in Greece when the combined fleets of Spain, Malta, Venice and the Pope, altogether 208 well-equipped galleys and galeases, gained a crushing victory over the less well-equipped Turkish fleet of galleys (273). Naturally the great victory was pictorially recorded by many contemporary artists, and the main point of interest for many of them seems to have been the heavy powerful galeasses. In these vessels an attempt had been made at combining the manoeuvrability and independence of wind with a heavy ship's strength, capacity for carrying guns and ability to sail when this was considered necessary.

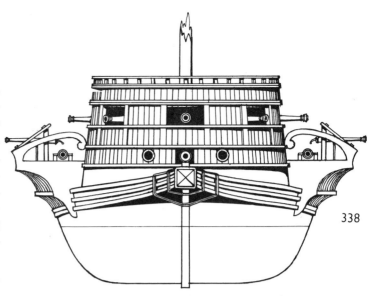

338

The galeasses in the Lepanto pictures (335) all seem to be in agreement with the picture of a Spanish galeass on a fresco in the Escorial (334) illustrating the Battle of the Azores of 1582. In Anthony Anthony's illustrations of the vessels in the English fleet of 1545 there are also galeasses (336), but, exactly as one might have expected of a northern country unfamiliar with galleys, what was built was a sailing-ship, perhaps a little longer and lower than usual, which had been fitted with oars. Contrary to this the Mediterranean galeasses give the impression of being high-sided galleys.

In his manuscript Pre Theodoro also describes the building of oar-propelled galleons, the largest of them 145 feet from stem to stern-post, 27 feet wide, 9 feet deep, and "two men to each oar and two oars to each thwart" — thus being rowed according to the old system. I believe that we ought to regard these "rowing galleons" as galeasses. Yet it was not so very long before Pre Theo-

doro wrote his manual that the galleons first made their appearance, and it may be that his writings give us a clue as to the origin of the galleons.

The reconstruction (337, 338) has been based on the galeasses at Lepanto and the Azores with a touch of Pre Theodoro's measurements. We can count eight heavy guns in the round forecastle and two more heavy pieces sit in carriages on the aftercastle. Furthermore we seem to see the possibility of there being some 12—14 lighter guns and perhaps as many small railing pieces. The largest galeasses at Lepanto were rigged with three lateen masts plus a fourth mast — or bowsprit? — leaning over the stem and fitted with a square sail, an artemon or spritsail (335). The ram appears to be so powerful and moreover reinforced with iron that it still very likely could be used for its old purpose. The oarsmen, as on Pieter Brueghel's galley (325), are protected by a long, sloping breastwork.

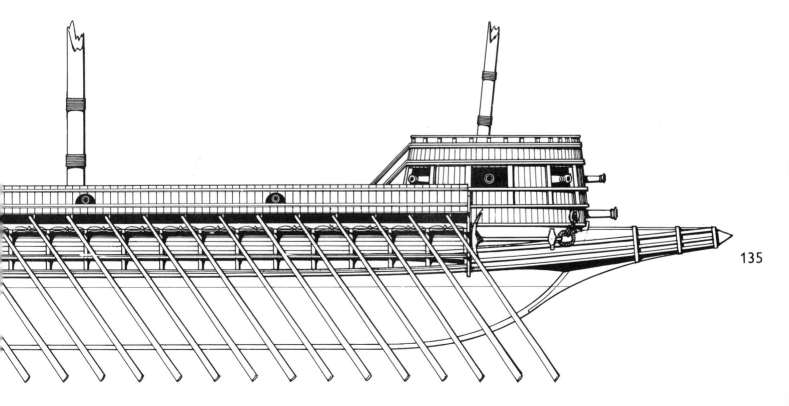

135

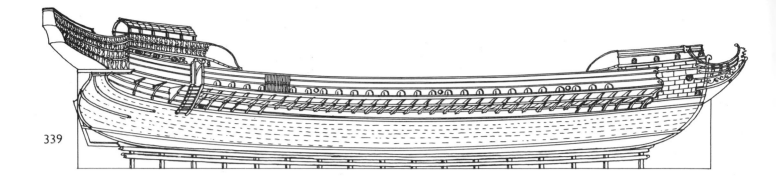

Galeasses, seventeenth century

During the seventeenth century France became the leading power in Europe. At the beginning of the reign of Louis XIV the country had little or no navy, but it was soon to be built up according to the most modern methods so that it was well able to contend with the English and Dutch navies. The most important group consisted of pure sailing-ships intended for warring in the English Channel, the Baltic and on the Atlantic coastline. But France also had a Mediterranean coast, and here Louis XIV secured his realm with a fleet which included both galleys and galeasses.

During the hundred years which had passed since the Battle of Lepanto the Mediterranean galeass had not undergone much change. An Italian drawing (339) dated 1669 shows a galeass whose dimensions have been calculated to be: length from stem to stern 164 feet and

beam 42½ feet. It was propelled by 300 or 350 oarsmen at 50 oars. It probably had the same rig as contemporary galeasses with three lateen masts and a bowsprit with spritsail. (Reconstruction 340). The poop with the long extension over the rudder is found a hundred years earlier. The after part of the forecastle has been given a straight bulkhead, and the ram has disappeared entirely, being replaced with a beak-head typical of the sailing-ships of those days.

In comparison with the broadsides that could be fired by the large men-of-war the armament of the galeass seems to be remarkably weak. On the Italian drawing we are unable to find arrangements for more than about twenty guns. Other pictures of galeasses from the same period do certainly show up to fifty guns, but they appear to be small for the most part. Both the galley and the galeass had really become outmoded during the sixteenth century, and that they continued to be built may have depended on the dogmatic belief that sea-fights in the Mediterranean could only be carried out with oar-propelled vessels.

340

La Réale, 1680

The name *La Réale* meant that the ship belonged to the king, and from the year 1526 the flagship of the French galley commander was called *La Réale* and carried the flags of both the king and her commander. It is likely that the most complete version of the galley had already come into being about the beginning of the seventeenth century although the Mediterranean galley-builders by no means constructed their masterpieces in co-operation; they were built according to principles and secret rules that were enviously guarded within arsenal and ship-building family.

The seventeenth-century French galleys were classified as *ordinary* with 26 pairs of thwarts and *extraordinary* which could have as many as 33 pairs. Normally a galley had 5 oarsmen on each thwart, bringing the total number on an ordinary galley to 260. But the very largest, and belonging to these were of course the *réales*, could have up to 7 men per thwart, thus being driven by a total of 462.

341

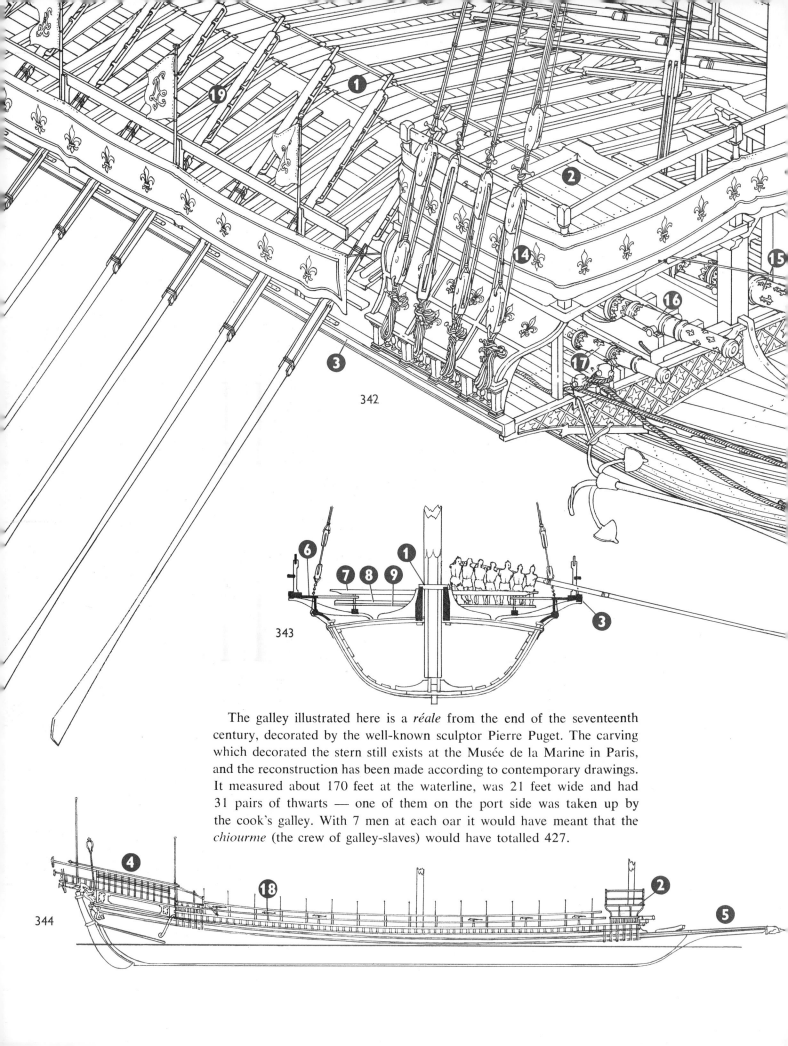

342

343

The galley illustrated here is a *réale* from the end of the seventeenth
century, decorated by the well-known sculptor Pierre Puget. The carving
which decorated the stern still exists at the Musée de la Marine in Paris,
and the reconstruction has been made according to contemporary drawings.
It measured about 170 feet at the waterline, was 21 feet wide and had
31 pairs of thwarts — one of them on the port side was taken up by
the cook's galley. With 7 men at each oar it would have meant that the
chiourme (the crew of galley-slaves) would have totalled 427.

344

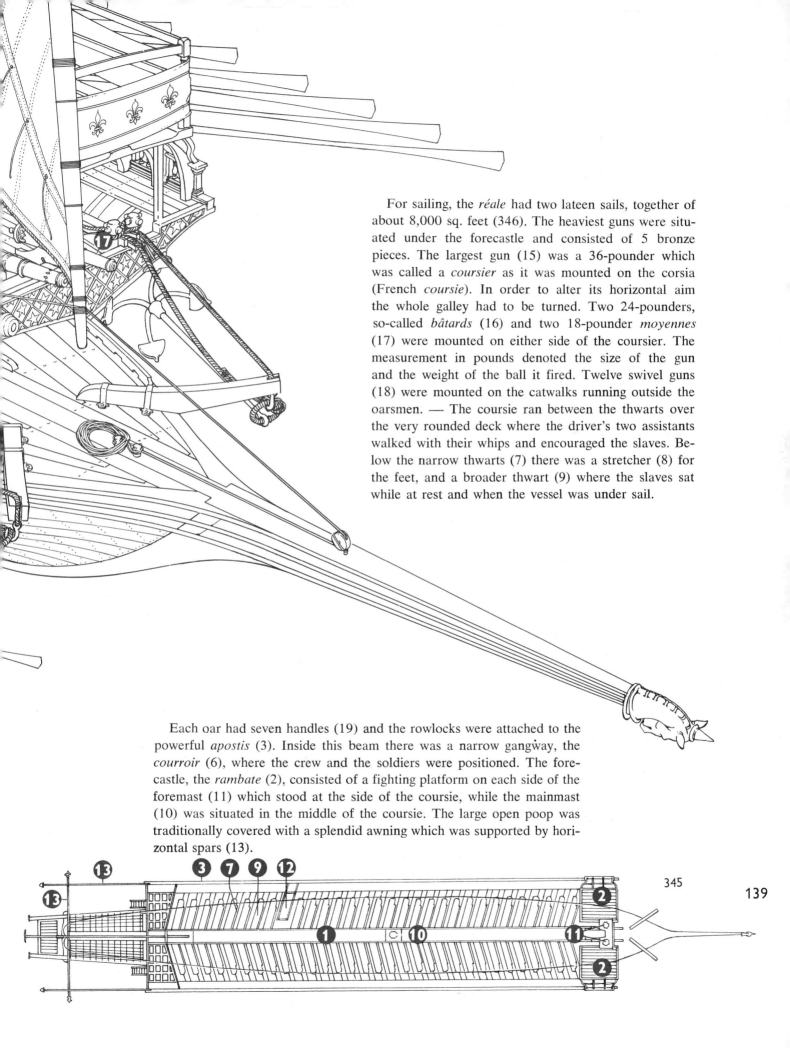

For sailing, the *réale* had two lateen sails, together of about 8,000 sq. feet (346). The heaviest guns were situated under the forecastle and consisted of 5 bronze pieces. The largest gun (15) was a 36-pounder which was called a *coursier* as it was mounted on the corsia (French *coursie*). In order to alter its horizontal aim the whole galley had to be turned. Two 24-pounders, so-called *bâtards* (16) and two 18-pounder *moyennes* (17) were mounted on either side of the coursier. The measurement in pounds denoted the size of the gun and the weight of the ball it fired. Twelve swivel guns (18) were mounted on the catwalks running outside the oarsmen. — The coursie ran between the thwarts over the very rounded deck where the driver's two assistants walked with their whips and encouraged the slaves. Below the narrow thwarts (7) there was a stretcher (8) for the feet, and a broader thwart (9) where the slaves sat while at rest and when the vessel was under sail.

Each oar had seven handles (19) and the rowlocks were attached to the powerful *apostis* (3). Inside this beam there was a narrow gangway, the *courroir* (6), where the crew and the soldiers were positioned. The forecastle, the *rambate* (2), consisted of a fighting platform on each side of the foremast (11) which stood at the side of the coursie, while the mainmast (10) was situated in the middle of the coursie. The large open poop was traditionally covered with a splendid awning which was supported by horizontal spars (13).

345

La Réale

Proceeding from the stern the layout of the galley under deck began with the captain's cabin, then a smaller room for the belongings of the principal officers and the furniture that was used on the afterdeck when the vessel was not on active service, then a store room for drink and fresh food and another store room for dry foodstuffs. Amidships there was a room called the *taverne,* and, apart from housing reserve sails and a large awning which could be rigged up over the whole galley, this was the cellar for the wine which the driver sold to the crew. A room led from the taverne to the powder room which was in the charge of the master gunner. The room farthest forward was occupied by the anchor cables and other material, and when necessary was used as a hospital for the sick and wounded.

La Réale carried two ship's boats, a heavier called *caique* which was used among other things for weighing anchor, and a lighter which was called *canot.* Each was rowed by twelve freemen. They were usually carried in tow but could be lifted up onto gallows above the oarsmen when necessary.

The hull of the galley was very low in the water and waves swamped the deck even in a slight sea. When sailing in a fairly strong wind the whole leeside of the deck was under water

346

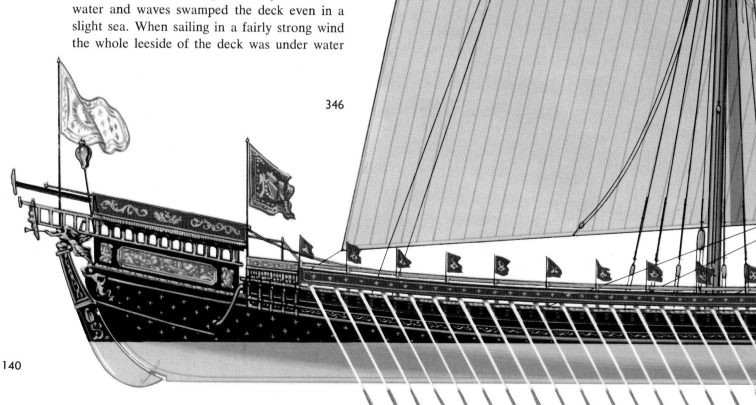

and the oarsmen often sat up to their waists in it. The sails were always furled before battle and the long yards were made safe to the masts with chains so that they could not so easily be shot down and interfere with manoeuvring the vessel. A galley was generally speaking very loth to give battle to a sailing-ship in fresh wind. Because of their length they were very slow on the turn, and to facilitate manoeuvring it was attempted — without much success — to rig a third sail near the poop. With a similar object in mind experiments were made during the eighteenth century with another rudder in the bows.

The galleys could only effectively give battle to the heavily armed seventeenth-century men-of-war in calm weather when they had the possibility of turning from the broadsides and choosing the position of battle themselves. But as they were relatively lightly armed many of them were necessary to overcome a well-armed man-of-war.

There were many experts who advised Louis XIV to abandon the galley fleet, eagerly telling him of how the 26-gun frigate *Lion Couronné* had fought an undecided battle for hours against eleven galleys in June 1651, and of the ship *Le Bon* which had defeated thirty-five galleys in July 1684.

The last naval battle in which galleys were actively employed was fought at Matapan in 1717. The last French *réale* was built three years after.

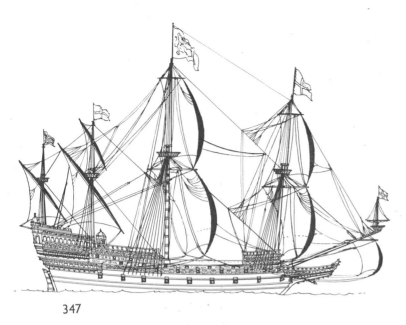

347

The Prince Royal, 1610

Nothing really sensational occurred in the development of the ship during the seventeenth century and the reason for the extensive treatment of just this century by books on the ship is because this is when sources of reliable information begin to appear. There are detailed paintings and engravings from even the first decade which reproduce vessels in correct proportion, there are manuals where the building of ships has been accurately and clearly accounted for, and finally there are the exceptionally detailed scale models of the middle of the

century where even the rigging has in some cases been preserved, where there are not many questions of doubt left unanswered. This is why I have not thought it necessary to present any further pictures of the sources to my reconstructions as the reader's interpretations cannot much diverge from my own any longer.

A Dutch engraving from 1613 which is supposed to be the first showing a ship with three complete gun decks, the English *Prince Royal,* seems to be a purely imaginative vessel drawn up on Dutch originals. With this as a model I have drawn a ship (347) which might be representative of a large Dutch man-of-war. It has double galleries and small turrets around the aftercastle, and right out at the end of the bowsprit is an innovation: a mast has developed out of the flagstaff (cf. 293, 305) to carry a new sail, the *spritsail topsail.*

A painting by the Dutch artist Hendrik Vroom shows an East Indiaman. The rig is in no way extreme, and we notice that the inconvenient lateen topsail on the mizzenmast has gone (348). The English ship *Red Lion* (349) is to be found on another large painting by Vroom together with the well-known *Prince Royal* (350). The *Red Lion* was an old ship which was rebuilt in 1609 and then fitted with a *mizzen topsail* which was no longer a lateen but a square sail between two yards, the *mizzen topsail yard* and the *crojack yard.* On Vroom's painting the four-masted *Prince Royal* carries a similar sail on the bonaventure topmast as well, and both ships carry a furled sail on the crojack yard. I have also drawn

142

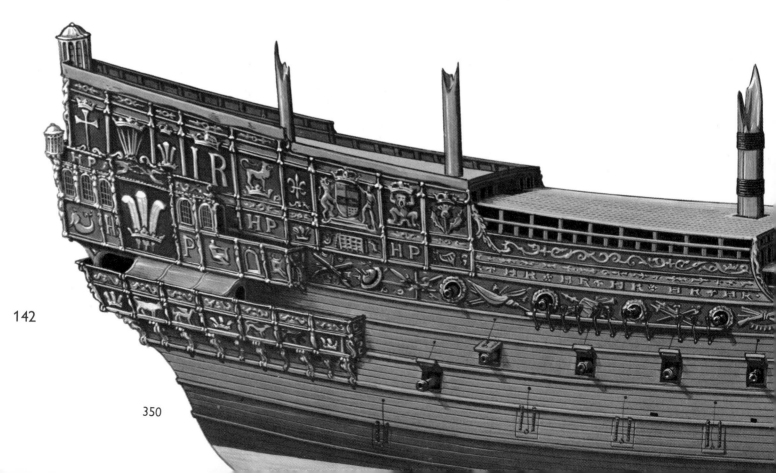

350

348

349

this on the *Red Lion,* but no future illustrations have such sails, and it is possible that Vroom misinterpreted his own sketch when painting the picture. The square mizzen topsail would have been a novelty to him as well.

The *Prince Royal* was built in 1610 by the renowned Phineas Pett, a man of an old shipbuilding family, of excellent technical education for his time and one of the foremost master shipbuilders known to history. Vroom's painting is from 1620 and she is illustrated here according to it (350). A manual on shipbuilding from about the same year gave impulse to the diagram of her shape amidships (351). As already mentioned she

had three complete gun decks with a total of 56 guns. Later she was rebuilt twice, finally to be armed with 90 guns. She had three galleries, but the two uppermost were connected with a row of windows and the large coat-of-arms with the three plumes of the Prince of Wales. Only these plumes and certain small details were painted in white. All other carving was gilt on a green background, and the account for the decorations still exists. The carving cost £441 0s 4d and the painting and gilding went to as much as £868 6s 8d. But the *Prince Royal* was indeed the most decorated vessel hitherto seen.

351

The Saint Louis, 1626

It may be said that Richelieu was the maker of the French navy. When he came to power in 1624 the country did not have a single ship which could vie with the modern English and Dutch men-of-war, and the French shipbuilders lacked both the knowledge and the resources to create a new fleet. In order to obtain new ships at once, ships which would furthermore have been good models for the French shipbuilding yards in the process of being fitted up, Richelieu ordered five ships as well as some smaller vessels from yards in Holland. They were delivered in 1626 and the Dutch engraver Hendrik Hondius made a picture of one of the ships, probably the *Saint Louis*.

It was a ship with two gun decks and about 60 guns. As boarding was now no longer the rule, sea-fights having turned into artillery battles, the boarding nets were no longer necessary. As on the *Prince Royal* (350) they had been replaced by a grating roof over the deck to protect the crew from spars and other parts of the rigging which could be shot down during battle. To disperse the powder smoke more quickly a number of the planks in the quarter-deck and forecastle deck were replaced with gratings.

The rig was modern with spritsail topsail and mizzen topsail, and it may be noticed that the topping lifts for both fore and mainsail were furled with martnets, *buntlines* and clewlines. The topsails had no martnets and were furled with buntlines and clewlines. As on the *Red Lion* and the *Prince Royal* the fore tack tackles were led through holes in a fixture on the cutwater under the beakhead. Contrary to the *Prince Royal* the *Saint Louis* shows no cat-heads.

144

352

145

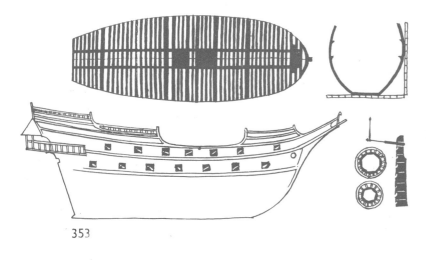

353

ferent perspectives and also in section (354, 355). The shape of the frame is roughly drawn but correctly understood.

In order that the vessels would be roomy as well as of shallow draught they were made flat-bottomed or almost so. As we have already seen, the sides of the carrack had sloped inwards, and when the ships began to carry long rows of heavy guns the gun decks were made narrower, moving the centre of gravity more amidships to achieve better stability. These very sloping sides naturally made boarding more difficult — the railings of two such vessels lying hull to hull could be yards apart. The Dutch built shallow-draught vessels very long in comparison to their width to maintain a high standard of seaworthiness.

The Portuguese drawing (353) shows a gallery roofed-in farthest aft. Dutch ships were built with completely roofed galleries at an early date. Furttenbach's ship (reconstruction 356) gives a very modern impression with quarter-deck and half deck well to aft and the only slightly raised forecastle, so low in fact that it was necessary to arch the deck to enlarge and protect the ladderway. On the Dutch-built *Saint Louis* (352) there were no catheads. Here we can see a long beam lying across the *beak-head rails,* and in the future we are to see how the cat-heads were always to proceed from the beak-heads of Dutch vessels while on English ships they emerged from the forecastle. On northern ships the lateen mizzen was carried inside the shrouds — its main object was not to propel but to aid steering. On contemporary pictures of ships running before the wind it is nearly always furled, usually being set when going to windward.

"Architectura Navalis"

An illustrated manuscript in the spirit of Matthew Baker but perhaps written without the same artistic finesse is the "Livro de Tracas de Carpintaria" of 1616 by the Portuguese, Manuel Fernandes. He has drawings of naos and galleons with frame, deck and rudder constructions, tops etc. (353).

Joseph Furttenbach, a German, published a printed work in 1629, "Architectura Navalis", in which he describes the construction of different types of vessels and also gives us some idea of the naval strategy of the period. The woodcut illustrations are not wholly satisfactory, once again they give the impression that the artist has drawn from roughly-made models. A small Dutch ship, probably a merchantman, is shown in dif-

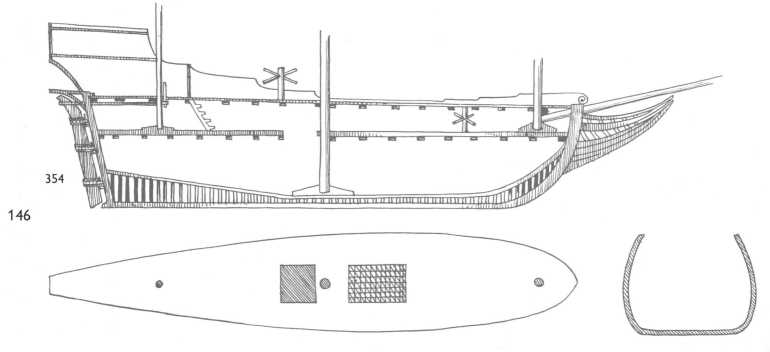

354

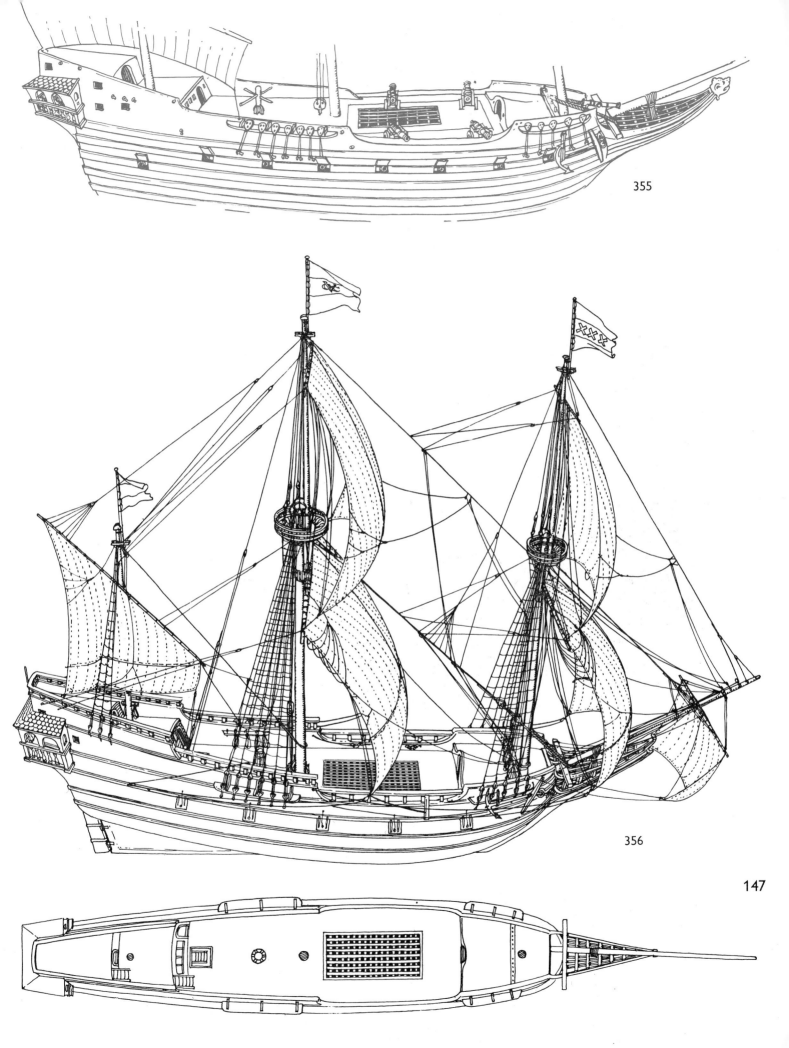

355

356

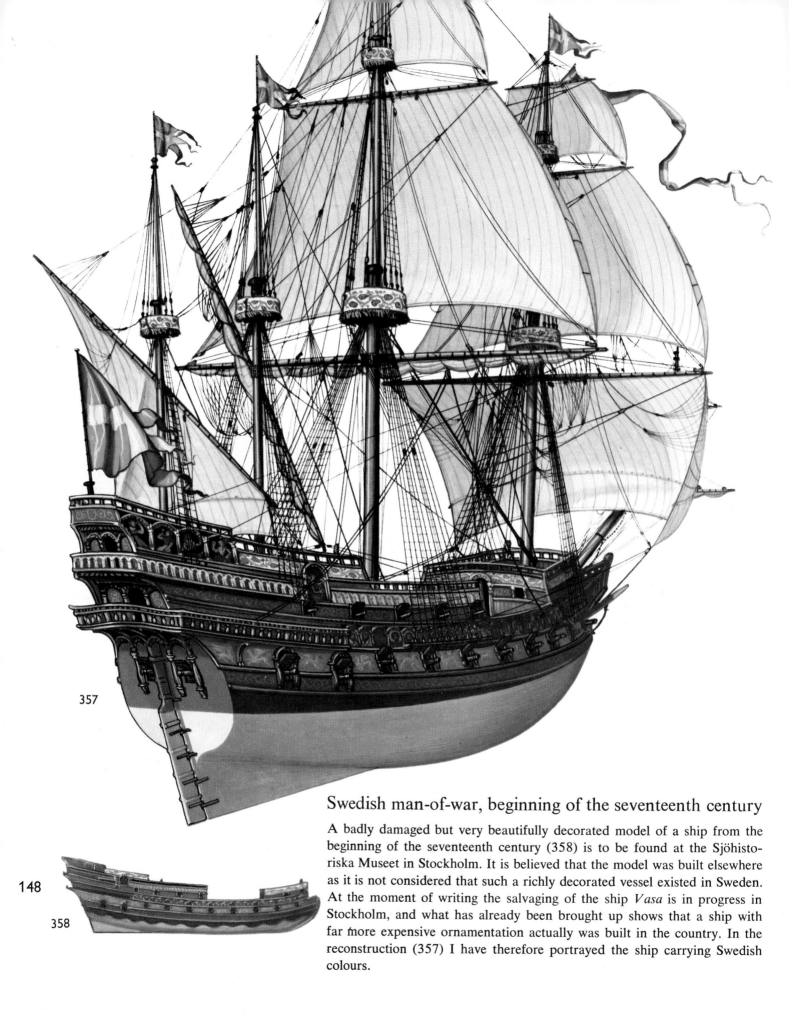

357

148

358

Swedish man-of-war, beginning of the seventeenth century

A badly damaged but very beautifully decorated model of a ship from the beginning of the seventeenth century (358) is to be found at the Sjöhistoriska Museet in Stockholm. It is believed that the model was built elsewhere as it is not considered that such a richly decorated vessel existed in Sweden. At the moment of writing the salvaging of the ship *Vasa* is in progress in Stockholm, and what has already been brought up shows that a ship with far more expensive ornamentation actually was built in the country. In the reconstruction (357) I have therefore portrayed the ship carrying Swedish colours.

Sovereign of the Seas, 1637

On 26th June 1634 Charles I visited the shipyards at Woolwich on an official inspection of the half-completed ship *Leopard,* but down in the bowels of the vessel he called master shipwright Phineas Pett aside and gave him orders to build the largest ship ever seen. Pett and His Majesty presumably discussed the dimensions of the giant at the time because only a few weeks later a protest was made against the Royal decision by Trinity House, representative of naval authority, in a letter to the Secretary of State. It was stated that the ship as ordered was to be 124 feet in the keel, 46 feet wide and to have a draught of 22 feet, and Trinity House was of the opinion that such a vessel was unmanageable and could not be used in English waters.

But the king was to have his giant at any price — she was in actual fact to be larger than Trinity House had imagined: 127 feet in the keel, 48 feet wide and a draught of 23½ feet. It may be somewhat of an exaggeration to say that the *Sovereign of the Seas,* as she was called, finally cost the king his head on account of the dissatisfaction that arose with the extra taxes he levied to finance his naval programme. At the time a ship of 40 guns cost about £6,000. When she was ready the *Sovereign* cost a total of £65,586 16s 9½d.

She was launched in 1637. It is often asserted that she was the first three-decker and the first to carry *royals,* a sail above the topgallant. But Phineas Pett had already built the three-decker *Prince Royal,* and in a manuscript from 1625 it is stated that flagpoles could also carry royals. Regarding size, however the *Sovereign* was a hundred and fifty years before her time.

359

Sovereign of the Seas

The *Sovereign's* rig of 1637 as it appears in J. Payne's well-known engraving is shown here in the reconstruction. It may be observed that the length of the top yard, as we have already seen before, is about half of the course yard, the length of the topgallant yard a half of the top yard and finally the royal yard a half of the topgallant yard. Contrary to other ships of the times the *Sovereign* also carries martnets on the main topsails.

1. Spritsail
2. Spritsail topsail
3. Foresail
4. Fore topsail
5. Fore topgallant
6. Fore royal
7. Mainsail
8. Main topsail
9. Main topgallant
10. Main royal
11. Mizzen topsail
12. Mizzen topgallant
13. Mizzen
14. Spritsail topmast
15. Forestay
16. Fore topmast stay
17. Fore topgallant stay
18. Fore royal stay
19. Mainstay
20. Main topmast stay
21. Main topgallant stay
22. Main royal stay
23. Mizzen stay
24. Mizzen topmast stay
25. Mizzen topgallant stay
26. Fairleads for the fore tacks
27. Gammonings
28. Mainstay collar
29. Clewgarnet
30. Buntline
31. Bowlines
32. Martnets
33. Mizzen martnet
34. Winding tackle
35. Mizzen lift

150

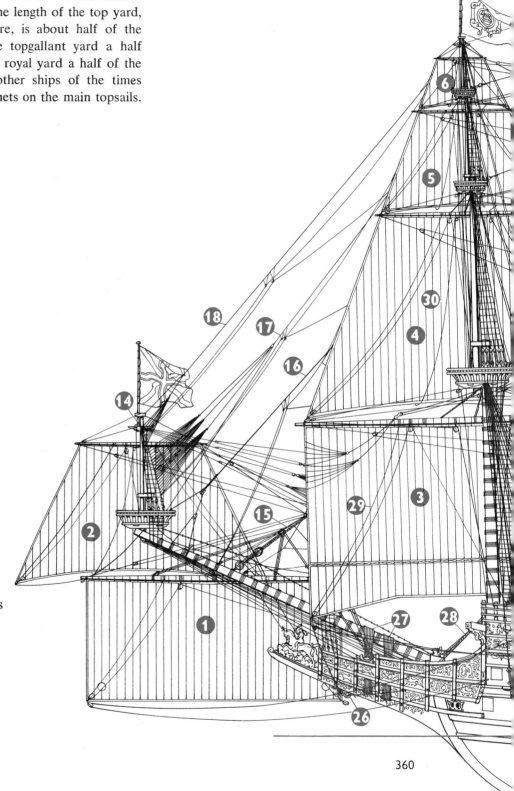

360

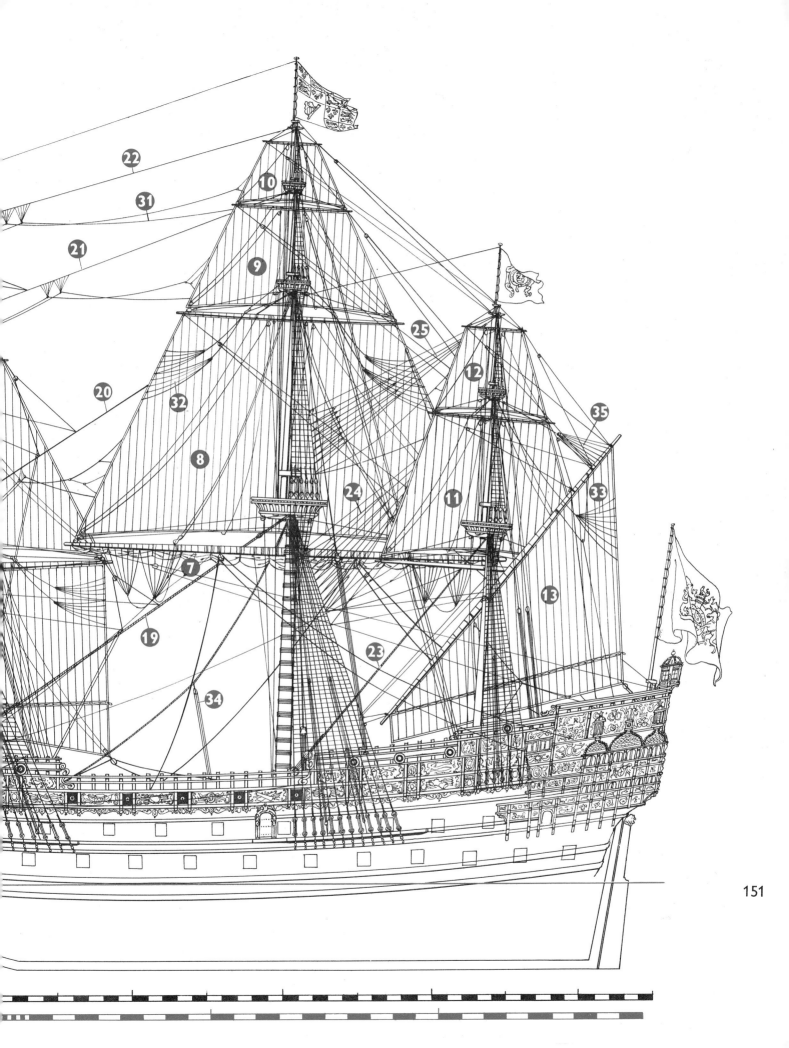

361

Sovereign of the Seas, 1637

A flat stern had been common on all European men-of-war ever since the beginning of the sixteenth century but the stern of the *Sovereign* was made round, first flattening out about ten feet above the waterline. Such sterns were to be characteristic of English men-of-war well into the nineteenth century while the Dutch and French retained the flat stern.

From the beginning the *Prince Royal* had carried 56 guns, but the *Sovereign* had 100 and could very well have been included as a first rate ship of the line in Nelson's fleet. And if she was superior to all previous ships as to size and armament she was also superior in another way to all ships that were to come after her:

she was the most richly decorated ship in the world. Her ornamentation was believed to have been carried out by the royal master carver Gerard Christmas, his sons and assistants after drawings by van Dyck. The Dutch in their many sea-fights and smaller engagements with her praised her and called her "The Golden Devil", and her gilding must indeed have glittered far more than any picture can show.

The figurehead represented Edgar the Peaceful riding down seven enemy kings. The beak-head railings were decorated with the greyhounds of Henry VII and the dragon of Cadwallader, with the lion and the unicorn, with the roses of England, the thistle of Scotland, the fleur de lis of France and the harp of Ireland, with royal monograms and various heraldic beasts. The fore-post was topped with a cupid mounted on a lion, and two satyrs grinned from under the cat-heads on the

forecastle. Between the satyrs the whole forepart of the forecastle was decorated with six beautiful goddesses symbolising Counsel, Care, Industry, Strength, Valour and Victory. The sides were decorated with three friezes. The lowest was the simplest and consisted only of coats-of-arms and volutions. The central frieze, interrupted by the gunports, had helmets, cuirasses, musical instruments and all sorts of weapons. The upper which decorated the sides of the forecastle and half deck portrayed the Signs of the Zodiac alternating with representations of Roman Emperors. The galleries with their cupolas and long rows of windows were covered with mythological figures and scenes, royal coats-of-arms and monograms. The high stern (359) was dominated by the Goddess of Victory surrounded by Neptune and Jupiter, Jason and Hercules. On either side of the rudder was the following inscription:

Qui mare, qui fluctus, ventos, navesque gubernat,
Sospitet hanc arcem, Carole magne, tuam.

Roughly meaning: May He whom sea and tides obey, and the winds that blow and the ships, Guard this, great Charles, thy man-of-war with sustenance Divine.

The *Sovereign of the Seas* was in fact protected longer than her king, but she was to suffer so many alterations that she finally looked quite different from the *Sovereign* that was launched in 1637. The rig was reduced and it may be questioned whether she ever set her royals except on parade. A great deal of the upperwork was cut down because she lay so deep that it was nearly impossible to use the lowest leeside battery when only heeling over slightly. She was finally rechristened the *Royal Sovereign*. She took a very honourable part in many sea-fights and was never defeated, but an overturned candle sealed her fate in 1696 and she went up in flames.

153

The fluyt and the pinnace

It is recorded that the Dutch at the beginning of the seventeenth century had over 10,000 merchantmen of different sorts in their service with a total number of 100,000 crew members. Even if the numbers are exaggerated they indicate the dominance of Dutch trade, and we know that 55 % of all ships that passed Øresund and were controlled by the Danish Customs at Elsinore were Dutchmen. The most important merchantman, in European waters anyway, seems to have been the *fluyt* (362, 364, 365), a round-sterned, flat-bottomed and relatively narrow vessel. As the Øresund duty was based on tonnage which was calculated among other things by the bulk of the vessel amidships, the sevententh-century fluyts were built with the sides sloping sharply inwards. A new system of measurement was introduced in 1669, however, and from then on the decks of the fluyts gradually became broader.

Around the middle of the century the topsails of all vessels had become so much larger that they were soon to outgrow the course. Many ships, both merchantmen and warships, sailed without topgallants, and because of the great demand for seamen the Dutch ships were made so easy to handle that as early as 1603 Walter Raleigh complained that where an English ship of 100 tons needed a crew of 30 a corresponding Dutch ship could make do with 10.

The *pinnace* was used both for warfare and for trading. As opposed to the fluyt it was flat-sterned, and it differed from an ordinary full-rigged ship only in being smaller. Perhaps the oldest constructional drawing in

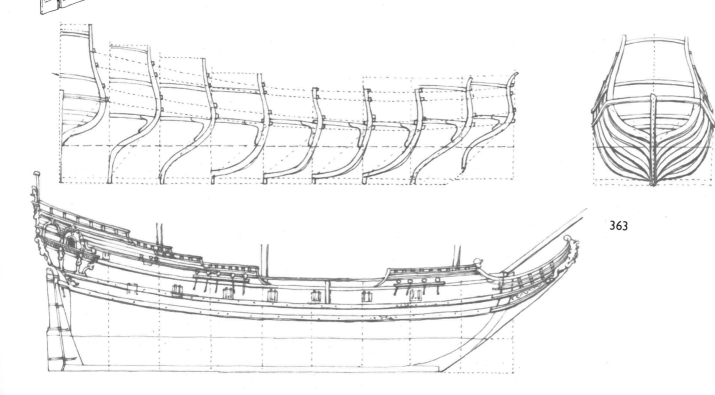

362

363

364

the modern sense with the ribs included so that we can form a clear idea of the shape of the hull (363) is of a pinnace from 1670. It has one single deck, a short quarter-deck, half deck and a high forecastle, but the bulwarks, which are high around the open deck, hide all sharp contours and create a very harmonious little vessel. There were also larger types, two-decked pinnaces, and it is difficult to draw a sharp line between these and ordinary ships. And then there were small, full-rigged ships, which would immediately be thought of as pinnaces but which were in actual fact called *jachts*. The word "jacht" originally had nothing to do with pleasure sailing but meant "swift craft" or "hunter".

155

365

Dutch men-of-war, 1670

While England and France built many three-decked ships during the seventeenth century the Dutch satisfied themselves with only a few. The most common Dutch man-of-war had two gun decks, presumably because the Dutch preferred shallow-draught vessels. Their ships were also lighter built in proportion to the English, yet even though they were swifter and more easily manoeuvred the light construction many times proved to be disastrous in exchanges of gunfire. Even so, Dutch shipbuilding came to be the model for many foreign powers. Peter the Great made a personal study of shipbuilding at Zaandam in Holland in 1667, and Frenchmen, Swedes, Danes and Germans had earlier profited from Dutch skill.

Outwardly the Dutch ships differed from the English and the French only in their comparatively sparse ornamentation, the sides being as a rule completely plain. During the seventeenth century the beak-head gradually curved upwards more and more mainly because a low beak-head, especially on smaller vessels, became too "wet", but very likely also because the forecastle called for more harmonious lines. The cutwater supporting the beak-head was usually perforated above as a convoluted vine, and was itself supported at the sides by the sturdy knees of the beak-head. The uppermost beak-head rails began up by the forecastle railings, most often capped with a helmeted head, and then curved gracefully forwards, ending in a convolute where they met above the red lion which was always the figurehead of Dutch ships. Depending on the size of the vessel there were three or four rails on each side joined to the vertical *beak-head timbers*. The beak-head was traditionally the crew toilet. A part of the foredeck projected forward from the forecastle from which the cat-heads proceeded, later to rest on a clamp on the beak-head rail. The quarter galleries in the stern which had become the officers' toilets were completely covered in with clinker-laid planks. The planking of the poop and the upper part of the bulwarks around the half deck were also clinker-laid to combine lightness with strength. The stern was decorated with a coat-of-arms framed in the various ornamentations of Dutch baroque architecture with lions, soldiers, cupids

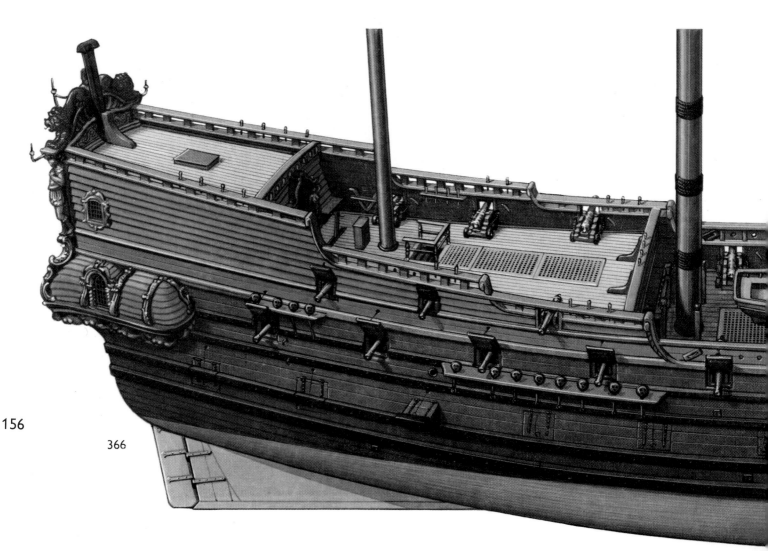

366

and caryatids bearing friezes, convolutes and other whorles. At the beginning of the century the stern was usually topped with a single, enormous lantern, but later there were commonly three or even five.

The broad, protective gratings above the deck (350, 352, 361) had disappeared, but the batteries under deck were ventilated through large gratings which sat inside the frames of the hatches. In heavy weather these gratings were covered with tarpaulins. On many ships the whipstaff (cf.309) was brought up through the quarterdeck so that the helmsman could be outside. In the picture (366) the whipstaff can be seen immediately forward of the entrance to the poop, and between it and the mizzenmast is the compass in its *binnacle*. The railings are raised amidships into a breastwork with apertures for the barrels of the soldiers' hand-guns.

On the forecastle, amidships and on the half deck there are large V-shaped *cavils* on the planked inside of the bulwarks for securing the sheets. Around the main and foremast there are knights with *pin rails,* and around the forecastle, quarter-deck and half deck there are further pin rails on the railings for securing all the halyards, ropes, lines, tacks and sheets which controlled the rig.

367

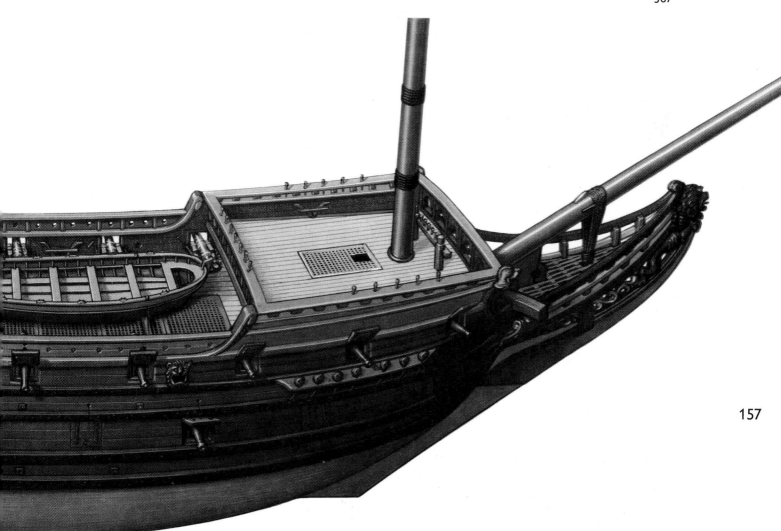

157

368

The frigate

We hear of "frigates", small swift craft armed with 6—
12 guns, as early as the beginning of the seventeenth century, but soon both the vessels and their armament were
to grow so that by the middle of the century we hear of
an English frigate of 64 guns. Even so, what usually
seems to have been meant by a frigate during the seventeenth century was a full-rigged man-of-war with only
one complete gun deck. — A Dutch frigate of 1665
drawn by Wilhelm van de Velde he Younger (368)
does show a complete gun deck under the main deck,
but it seems as if the vessel lacks a forecastle deck, and
only the high forward bulkhead and the slightly raised
sides mark the forecastle.

Dutch jachts

By *jachts* the Dutch originally meant small, swift-sailing
vessels of varying type. During the seventeenth century
the single-masted, so-called *staten jacht* was the most
important. It was used both as a scout and as a dispatch
boat, and furthermore as a swift transport for persons
of importance. But even ordinary sailing-craft intended
for transport and fishing could be designated jachts were
they but a little lighter and more elegant than usual. And
finally all the small open boats with variously shaped
hulls and rigs used by the inhabitants of the seaports
for pleasure were also called jachts.

By the middle of the century the Dutch had given
over the somewhat inconvenient, fore-and-aft spritsail
rig to their jachts, using instead an easily-manageable
rig with a long, standing *gaff* in which the mainsail could
be easily furled with clewlines (370). It was such a jacht
that Amsterdam presented to Charles II in 1660. He
was later to build a whole flotilla of them and arrange
races for them — thereby introducing the term *yachting*.

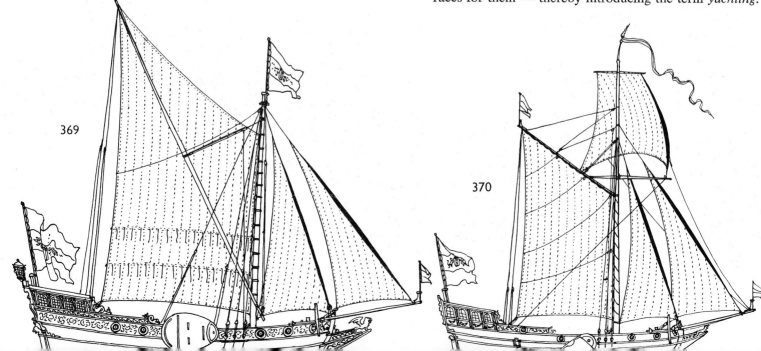

369

370

Innovations in the rigging

For some unknown reason reef-points do not seem to have been used on larger vessels for a period of more than a hundred years. We saw them on the seals from the beginning of the fifteenth century (200) and they were to appear right up to the beginning of the following century, but then they vanish. They make their return about 1660 on the large topsails (371). In order to be able to reef the very tapering sails the yard has been lengthened. — The topping lifts of the main and top yards run together through *fiddle blocks* (blocks with two sheaves after one another) and the sheets of the topgallant and topsail are rove through the same blocks and from there through a block on the yard near the mast down to the deck. — The picture is of the Dutch 72-gun ship *Gouda,* built in 1665.

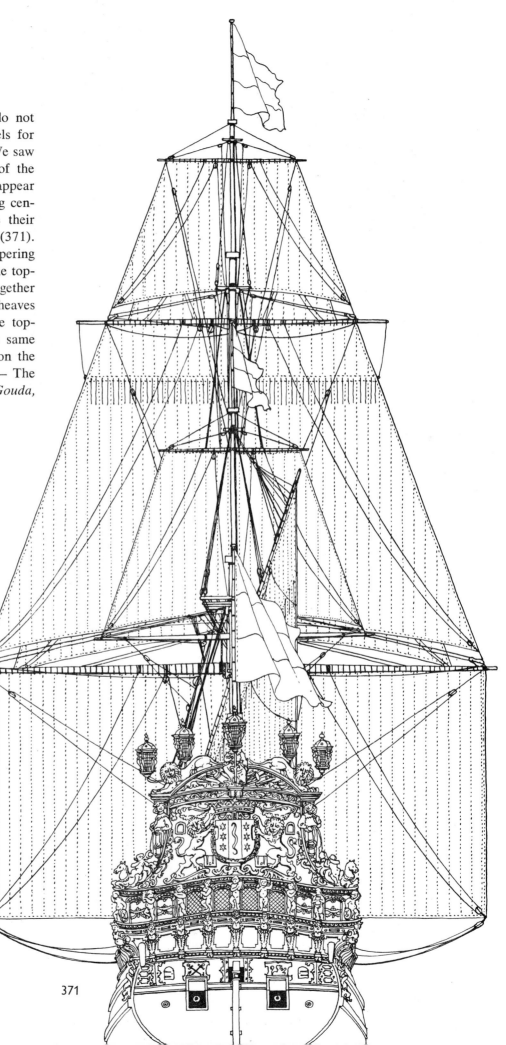

371

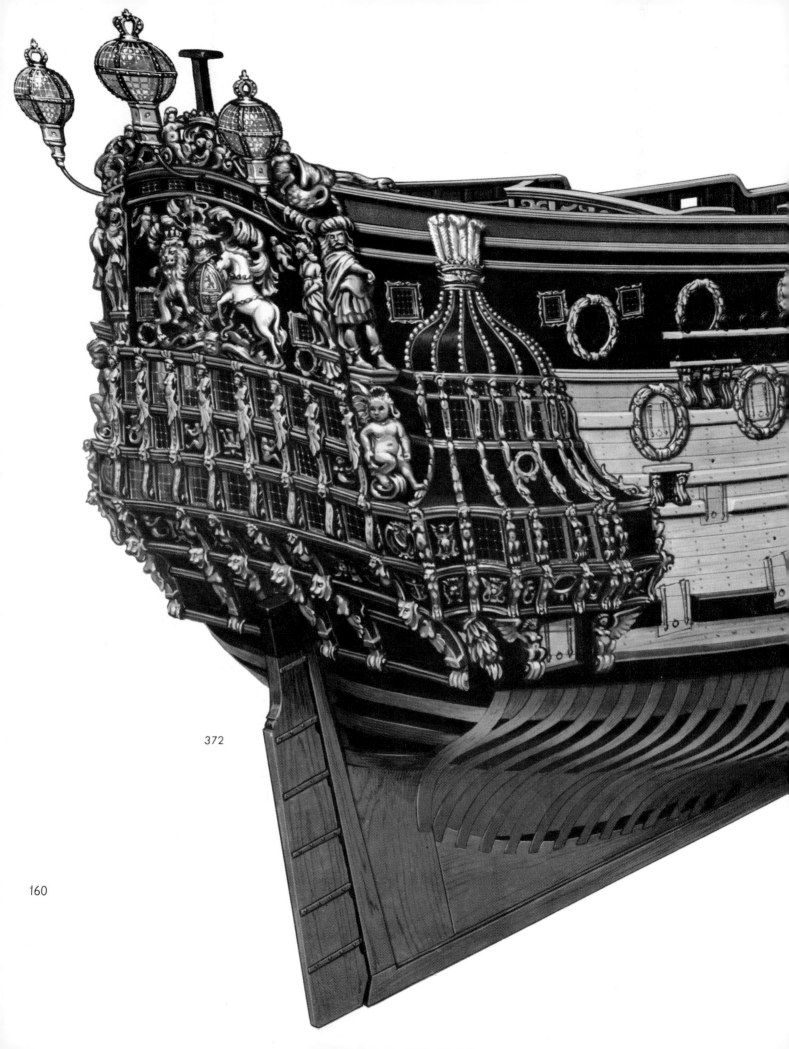

372

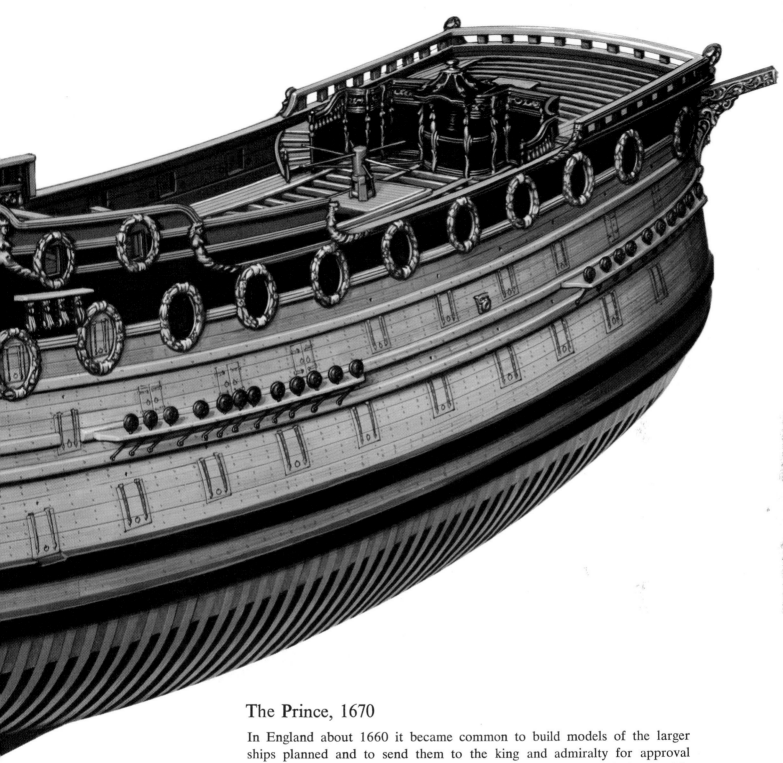

The Prince, 1670

In England about 1660 it became common to build models of the larger ships planned and to send them to the king and admiralty for approval before the actual vessels were built. One of the oldest admiralty models (372) representing the 100-gun ship *Prince* of 1670 is preserved at the Science Museum in South Kensington. The English men-of-war were so-built that they would afford steady platforms for the heavy artillery, and as a result of this became both heavy and deep-going. The forecastle hides the richly decorated beak-head, but we do see that the cat-heads proceeding from the forecastle itself, the wreaths around the gun-ports and nearly all ornamentations are gilt on a black background, as on the *Sovereign*. But what was gilt on the models was usually yellow paint in reality, and only the royal arms always to be found on the sterns of the English ships was accorded true gilding.

161

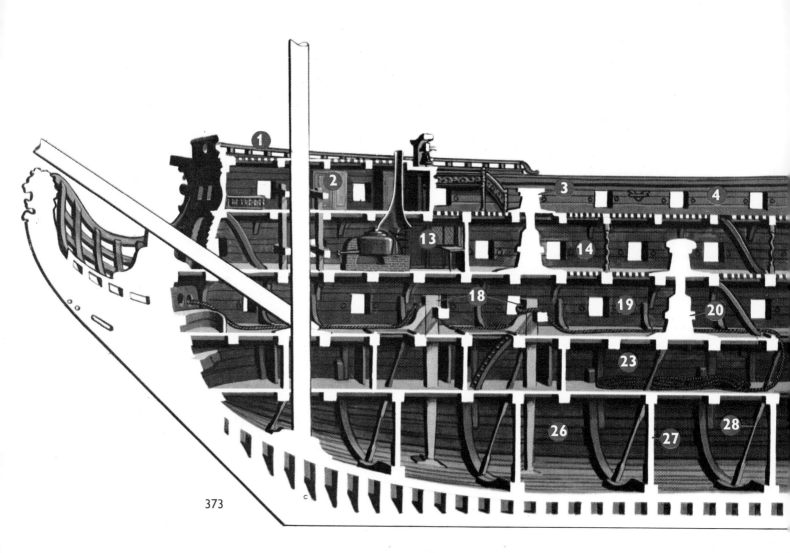

373

The ship of the line

Right up until the middle of the seventeenth century all the ships of various size and armament which constituted a fleet in naval engagements had fought without any real order of battle. In 1653, however, the British Admiralty issued an order that ships were to give battle in line, in single file that is to say, so that broadsides would be most effective. Apart from good drilling and discipline it presupposed that the ships were able to sail with the same speed and that they were approximately equally armed, otherwise a more weakly armed vessel in the line might be forced to fight with a superior enemy.

The result was that the ships were divided into rates. A first rate ship had over 90 guns, a second over 80 and a third rate over 50. These first three rates were considered strong enough to fight in the line and were therefore called *ships of the line*. A fourth rate ship had over 38 guns, a fifth over 18 and finally a sixth over 6. Moreover the officers' pay was in proportion to the rate of ship they served on. The boundaries between the rates were to vary somewhat and were often to be adjusted during the years to come, but generally speaking they were to become norms for the classification of ships, even of those belonging to foreign navies.

A first rate ship

The vertical section of an English first rate ship from the end of the seventeenth century (373) is based on a contemporary engraving. The guns are not included, but gun-ports are to be seen, even in the admiral's lounge. The numbers indicate:

1. Forecastle deck with gratings for ventilation. 2. Forecastle with knights for the halyards etc. 3. Warping

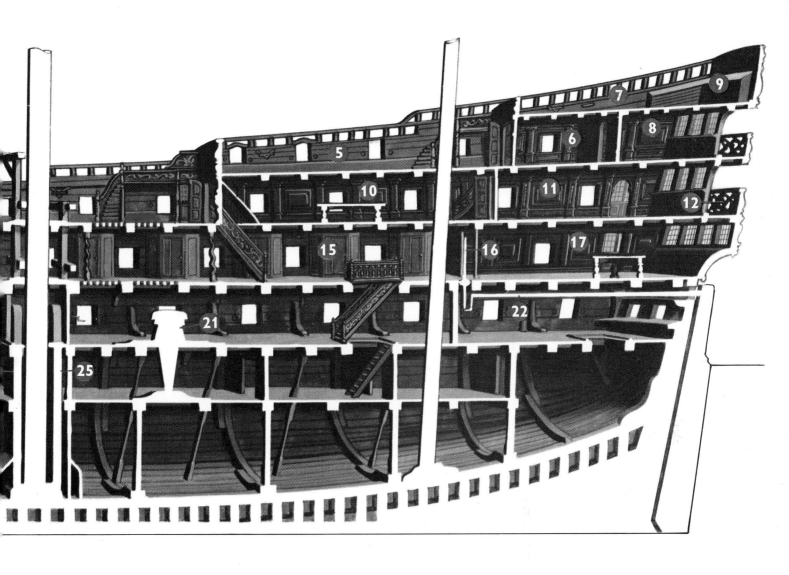

capstan. 4. Upper deck with gratings for ventilation. 5. Quarter-deck. 6. Cabin for the mate and navigation officers. 7. Poop deck. 8. Cabins for the captain and lieutenants. 9. Boxes for signal flags etc. 10. Ward room. 11. State room with sleeping-compartment for the commander-in-chief. 12. Gallery. (Open galleries on the stern became common on English ships towards the end of the century.) 13. Galley with chimney up to the forecastle deck. 14. Upper gun deck with gratings for ventilation. 15. Officers" cabins. (They consisted of screens which were stowed away before an action so that the deck around the guns was clear.) 16. Whipstaff. 17. Ward room for volunteers and land officers. 18. Riding bitts for the anchor cables. 19. Lower gun deck. 20. Capstan for weighing the anchor. 21. Warping capstan. 22. Gun room and tiller. 23. Orlop. (The deck aft of the mainmast served as a dressing station and hospital under action.) 24 & 25. Pumps. 26. Hold. 27. Deck-beam supports. 28. Cross supports.

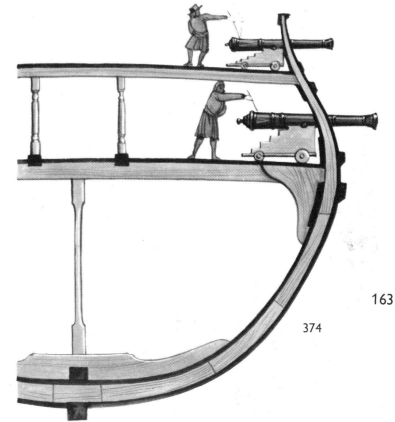

163

374

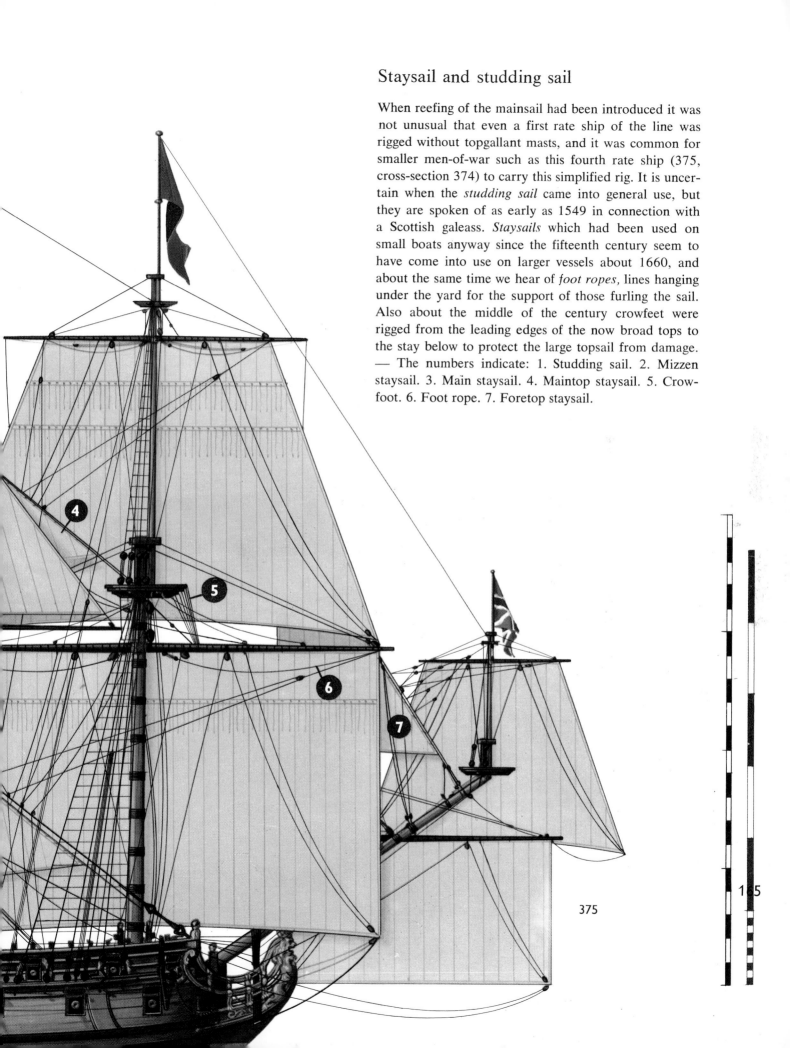

Staysail and studding sail

When reefing of the mainsail had been introduced it was not unusual that even a first rate ship of the line was rigged without topgallant masts, and it was common for smaller men-of-war such as this fourth rate ship (375, cross-section 374) to carry this simplified rig. It is uncertain when the *studding sail* came into general use, but they are spoken of as early as 1549 in connection with a Scottish galeass. *Staysails* which had been used on small boats anyway since the fifteenth century seem to have come into use on larger vessels about 1660, and about the same time we hear of *foot ropes,* lines hanging under the yard for the support of those furling the sail. Also about the middle of the century crowfeet were rigged from the leading edges of the now broad tops to the stay below to protect the large topsail from damage. — The numbers indicate: 1. Studding sail. 2. Mizzen staysail. 3. Main staysail. 4. Maintop staysail. 5. Crowfoot. 6. Foot rope. 7. Foretop staysail.

375

376

French shipbuilding

The French made an early reply in 1638 to the English three-decked, 100-gun ship *Sovereign of the Seas* by building a vessel roughly as large but with only two decks and 72 guns, the *Couronne,* which was a better sailer and in fresher wind could probably fire as many deadly broadsides as the heavy, deep-going *Sovereign.*

Richelieu died in 1642, and his death was followed by a period of misrule which allowed the French navy to rot in port until Colbert came to power nineteen years later. Like Richelieu he had to begin from the beginning. While the French dockyards were being put into service he ordered ships from Holland and other countries, and during his lifetime he was to see French shipbuilding become the foremost in the world.

In his diary Samuel Pepys, then Secretary to the Admiralty, says that the French built a two-decked ship of 70 guns in 1663 whose lower deck was 4 feet above the waterline whereas the English ships, being narrower and more deep-going, had their lower deck only a little over 3 feet above. French three-deckers were about 44 feet wide, the English not being more than 41 as a rule. The Frenchmen were better platforms for the artillery and far better sailers moreover.

During a French visit to Spithead in 1672 a great deal of interest was given to the Frenchman *Superbe* of 74 guns. She was 40 feet wide and the lower gun deck was considerably higher out of the water than those of the Englishmen. The chief English designer Sir Anthony Deane, was thus ordered by the king to make a copy of the *Superbe,* and the copy, the *Harwich* of 70 guns, was such a success that nine new ships of the same size were ordered. Samuel Pepys noted that the English master shipbuilders had not observed that only ships broad enough were sturdy enough. Later, when the English were at war with France, attempts were made to copy

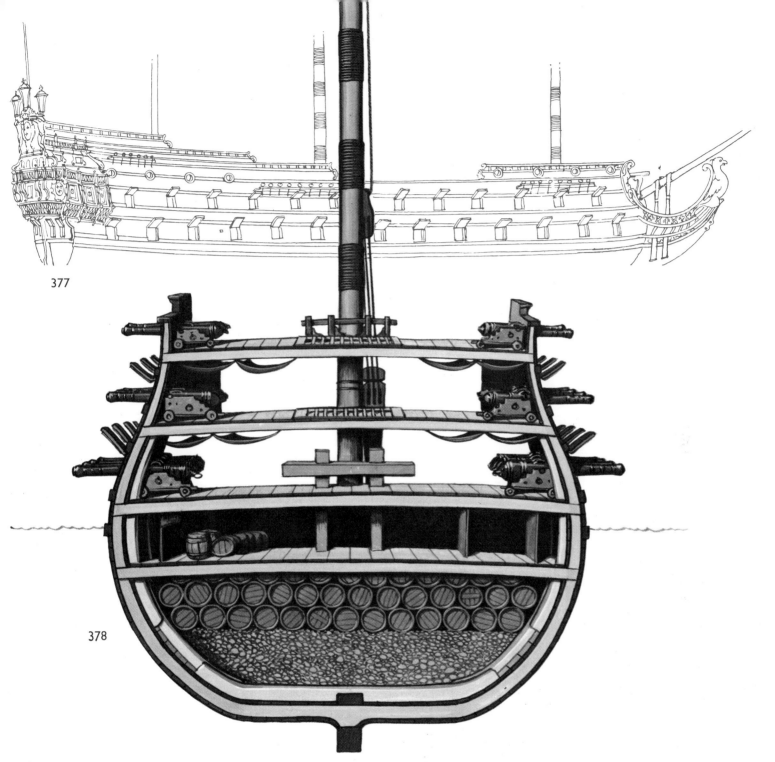

377

378

the best French prizes. When the French in their turn captured English ships and included them in their fleet they always reduced the number of guns.

In the so-called "Atlas de Colbert" from 1664—1669 there are, among many other pictures, drawings of a ship of 84 guns with two complete gun decks (376, 377, 378). It has no raised forecastle, and the quarter-deck first begins at the mizzenmast. Its overall length has been calculated to about 180 feet, length of keel to 128 feet,

width 42½ feet and draught to 19½ feet. — The English three-decker *Prince* of 100 guns from 1670 (372) had about the same proportions except for the draught which was over 21½ feet. — The French ships were built even with an eye to fighting the galleys in the wind-impoverished Mediterranean and were therefore strongly armed both fore and aft. In order to have a free arc of fire the beak-head and its rails swept down in a deeper curve than on other ships of the times.

167

379

French shipbuilding

The ornamentation about the stern of the ship in the "Atlas de Colbert" (376) differs in many respects from the decorations on contemporary Dutchmen and Englishmen (367, 371, 372). The galleries are open, and it seems as if balustrades, window-frames, strip-work and other decorative elements had been directly taken over from contemporary French palatial architecture.

The well-known Pierre Puget who carved the decorations on *La Réale* (341) was also responsible for the ornamentations of many men-of-war, and it is said that he often covered the stern with such a number of heavy figures that the despairing captains had most of the decorations cut away when well out to sea so that the ships would be made more seaworthy.

Towards the end of the century the ornamentation of even the French ships became more sensible and the figures usually carved in low relief. The *St. Philippe* (379), a first class ship of the line, was very tastefully decorated like all French ships of her time even if the stern with its almost right-angled proportions still gave the impression of a miniature palace not quite following the natural lines of the ship to the full.

The picture of a Frenchmen of 56 guns (380) rigged only with the lower masts and bowsprit clearly shows the crowfeet from the tops to the stays underneath. Between the shrouds and the tops we can see the *futtock shrouds* which give support to the tops and topshrouds. The futtock shrouds proceed from a bar, the *futtock staff* which lies across the shrouds proper. A system of lines, the *catharpins,* run between the port and starboard staffs to secure them. The *cap* rests on the square masthead and together with the trestle-trees supports the topmast. On Englishmen the cap had straight edges like a brick (cf. 375) whereas the Dutch (cf. title-page) and French ships had a curved upper surface so that it was thinnest around the hole for the topmast.

About 1690, perhaps even ten years earlier, the *bobstay* was first introduced on French ships. It fixed the bowsprit to the beak-head's cutwater (later to the forepost itself).

380

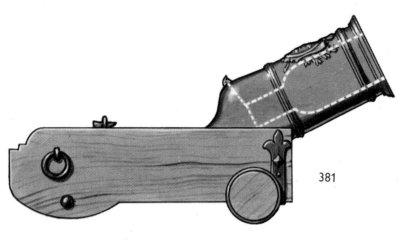

381

The bomb ketch, 1682

In 1682 the French naval hero Abraham Du Quesne introduced a new weapon on a new type of vessel. Mortars had already been used on land for a hundred years, but the first mortar bombardment from sea was suffered by the pirate town of Algiers from Du Quesne's *bomb ketches*. It is said that a Frenchman was to have constructed the first bomb ketch about 1679 which was quite simply a broad vessel with the foremast removed (382) to make room for the heavy mortars (381). The bomb ketches were much more strongly built than ordinary vessels, and sturdy beam bridges supported the deck from below and distributed the shock of recoil when the mortars were fired. The bombs weighed about 200 lbs which was a great deal when one considers that the balls from the largest guns were of 48 lbs.

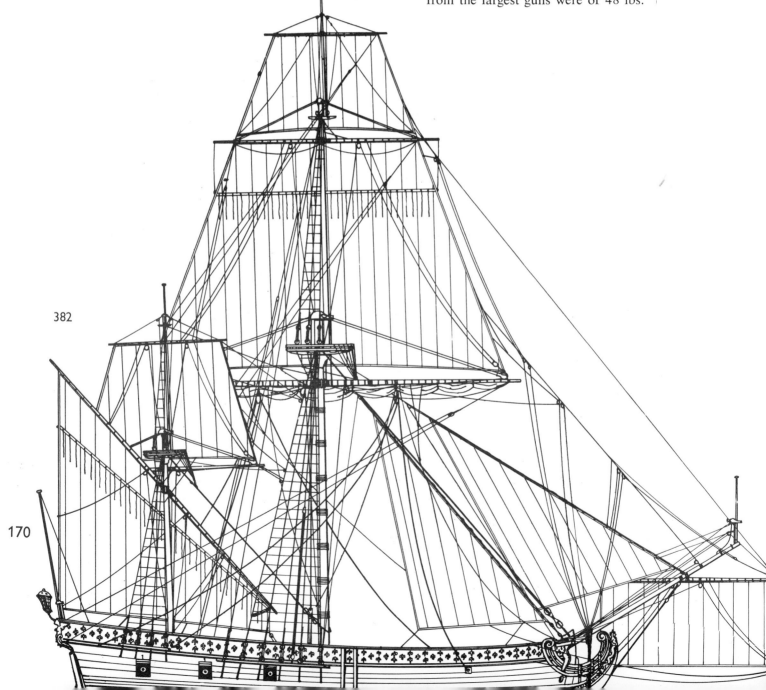

382

170

383

Polacca, barque etc.

A *polacca* is usually understood to be a large, square-rigged Mediterranean vessel with two or three single-piece masts which makes it possible for an upper yard to be hoisted close to the lower so that all wind can in this way be taken out of the sail. But in a series of ship portrayals made by Jean Jouve in Marseilles in 1679 there is a small French man-of-war with tops on both main and mizzenmast and lateen sail on the foremast-designated as a *polacre,* i.e. polacca (383).

It is at times a hopeless job trying to straighten out the terminology especially as regards small vessels. A ship in Jouve's series with identical hull but with lateen sails on all masts is called a *barca.* Yet ships which both in hull and rig were identical with Jouve's polacca are also called barca in other parts of the Mediterranean. And barca is the same word as barque and barge. Experts say that the word comes from the Latin *baris* which meant an Egyptian vessel.

Finally we find different types of barques in all the larger ports of the Mediterranean, right up the Atlantic coast and even on the rivers. Wine barques ply the Rhone. The English and Dutch have fishing barques, and in a Swedish book on shipbuilding from 1691 we find there is an English "Barque or galleya which serves only for rowing up or downstream, of 41 feet from stem to stern."

171

384

385

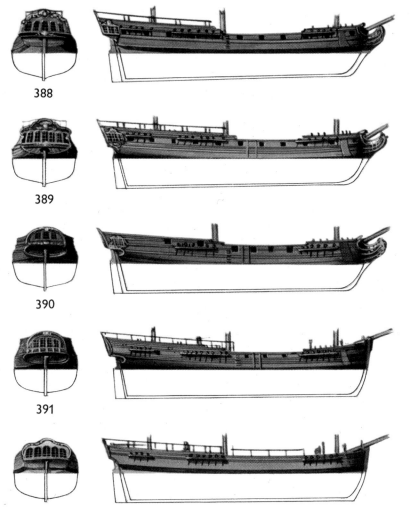

388

389

390

391

392

Ships of the line, eighteenth century

The eighteenth century was not to introduce any radical changes in the large men-of-war either. The rig was gradually made more efficient, the English system of the rounded stern (cf. the Sovereign 359) was taken up by other sea powers, and the channels which on English three-deckers were situated at the level of the middle gun deck were moved upwards according to foreign practice (373, 377, 384, 386). Immediately after the turn of the century the bowsprit was extended with a *jib-boom* for the *jib* (384), and it was not too long before the spritsail topmast disappeared and its sail set under the jib-boom (386). On smaller ships the long mizzen spar soon vanished and was replaced with a gaff (385), but large ships retained it for nearly the whole century as a reserve spar should one of the important yards be damaged. Towards the end of the century it was common for the mizzen of smaller vessels to be fitted with a *boom*, that both spritsail and spritsail topsail were done away with and were replaced by a *flying jib* furthest out on the jib-boom which was supported by a stay over a *martingale-boom* or *dolphin-striker* pointing downward from the end of the bowsprit (387).

386

387

Merchantmen, eighteenth century

In his major work "Architectura Navalis Mercatoria" of 1768 the Swedish master shipwright Fredrik Henrik af Chapman gives a classification of the variegated flora of sea-going merchantmen that were to be seen in the ports of northern Europe. He divides them into five main groups according to details of the hull.

A *frigate* (388) was flat-sterned in that the planking came to an end at the *counter* under the decorated upper part of the stern. On a *hagboat* (389) the planking continued up to a beam just under the taffrail. The *pink* (390) seems to have been a development of the Dutch

fluyt (362), round-sterned and narrowing above. All these three groups had a beak-head of the same type as contemporary men-of-war, but without a beak-head and therefore much more blunt in the bow were the *cat* and the *barque* (392).

Yet a merchant frigate could carry schooner or jacht rig and still be called frigate, just as a barque or cat with frigate or brigantine rig could still be called barque or cat. It was only during the nineteenth century that it was found easier and more natural to denominate a merchantman according to the rig it carried.

Three midship sections show — approximately — how French (393), Dutch (394) and English (395) merchantmen differed from eachother in construction.

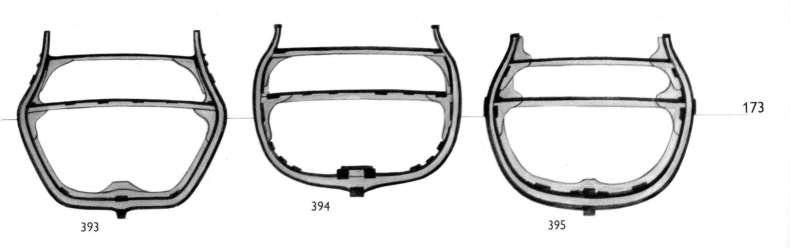

393

394

395

173

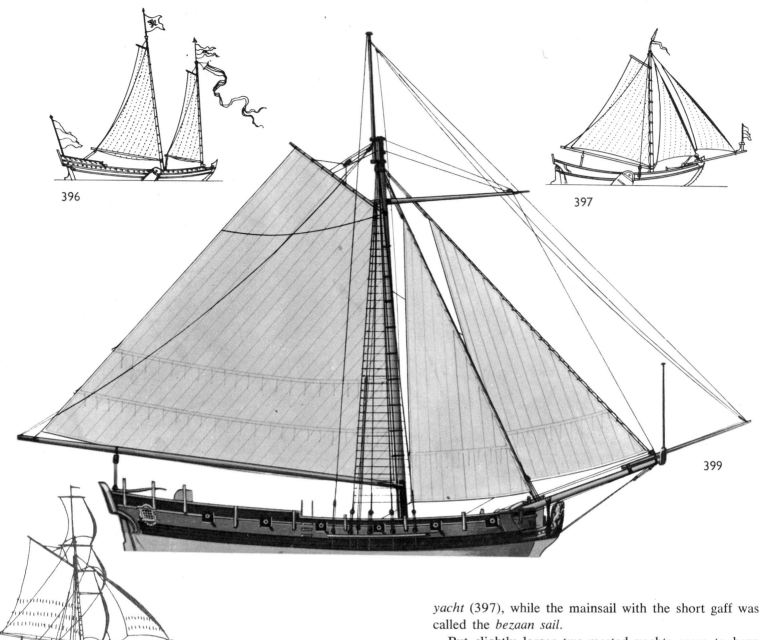

396

397

399

400

The cutter and the schooner

During the seventeenth century, Dutch inland waters were traversed by a small two-masted jacht (396), a pleasure boat with main and fore gaffs which would be called a *schooner* today. It was presumably found that two masts on such a small vessel were too many, and so the foremast was removed and a three-cornered foresail was rigged on a stay between the fore-post and masthead. The gaff-rigged craft was further given a jib on an easily detachable jib-boom and was called a *bezaan*

yacht (397), while the mainsail with the short gaff was called the *bezaan sail*.

But slightly larger two-masted yachts seem to have changed in another way. In a drawing by Willem van de Velde the Younger from about 1700 we can see a two-masted yacht with a jib-boom and the jib hoisted to the top of the foremast, and this yacht must quite definitely be called a *schooner* (398).

The gaff-rigged *cutter* which was common as a dispatch and patrol vessel during the eighteenth century seems to have developed in part from the bezaan yacht and in part from the staten jacht with its standing gaff (370). An English cutter from 1711 (399) has bowsprit, jib-boom and a long yard for a square sail, the *running square-sail,* which was hoisted when running before the wind. The vertical timbers on the outside of the bulwarks are supports for the swivel guns. A further English naval

401

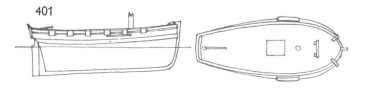

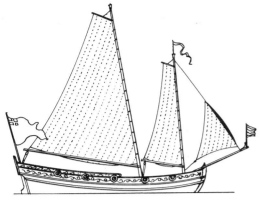

398

cutter from 1768 has no beak-head and carries double, *square topsails* (400, 401). The length of the jib-boom is 4/5ths of the hull, and at first glance the vessel gives the impression of being over-rigged. But the hull is broad and deep-going and would need much sail in slight wind. In fresh. wind the topmast could be lowered and the jib-boom drawn in, and there are three rows of reef-points on the mainsail.

A schooner is usually understood as a two-masted vessel carrying chiefly fore-and-aft sail whose after mast is not shorter than the forward. Popular tradition says that the first schooner was built in Gloucester, Massachusetts in 1713, but we have seen that the schooner rig was already in use in Holland during the seventeenth

century. The name *schooner* is, however, American, and as Chapman named merchantmen according to the different details in the construction of the hull it is possible that the inhabitants of Gloucester gave a name to the first schooner with regard to special hull characteristics. However this may be, the rig itself was soon to become the characteristic of the schooner, and under the heading "rigging" Chapman's manual does in fact include a "scooner" (402).

The English systematically took measurements and made drawings of the ships they captured, and in the admiralty archives there are drawings of a small American schooner built during the 1760's (403). It carries topsails both on the main and foremast and also a running square-sail with a yard at the foot as well. It is also possible that a square sail was set under the running square-sail yard on the mainmast, and rigged in this fashion a schooner could be called a *brigantine*. A main staysail could be carried as well.

The well-known, swift-sailing "Baltimore clipper" which was to be used by pirates, smugglers, slave-traders and the U.S. Navy is already mentioned in 1746. It is uncertain whether it was schooner-rigged at that time, but later it was always portrayed as a schooner (448).

402

403

175

Brigantines, snows and brigs

The name *brigantine* is first come across at the end of the seventeenth century, and it seems then to have designated a fairly small, two-masted vessel with square sails on both masts (404). But a similar ship could also be called a *snow,* and it is once again difficult to decide whether the appearance of the hull, size, or the rig was the deciding point. Both the brigantine and the snow were employed in fleets, mainly as dispatch vessels. As early as 1669 a brigantine with main gaffsail was built in Sweden, and during the eighteenth century the name brigantine definitely seems to have been intended for a vessel with square sails on the foremast and fore-and-aft sails on the mainmast (406). A fore-and-aft topsail was still often carried above the mainsail.

As the brigantine gradually grew in size topgallants were rigged on the fore and mainmast, and a ship rigged in this way Chapman calls a "brigantine or brig". But Chapman also reproduces a vessel which he calls "snow" (407) where the gaffsail, the *brigsail,* is latched to a spar just aft of the mainmast between its top and the deck. On a snow the gaff could be hoisted higher than the main yard and quite independently of it, nor was it hindered by the iron collars fitted to larger vessels whose masts consisted of several parts. Towards the end of the eigthteenth century when snows and brigs had both fore-and-aft mainsails and brigsails, the snow was called first snowbrig and then the name brig became attached to both of them. The designation snowmast, in England the *trysail mast,* was retained in certain countries, and such masts were to be found on both barques and full-riggers.

A U.S. Navy brig from 1778 (408) shows a high rig with royals on both masts. The brigsail is brailed to the standing gaff and mast. Double upper main studding sails and main topgallant studding sails are set, but the foremast has only fore topgallant studding sail, upper foresail studding sail and lower foresail studding sail on the port side. The spritsail under the bowsprit has holes at the sheeted corners so that if it was swamped the water would drain away more easily.

404

405

406

407

408

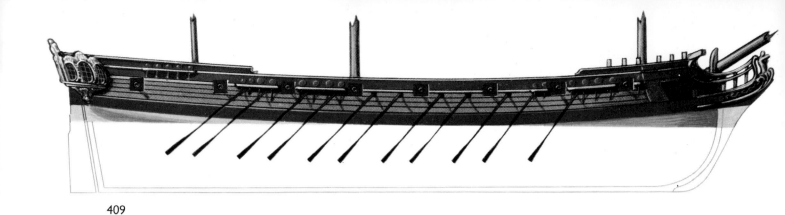

409

The frigate

The greater part of the eighteenth century was a period of stagnation for English shipbuilders mainly because of a number of rigid regulations which bound their hands. The result of this was that Spanish and French ships continued to be larger and better than Englishmen of the same class.

The frigate had gained in importance in nearly all navies. It was built to be a strong swift vessel for all-weather purposes and was mainly used in convoy and privateering service. It was well-armed for its size, and during the eighteenth century the guns were generally mounted on a single deck. The early frigates usually

carried from 24 to 28 and a crew of about 160. By the middle of the century many were being built which had 32 or even 36 guns, and towards its end there were frigates armed with over 40.

Nearly all French eighteenth-century men-of-war were built with very slightly inclined end-posts which naturally resulted in concave waterlines near the keel. The frigate *La Flore* (410, 411) from the 1780's has these typically French characteristics. Also typical of the times were the gangboards which ran beside the railings leaving room amidships for the boats. *La Flore* was armed with thirty 9-pounders and her dimensions were: total length 154 feet, length of keel 124½ feet, beam 34 feet and draught 16½ feet.

The numbers in the picture indicate: 1. Capstan. 2. Ventilators for the galley. 3. Ship's bell. 4. Sheave hole for the main tack (chesstree). 5. Gangboard. 6. Sheave

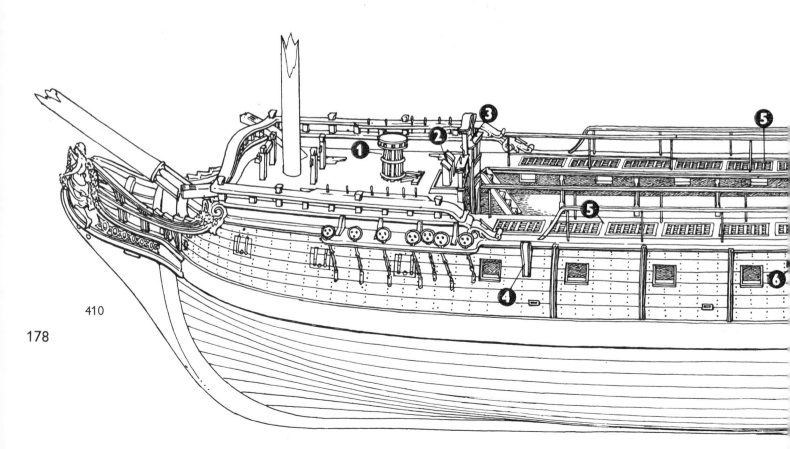

410

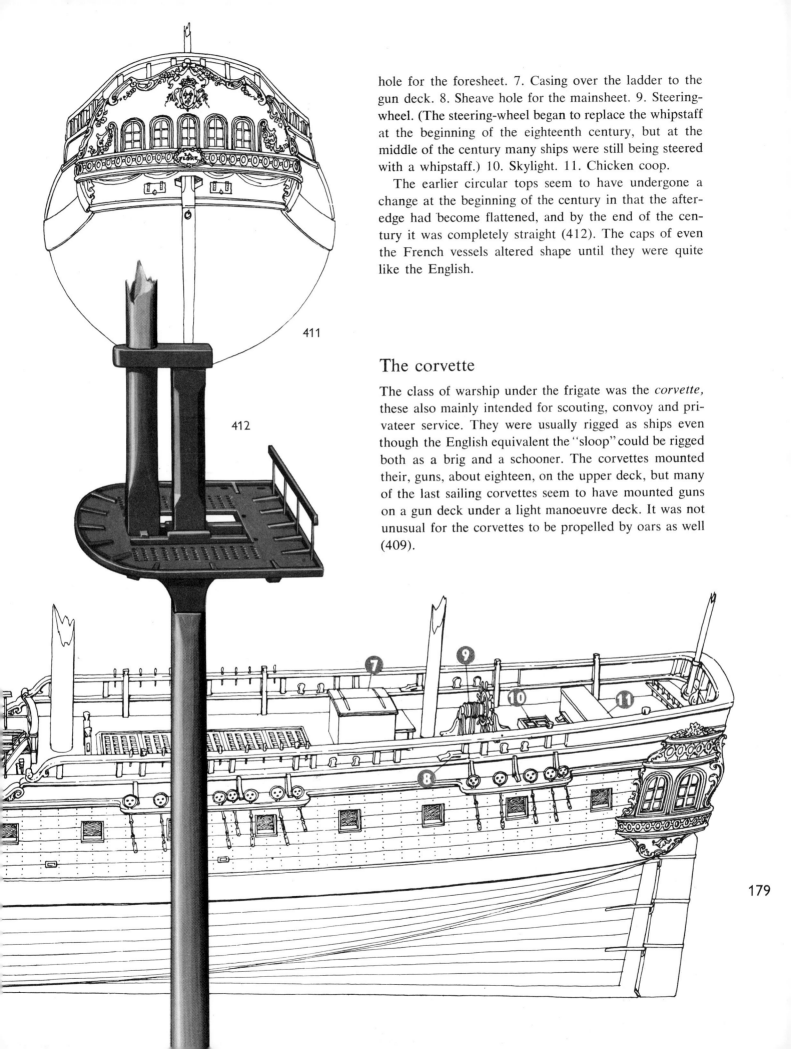

hole for the foresheet. 7. Casing over the ladder to the gun deck. 8. Sheave hole for the mainsheet. 9. Steering-wheel. (The steering-wheel began to replace the whipstaff at the beginning of the eighteenth century, but at the middle of the century many ships were still being steered with a whipstaff.) 10. Skylight. 11. Chicken coop.

The earlier circular tops seem to have undergone a change at the beginning of the century in that the after-edge had become flattened, and by the end of the century it was completely straight (412). The caps of even the French vessels altered shape until they were quite like the English.

411

412

The corvette

The class of warship under the frigate was the *corvette*, these also mainly intended for scouting, convoy and privateer service. They were usually rigged as ships even though the English equivalent the "sloop" could be rigged both as a brig and a schooner. The corvettes mounted their, guns, about eighteen, on the upper deck, but many of the last sailing corvettes seem to have mounted guns on a gun deck under a light manoeuvre deck. It was not unusual for the corvettes to be propelled by oars as well (409).

179

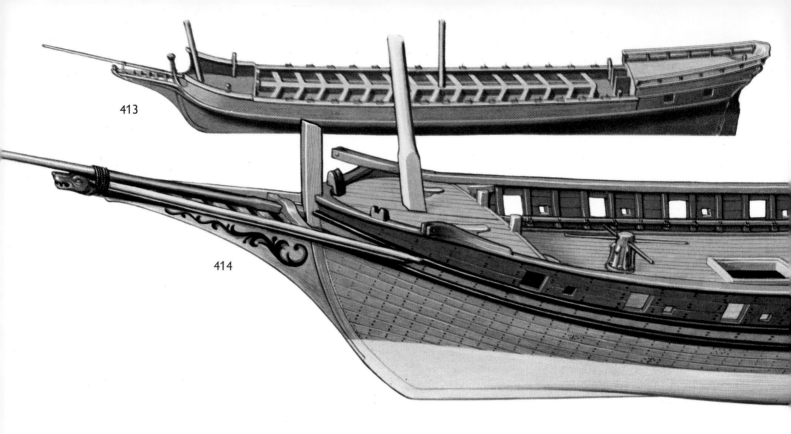

413

414

The chebeck

Like much else in this book the origin of the *chebeck* is very obscure. It is known that the pirates of the Barbary States used the chebeck during the seventeenth century, and in the eighteenth century we find both Spanish and French chebecks, Russian towards its end even. It is said that the Spanish built their first chebecks to fight the Algerian pirates with their own weapon.

A Spanish model at the Museo Maritimo in Barcelona is of the elegant and swift chebeck (414, 415). It is a shallow-draught vessel with concave waterlines in the bows and sides sloping outwards, and the hull has so much in common with the picture we have created of the caravel (277) that some connection may be suspected. It is, on the other hand, possible to discern some connection between nearly all swift sailing vessels in the Mediterranean, and there are pictures of older Spanish *feluccas* that hardly differ outwardly from the chebeck at all.

415

In the chebeck we can also see a development from the galley. The Venetian *galeotta* (413) was an oar-propelled vessel with auxiliary sails, and if we think of her as a little broader we almost have a chebeck before us. The midship section of the galley (343) is also very like that of the chebeck (416). But the chebeck was above all a magnificent sailer, and for her the oars were a mere auxiliary. Like so many other Mediterranean vessels she had a ram-like "beak-head". A "grating deck" projected far out over the round stern as an extension of the quarter-deck.

It is very likely that all chebecks were from the beginning rigged with lateen sails on all three masts, but from the middle of the eighteenth century we find both Moroccan and French chebecks with mainmasts square-rigged à la polacca. Such a polacca-chebeck is to be found in the "Souvenirs de Marine Conservés" by Admiral Paris (417), but in it is also another chebeck rigged approximately like an ordinary eighteenth century frigate.

416

417

181

419

418

"The Finnish archipelago fleet"

The vessels built by Fredrik Henrik af Chapman for Swedish operations in the Finnish archipelago were very singular and in theory partly revolutionary. As early as 1760 he had made a constructional drawing of a very shallow-draught vessel which we might call a galeass (418, 419, 420) with ten guns mounted on swivel carriages in the centre-line of the ship. It was to be rowed by 72 men at 18 pairs of oars and sailed with a low rig consisting of two fore-and-aft spritsails, a gaffsail, a fore-stay sail and jib. The ship was never built but the drawings were to be the basis for other constructions in the archipelago fleet.

The skeleton of the fleet was to be four vessel types called *hemmema*, *pojama*, *udema* and *turuma* which were thought to be the Finnish names of provinces in Finland. The *turuma* type was rigged with square sails whereas the others had a form of the lateen rig to begin with. On a *hemmema* (421) we can see how the sails on the main and foremast are cloven so that the yard could be moved within the shrouds and need never be

transferred from the one side to the other. All four types were combined rowing and sailing vessels, but, as others long before his time, Chapman had to admit that the combination was not a happy one. On account of the shallow draught the ships were bad sailers, and on account of their weight they were difficult to row. At the battle of Svensksund in 1790 when the Swedish fleet utterly defeated the Russian, their service was chiefly as floating batteries, the offensive action mainly being carried out by *gunsloops* and *gun launches*.

In 1775 Chapman came forward with a suggestion for two different types of gunsloop which were built that winter and demonstrated for the king the following summer (424, 425). Chapman reports this himself: "When these gunsloops had been built I armed one of them myself, took it up to Värtan in Stockholm where the King himself came on board, and then rowed it, fired salvoes, made for land and set out gangplanks, landed with the guns and advanced firing all the time, then retreated still firing until the guns were once more in position in the sloop, all finally coming to an end in that His Majesty made me lieutenant-colonel."

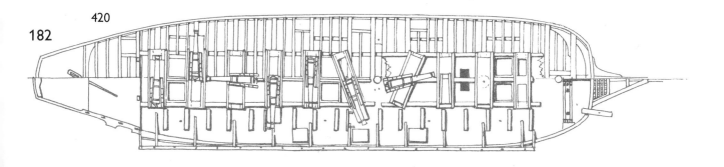

420

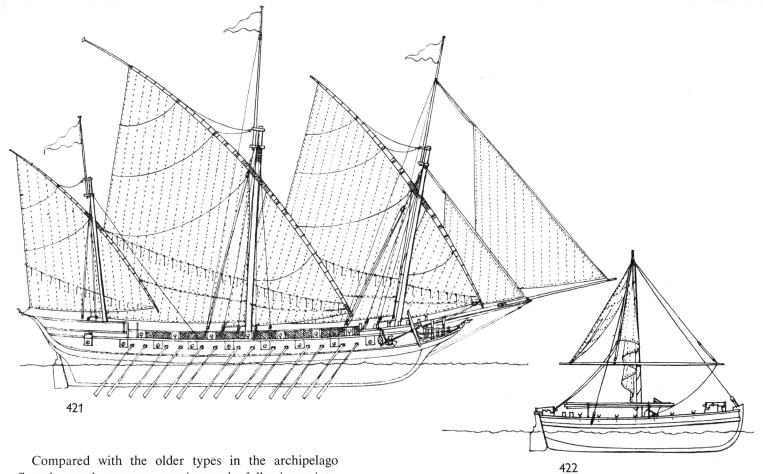

421

422

Compared with the older types in the archipelago fleet the gunsloops were superior on the following points: they were strongly armed considering the size of the crews (two 18-pounders and 55 men), they offered a relatively small target, they were of shallow draught (2½ feet), they were easily manoeuvred and could therefore be manned by comparatively inexperienced men. The crews could not sleep on board, however, and had to pitch tents on land. — Later, gunsloops for 24-pounders were also built, and in 1778 gun launches for both 18 and 24-pounders began to appear.

On the small gun launches (423) the gun carriage was a hull fixture so that the whole vessel recoiled when the gun was fired. The strangely extended stern gave buoyancy to the boat so that the mouth of the gun did not need to be retracted within the railings. The oarsmen sat in apertures in the deck. Both sloops and launches were rigged with *lug sails* while the *bomb vessels* (422) had stay sail and fore-and-aft spritsail.

423

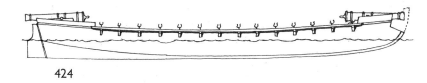

424

425

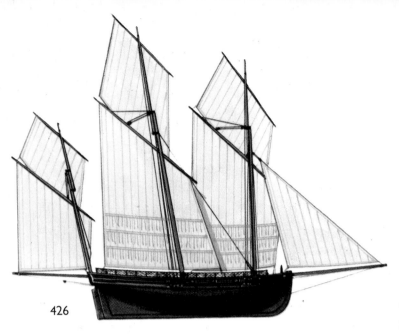

426

East Indiamen

Thus called were the small broad, roomy ships used by the Dutch for trade with the East Indian Colonies (427). They were the successors of the merchant pinnaces, rigged as frigates (432) and powerfully armed partly from fear of pirates and partly because they had to serve as fighting craft during a war.

The Endeavour, 1768

The first discovery ship of which there are accurate details is James Cook's barque *Endeavour* (428, 429). Earlier she had borne the name *Earl of Pembroke* and carried coals from England to Scandinavia, and when she was bought and equipped by the admiralty for expedition, careful measurements were taken of her in the customary way and an extensive description with diagrams made. The length of the lower deck of the *Endeavour* was 97 feet 8 ins from the forward edge of the sternpost to the after edge of the stempost. The length of the keel was 81 feet ⅜ ins and her greatest width was 29 feet 2 ins.

Before departure she was equipped with great care. Almost the whole rig was replaced, cabins were built for her officers, scientists and other persons of importance, and a new deck was built in the hold. In order to protect her from the destructive shipworm a layer of thin oak planks was attached to her underwater planking with nails whose large flat heads were driven in close together. She was armed with ten guns on carriages and twelve swivel guns. There were five anchors and three boats on board, and with her officers, scientists, servants and crew there was a total of ninety-four persons on board when she sailed from Plymouth on 26th August 1768.

French lugger

Lug-rigged fishing and transport craft had sailed the French channel coast and around Brittany ever since the Middle Ages. One type gradually came to be called *chasse-marée,* sea-hunter, a name corresponding to the Dutch word "jacht". As the chasse-marée was much used by smugglers the French Customs took up use of them about the end of the eighteenth century, and about this same time they began to make an appearance in the navy as a dispatch boat. During the Napoleonic wars large chasse-marées were equipped for privateers and were then armed with 8—10 guns and had a crew of 40—50 men (426).

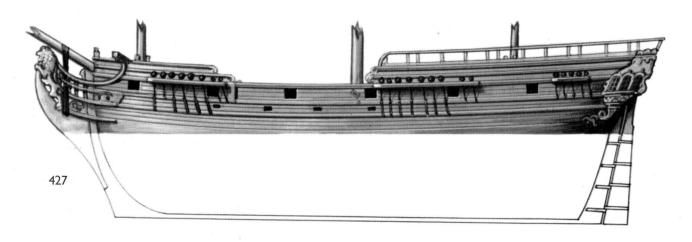

427

428

429

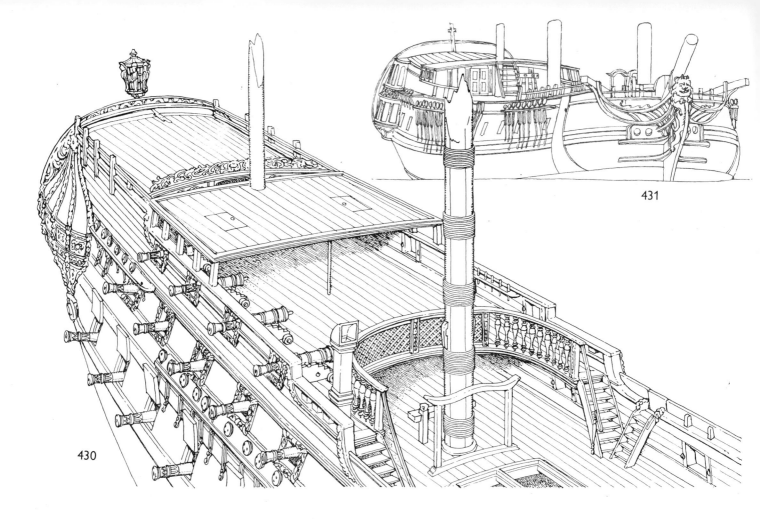

431

430

432

Merchantmen, eighteenth century

Most of the larger merchantmen during the middle and end of the eighteenth century were probably rigged as the frigate Chapman considers as representative in his "Architectura Navalis Mercatoria" (432) although many

vessels were still without topgallants and the very largest — or those of the most extrovert shipowners — could carry royals. The large ships of the Dutch East India Company were built, rigged and armed as complete men-of-war, and as loss of life was still great due to the length of the voyage and bad food a large crew was always taken from home.

On a model of the 54-gun East Indiaman *den Ary* of 1725 (430) we can still see the clinker-laid planks covering the sides of the quarter-deck and half deck (cf. 366) which was to be retained on Dutchmen almost right to the end of the century. The quarter-deck is built forward in a sweeping curve around the mainmast, hardly of any use, yet found on most of the Company's large ships. The *sun deck* forward of the poop deck and half deck ventilator is easier to understand on ships which sailed in tropical waters, and these details were also considered modern. We also find the sun deck in Chapman on a vessel of "Hagboat built, Ship's rigging" (431). The taffrail also appears to have been à la mode about the middle of the century but later seems to have vanished.

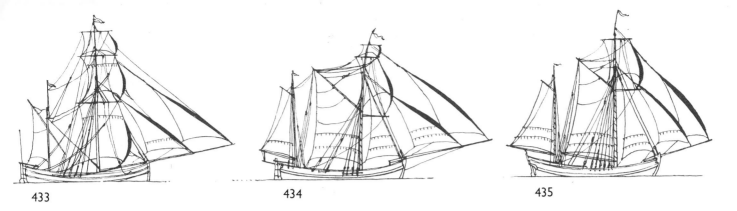

433   434   435

Whalers

The Dutch seem to have been whaling in the Arctic Ocean ever since the beginning of the seventeenth century, primarily using fluyts (362, 364) as parent ships for the whaling boats. During the eighteenth century too a modernised type of fluyt with broader deck seems to have been used, but the fluyt was later to be superseded by a so-called *bootschip* (436). It had roughly the same hull as the *galiot,* stubby at the ends, but differed from it mainly in the broad, richly ornamented stern. The stem also seems to have been higher than normal for the times. The *bootschips* that were equipped for whaling had sturdy fender cleats nailed to the sides, and furthest astern, above the half deck, a long, thick spar was erected for raising the sterns of the whaling boats. Their bows were raised with tackle from the mainmast. A *bootschip* usually carried from 6 to 8 whaling boats.

Small craft

The smaller trading vessels were rigged as snows, brigantines or schooners (403—407), and the small coastal vessels showed a multifarious collection of sails, all in the way of square sails in the North to different variations of lateen sails in the Mediterranean (cf. 477—510). Chapman shows for example a *hooker* (433), a *galiot* (434) and a *galeass* (435).

436

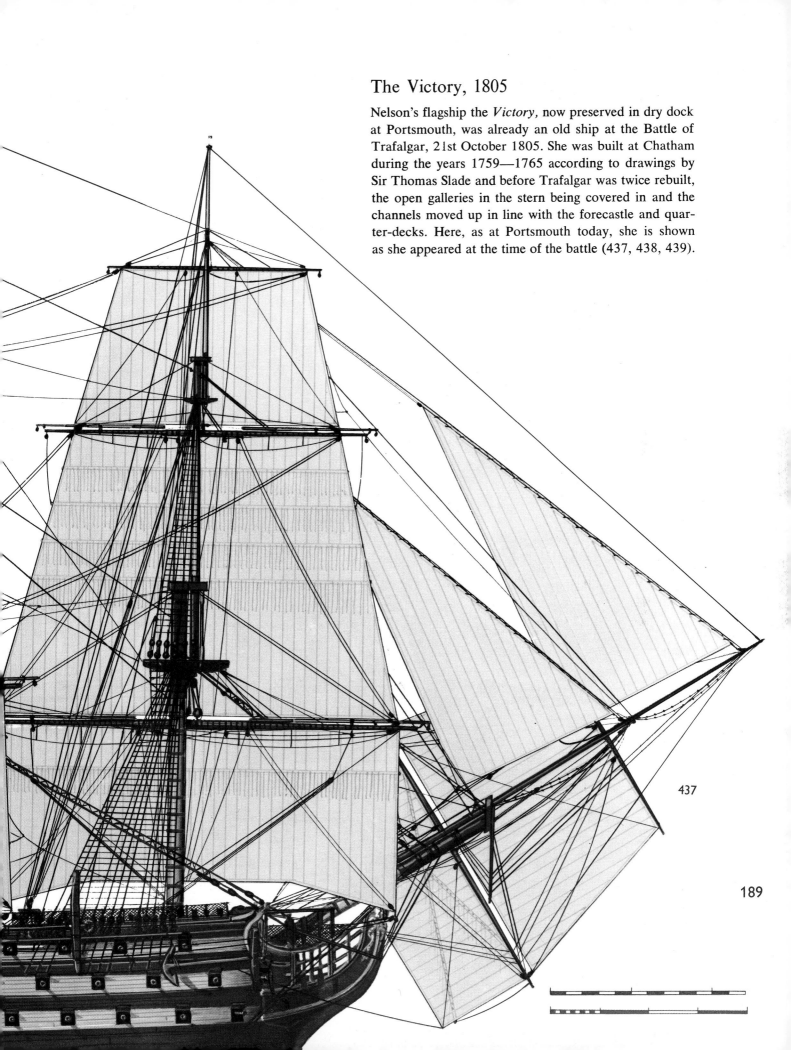

The Victory, 1805

Nelson's flagship the *Victory,* now preserved in dry dock at Portsmouth, was already an old ship at the Battle of Trafalgar, 21st October 1805. She was built at Chatham during the years 1759—1765 according to drawings by Sir Thomas Slade and before Trafalgar was twice rebuilt, the open galleries in the stern being covered in and the channels moved up in line with the forecastle and quarter-decks. Here, as at Portsmouth today, she is shown as she appeared at the time of the battle (437, 438, 439).

437

189

The Victory, 1805

The total length of the ship from the figurehead to the *taffrail* (the uppermost part of the stern) is 226·3 feet, the length of the keel 150·1 and greatest width 51·5 feet. The keel is of elm and the ribs and planking of oak. The underwater hull is protected from shipworm with copper plating. The armament at Trafalgar was: on the lower gun deck thirty 32-pounders, on the middle deck twenty-eight 24-pounders, on the upper deck thirty 12-pounders, on the half deck ten 12-pounders, on the forecastle deck two 12-pounders and two 68-pounder *carronades* (stubby guns for close-quarter work named after the town of Carron in Scotland where they were first made, cf. 446). The total number of guns carried by the *Victory* was thus 102. The crew amounted to 850.

The forecastle and quarter-decks are joined by two gangboards, and between them on the beams there are places for the four ship's boats. Round the whole deck (here only shown on the starboard side) the *hammock netting* is fitted up on the railings, a row of U-shaped iron prongs and strong netting where the tightly-rolled crew hammocks were stowed during daytime partly to be out of the way of the guns and partly to serve as protection from shrapnel and light enemy fire. The galleries are completely covered in and the decoration is very restricted. Only the coat-of-arms on the figurehead is gilt.

It was presumably seldom that the spritsail and spritsail topsail were set, but their yards were carried, their braces and lifts giving bowsprit and jib-boom good support at the sides. The *bumpkins* for the foretacks with their blocks jut obliquely forwards over the beak-head rails from the sturdy riding bitts on each side of the bowsprit. Up to the eighteenth century the foretacks had been rove through holes in the cutwater. In 1710 the double foretack davits were introduced on English ships, but they were only to become general by the middle of the century.

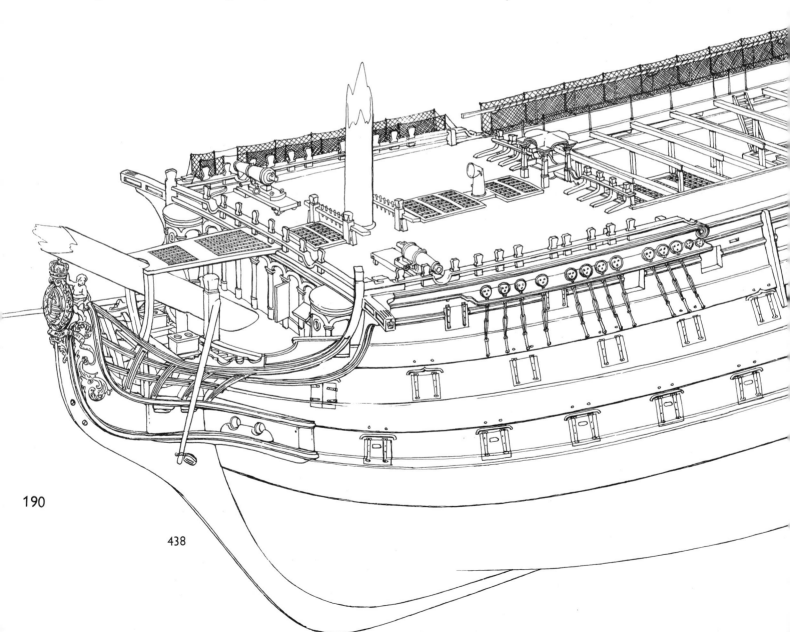

438

190

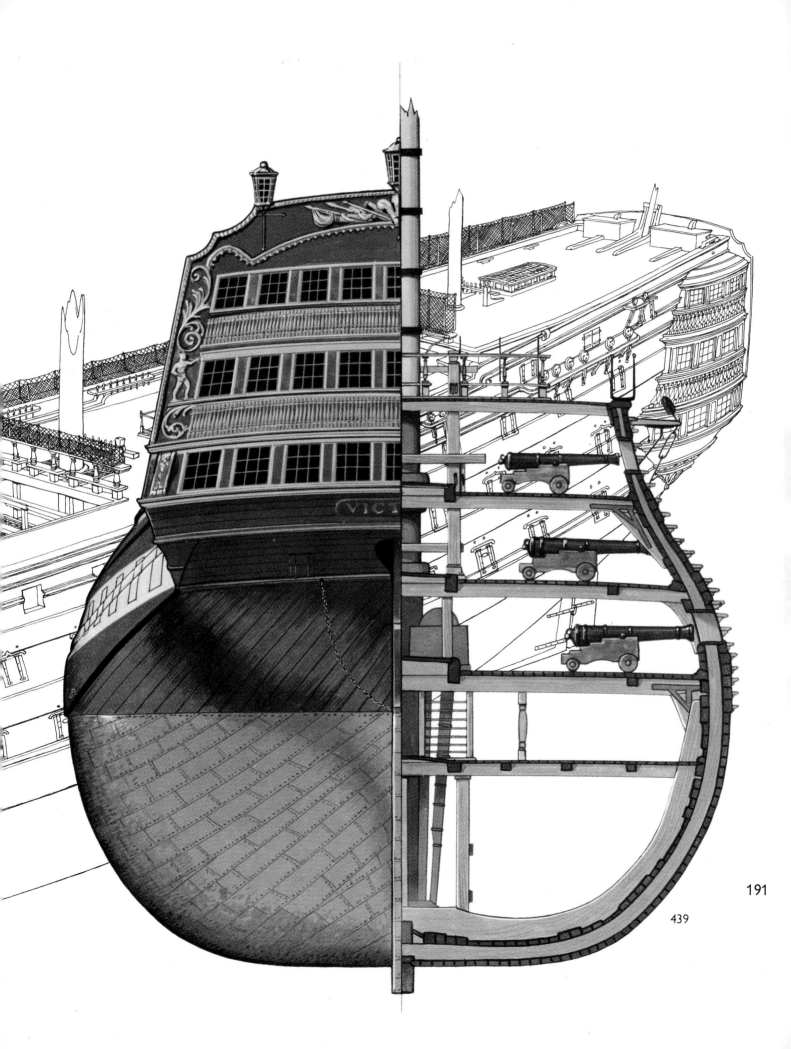

439

American frigates

During the last decade of the eighteenth century the keels of three frigates were laid in the United States which were to be the largest the world had hitherto seen and perhaps the finest ever to be built. The *United States* and the *Constitution* were launched in 1797, and the *President,* which was the best sailer, first entered the water in 1800 due to various delays. From figurehead to stern they measured 204 feet, the keel was 146·4 feet and at their widest they were 44·3 feet. Officially they were called 44-gun frigates, but their real armament was thirty long 24-pounders on the gun deck and twenty to twenty-two 12-pounders on the forecastle and half decks plus another two long 24-pounders on the forecastle.

The American frigates were 20 feet longer and 3 feet broader than the most modern English 44-gun frigates and 13 feet longer than contemporary French 40-gun frigates. The *President* (440) which was captured by the English in 1815 had a fantastic rig with *skysails* on all masts above the royals. We also see a *gaff topsail* above the mizzen.

One of these frigates, the *Constitution,* is still in ex-

istence. It has been restored and is to be found at the naval shipyards in Boston. It is said that she was able to make 13½ knots in her time, and it is known that the *President* was even faster.

The painting of ships

It was only at the beginning of the nineteenth century that the ships of the different navies began to be painted somewhat uniformly. During the eighteenth century it still seems to have been a matter of personal choice by the captains, and at the Battle of Abukir in 1798 one ship was painted with red sides and narrow yellow stripes and another with red sides and narrow black stripes, while most Englishmen were yellow with black stripes. Even at Trafalgar the Spanish *Santissima Trinidad* was dark red with white stripes and another Spaniard was completely black. At that time most of the English ships were painted black according to Nelson's wishes with yellow bands broken by the black hatches of the gun-ports. About 1815 the bands generally began to be painted white. This fashion was to stay as long as warships were sail-propelled, and long afterwards peaceful merchantmen were still painted "Nelson-style".

440

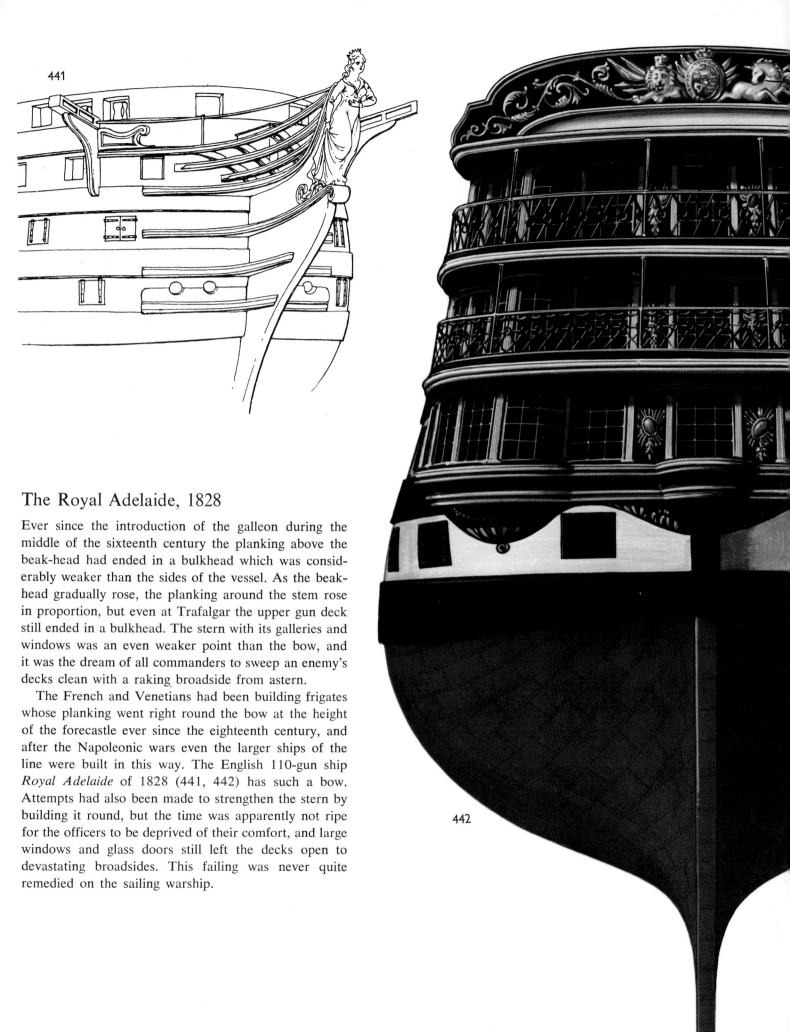

441

442

The Royal Adelaide, 1828

Ever since the introduction of the galleon during the middle of the sixteenth century the planking above the beak-head had ended in a bulkhead which was considerably weaker than the sides of the vessel. As the beak-head gradually rose, the planking around the stem rose in proportion, but even at Trafalgar the upper gun deck still ended in a bulkhead. The stern with its galleries and windows was an even weaker point than the bow, and it was the dream of all commanders to sweep an enemy's decks clean with a raking broadside from astern.

The French and Venetians had been building frigates whose planking went right round the bow at the height of the forecastle ever since the eighteenth century, and after the Napoleonic wars even the larger ships of the line were built in this way. The English 110-gun ship *Royal Adelaide* of 1828 (441, 442) has such a bow. Attempts had also been made to strengthen the stern by building it round, but the time was apparently not ripe for the officers to be deprived of their comfort, and large windows and glass doors still left the decks open to devastating broadsides. This failing was never quite remedied on the sailing warship.

443

La Belle Poule, 1834

from the railings and bulwarks proper as we can see on the French 120-gun ship *Ville de Paris* of 1851 (443) and on the 60-gun frigate *La Belle Poule* of 1834 (444).

During the nineteenth century the space between the gangboards began to be covered in so that the forecastle, quarter and half decks finally became one long deck, but on men-of-war the old names were retained so that the part aft of the mainmast was called quarter deck and the part around the foremast forecastle. The portions corresponding to the earlier gangboards were called port and starboard *gangways*.

The French *La Belle Poule* was even larger than the large American frigates. From figurehead to stern she measured 209 feet, length of keel 166½ feet and greatest width 48½ feet. She was called a frigate and had the lines of a frigate, but the mounting of the guns on two complete decks and their number made her almost as powerful as a third rate ship of the line from the previous century. On the gun deck she carried twenty-eight long 30-pounders and two 80-pounders, and on the upper deck there were four 30-pounders and twenty-six 30-pounder carronades (446).

As on most men-of-war from those times her railings ran uninterruptedly in a sweeping line from stem to stern, the hammock nettings developing into wooden hammock barricades. Forward of the foremast there was an *anchor deck,* and furthest aft a short poop deck. The gun-ports were of a new construction which made it possible for the guns to rest closer to the ship's side when not in use. Davits for a boat projected over the stern and a further four pairs of swivel davits projected above the long channels aft of the mainmast.

About this same time the anchor cables began to be made of iron chain, the square sails were no longer bent directly to the yards but to a *jackstay* which was stretched along the upper edge of the yard (453, 461), and the sails under the bowsprit and jib-boom disappeared for good.

The beak-head, like the ornamented stern and the galleries, was to remain with the sailing warship to the end. But the beak-head rails changed from a gently curving trellis-work to straight bulwarks continuing directly on

444

194

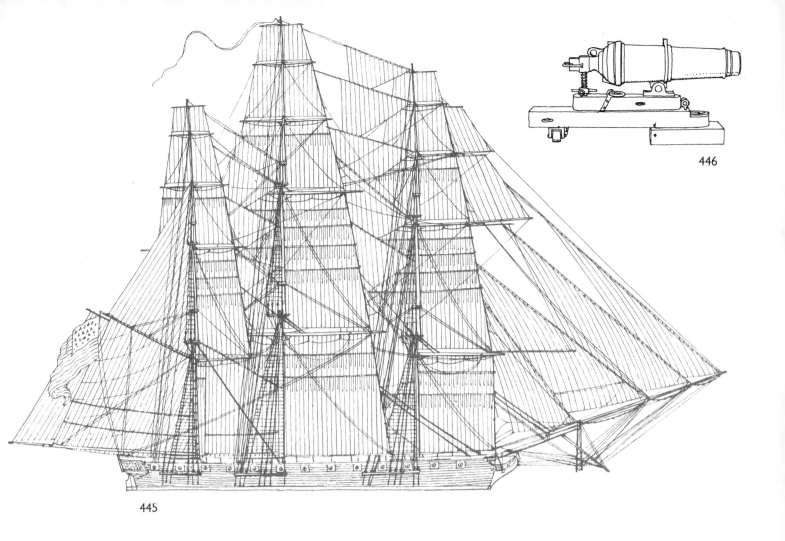

445

446

The General Pike, 1813

The keel of the American corvette *General Pike* was laid one day in 1813 and she was launched 63 days later. Officially she mounted 24 guns, but in reality was armed with twenty-six long 24-pounders and two 24-pounder carronades. She measured 174 feet from figurehead to stern and was 37 feet wide. Her rig, drawn here from the official diagram of the rigging (445), was very high indeed and the flagstaff on the main topgallant mast was 195 feet above the deck. She has skysails on all three masts and the following staysails: (between mizzen topmast and mainmast from above) mizzen top skysail, staysail, mizzen royal staysail, mizzen topgallant staysail, mizzen topsail staysail; (between the mainmast and foremast from above) main skysail staysail, main royal staysail, upper and lower main topgallant staysails, main topgallant mast staysail, main topmast staysail. On the jib-boom moving forwards she carries: fore topmast staysail, jib, flying jib, outer flying jib (fore royal staysail).

447

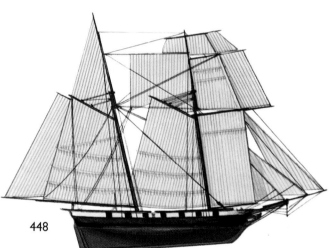

448

The Baltimore clipper

Almost more books have been written about the so-called *clipper ships* than about all other ships put together. Now one ship, now another has been pointed out as the first clipper, but it seems to be with clippers as with most other things in seafaring, that they made a gradual appearance as a result of natural development, and then one day someone called a certain type of swift, nineteenth-century sailing-ship a "clipper".

The so-called *Baltimore clipper* (448) has already been mentioned. She was a very swift ship first remarked in Baltimore and from the beginning perhaps rigged as a cutter, but during the latter half of the eighteenth century was most often schooner-rigged. The Baltimore clipper differed from other small contemporary vessels mainly in its sharp bows, but it probably did not have concave waterlines like the contemporary chebeck (414) and clipper ships to come.

The Blackwall frigates

About the beginning and middle of the nineteenth century there were many circumstances which combined to increase the demand for large, swift merchantmen. The monopoly of trade with the colonies enjoyed by the various trading companies was no longer the rule — the sea routes to the ports of India and China were now open to all, and gold rushes to California and Australia called for new vessels for the transport of emigrants and goods. The large East Indiamen of both the English and Dutch had been built approximately like the naval frigates, and the so-called *Blackwall frigates* which

449

began to be built in 1837 at Blackwall on the Thames were in actual fact not so very different from large naval frigates of the times. The first, the *Seringapatam* (447), was of 818 tons, and the largest of them was about 1,400 tons and measured 183 feet from stem to stern and about 40 feet in width.

U.S. clipper ships

The *Rainbow,* which is considered to be the first clipper by most authors, was constructed by John W. Griffiths and launched in New York in 1845 (450). She had slightly concave waterlines in the fore, a deep keel and more speedy lines than later clippers which were swifter because of their great length, and could therefore be built with more consideration to cargo capacity. She was 154 feet long at the waterline and 31·5 feet wide.

The *Flying Cloud* (449) which was launched in 1851 was 209·5 feet at the waterline and 40·7 feet wide. She was considered to be the fastest of all American clippers and twice covered the route from New York to San Francisco via Cape Horn in 89 days.

The largest of all clippers and the largest wooden vessel ever to be built was the *Great Republic,* launched in 1853. She was 325 feet long, 53 feet wide and had four masts. The three first were square-rigged, the last carried a fore-and-aft sail, and today we should call her a four-masted *barque*. To ease manipulation of the rig the topsails were divided into *upper topsails* and *lower topsails*. As she was about to start her maiden voyage a fire broke out on board, and, during the extensive repairs that followed, her hull and rig were cut down so much that she never had the chance of showing what sort of a sailer she could have been.

450

The Cutty Sark, 1869

The most famous clipper, the *Cutty Sark,* has been preserved for posterity and is to be found today in dry dock at Greenwich. She was built to bring tea from China and was constructed by Hercules Linton with the sole purpose of out-sailing the *Thermopylae* which was thought to be the fastest ship of the times. Both vessels measured roughly the same: length 212 feet, width 36 feet, depth 21 feet. *Cutty Sark* had a net tonnage of 921 tons against *Thermopylae's* 948. Due to the many hundreds of years of shipbuilding it was difficult to find good oak in England, and as it had been observed that oak frames took up so much valuable hold space it had become modern with so-called composite construction, i.e. that the hull was built of wooden planking on iron frames. The *Cutty Sark* was built on an elm keel with planking of teak.

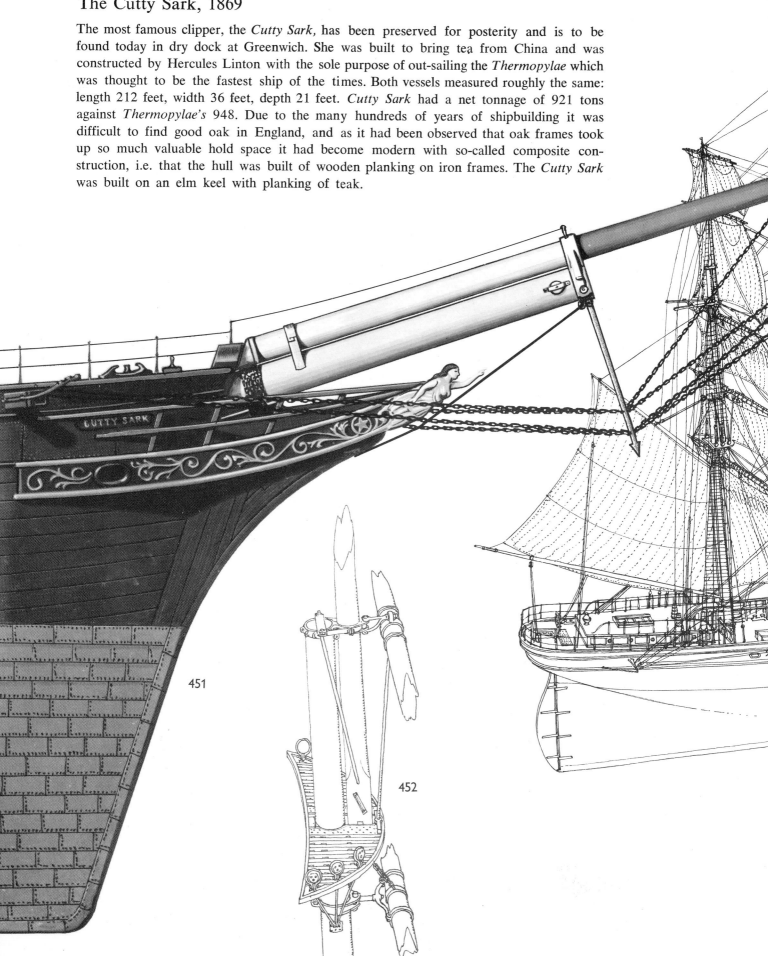

451

452

453

Aft of the mizzenmast the *Cutty Sark* has a raised poop deck, and in the bow an anchor deck. The deckhouse aft of the foremast contains crew quarters and galley. The deckhouse aft of the mainmast contains accommodation for apprentices. The captain's and first officer's accommodations are sunk into the poop deck. She carries a skysail on the mainmast alone and only the topsails are divided. The cap and other rig details are of iron (452). In the picture (453) she carries topgallant studding sail, upper studding sail and lower studding sail on the foremast.

454

The Preussen, 1902

Towards the end of the nineteenth century all large sailing-ships were built of iron and later steel. Even the masts, spars and yards were made of steel tubing, and steel wires replaced a good deal of the hemp lines in the rigging. The bowsprit and jib-boom were made in one piece, and on many vessels the lower mast and topmast were also a single construction. Channels disappeared and shrouds and stays were made fast with rigging screws.

A *full-rigged ship* is a ship with at least three masts, all of which are square rigged. The *Cutty Sark* was a three-masted full-rigger. The German *Preussen* (454) was the only five-masted full-rigger in the world. She was launched in 1902 and was 407·8 feet long and 53·6 feet wide. Like all sail-propelled vessels from the last days of the sailing-ship she also had double topgallants. With her 47 sails she had a total sail area of 50,000 sq. feet.

The Archibald Russell, 1905

The *barque* is a vessel with at least three masts where the last mast alone is rigged with fore-and-aft sails and the remainder with square sails. The *Archibald Russell* of 1905 (455, 460) was a four-masted English-built steel barque about 291 feet long and 43 feet wide. The masts from the bow aft are: foremast, mainmast, mizzenmast and spanker mast. The numbers in the drawing indicate: 1. Jigger topsail. 2. Spanker. 3. Jigger topgallant staysail. 4. Jigger topmast staysail. 5. Jigger staysail. 6. Mizzen royal. 7. Mizzen upper topgallant. 8. Mizzen lower topgallant. 9. Mizzen upper topsail. 10. Mizzen lower topsail. 11. Mizzen crojack. 12. Mizzen topgallant staysail. 13. Mizzen topmast staysail. 14. Mizzen staysail. 15. Main royal. 16. Main upper topgallant. 17. Main lower topgallant. 18. Main upper topsail. 19. Main lower topsail. 20. Mainsail. 21. Main topgallant staysail. 22. Main topmast staysail. 23. Main staysail. 24. Fore royal. 25. Fore upper topgallant. 26. Fore lower topgallant. 27. Fore upper topsail. 28. Fore lower topsail. 29. Foresail. 30. Fore topmast staysail. 31. Inner jib. 32. Outer jib. 33. Flying jib.

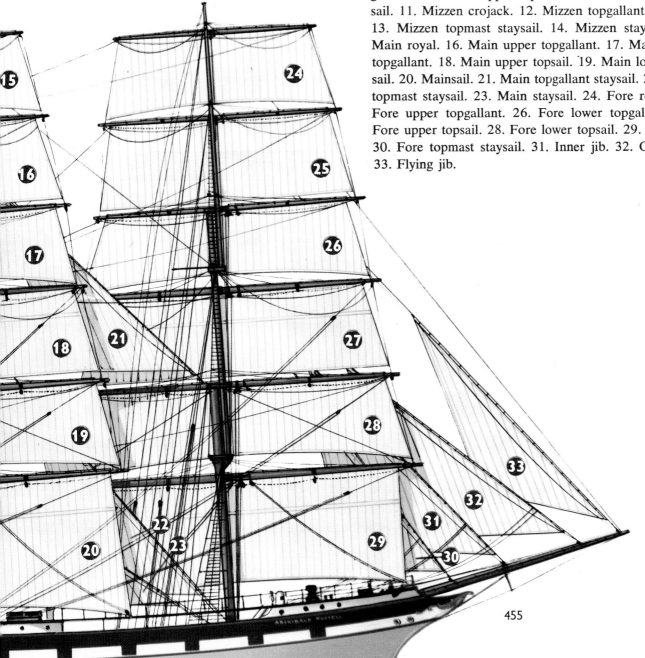

455

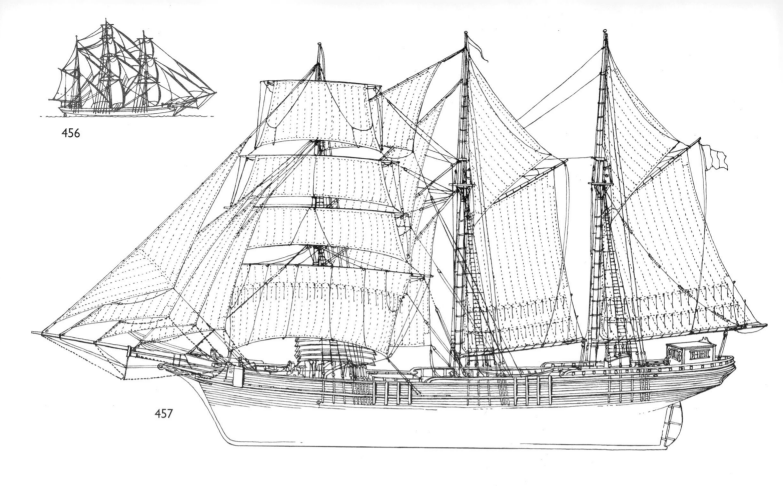

456

457

The Archibald Russell

In the hull drawing of the *Archibald Russell* (460) the numbers indicate: 1. Wheelhouse with steering-wheel. 2. Steering compass in binnacle. 3. Skylight above the captain's cabin. 4. Chart house. 5. Standard compass. 6. Monkey bridge leading over the deckhouses from poop to forecastle. 7. After deckhouse with accommodation for petty officers and apprentices and companion way leading down to the "tween decks". 8. Midships house with donkey boiler (boiler for winches etc.) and galley. 9. Seamen's house. 10. Port and starboard lanterns. 11. Anchor davit.

In the picture of the square-rigged mast (461) the numbers indicate: 1. Royal halyard. 2. Royal clewline. 3. Upper topgallant buntline. 4. Upper topgallant halyard. 5. Upper topgallant topping lift. 6. Upper topgallant downhaul. 7. Upper topgallant foot with buntlines. 8. Upper topgallant sheet. 9. Lower topgallant clewline. 10. Lower topgallant sheet. 11. Footrope. 12. Upper topsail halyard. 13. Upper topsail downhaul. 14. Lower yard topping lift. 15. Lower topsail clewline. 16. Lower sail clewline.

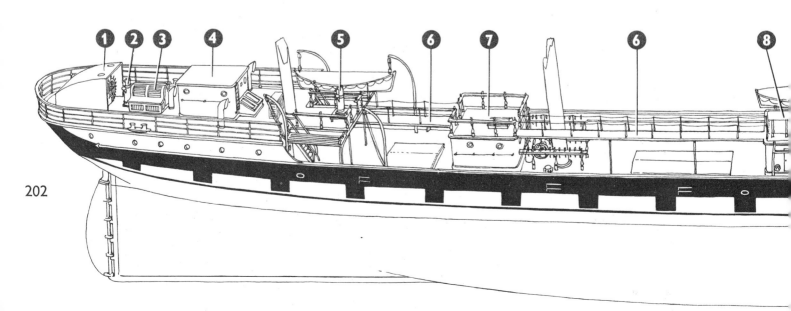

202

Barques and barquentines

The three-masted *barque* (456) was the most important vessel in the northern merchant fleets at the end of the nineteenth century. When the steamship came into general use and competition increased, many earlier barques were rerigged so that maintenance would be cheaper and the number of crew reduced. Yet the *barquentine* did not come into existence merely by rerigging the barque although no more was necessary than that the mainmast was fitted with fore-and-aft sails for the barque to become a schooner-type ship. The French vessels that still fished the Newfoundland banks after the First World War were often rigged as barquentines (457). The masts retained their old names and the only new sail was the *main gaff topsail*.

But it sometimes occurred that a ship was rigged for example with a fore-and-aft sail on the lower mainmast and square sails on the top and topgallant masts (458), the usual terminology then not covering the new type. In England all such types of pseudo-barques were called *jackass barques*.

Twentieth-century full-riggers and barques were only built for really long-distance trading and as school ships. In order to make seafaring under sail at all profitable even for coastal work, large barquentines were built which could be manned by a very small crew. Thus came the four, five and six-masted ships (459) to continue the battle against the steamship.

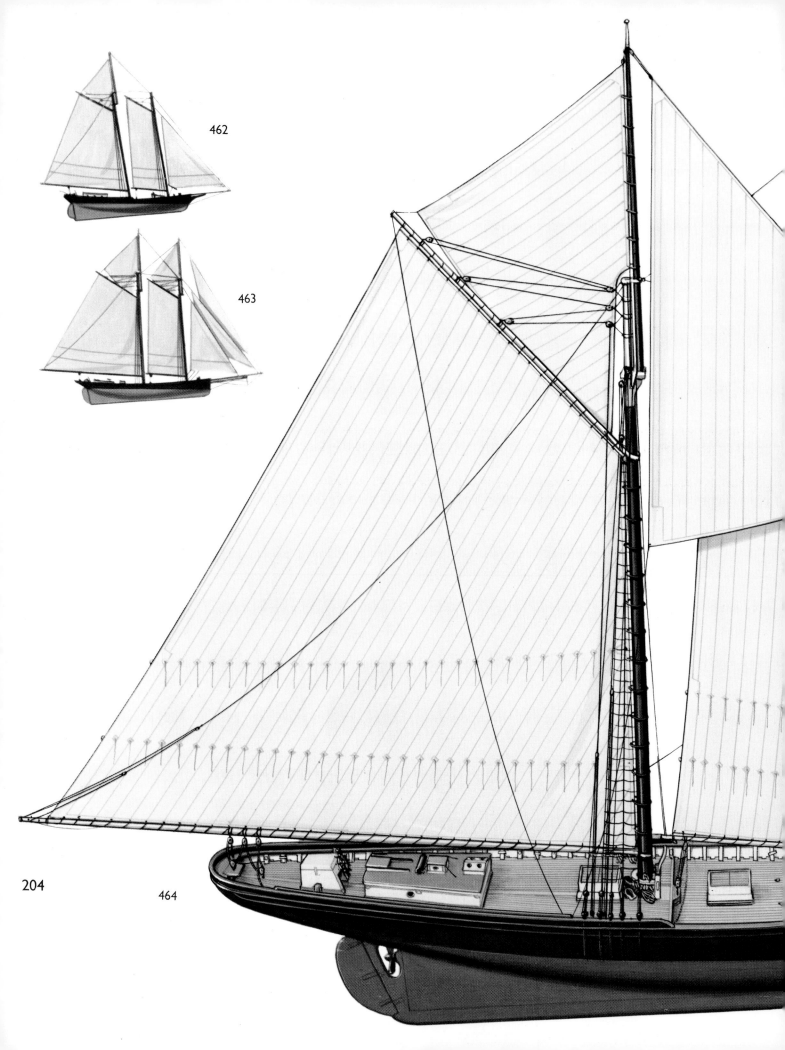

462

463

204

464

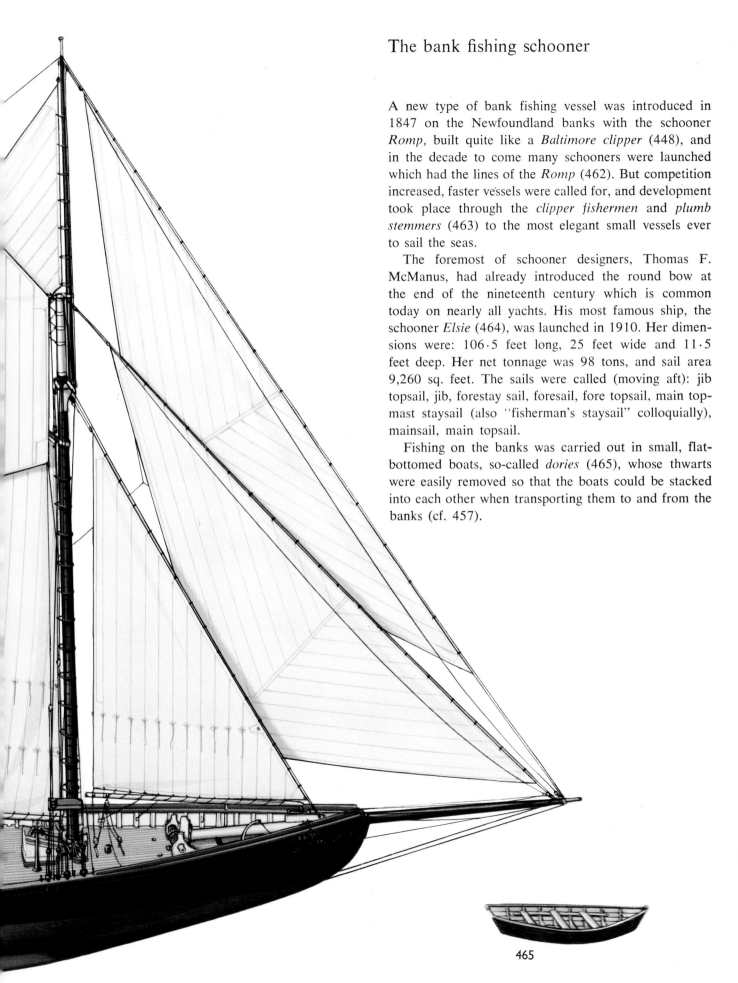

The bank fishing schooner

A new type of bank fishing vessel was introduced in 1847 on the Newfoundland banks with the schooner *Romp,* built quite like a *Baltimore clipper* (448), and in the decade to come many schooners were launched which had the lines of the *Romp* (462). But competition increased, faster vessels were called for, and development took place through the *clipper fishermen* and *plumb stemmers* (463) to the most elegant small vessels ever to sail the seas.

The foremost of schooner designers, Thomas F. McManus, had already introduced the round bow at the end of the nineteenth century which is common today on nearly all yachts. His most famous ship, the schooner *Elsie* (464), was launched in 1910. Her dimensions were: 106·5 feet long, 25 feet wide and 11·5 feet deep. Her net tonnage was 98 tons, and sail area 9,260 sq. feet. The sails were called (moving aft): jib topsail, jib, forestay sail, foresail, fore topsail, main topmast staysail (also "fisherman's staysail" colloquially), mainsail, main topsail.

Fishing on the banks was carried out in small, flat-bottomed boats, so-called *dories* (465), whose thwarts were easily removed so that the boats could be stacked into each other when transporting them to and from the banks (cf. 457).

465

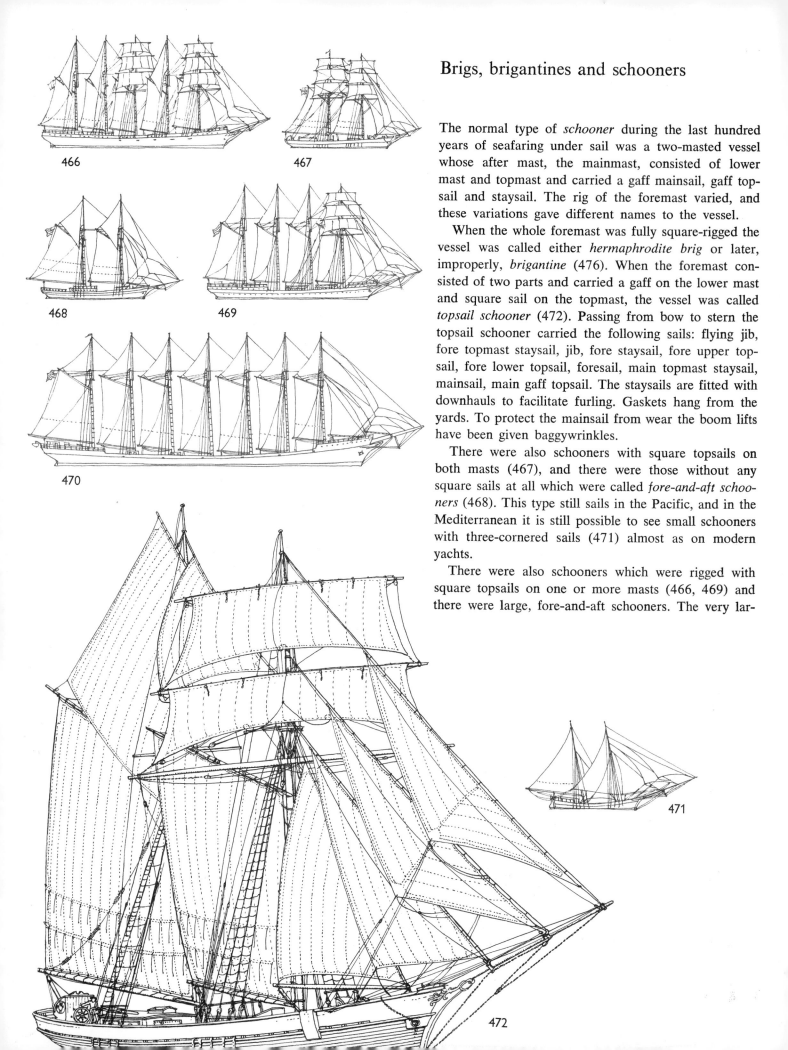

466

467

468

469

470

Brigs, brigantines and schooners

The normal type of *schooner* during the last hundred years of seafaring under sail was a two-masted vessel whose after mast, the mainmast, consisted of lower mast and topmast and carried a gaff mainsail, gaff topsail and staysail. The rig of the foremast varied, and these variations gave different names to the vessel.

When the whole foremast was fully square-rigged the vessel was called either *hermaphrodite brig* or later, improperly, *brigantine* (476). When the foremast consisted of two parts and carried a gaff on the lower mast and square sail on the topmast, the vessel was called *topsail schooner* (472). Passing from bow to stern the topsail schooner carried the following sails: flying jib, fore topmast staysail, jib, fore staysail, fore upper topsail, fore lower topsail, foresail, main topmast staysail, mainsail, main gaff topsail. The staysails are fitted with downhauls to facilitate furling. Gaskets hang from the yards. To protect the mainsail from wear the boom lifts have been given baggywrinkles.

There were also schooners with square topsails on both masts (467), and there were those without any square sails at all which were called *fore-and-aft schooners* (468). This type still sails in the Pacific, and in the Mediterranean it is still possible to see small schooners with three-cornered sails (471) almost as on modern yachts.

There were also schooners which were rigged with square topsails on one or more masts (466, 469) and there were large, fore-and-aft schooners. The very lar-

471

472

473   474   475

gest of them was the *Thomas W. Lawson* of over 5,000 tons and rigged with seven masts (470). She was 385 feet long and 50 feet wide and sailed with a crew of only sixteen.

The brig was a two-masted vessel rigged as the fore and mainmast of a barque were with the addition of a large main gaffsail. About the middle of the nineteenth century the brig was still common as a small vessel on long ocean routes, but, for the same reason as the full-rigger and barque were rerigged, the brigs proper also began to disappear towards the end of the century. But the snow-brig with brigsail on the snowmast aft of the mainmast (473 and cf. 407) was still sailing in this century, and the common brig (474) has long remained as a collier transporting coal from the English mining towns to London, Scandinavia and Spain.

The true brigantine (475) had no square mainsail. The mainmast often consisted of two parts and always carried a square topsail. When the square topsail on the mainmast was later replaced with a gaff topsail the vessel continued to be called brigantine by some. Others called it a hermaphrodite brig (467).

476

European coastal vessels, 1850-1960

We have now followed the European — and in part North American — history of the ship to the last days of sailing. The small craft have only just been touched upon — the hundreds of types of coastal vessels that have made a short-lived appearance during the centuries, the vessels which from the beginning have been the prototypes of the large ships, many times leading development along certain lines. Their history is a blank page right into the seventeenth century, and we know far too little of them even in more modern times as artists have not considered them worth depicting and the learned have given them no words. But in many of the types that still sail today or anyway have sailed during this century we are able to discern that development has taken place very slowly. Especially in the small Mediterranean vessels we are able to see details which we can trace right back to classical times.

Norwegian Nordland jagt

477

478 Swedish Roslag jagt

479 Swedish galeas

480 Finnish jagt

481 Finnish galeas

482 Danish jagt

483 Danish galeas

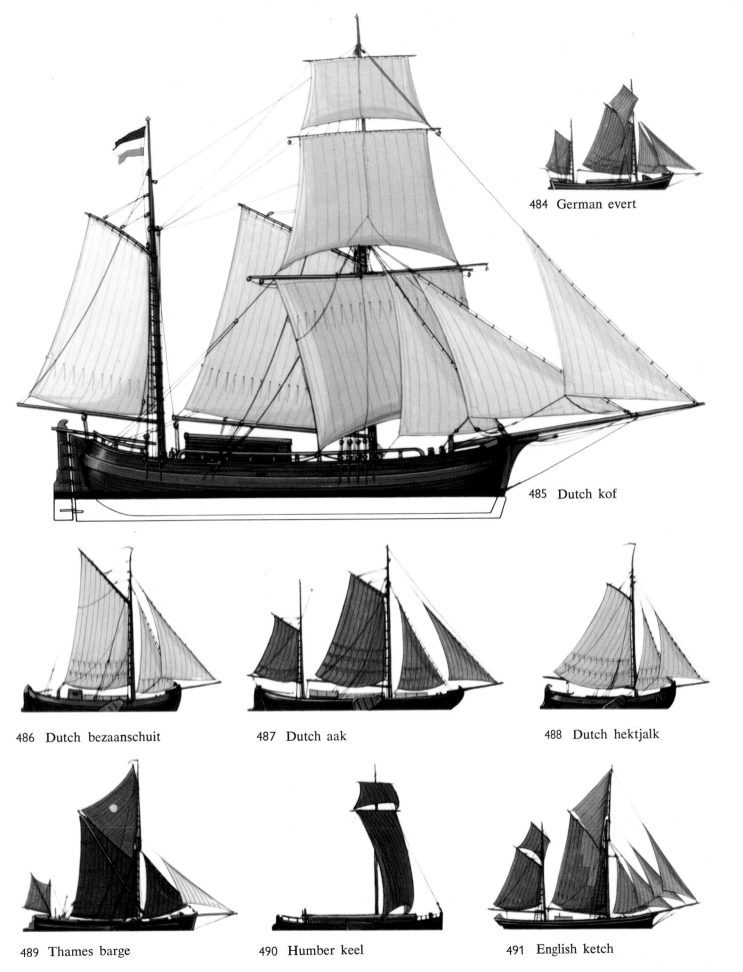

484 German evert

485 Dutch kof

486 Dutch bezaanschuit

487 Dutch aak

488 Dutch hektjalk

489 Thames barge

490 Humber keel

491 English ketch

209

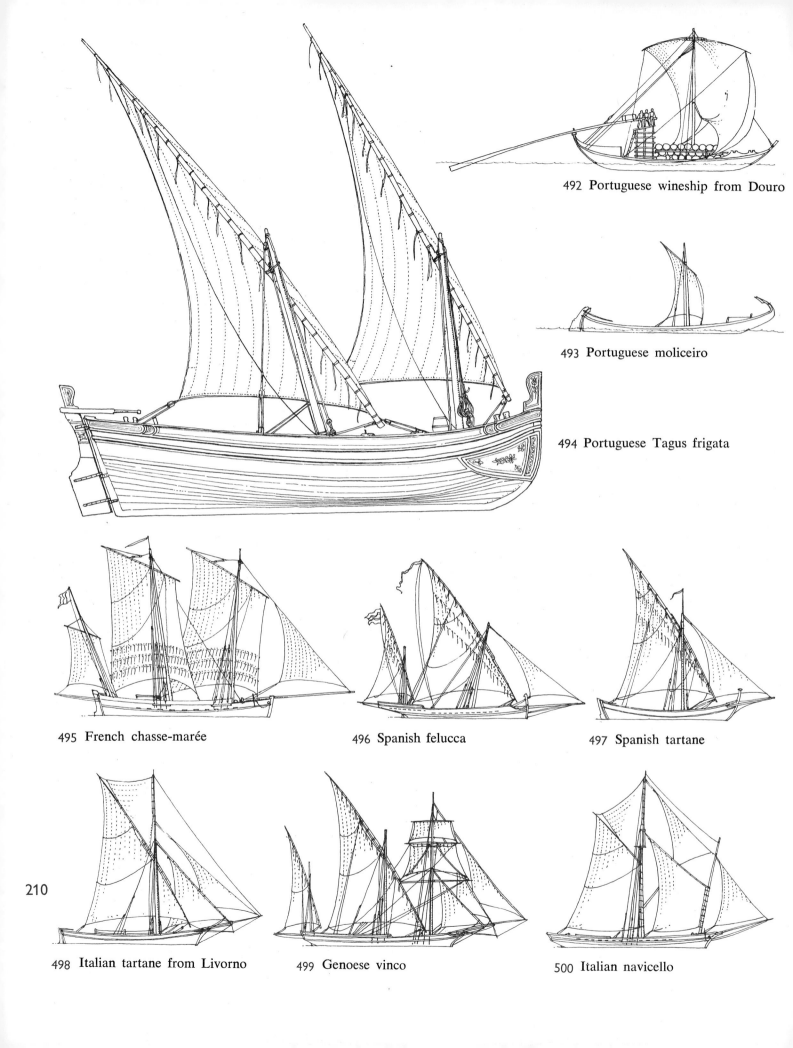

492 Portuguese wineship from Douro

493 Portuguese moliceiro

494 Portuguese Tagus frigata

495 French chasse-marée

496 Spanish felucca

497 Spanish tartane

498 Italian tartane from Livorno

499 Genoese vinco

500 Italian navicello

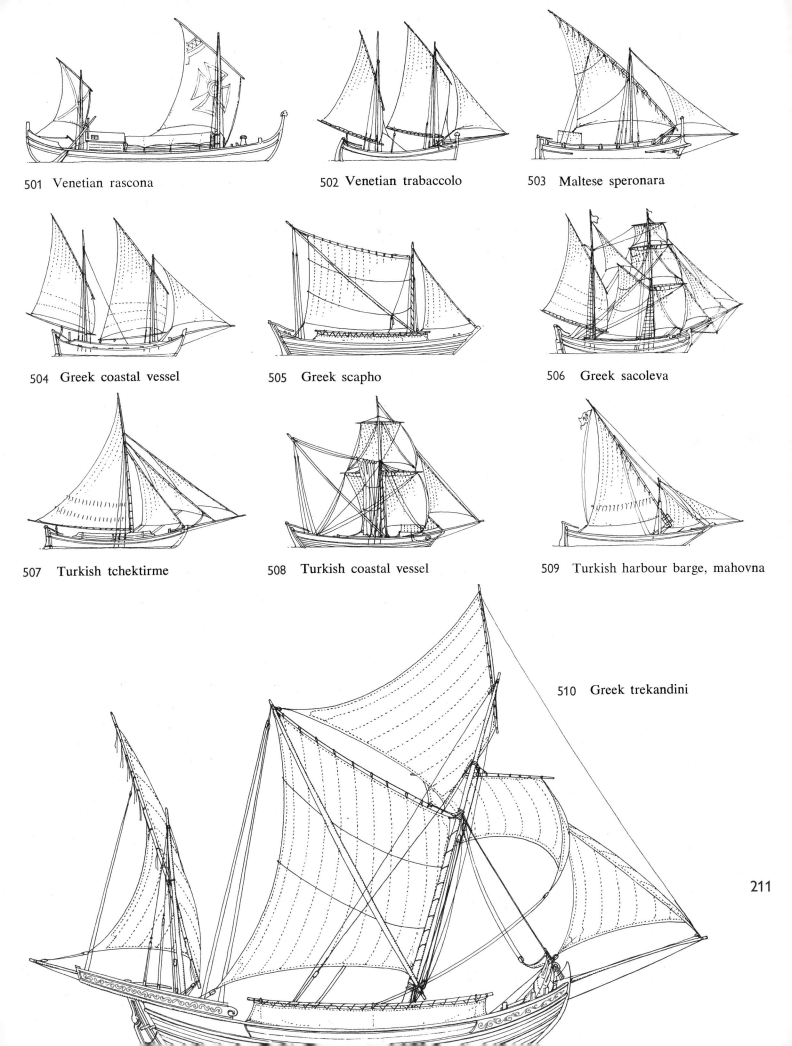

501 Venetian rascona

502 Venetian trabaccolo

503 Maltese speronara

504 Greek coastal vessel

505 Greek scapho

506 Greek sacoleva

507 Turkish tchektirme

508 Turkish coastal vessel

509 Turkish harbour barge, mahovna

510 Greek trekandini

211

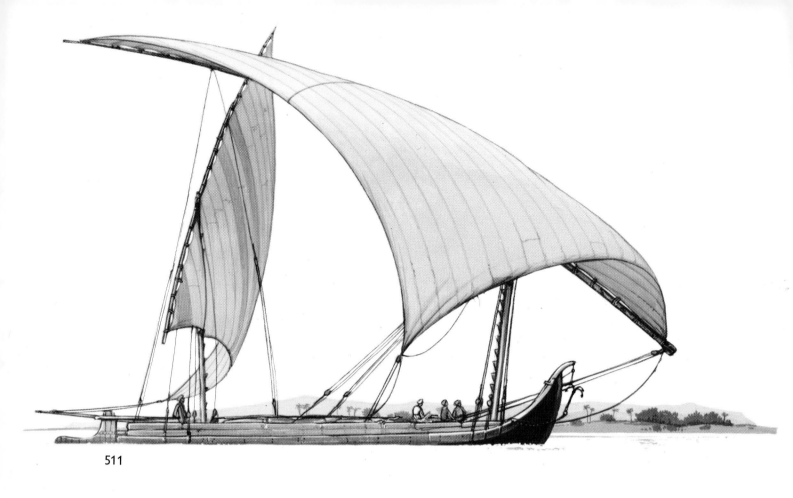

511

Vessels on the Nile

We know too little of the sailing vessels whose home waters lie outside of Europe and North America to be able to say anything of their historical development and origin. We must satisfy ourselves with the most important of them that still sail today or have sailed during the past hundred years and that have been portrayed and described in a satisfactory manner.

The Nile *gaiassa* (511) which sails upstream and floats downstream is nothing more than a long, shallow-draught cargo barge with curved stem, straight stern and large rudder. The smallest gaiassas have one sail and the largest can have three, but two tall, elegant sails hoisted right to the masthead like the first European lateen sails we saw (209) are the most common. Before the advent of motor-propelled vessels the *dahabia* (512) was the luxury boat of the Nile with passenger accommodation and sun roof, and except for its large sail it only carried a small mizzen which helped steering.

513

514

515

Arabian ships

Both the large Arabian sailing vessels and their sisters on the Coromandel Coast are called *dhows* by Europeans although there is no vessel which the Arabs themselves call *dhow*. The *baghla* is the most elegant of the vessels which sail the seas and bays around Arabia (513, 517), and in the baghla and the other large craft which are called *sambuk* (514), *boom* (515) and *ghanja* (516) there are many who see direct descendants of the Portuguese ships which traded and spread terror in the present waters of the dhow during the sixteenth century and after.

The baghla's stern is without doubt shaped on an early eighteenth-century European model, the midship sections are roughly similar to those of the caravel reconstruction (276), but we know of no European counterpart to the long, straight bow — if we do not seek right up to the North and find the cog stem, that is. The large boom with the long bow pointing skywards belongs to the Persian Gulf and is said to be built in the shipyards around Kuwait to this day. It is an ocean-going ship, traverses the Indian Ocean to Bombay and Zanzibar, first always waiting for the right season and the right wind of course because all seamen who sail in dhow waters say: "No one but a madman or a Christian would sail to windward".

Perhaps the ghanja no longer sails. I have only come across her mentioned in a book and in a drawing by an Arab. She seems to have been longer and more slender than the other dhows and the sole three-master in these waters. None of these ships has reefing arrangements, and if the wind becomes too fresh it is common practice to unbend the sails and bend other smaller ones instead.

512

516

517

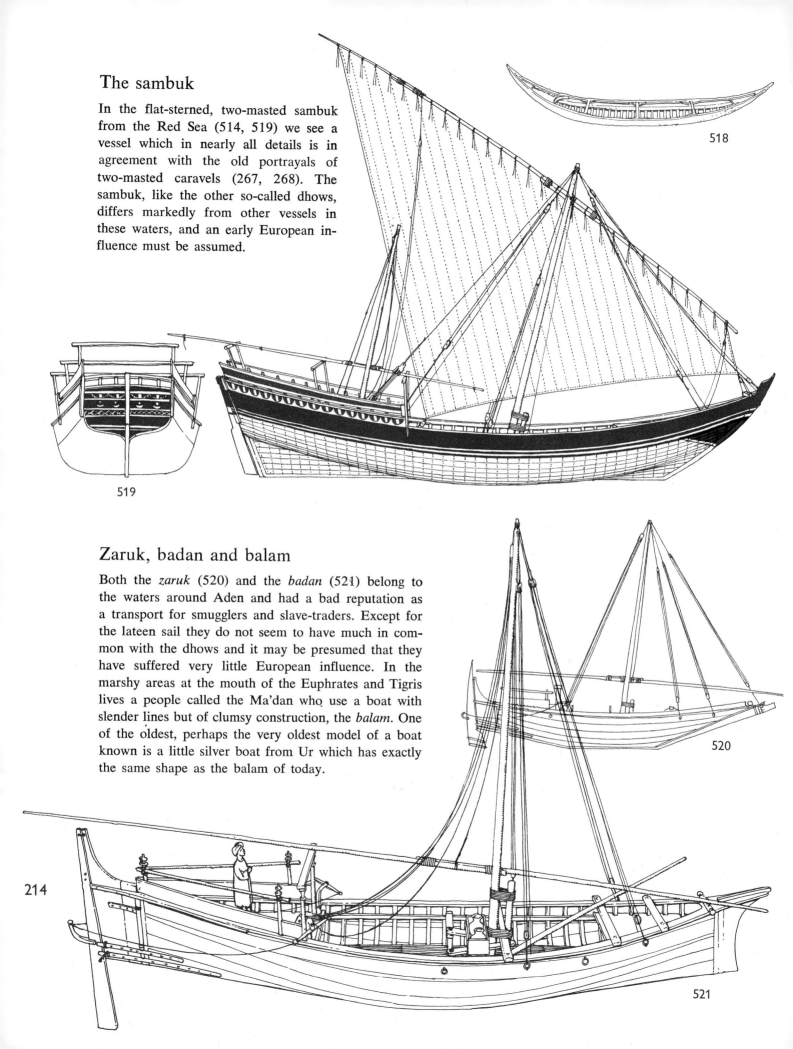

The sambuk

In the flat-sterned, two-masted sambuk
from the Red Sea (514, 519) we see a
vessel which in nearly all details is in
agreement with the old portrayals of
two-masted caravels (267, 268). The
sambuk, like the other so-called dhows,
differs markedly from other vessels in
these waters, and an early European influence must be assumed.

518

519

Zaruk, badan and balam

Both the *zaruk* (520) and the *badan* (521) belong to
the waters around Aden and had a bad reputation as
a transport for smugglers and slave-traders. Except for
the lateen sail they do not seem to have much in common with the dhows and it may be presumed that they
have suffered very little European influence. In the
marshy areas at the mouth of the Euphrates and Tigris
lives a people called the Ma'dan who use a boat with
slender lines but of clumsy construction, the *balam*. One
of the oldest, perhaps the very oldest model of a boat
known is a little silver boat from Ur which has exactly
the same shape as the balam of today.

520

214

521

Pattamar, mashwa and doni

A strange vessel which is usually referred to the dhow family is the *pattamar* from the Coromandel Coast, the east coast of India north of Ceylon. The stem of the pattamar is reminiscent of the baghla's except for the lowest part where it meets the downward sloping keel in a shape which would certainly improve its sailing ability (522). The stern is round and buoyant, and with its two large lateen sails the pattamar is a good sailer. There are larger pattamars that carry as many as three sails but they are quite without decks and by no means ocean-going like the boom.

The *mashwa* seems to be the name for small vessels in general around the Indian Ocean. Large dhows carry a "mashwa" on deck as a ship's boat, and the mashwa occurs as a fishing and transport vessel around Zanzibar, Bombay and Ceylon. On the Coromandel Coast the mashwa seems to be a reduced pattamar rigged with one sail (523).

A craft called *doni* shows the ancient system of stitched planking. To make the boat anyway fairly watertight further long ribs have been stitched over the seams. The doni has been reinforced with through-beams in the same way as hulls were reinforced in the Mediterranean back in the sixteenth century. Lug sails are common round Ceylon, and it is possible that the lateen sail — in the Arab world not shaped like a triangle but like a trapezium — has developed from the Asiatic lug sail.

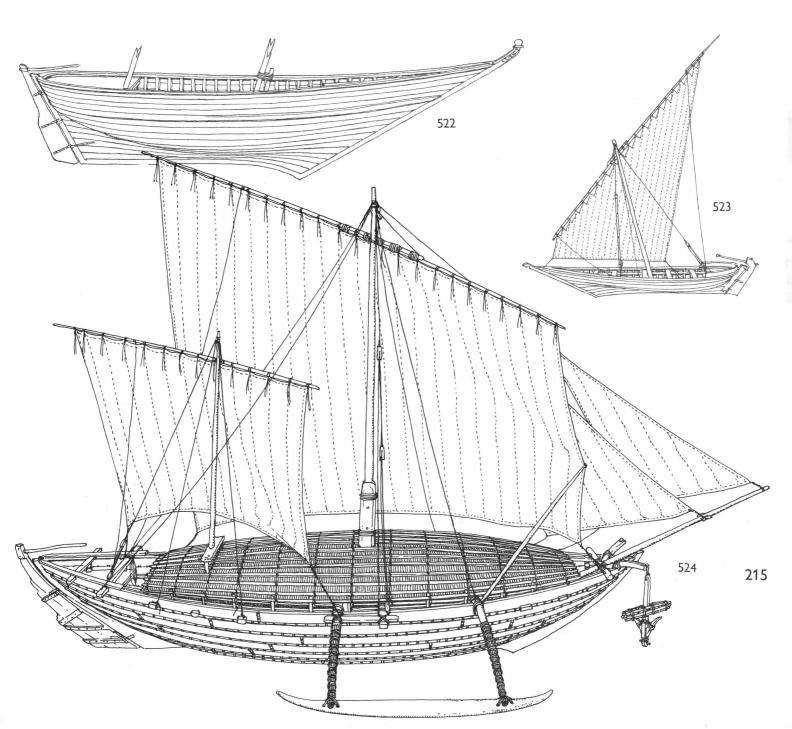

522

523

524

215

525

526

India and Indochina

The Ganges has a transport vessel, a large barge called a *patile* (525). Like other Indian vessels it has a large balanced rudder which is easy to manoeuvre because a part of the blade lies in front of the stock. But it is most remarkable in that it is clinker-built, and not even by the greatest stretch of imagination can we believe that there has been influence from the North.

Nor is it really possible to believe in an exchange of influence or a connection between ancient Egypt and India although there are two other Ganges vessels which could just as well have been sailing the Nile four thousand years ago. The one is called *pallar* and carries passengers and goods over the river (526). Admittedly it has only *one* side rudder, but the ends and the through-beams take our thoughts to the vessels which towed Queen Hatshepsut's obelisk barges (36). The other vessel

(528) also carries passengers, and were it not for the lug sail it could well have been found in Mehenkvetre's tomb (30, 31).

The large vessel that carries rice and other goods on the Irawadi in Burma (530) is, on the other hand, quite original. The main part of the hull is a large wooden dug-out which is soaked and then gradually heated over a slow fire until the sides can be forced out. They are then made higher with several planks (cf. 130). When the cold season comes to an end in Burma a good southerly breeze blows up along the Irawadi for several months. It is then the bipod masts of the rice boats are raised, the long yard hoisted with many topping lifts, an enormous sail of the thinnest cloth set with a further topsail above and the up-river journey begun. It is a complicated and fragile rig, but the wind is to be relied on and the river does not make many turns.

Siamese waters are trafficked by a small, high-stem-

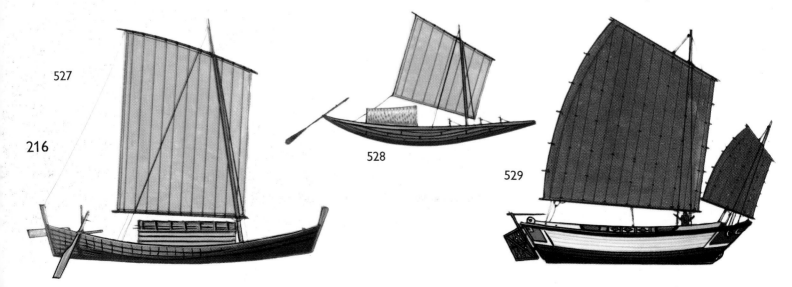

527

216

528

529

530

531

med coastal vessel called *rua chalom* (527), steered with two rudders like the ships of ancient times. And a small, gaily-painted, flat-bottomed vessel having two lug sails with long battens (529) reminds us of the proximity to the great seafaring nation China. It is called *twaqo,* and although it belongs to the waters around Singapore it must be called a *junk.* The junk is a vessel, a ship, whereas the *sampan* is a boat. There are also other junks of indisputable S. Chinese type (531) which have had a home in Siam for hundreds of years.

In Cochin-China which lies even closer to China proper we can find dozens of different vessel types quite on their own as regards hull and rig. A long, narrow riverboat, a *ghe ca vom* (532), has a sail which seems to be something between an Asiatic lug sail and a gaff-sail, and a vessel from the coast north of Saigon, a *ghe luoi rung* (533), has a very elegant *gunter rig* on its three short masts.

532

533

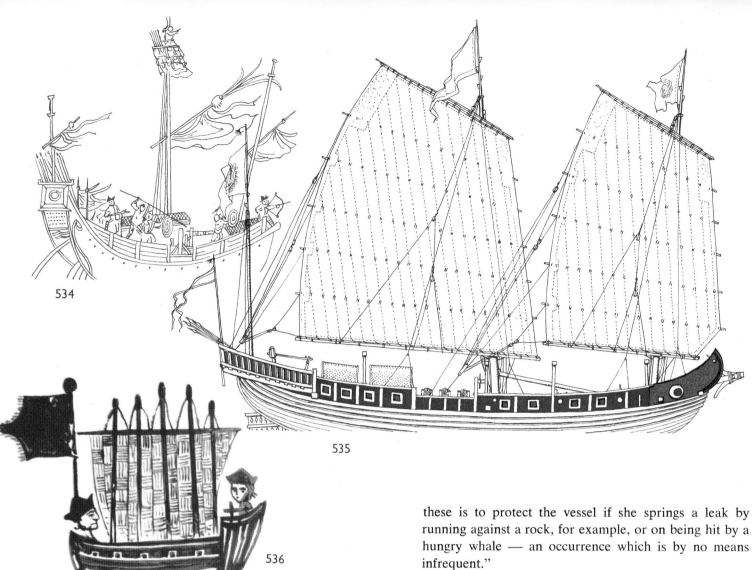

534

535

218

Chinese junks

The oldest-known description of a Chinese junk was given by Marco Polo in 1298 while dictating his voyage of discovery in a prison in Genoa: "We shall begin with a description of the merchants' ships which are built of deal. They have a single deck, and under this the space is divided into sixty small cabins — more or less according to the size of the vessel — of which each is furnished as a small living quarters for a merchant. They are fitted with only one rudder. They have four masts with as many sails, and some have a further two which can be raised and lowered when necessary. In addition to the cabins already spoken of, some vessels of the larger sort have their hulls fitted with thirteen partitions which are made of thick planks joined together. The purpose of

536

these is to protect the vessel if she springs a leak by running against a rock, for example, or on being hit by a hungry whale — an occurrence which is by no means infrequent."

The oldest representation which is supposed to be of such a vessel is to be found in the "Catalan Atlas" of 1357 (536), but apart from the five masts with woven matting sails it shows nothing particularly foreign to Europe and it was presumably drawn according to Marco Polo's decription. A Chinese woodcut from the middle of the sixteenth century, however, portrays a fighting junk (534) which is in good agreement with the fighting junks that were still used during the nineteenth century (535).

Nearly everything that Marco Polo says that he had experienced and seen with his own eyes seems to be true to fact, and there is nothing that gainsays his description of the junk. He makes a definite point of saying that the ships had only one rudder — this would have been a novelty for him as all ships in the Mediterranean of those days still had two. It seems then as if the Chinese came before Europeans with the stern-rudder as with so many other things.

There may still be one or two of the old, so-called *pechili junks* (538, 539) in existence today, a trading

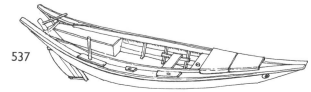

537

538

junk from northernmost China which seems to have much in common with the giant junks of the thirteenth century. At the beginning of the twentieth century the largest of the pechili junks were about 180 feet long and 30 feet wide. The remarkable, flat-bottomed pontoon hull (transverse section 539) was divided into compartments by some twenty watertight bulkheads like Marco Polo's vessel, and of the five masts the foremost and the next aftermost could be raised or lowered as required. The sails, which during previous centuries had consisted of fibre matting, were usually made of cloth with matting reinforcements during the last hundred years. The through battens made the sails most efficient, as they still do today on other junks, and reefing was simple as a system of sheets ending in crowfeet controlled the whole afterleech and it was only really necessary to lower the sail to a suitable reduction of area.

A flat deck ran from fore to aft above the arched pontoon deck and a row of hatches amidships covered the entrances to the many holds. Captain and crew were accommodated under the quarter-deck. The decoration was often merely a little sparse carving. — Most of the larger junks carried one or more sampans as ship's boats. The sampan here (537) is of a type to be found all over the Far East from Singapore to northernmost China.

539

219

540

541

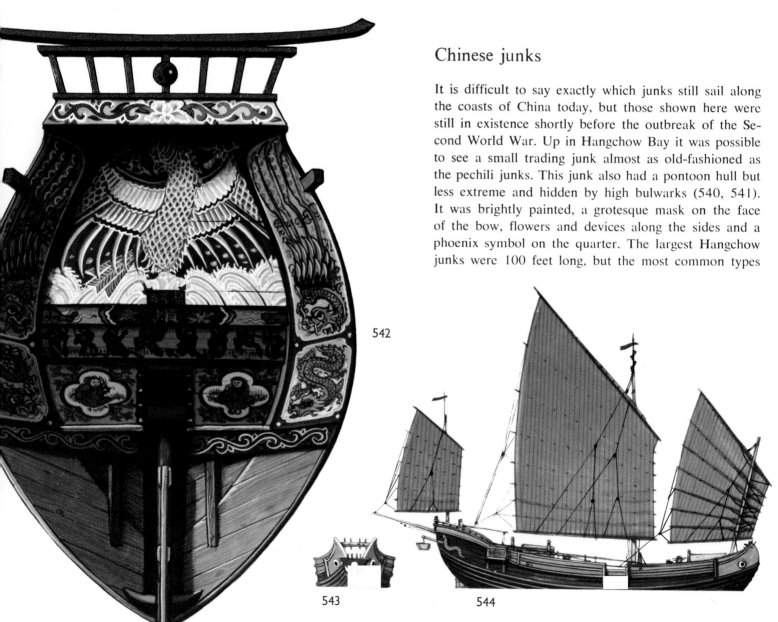

Chinese junks

It is difficult to say exactly which junks still sail along the coasts of China today, but those shown here were still in existence shortly before the outbreak of the Second World War. Up in Hangchow Bay it was possible to see a small trading junk almost as old-fashioned as the pechili junks. This junk also had a pontoon hull but less extreme and hidden by high bulwarks (540, 541). It was brightly painted, a grotesque mask on the face of the bow, flowers and devices along the sides and a phoenix symbol on the quarter. The largest Hangchow junks were 100 feet long, but the most common types

542

543

544

545

were about 75 feet long and 22 feet wide.

Models of the beautiful Foochow *stock junk* (542, 543, 544) are still built for tourists. It is called stock junk because it chiefly carried timber along the coast from Pei Ho in the north to Canton in the south. The hull was strengthened with fifteen watertight bulkheads and was very strong. The decoration on the face of the bow and the eyes on the bulwarks are to be found on many other junks, but the Foochow junks were the only ones which had the beautifully shaped and richly decorated stern. The figures were painted with distemper on a white distemper background and quite naturally had to be touched up now and again. The phoenix, symbol of immortality, was always the dominating figure and was generally framed with dragons, of figures symbolising the eight immortals, of symbols for power and greatness, riches and independence. A crimson sea monster on the quarter indicated that the vessel belonged to the province of Fukien.

To our eyes the S. Chinese junks are less extreme (545, 546, 547), probably due to western influence having caused a great yet gradual change. The large efficient rudder which can be adjusted to a desired depth with tackle is common to all junks. In the south a wide housing is often built around it (545) and a square platform projects over the railings in the bow.

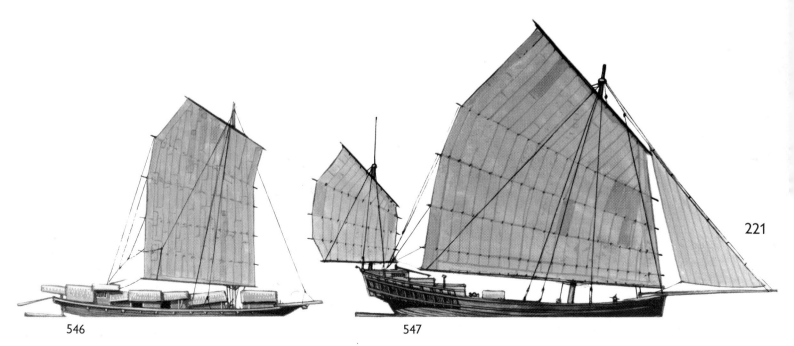

546   547

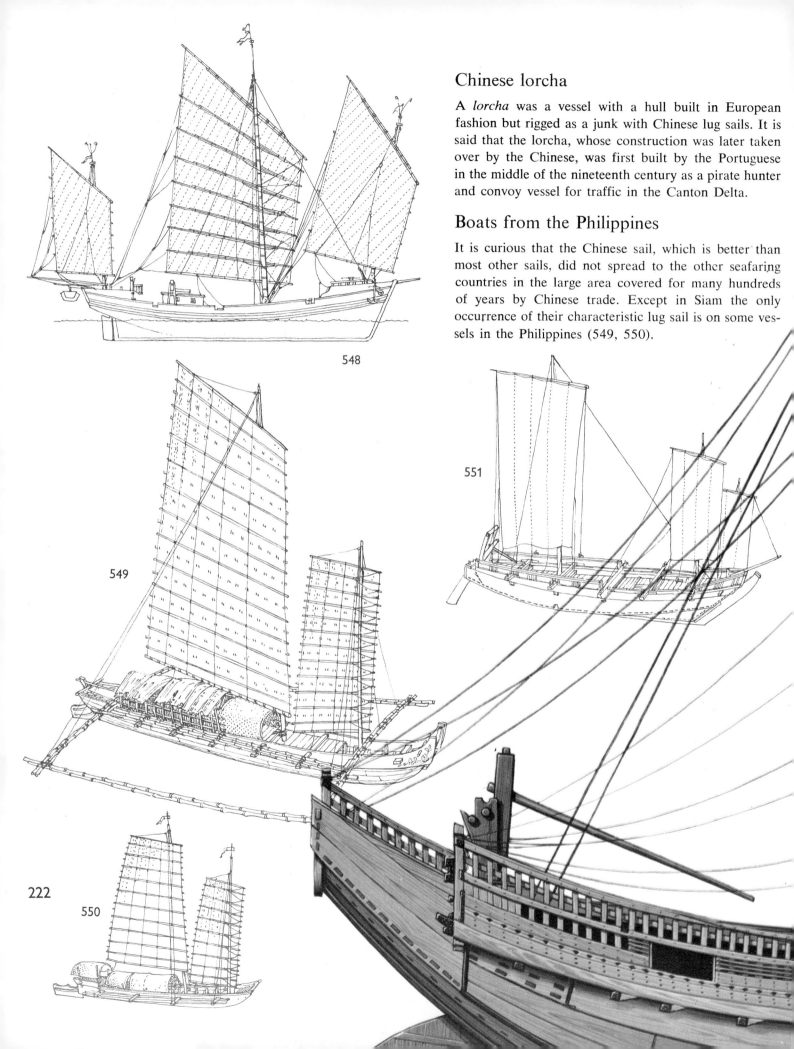

Chinese lorcha

A *lorcha* was a vessel with a hull built in European fashion but rigged as a junk with Chinese lug sails. It is said that the lorcha, whose construction was later taken over by the Chinese, was first built by the Portuguese in the middle of the nineteenth century as a pirate hunter and convoy vessel for traffic in the Canton Delta.

Boats from the Philippines

It is curious that the Chinese sail, which is better than most other sails, did not spread to the other seafaring countries in the large area covered for many hundreds of years by Chinese trade. Except in Siam the only occurrence of their characteristic lug sail is on some vessels in the Philippines (549, 550).

548

551

549

222

550

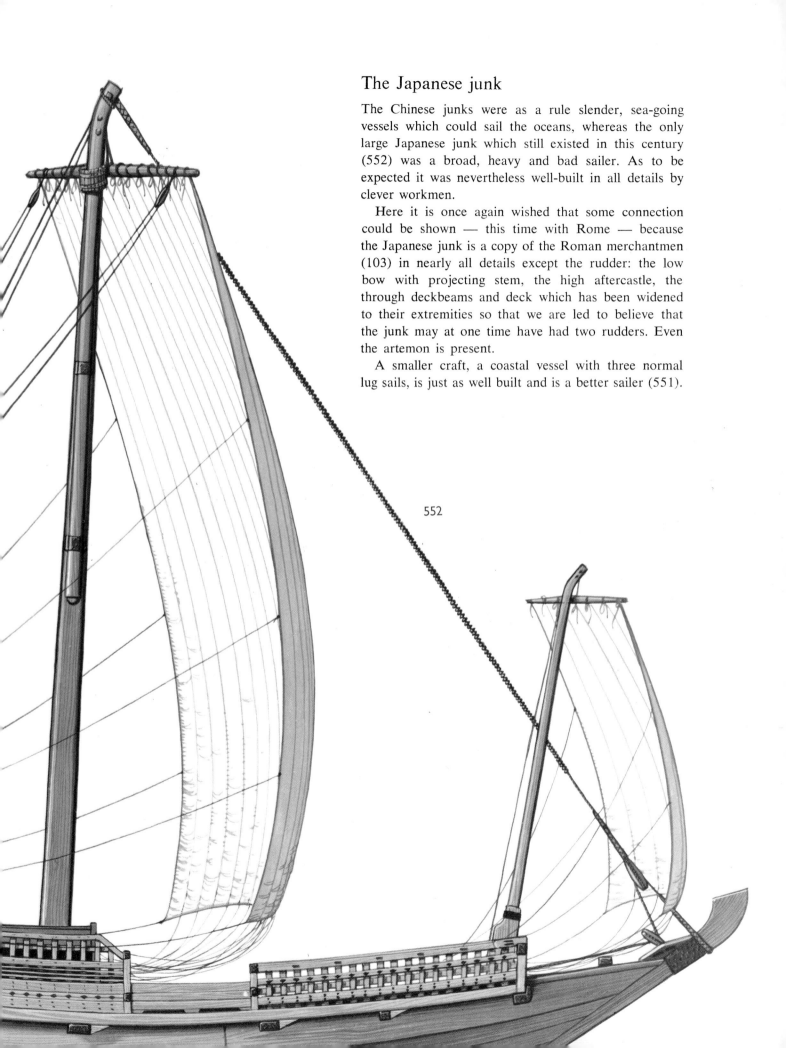

The Japanese junk

The Chinese junks were as a rule slender, sea-going vessels which could sail the oceans, whereas the only large Japanese junk which still existed in this century (552) was a broad, heavy and bad sailer. As to be expected it was nevertheless well-built in all details by clever workmen.

Here it is once again wished that some connection could be shown — this time with Rome — because the Japanese junk is a copy of the Roman merchantmen (103) in nearly all details except the rudder: the low bow with projecting stem, the high aftercastle, the through deckbeams and deck which has been widened to their extremities so that we are led to believe that the junk may at one time have had two rudders. Even the artemon is present.

A smaller craft, a coastal vessel with three normal lug sails, is just as well built and is a better sailer (551).

552

Indonesia and the South Pacific

553

554

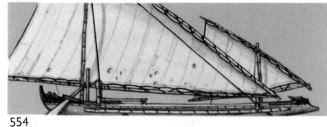

555

Prau or *prahu* is Malayan and means boat or vessel. The prau (553) from Madura, near Java, is built of thick teak planks without a frame and the hull is supported in the old Egyptian manner with cross-beams fitting into the planking. The Madura prau is usually about 50 feet long and 13 feet wide. The two short masts carry three-cornered sails which seem to be something between lug and lateen. It is sometimes, not always, fitted with outriggers, but it is not an especially good sailer, and on its long journeys it follows the routes decided by the monsoon winds.

A vessel with double outriggers called a *prau beduang* (554) comes from the same waters and has the same indefinite rig as its neighbour from Madura. Larger Javanese vessels generally have

556

a wide, low lug sail. Such sails have been found on seventh century reliefs, and when Europeans came to these waters in the sixteenth century they still found the same type. A large, round cargo vessel, a *prau mayang,* was sailing anyway a hundred years ago with this lug sail, and it also had a fore staysail in the European manner (557).

The large *caracor* (555) is to be found in the waters around Java, Borneo, Celebes and New Guinea. The hull is reminiscent of that of the Viking ships, but it is carvel-built and fitted with outriggers on each side. The caracor is a swift vessel, and when it is paddled by many rows of men, both within the hull and sitting on the outriggers, it is faster than most other vessels in the East Indies. This is why the Dutch were still using it in this century as a coastal patrol craft.

224

557

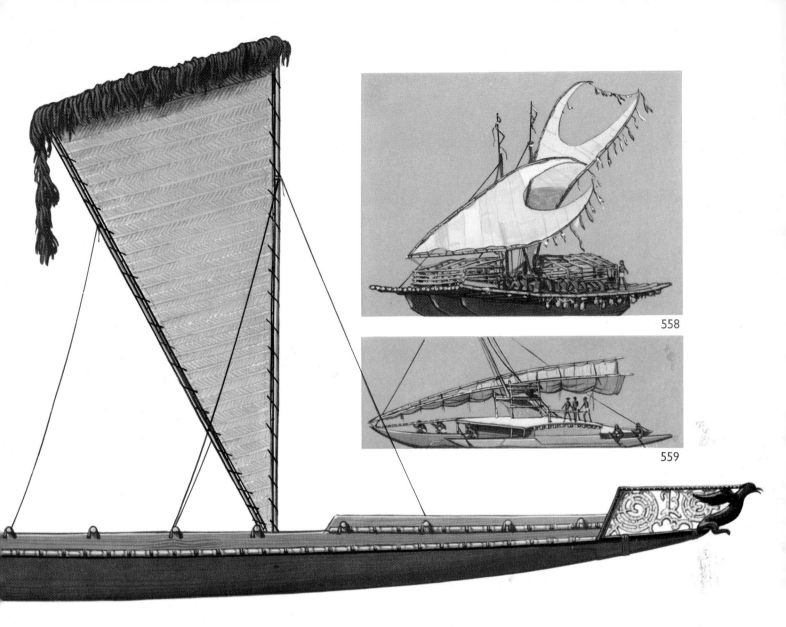

A singular vessel from New Guinea called *lakatoi*
(558) consists of three or more dug-outs joined side to
side with through-beams and supporting a bamboo platform. It is usually about 60 feet long and 50 feet wide.
Two masts abreast roughly amidships carry the claw-
like sails which earlier had been found over the whole
of the South Pacific and even as far north as the
Hawaiian Islands.

Double canoes are very common in the South Seas.
A large vessel from the Tonga Islands called a *calie*
(559) is asymmetrical and the smaller half gives the impression of being a hollow outrigger, but Captain Cook
was met at Tahiti with stately double canoes (560) where
both hulls were of the same size. The most elegant of all
vessels in the South Pacific is without doubt the New
Zealand war canoe, the *waka taua* (556). It is made of
a dug-out fitted with wash boards, often over 65 feet
long yet only 5 feet wide. The decoration in the stern
can be up to 20 feet high, and the canoe is most often
paddled, seldom sailed.

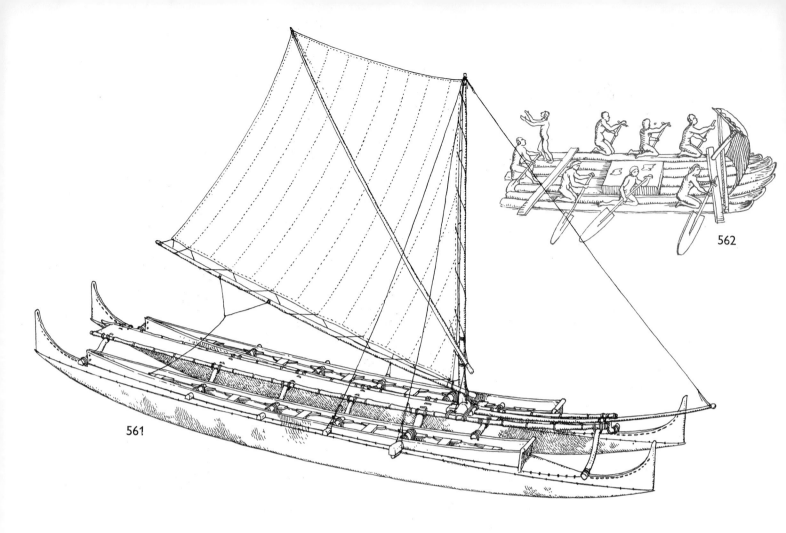

562

561

A royal canoe and a balsa

A hundred years ago a certain Captain Paris at Hawaii made a drawing of the king's canoe, a beautifully shaped double canoe (561) and prototype of the large double canoes that give rides to tourists in the same waters today and are strangely enough called catamarans (cf. 4). The sail appears to be almost like the European fore-and-aft spritsail and has perhaps come into use through European influence since Captain Paris says

that the Hawaiian canoes were previously rigged with claw sails.

In the western part of South America the word *balsa* seems to mean boat or vessel. On Lake Titicaca, almost 12,500 feet above sea level, there are grass boats called balsas, and the large raft used by Heyerdal on his Kon-Tiki expedition was a balsa. The balsa raft had already been noticed in the sixteenth century (562), and to this day primitive balsa rafts are sailed and punted along the coasts of South America (563).

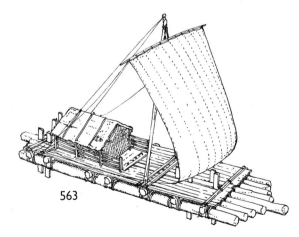

563

574

575

The paddle wheels were placed between the hulls and were rotated by hand. The vessel could be driven forward — but it was too heavy for the "machinery". Miller therefore started to co-operate with William Symington, constructor of steam engines, who built him a two-cylinder engine. In the new vessel, this time with only two hulls, the engine was placed in the one and the boiler in the other, and the two paddle wheels which were situated behind eachother between the hulls managed to propel the little vessel with a speed of 5 knots.

William Lyttleton, a London merchant, experimented in 1794 with something he called an "aquatic propeller" (573). It consisted of three coils of plate wound around an axle like the threads of a screw, each coil making one complete turn around the axle. The propeller was hung in a carriage over the stern of the boat and was rotated by hand, but the speed was not breathtaking.

Many people experimented with steamships about the turn of the century, but the first to be of practical use was the little Charlotte Dundas. Lord Dundas wished to replace the horses which pulled barges along the Forth and Clyde Canal with two boats, and for the purpose had a paddle vessel constructed which was driven by a Symington machine (575). The wheel was situated in a drum furthest aft, the 10 H.P. engine stood on the port side of the deck and the boiler was under deck on the starboard side. In March 1802 the Charlotte Dundas towed two 70-ton vessels 19½ miles along the canal against a strong wind for 6 hours. The feat made quite an impression although it was believed that horses were still to be preferred in the long run because of the damage soon to be caused the canal banks by the eddies from the whirling blades. So the Charlotte Dundas was laid up and allowed to rot. Symington, constructor of the engine, was given no further work and died in poverty. — The dimensions of the Charlotte Dundas were: length 56 feet, width 18 feet, depth 8 feet.

The many-sided American inventor Robert Fulton was a smart businessman whose abilities were partly due to the fact that he profited from the hard work, successes and failures of other inventors. He had made himself acquainted with John Fitch's inventions and plans and even taken a trial spin in the Charlotte Dundas when his first steamboat was built in Paris (576). The long, slender hull wihtout an outer keel he had designed himself, and like the Egyptians during the reign of Pharaoh Sahure he had reinforced it fore-and-aft — not with a rope cable but with long beams.

When the vessel was to set out on trial a storm broke out which snapped the hull, and lock, stock and barrel sank to the bottom of the Seine. Fulton managed to salvage the machinery with great difficulty and then constructed a new, stronger hull which was ready to be tried out by 9th August 1803. Part of a report of the event in a French newspaper ran as follows: "At 6 p.m. with the aid of only three others he started his boat with two boats in tow, and for one and a half hours he presented the remarkable drama of a boat moved by wheels like a cart, wheels that were fitted with blades or flat oars and turned by a fire machine".

229

576

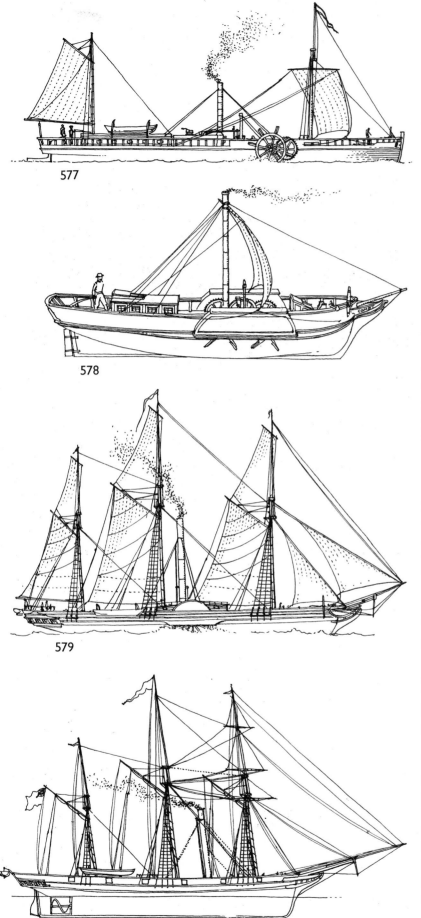

577

578

579

580

Steamships at work

The *Charlotte Dundas* could have been the first steamship in commission, but she was not trusted. Robert Fulton's *Clermont* (577) has the honour instead. She was built in 1807 and began in traffic on the River Hudson between New York and Albany. As Fulton had the monopoly of steam navigating on the Hudson, another vessel, the *Phoenix,* was built the following year for the River Delaware, but it first had to travel from New York to Philadelphia and thus became the first sea-going steamship.

In 1812 the *Comet* (578) was launched on the Clyde and was to be the first merchant steamship in Europe. As opposed to the *Clermont's* 4·7 knots the *Comet* made 6·7 and she was put into traffic between Glasgow, Greenock and Helensburgh on the Clyde.

It is said that the *Savannah* was the first steamship to cross the Atlantic, and this is true insofar as we look upon her as a steamship proper. She was in fact a full-rigged ship (587) with accessory engine and collapsible paddle wheel. She crossed the Atlantic from the River Savannah to Liverpool during the summer of 1819, very seldom using her machinery.

The largest steamship of the times was the *James Watt* (579) which went into coastal service between London and Leith. She was 141·8 feet long and 47 feet wide over the paddle boxes. The wheel was 18 feet in diameter and was driven by 100 H.P. from two cylinders with a diameter of 20 ins. — The first iron steamship was the *Aaron Manby* which was built in England in 1822 for traffic on the Seine (581). —- When the *Sirius* (588) was built it was intended that she should run between London and Cork, but due to certain circumstances she was chartered for traffic to America in 1838 and in this way came to be the first vessel to cross the Atlantic with the aid of an engine. The journey was made with an average speed of 6·7 knots, but she had to battle against strong winds — in smooth water she could make as much as 9 knots.

There were many during the eighteenth century who believed that a screw, a propeller, was a better and safer means of propulsion than the relatively fragile paddle wheel, and by the middle of the nineteenth century some thirty or so different propeller types had patents applied for in various countries. There was Shorter's propeller of 1800 (582), Smith's screw of 1836 (583) which broke on trial and was shown to be more efficient when shortened (580, 585), John Ericsson's double propeller of 1836 (584) and finally his improved and almost "modern" propeller of 1839.

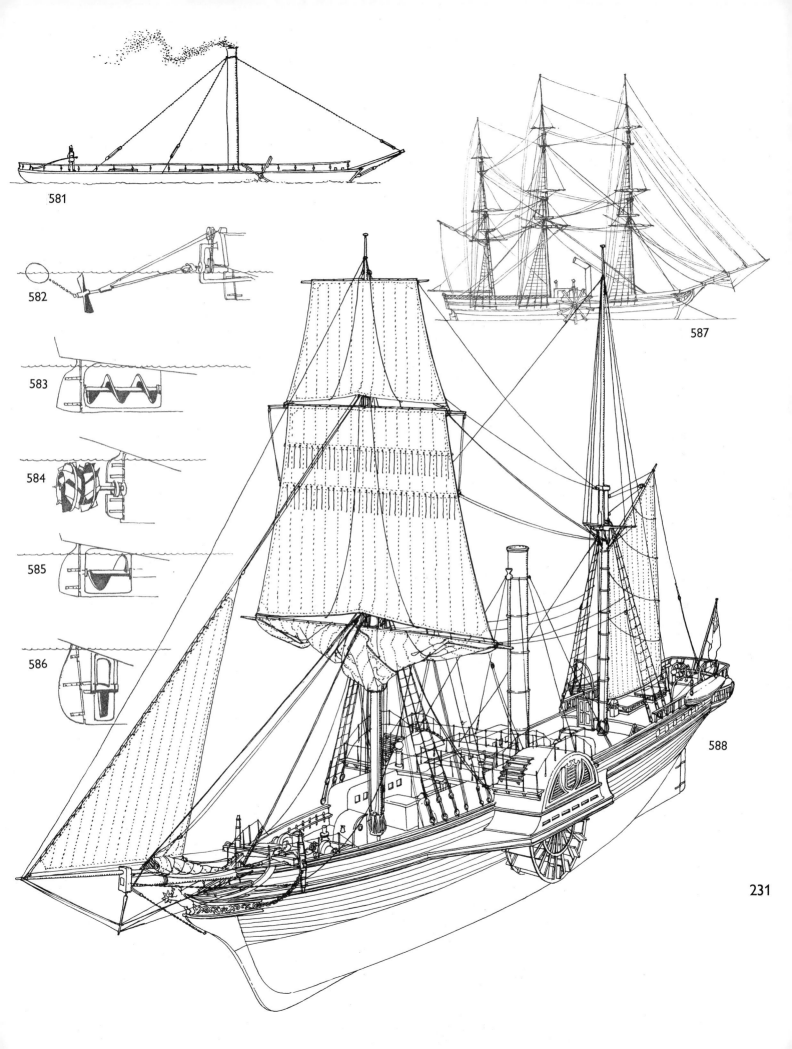

581

582

583

584

585

586

587

588

231

589

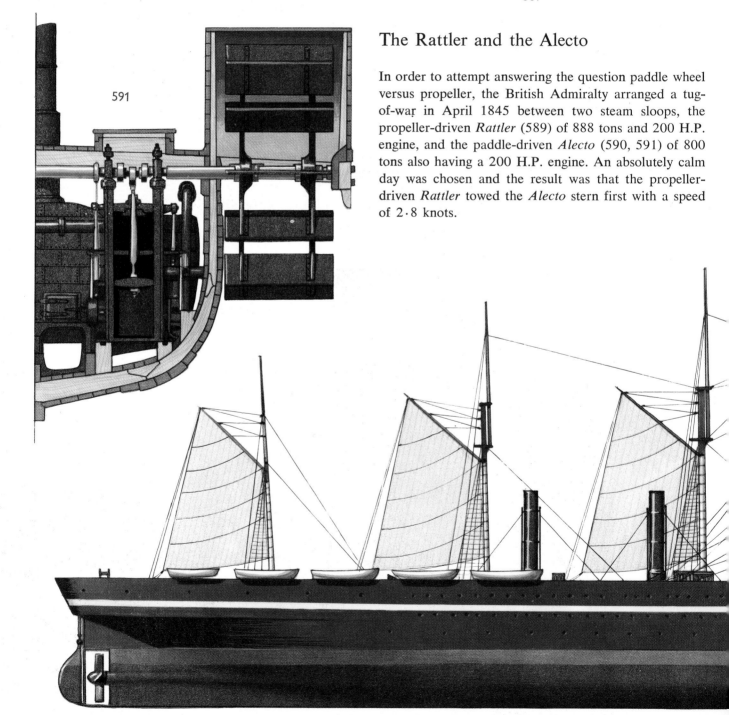

591

The Rattler and the Alecto

In order to attempt answering the question paddle wheel versus propeller, the British Admiralty arranged a tug-of-war in April 1845 between two steam sloops, the propeller-driven *Rattler* (589) of 888 tons and 200 H.P. engine, and the paddle-driven *Alecto* (590, 591) of 800 tons also having a 200 H.P. engine. An absolutely calm day was chosen and the result was that the propeller-driven *Rattler* towed the *Alecto* stern first with a speed of 2·8 knots.

590

The Great Britain, 1843

The first propeller-driven vessel to cross the Atlantic was the *Great Britain* (592) designed by the prominent engineer Isambard Kingdom Brunel. She was built wholly of iron without any outer keel, but to diminish rolling she was fitted with two bilge keels. Her engines of four 88-inch cylinders developed 1,500 H.P., the propeller shaft rotated at 53 r.p.m., and the propeller was six-bladed with a diameter of 15·5 feet. Her dimensions were: length 322 feet, width 50·5 feet, depth 32·5 feet, displacement 3,618 tons. On her trials she reached a speed of 9 knots. — But neither shipowners nor passengers yet quite trusted the steam engine, and the *Great Britain* like other steamships of the times was fitted with sails, a total of 15,000 sq. feet on six masts.

On 1st May 1854 construction was started on a ship which was to be the largest yet seen by the world. Isambard K. Brunel had persuaded the Eastern Steamship Navigation Company that a ship five times as large as any other steamship would be more economical. The vessel was to be called the *Leviathan,* but when she was finally launched she was christened the *Great Eastern* (593).

593

592

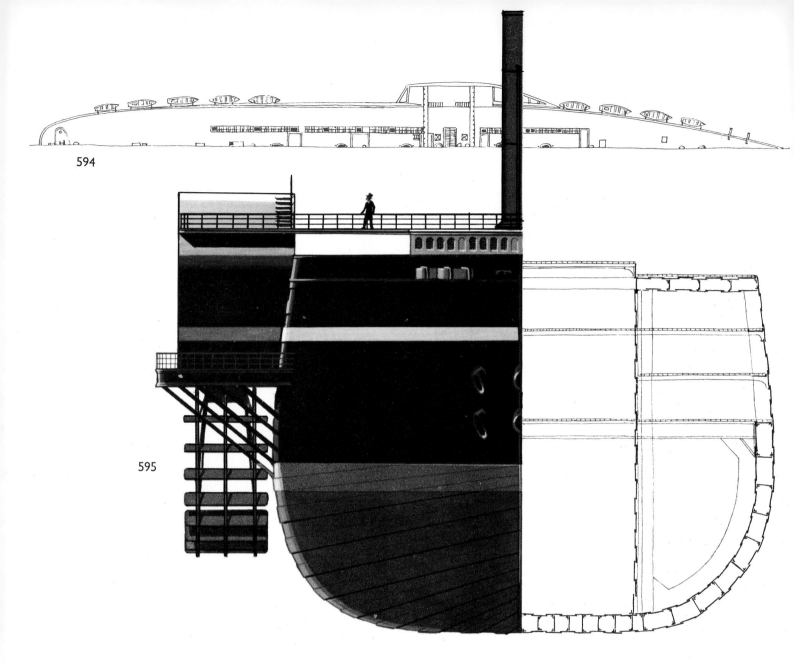

594

595

The Great Eastern, 1858

The hull of the giant vessel was divided into ten water-tight compartments. The iron plating was double from the keel to the waterline, and the space between the outer and inner plates was 2 feet 9 ins. The main deck was also constructed in the same way. The dimensions of the *Great Eastern* were: length 692 feet, width 82·7 feet, width over the paddle boxes 118 feet, draught 30 feet, fully loaded displacement 27,400 tons. She was the only vessel in the world to have both paddle wheels and propeller. The diameter of the wheels was 56 feet and the diameter of the four-bladed propeller 24 feet. Her speed was about 15 knots. The six masts could carry a total sail area of some 58,000 sq. feet. The *Great Eastern* had passenger accommodation for 800 in the 1st class, 2,000 in the 2nd class and 1,200 in the 3rd class. She carried a crew of 400 and there was room for a cargo of about 6,000 tons.

It had been hoped that she would give the passengers a smooth crossing over the sea because of her size, but in actual fact she had a pronounced roll and passengers were scared away. Her engines did not give her enough speed, it was difficult to find ports for her and she became an enormous economic failure. Her greatest significance was attained as a cable layer, in 1865 for example she laid the line between the United States and Europe. She was sold as scrap in 1888 and another eleven years were to pass before a vessel larger than the *Great Eastern* was built.

234

596

Warships and steam propulsion

A long time was to pass before warships were fitted with steam engines, and there were many reasons for the delay. The official objections from admiralty quarters ran thus: the large, fragile paddle wheels increased the target for the enemy, and were they damaged the vessel would be as helpless as a ship without masts. It was by no means seldom that boilers exploded and fires broke out on board merchantmen, and all were agreed as to the extra danger this would mean for a naval vessel. The machinery was large and heavy and had furthermore to be allowed much space for fuel, and all space on navy ships was already occupied.

It did not avail the pioneers of the steamship to explain that a warship powered by steam had no worries about wind or weather and could choose battle positions at will. Such a ship could not carry enough guns, it was said, and would not be able to stand up to a sailing opponent. The conservative admirals who were quite incapable of imagining the seas dotted with smoking sail-less ships finally went so far as to accept engine-propelled tugs and even corvettes for coastal work, but at the same time they stated that seafaring nations would always be dependent on their ships of the line.

During the 1830's suggestions were also made for building warships of iron. The admirals objected that iron ships would be more difficult to repair than the old wooden walls, but it was soon shown that ships of iron were both easier to repair and much cheaper to run. An iron frigate was built in England in 1842 and was offered to the Admiralty who refused to have anything to do with such vessels, however, and it was sold to Mexico. Shortly before, John Ericsson had demonstrated a propeller-driven ship to the British Admiralty, but the admirals found that the propeller could not be of any use to the navy so Ericsson took himself and his invention to the United States. Brunel's large steamship the *Great Britain* (cf. 592) went hard aground off Ireland in 1844. She was towed off eleven months later, and after repairing could be put into traffic again, this being an eye-opener for those who had previously had no faith in the superiority of the iron ship.

Experiments were made with small craft, corvettes were built which were driven by paddle wheels or propeller — and for safety's sake always with sails too. Tugs-of-war were arranged to investigate the effect of paddle wheel and propeller (cf. 589, 590), and finally, about the middle of the nineteenth century, steam engines were risked on the large ships of the line (596). When the Crimean War began in 1853 both the United Kingdom and France had only a few steam-propelled ships of the line and frigates, but the war convinced everyone of the superiority of steam propulsion.

597

The shell gun

The French general Paixhans suggested in a book entitled "Nouvelle Force Maritime" which was published in 1822 that mortar shells ought also to be used in direct-aim guns, not shooting them in a high trajectory from mortars as before. He constructed new, heavy calibre guns for the purpose, and these "shell guns" were first to be used at the Battle of Sinope in 1853 where the Russian Navy utterly defeated the Turkish. Earlier rumours had made the admirals of wooden navies suspicious, and experiments had been made on the reinforcement of ships' sides with thick iron plating, but this only resulted in heavy vessels which were difficult to manoeuvre.

The Gloire, 1859

Even after the Crimean War Britain launched a ship of the line in 1858 which was built wholly of wood, but the following year it was understood that the age of the wooden ship was past when the French launched the first so-called armoured ship. The gifted designer Dupuy de Lôme had realised his ideas in the armoured frigate *Gloire* (597).

From the beginning she was thought of and built as a regular 90-gun ship of the line, but she was launched as a 60-gun armoured frigate. She was still built of wood, but along the waterline and in part up to the guns she was protected by almost 5-inch armour plating. Her engines developed about 4,200 H.P. and propelled the 5,675 ton vessel with a speed of 13 knots. Her dimensions were: length 252·5 feet, width 55 feet, draught 25 feet.

The Warrior, 1860

Britain countered at once with the elegant frigate *Warrior* (598) which was built entirely of iron. In appearance she was not so very different from contemporary clippers except that she was very long — 380 feet. She was launched in 1860 and her 1,250 H.P. engines gave her a speed of 14½ knots. She mounted twenty-eight 7-inch smooth bore muzzle-loaders, two smaller smooth bore guns and two 20-pounder breech-loaders. On account of her length she could only be fitted with armour plating amidships for her to be seaworthy, and some 80 feet of the hull at each end were unprotected.

The Merrimack

During the American Civil War the one-time steam frigate *Merrimack* was to become known and feared as a floating ironclad armoury (599). When the Union troops retired from Norfolk they had burnt and sunk the vessels that were in the harbour, and the *Merrimack* was one of them. But the Confederates lifted her, cut away all that was burnt on the gun deck and fitted her with a casemate of oak beams protected with railroad rails and plating. She was then considered strong enough to withstand any gunfire that could be offered by the Union.

The bow was also reinforced and fitted with a ram of cast iron, but her armament was surprisingly weak. Reports do not seem to be entirely in agreement but she should anyway have had six 9-inch guns, two 6·4-inch rifled guns and two 7-inch guns.

The Monitor

The Swedish engineer John Ericsson had made early sketches of a vessel intended to withstand modern artillery fire and furthermore capable of giving devastating replies herself, and a year after the Battle of Sinope he

598

had presented drawings of such a vessel to Emperor Napoleon III. The Union was aware that the Confederates were equipping the *Merrimack* for the summer campaign of 1862, and after much intrigue John Ericsson was given the job of designing a ship which would immobilise the Confederate monster. In principle his work was based on the drawings previously shown to Napoleon III, and the result was the curious vessel the *Monitor* (600, 601, 602).

The hull consisted of two parts, an underwater body of ⅝-inch plating, 124 feet long, 34 feet wide and 5·8 feet deep. Above the underwater body there was an armoured teak hull 172 feet long, 41·5 feet wide and about 5 feet high (cf. transverse section 601). The armour-plated hull had a draught of 3 feet. The rotating, armour-plated gun tower with two 11-inch guns was situ-

ated amidships. Aft of the tower were two removable funnels and aft of them two ventilators, also removable. In action the deck was cleared except for the gun tower and a very low steering house forward. A fan led air from the ventilators to the different parts of the vessel and to the boiler fires which were constructed for forced draught.

The *Monitor* was no sea-going vessel, and on her journey from New York to Hampton Roads outside Washington where she put a definite end to the progress of the *Merrimack* she was close to sinking due to the water which came in through the holes in the deck. But she was not fully ready when forced out on her first operation, and it is surprising that her crew, unused as they must have been to all her innovations, ever succeeded in leading her to victory.

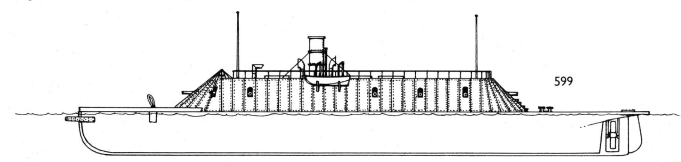

599

237

600

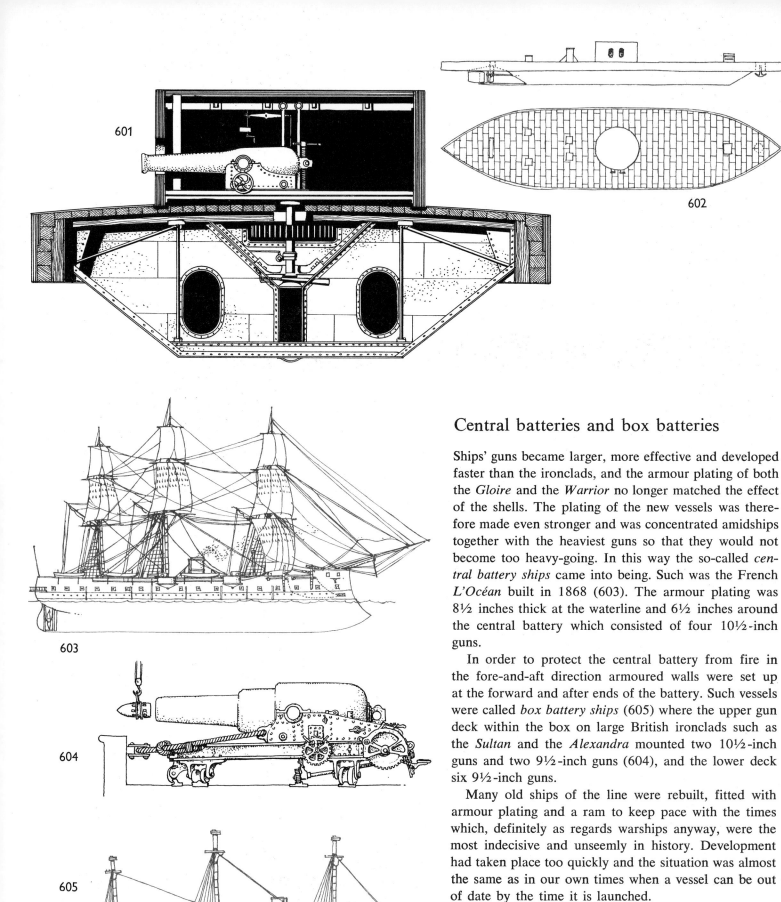

601

602

603

604

605

Central batteries and box batteries

Ships' guns became larger, more effective and developed faster than the ironclads, and the armour plating of both the *Gloire* and the *Warrior* no longer matched the effect of the shells. The plating of the new vessels was therefore made even stronger and was concentrated amidships together with the heaviest guns so that they would not become too heavy-going. In this way the so-called *central battery ships* came into being. Such was the French *L'Océan* built in 1868 (603). The armour plating was 8½ inches thick at the waterline and 6½ inches around the central battery which consisted of four 10½-inch guns.

In order to protect the central battery from fire in the fore-and-aft direction armoured walls were set up at the forward and after ends of the battery. Such vessels were called *box battery ships* (605) where the upper gun deck within the box on large British ironclads such as the *Sultan* and the *Alexandra* mounted two 10½-inch guns and two 9½-inch guns (604), and the lower deck six 9½-inch guns.

Many old ships of the line were rebuilt, fitted with armour plating and a ram to keep pace with the times which, definitely as regards warships anyway, were the most indecisive and unseemly in history. Development had taken place too quickly and the situation was almost the same as in our own times when a vessel can be out of date by the time it is launched.

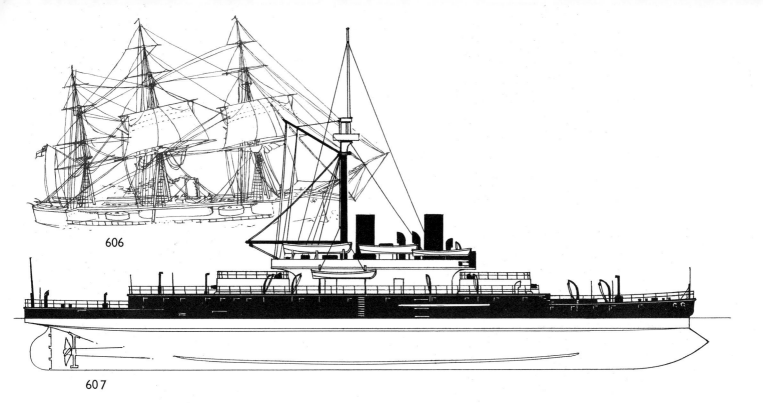

606

607

Ships with gun turrets

The most advanced attempt at combining a rotating gun turret with the traditional sea-going ship was made by Captain Coles, R.N., with the *Captain* (606). A spar deck for ship handling ran like a gangway above an open gun deck with two turrets, and the lower masts were tripod in form to simplify the rig. But the vessel was unstable and capsized and sank in a storm with all on board.

The chief naval designer Sir E.J. Reed who had tried to dissuade the Admiralty from building the *Captain* considered that the gun turrets could be made fully effective and the heavy hulls stable enough only if the traditional rig was done away with. The result of his work was the *Devastation* (607) which was a great blow

to all who had up to the very end thought sails necessary anyway on sea-going vessels.

The *Devastation* was 285 feet long and 62·3 feet wide, and two propellers gave her a speed of 12½ knots. She was armed with four 12-inch muzzle-loaders in two turrets whose armour plating was 10—14 inches thick. The armour on the hull sides was 8½—12 inches thick. The *Devastation* was the strongest and most efficient warship hitherto built and was to become a model for many later constructions.

An instance of the craze for experiment were the two circular vessels belonging to the Russian Navy, the so-called *popoffkas*, named after their designer Admiral Popoff (608). They were of 2,490 tons, and six propellers gave them a speed of 6 knots. They were armed with two 11-inch guns.

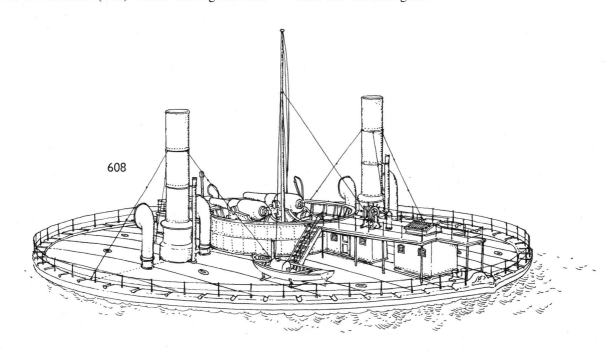

608

The Duilio and the Dandalo, 1876

Britain had been the greatest sea power ever since the Napoleonic wars, but foreign policy, as before, did not allow of arming or reinforcing unless some foreign sea power first gave the lead. As early as 1871 a British gun factory was able to report that it could manufacture guns considerably larger than those in use, but the Admiralty hesitated. It was Italy who was to build the first ships for the giant guns. The Italian designer Benedetto Brin went in for a combination of the largest guns on the most strongly armoured ships of the greatest possible speed, and he constructed the *Duilio* and the *Dandalo* with the sole purpose of their carrying four guns each of which weighed 38 tons. But the gun factories later said that they could supply 15-inch guns which weighed 50 tons, and the Italians accepted. On the new battleships (609, 610) the gun turrets were mounted so that the field of fire was more or less free in all directions. Their dimensions were: length 341 feet, width 64·7 feet, draught 26·4 feet, displacement 11,140 tons. At the waterline the armour was 22 inches thick and round the turrets 18 inches. The speed was calculated to 15 knots.

Britain replied immediately with the *Inflexible* of 11,880 tons with 24-inch armour plating and four 16-inch guns of 80 tons each. Italy countered by altering her order, asking this time for four 18-inch guns of 100 tons each for the *Duilio*.

Large breech-loading guns came into use during the 1880's. It had been found that a better effect was obtained if the shells were given a greater muzzle velocity, and this was attained by using coarse, slowly-

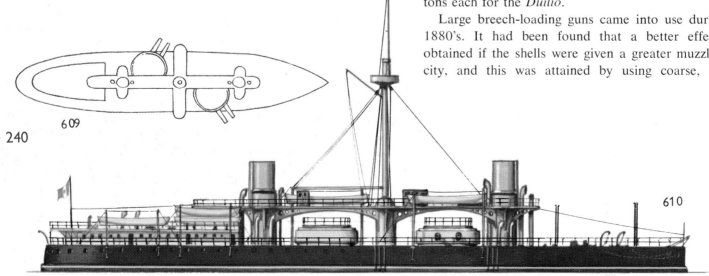

609

240

610

burning explosives in long gun barrels. The long barrels were naturally inconvenient for muzzle loading so that even the large guns became breech-loading. This in turn meant that the old type of gun turret also became unsuitable and guns began to be mounted on *barbettes*. In the barbette turrets the barrels were quite unprotected, and only when the gun was to be loaded was the breech end lowered into the turret. The French coastal defence battleship of the *Caiman* class (611) mounted two 16½-inch guns on barbettes.

The Royal Sovereign class, 1892

Sir William White constructed seven new battleships which were classified *Royal Sovereign* (612) after the first of them launched. Experience had shown that a vessel could not make use of her speed in heavy seas if the freeboards were not high enough to stop the waves breaking over the deck, and so these ships were built with freeboards higher than on previous British battle-

ships. The fastest in the class could attain a speed of 18 knots.

Steel plating was used for the first time and it was found possible to make the hull relatively lighter and stronger than before. At the waterline amidships the armour was no thicker than 18 inches, and towards the ends 14—16 inches. The heavy artillery, four 13½-inch guns, were mounted on barbettes and the ships were furthermore well-equipped with lighter guns and machine-guns for close-quarter work in order to be able to defend themselves against the *torpedo boats* which had by this time come into use. The dimensions of the ships were: length 380 feet, width 75 feet, draught 28 feet, displacement 14,150 tons.

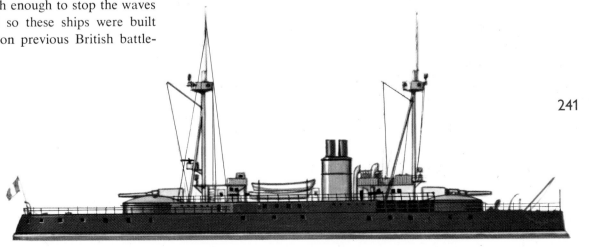

611

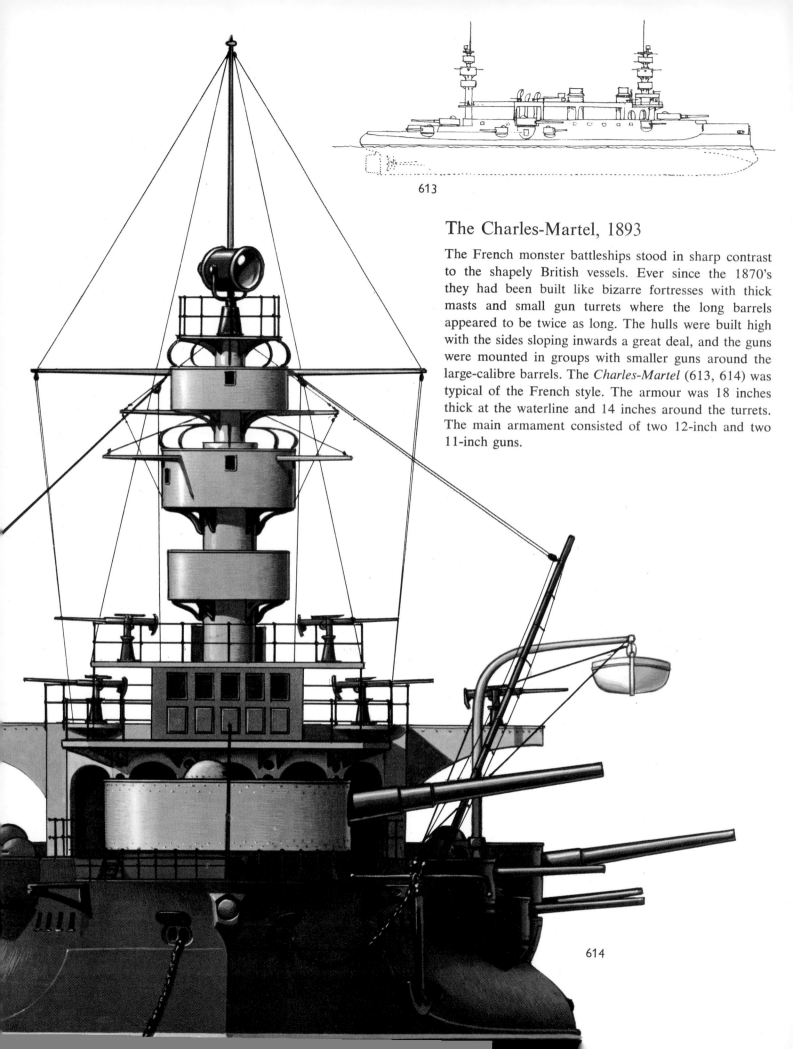

613

The Charles-Martel, 1893

The French monster battleships stood in sharp contrast to the shapely British vessels. Ever since the 1870's they had been built like bizarre fortresses with thick masts and small gun turrets where the long barrels appeared to be twice as long. The hulls were built high with the sides sloping inwards a great deal, and the guns were mounted in groups with smaller guns around the large-calibre barrels. The *Charles-Martel* (613, 614) was typical of the French style. The armour was 18 inches thick at the waterline and 14 inches around the turrets. The main armament consisted of two 12-inch and two 11-inch guns.

614

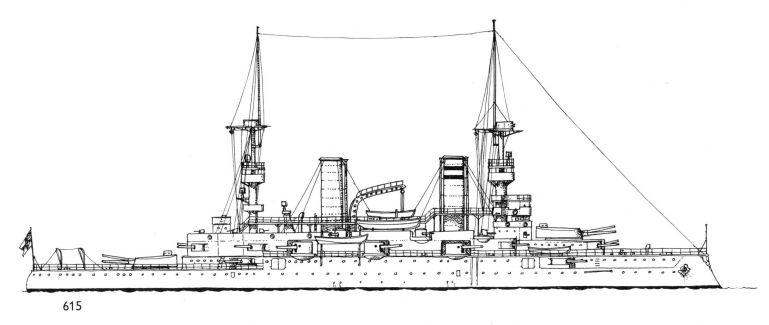

615

The Kaiser Barbarossa, 1900

Previously the few German warships had played a very
shy part on the seas, but when Admiral Tirpitz became
Secretary for Naval Affairs in 1897 a navy began to be
built which would be in proportion to the country's
foreign trade and seafaring. The energetic admiral managed to squeeze his naval programme through the
Reichstag, a programme which in effect would mean
that Germany was to build a navy of 19 battleships, 8
armoured coastal defence ships, 6 large cruisers and 16
smaller cruisers within a period of seven years.

The *Kaiser Barbarossa* (615), launched in 1900, was
one of the new battleships whose construction was
closest to contemporary French ships. Her dimensions
were: length 396 feet, width 67 feet, draught 25·5 feet,
displacement 11,150 tons. She was armed with four
9½-inch, fourteen 6-inch and fourteen 3½-inch guns.
Furthermore she had five torpedo tubes which had
become general on battleships towards the end of the
nineteenth century. The 13,500 H.P. engines gave her
with her three propellers a speed of 18 knots. The
French ironclad *Massena* of 1893 was probably one of

the first ships to be driven by three propellers. The
British preferred two until 1906 when ships began to
be built with four propellers. From the end of the
nineteenth century it was also common for ships to be
fitted with torpedo nets, metal nets which hung down
in the water on each side of the vessel from a row of
projecting booms. They could only be used when the
ships were at rest or moving at very low speed. (Torpedo
nets are shown in 612, 617, 619 and others).

The Tsesarevitch and the Asahi

The Japanese fleet which defeated the Russians at Tsushima in 1905 was mainly composed of British-built
ships. The majority of the Russian Navy had been built
at home, but among others the ironclad *Tsesarevitch*
(616) of 1901 had been built in France. Like other
French ships her sides sloped inwards a great deal and
her hull was very high. The main armament was four
12-inch guns. — The Japanese ironclad *Asahi* (617),
built in England in 1899, was not very different from
other British ships of the time, and its main armament
was the same as that of the *Tsesarevitch*.

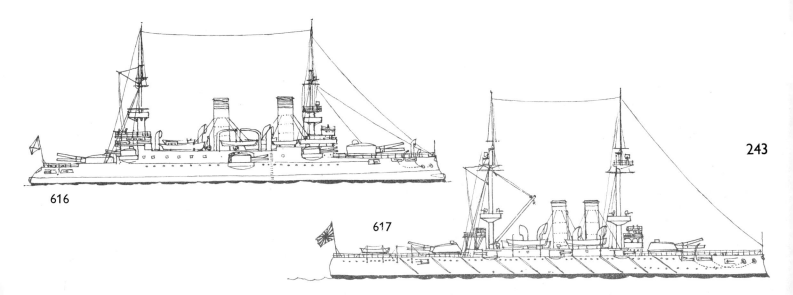

616

617

The Dreadnought, 1906

Even at the end of the nineteenth century it was considered that the guns of a battleship could not be used to effect at a range greater than 3,500 yards. After the British naval manoeuvres in the Mediterranean in 1899 Admiral Fisher came to the conclusion that future battle ranges at sea would be about 5,500 yards, yet only six years later at Tsushima the Russian battleships opened fire 20,000 yards from the enemy, and the first hits were recorded when the range had been reduced to 13,000 yards.

The danger of torpedoes made long-range fighting necessary. The only possibility of having some control over the effect of fire on distant targets was by discharging salvoes, and salvoes at long range meant that the ships had to be armed with many guns of the same large calibre. This had been foreseen before Tsushima, and the idea of a ship whose main armament comprised heavy artillery was not a new one when the British *Dreadnought* (618, 619) was built. She was to become the model for the battleships of the period.

She was built in record time according to the most modern methods. The first keelplates were laid on 2nd October 1905, she was launched on 10th February 1906 and was ready for trials by 3rd October the same year. Her ten 12-inch guns were mounted in five turrets, three in the centre line and two on the sides so that six guns could be fired forward, six aft and eight broadside. Twenty-seven small guns for repelling attacks by torpedo boats were mounted on the turrets, the upperstructure and the quarter-deck. She also had five torpedo tubes which discharged the missiles under water.

The *Dreadnought* was the first large warship to have turbine engines. Their 23,000 H.P. drove four propellers which gave her a speed of 21 knots. Amidships the armour plating was 11 inches thick and 6—4 inches towards the ends. The barbettes were also made of 11-inch armour. Her dimensions were: length 527 feet, width 82 feet, draught 26·5 feet, displacement 17,900 tons.

She was the fastest battleship in the navy and came up to all other expectations of her, especially as an excellent platform for the artillery. Replies from the other great powers were not long in coming. The same year that the *Dreadnought* was launched the Germans began building two "dreadnoughts" — the *Nassau* and the *Westfalen* (620).

The new German ships were shorter and wider than the *Dreadnought,* the displacement was 18,900 tons, the armour half an inch thicker than the British, and in reply to the *Dreadnought's* ten 12-inch guns the *Nassau* and the *Westfalen* mounted twelve 11-inch guns. Their speed was somewhat under 21 knots.

The French battleship *Danton* (621) of 18,400 tons and launched in 1909 still had not taken the full step to large guns alone, mounting in the forward and after turrets a total of four 12-inch guns and in the side turrets twelve 9½-inch guns. At this time the United States built ships of over 20,000 tons with the same armament as the *Dreadnought,* and in 1912 the *Texas* and the *New York* (622) of 27,400 tons were launched, being armed with ten 14-inch and twenty-one 5-inch guns. They were 573 feet long and 106 feet wide. Their speed was also about 21 knots.

618

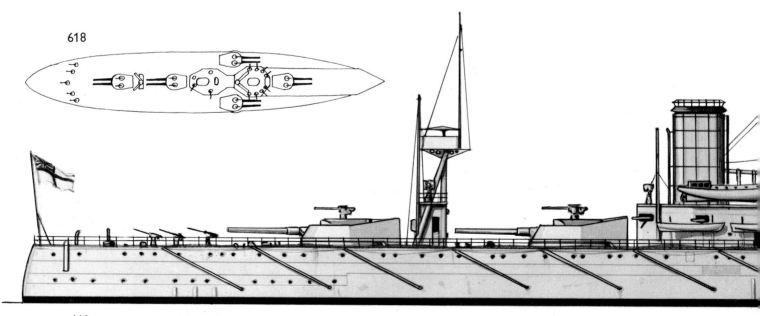

619

620

621

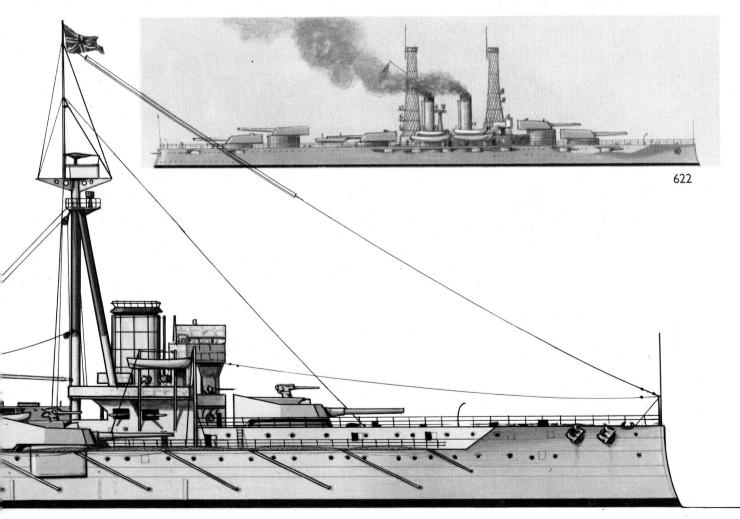

622

245

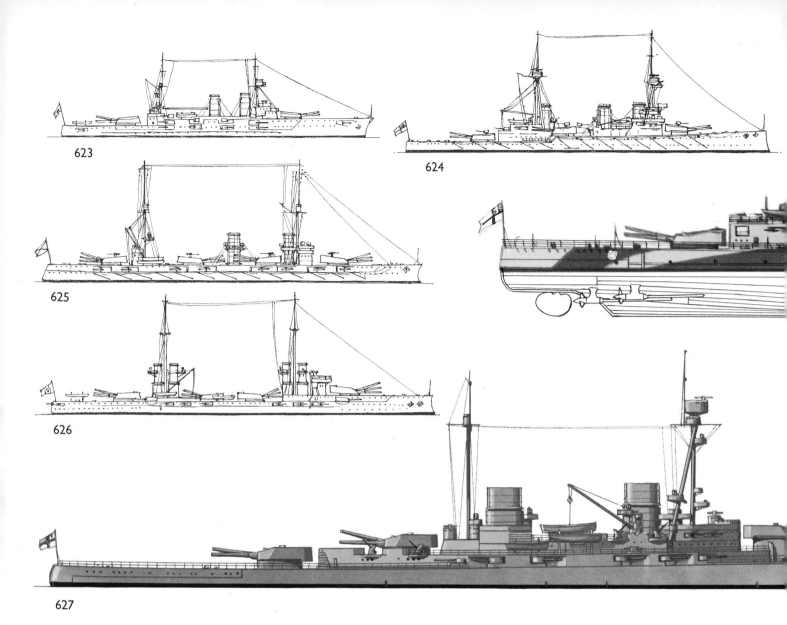

623

624

625

626

627

The battle-cruiser Invincible, 1908

The *Dreadnought* was the signal for rearmament within all naval powers. All earlier types of battleship were outmoded at once. Dreadnoughts and super-dreadnoughts were built, the number and calibre of the guns increased, the ships were made larger, and stronger engines installed to better the speed. And in 1906 a British naval shipyard began building a vessel which was later to be called the first *battle-cruiser*.

It may be said that the Japanese had already launched something which might be called a battle-cruiser in 1905 with a cruiser hull of 15,000 tons capable of making 21 knots and partly armed with heavy artillery. This was the *Tsukuba* (623) mounting four 12-inch and twelve 6-inch guns.

But the British *Invincible* (624) which was launched in 1907 and ready for trials a year later was something quite new. Outwardly she was not much different from the modern battleships, it was only her armour that was so much weaker. Against the *Dreadnought's* 11 inches hers was only 7, although her displacement was almost the same, 17,400 tons. She was 567 feet long and was propelled by the most powerful engines ever yet installed in a ship, turbines that developed 41,000 H.P. and gave her a speed of 26½ knots through her four propellers. Her main armament was eight 12-inch guns in two turrets in the centre line and one on each side. The *Indomitable* and the *Inflexible* were built of the same class as the *Invincible*.

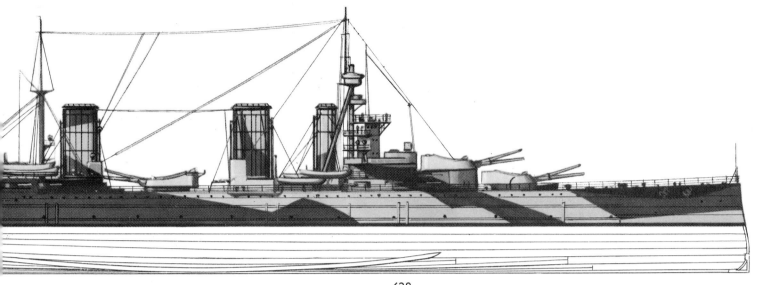

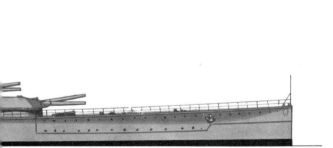

The Lion, 1912

New classes of battleships, heavier and larger but no faster, were built both in Britain and in Germany until the British naval shipyards began to build a battle-cruiser in 1910 which was to be larger than the largest battleship even, the fantastic *Lion* (628). She was ready for trials two years later. She had a fully loaded displacement of 29,680 tons and was 700 feet long, 88·5 feet wide and had a draught of 28·9 feet. Her armour at the waterline was 9 inches thick, narrowing to 6—4 inches towards the ends. She also had 9-inch armour around the barbettes and turrets.

The main armament of the *Lion* was eight 13½-inch guns all mounted in the mid-line of the ship where they were found to have a more stable platform. The crew consisted of 997 men. The turbines developing 70,000 H.P. gave her a speed of 28 knots, making her faster than any other large ship as well as being the world's largest warship. She was also the most expensive. Including guns the *Lion* cost £2,086,458. A further two ships of the same class were built, and the same year the *Lion* was completed work was begun on an even larger battle-cruiser, the *Tiger,* which when fully loaded was to have a displacement of 35,160 tons, and with her 108,000 H.P. engines she was one knot faster than the *Lion.*

The Derfflinger, 1914

Japan ordered a battle-cruiser of roughly the same size and strength as the *Lion* from Britain, but she was even more strongly armed with eight 14-inch guns. The Germans also built battle-cruisers, and the foremost of them — completed in time for the outbreak of war — was the *Derfflinger* (627). She had thicker plating than the British battle-cruisers, 12 inches at the waterline and 10—11 inches around the barbettes and turrets.

The dimensions of the *Derfflinger* were: length 689 feet, width 95 feet, draught 27 feet, displacement 26,180 tons. Her main armament consisted of eight 12-inch guns in the mid-line of the ship. Her 63,000 H.P. engines brought her speed up to 26½ knots.

The Gangut and the Dante Alighieri

Russia and Italy began to build their first dreadnoughts in 1909 and armed them with twelve 12-inch guns which were mounted in a new fashion in triple turrets in the mid-line of the ship. They were the Russian *Gangut* (625) of 23,400 tons and the Italian *Dante Alighieri* (626) of 19,500 tons, both capable of speeds up to about 23 knots. Shortly afterwards Austria, the United States and France also built battleships with such triple turrets.

629

248　630

The Queen Elizabeth, 1915

The foremost series of battleships ever built were the ships in the *Queen Elizabeth* class: the *Barham* (629), the *Malaya,* the *Queen Elizabeth,* the *Valiant* and the *Warspite.* Their keels were laid from 1912—13 and they were completed in 1915—16. Through two world wars they were to play a greater, longer and more important part than any other warships.

The new ships combined the speed of the battle-cruiser with the strength and great fire power of the battleships. The armour amidships was 13 inches thick and thinned out towards the ends to 6 inches. The plating of the barbettes was 10-inch and of the turrets 11—13-inch. Experiments had been made with 15-inch guns, and it was shown that their shells pierced the thickest armour plating that existed and that their explosive power was fifty percent greater than the shells of the previously largest ships' guns of 13½ inches. The new ships were thus given eight of the larger sort each. Earlier British battleships had also had a turret amidships; the large engines of the *Queen Elizabeth* class did not allow this, but it was compensated for by the more powerful armament. For short ranges they were given fourteen 6-inch guns, and for parrying attack from the air which by that time had become a possibility they were armed with two 3-inch guns.

The dimensions of the vessels were: length 645·9 feet, width 90·6 feet, draught 30·8 feet, displacement 27,500 tons. When fully loaded they displaced 33,000 tons. A revolutionary innovation for large ships was that the boilers were fired with oil. The 75,000 H.P. turbine engines gave a speed of 24 knots. The ships of the *Queen Elizabeth* class were thus both swifter and stronger than any other contemporary battleship. Each one of them cost about £2,400,000 to build.

They were more profitable than most warships. They took a successful part in the battles of the First World War and were still going strong when the second broke out. They were rebuilt during the 1930's to keep up with the demands of the times (630). The control tower and bridges were remodelled, the funnels made into one and the sides fitted with an arrangement for protection against attack by torpedoes. Four of them even outlived the Second World War. The *Barham* alone was sunk by German torpedoes in November 1941.

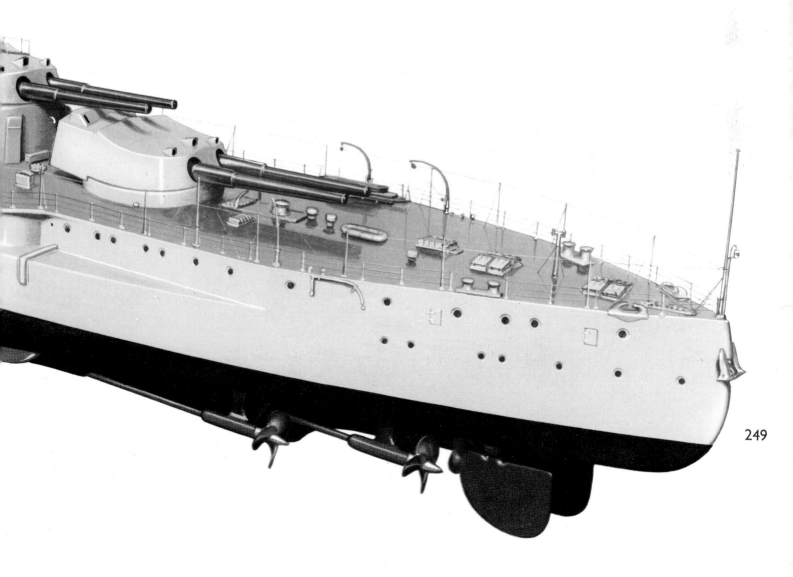

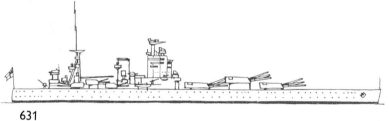

631

The Hood, 1920

During the First World War it came to the notice of the British that the Germans had begun building a battle-cruiser with 15-inch guns, and answer was made with the battle-cruiser *Hood* (632, 633) which was to be the largest warship of her time. The Battle of Skagerrak was fought while she was under construction and it was shown that speed in itself was not sufficient protection. Her side armour was therefore increased from 9 to 12 inches. Yet for her size her plating was still relatively weak.

Her dimensions were: length 860 feet, width 104 feet, draught 28·5 feet, displacement 41,200 tons. Her main armament consisted of eight 15-inch guns. Her secondary armament was twelve 5½-inch guns, four 4-inch anti-aircraft guns and nine smaller guns. The 144,000 H.P. engines gave her a speed of over 31 knots and she had a crew of 1,477. She was completed only after the Armistice and was sunk during the Second World War on 24th May 1941 after a salvo from the German battleship *Bismarck*.

The Washington Conference

In the naval treaty which was signed at the Washington Conference in 1922 by Great Britain, the United States, Japan, France and Italy, agreement was reached as to the naval tonnage allowed to each treaty country, and it was further decided that battleships were not to be built larger than 35,000 tons and that their guns were not to exceed 15 inches in calibre. Battleships could only be replaced with new vessels after at least twenty years had passed since they had been built. Rebuilding of battleships was to be restricted to alterations for defence against submarines and aircraft. — At the time, however, Japan was in the process of building two battleships with 16-inch guns, so it was decided to make this calibre the general rule instead.

The British *Nelson* and *Rodney* (631) were built according to the new regulations. Their dimensions were:

250

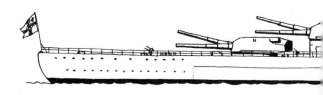

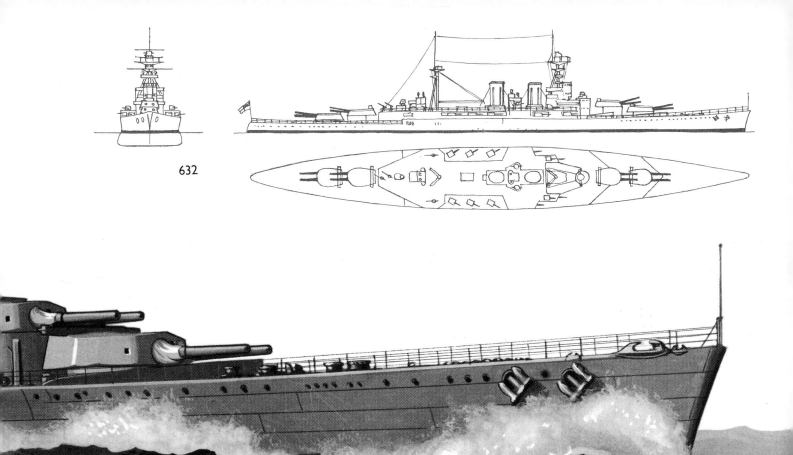

632

633

length 710 feet, width 106 feet, draught 30 feet, displacement 33,950 tons (38,000 tons when fully loaded). The heavy artillery, nine 16-inch guns, were mounted in three triple turrets on the foredeck. The armour was 14 inches thick and the speed 23 knots.

According to the Treaty of Versailles Germany was allowed to retain six battleships which were not to be replaced with vessels larger than 10,000 tons. The first German "pocket battleship" was the heavy cruiser *Deutschland* whose keel was laid in 1929. With her 26 knots she was swift enough to run from all battleships, and with her six 11-inch guns strong enough to defeat any cruiser. She was later followed by the *Admiral Scheer* (634) and the *Admiral Graf Spee* of the same type.

After that Hitler no longer felt bound by any treaty, and in 1934 construction was begun on the battleships

Gneisenau and *Scharnhorst* (635) of 31,300 tons which had the following dimensions: length 741·5 feet, width 98·5 feet, draught 24·6 feet. The main armament was nine 11-inch guns and the speed 32 knots. The even larger battleships *Bismarck* (636) and *Tirpitz* were launched at the outbreak of war in 1939. When fully loaded they displaced 52,600 tons and the dimensions were: length 791 feet, width 118 feet, draught 28 feet. The main armament was eight 15-inch guns and their speed over 30 knots.

634

635

636

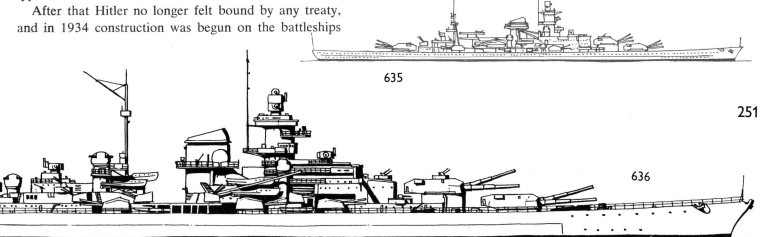

637

The Richelieu, 1940

The French battleship *Richelieu* (639) had been launched but was not completed by the outbreak of war. She was first able to complete her trials in April 1940. Her armour plating was 16 inches thick and on this point she was thus stronger than any other European ship. The main armament comprised eight 15-inch guns in two quadruple turrets and her 155,000 H.P. engines gave her a speed of 30 knots.

The Yamato, 1942

In all secrecy the Japanese had begun to build a battleship as early as 1937 which was to be the largest in the world, and in 1942 the powerful *Yamato* (637, 638) was ready for battle, followed the next year by a sister ship, the *Musashi*. Fully loaded the *Yamato* had a displacement of 70,321 tons. She was 862·5 feet long, 128 feet wide and had a draught of 35 feet. The engines developed 158,000 H.P. and her top speed was 27·7 knots. She was armed with nine 18-inch guns (the largest ever to have been mounted on a ship) and furthermore several hundreds of smaller guns of calibre varying from 6 inches to half an inch. She also carried seven aircraft which could be launched from catapults.

Both the *Yamato* and the *Musashi* were sunk by American planes. It is stated that forty direct bomb hits and eighteen torpedo hits were made before the *Musashi* was sunk in the Gulf of Leyte in 1944, and almost as much was needed to sink the *Yamato* in the final phase of the war. They had nevertheless been thought unsinkable.

The Iowa, 1943

The units in the last series of battleships begun in the United States in 1940 were longer than the *Yamato* yet narrower and considerably lighter. The first, the *Iowa* (641), was completed in February 1943. Her dimensions are: length 890 feet, width 108 feet, draught 36 feet, fully loaded displacement 57,950 tons. The 212,000 H.P. engines give her a speed of 33 knots, but she has made over 35. The thickest armour is 19 inches. Her main armament consists of nine 16-inch, twenty 5-inch and fifty-two 40 mm anti-aircraft guns. Two helicopters serve as scouts. Her wartime crew amounted to 2,700 men.

The Vanguard, 1946

The largest British battleship, the *Vanguard* (640), was begun in 1941. Before she was finished in 1946 it was already understood that the reign of the battleship was at an end. They are too large and expensive a target, far too easily destroyed by modern weapons. The £9 million expended on the *Vanguard* — excluding her large guns which were inherited from older ships — is money down the drain. Like U.S. battleships she has been taken out of commission.

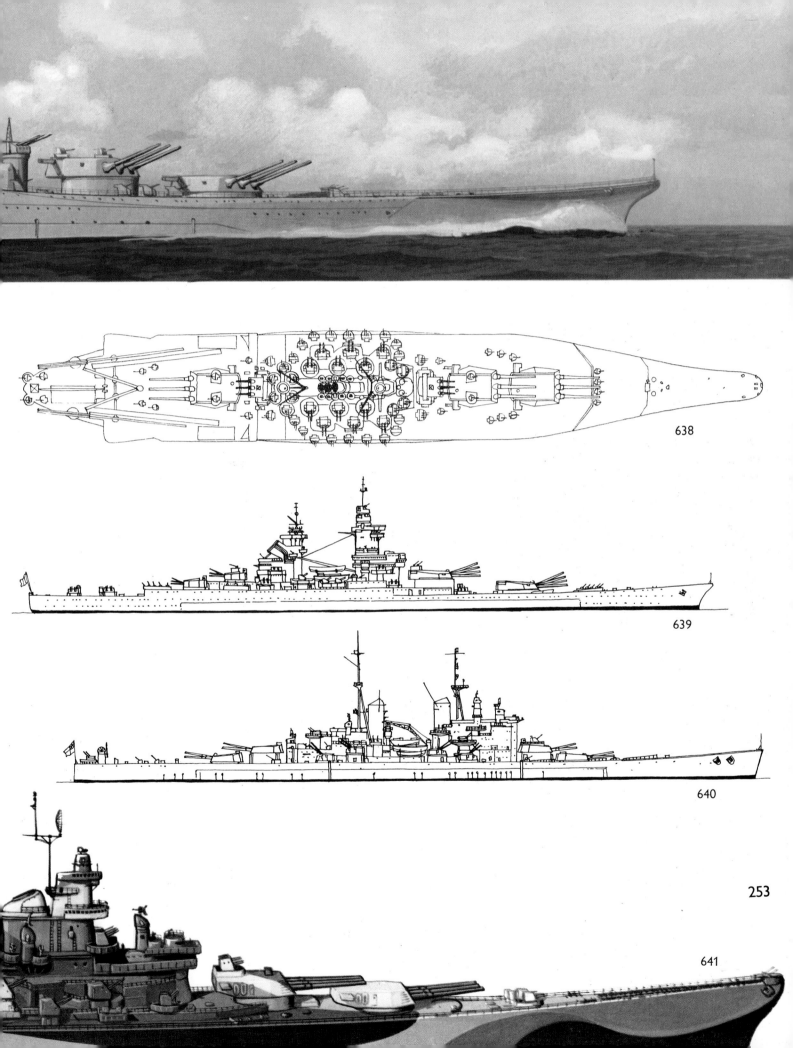

638

639

640

253

641

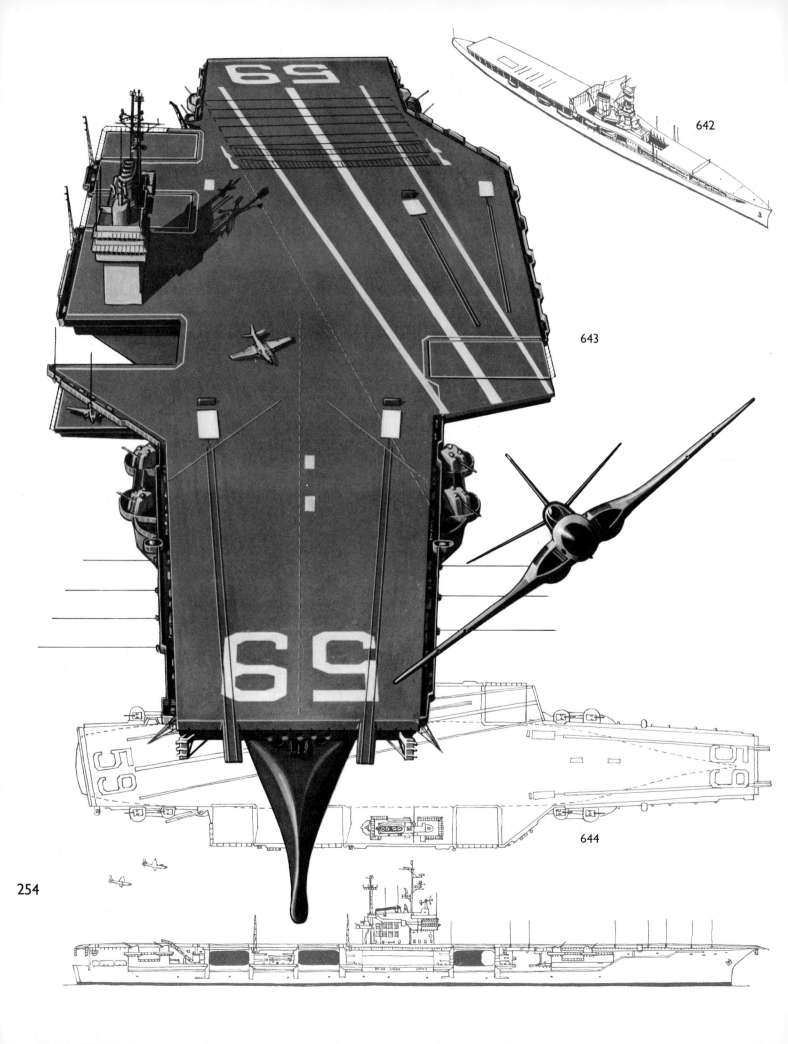

642

643

644

254

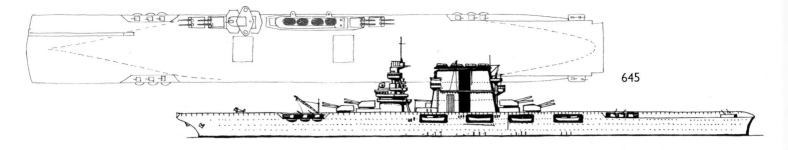

645

Aircraft carriers

Aircraft carriers are the largest units in today's navies. Their sole object is to carry and service planes, and in this capacity during engagements in the Pacific in the Second World War they made a more important contribution than any other type of vessel. The earliest aircraft carriers had no flight deck — they were merely floating hangars which transported seaplanes, lifting them out of the holds and placing them in the water with cranes. The old luxury liner *Campania* ended her days as an aircraft carrier, and she could in fact send off planes from her deck, but these were then forced either to try landing somewhere on the coast or in the water close to the ship to be lifted on board with cranes if possible.

The first aircraft carrier in the modern sense was the *Furious* (642), a converted cruiser with a flight deck where the planes could take off and most often land as well. But the landing deck was short and was disturbed by the swirling air from the bridge and the funnel. She was later rebuilt with a landing deck unbroken from fore to aft, and the smoke from the funnels was led to the side of the deck through horizontal pipes. (Cf. 646, the Japanese carrier *Ryuzyo*). Her dimensions were: length 786 feet, width 90 feet, draught 25 feet, displacement 22,450 tons. During the Second World War she was armed with twelve 4½-inch guns and a considerable number of anti- aircraft weapons. She was able to carry 36 planes.

The Lexington and the Saratoga, 1925

The U.S. carriers the *Lexington* and the *Saratoga* (645) were the most expensive warships of their time. When their keels were laid they were intended to be battlecruisers of 43,500 tons, but in conformity with the Washington Naval Treaty they were altered to carriers and the displacement stopped at 33,000 tons. (39,000 tons fully loaded).

The British carrier *Hermes* had already been built with bridge and funnel on one side of the deck in 1919, and this so-called "island type" is still the most common today. The *Lexington* and the *Saratoga* were built according to the same principle, and their four funnels were joined to a single, tall, elongated funnel which towered 130 feet above the water. The flight deck was 909·5 feet long and 105·6 feet wide. The turbo-electric engines developed a normal horsepower of 180,000 but this could be forced up to 210,000, then giving the large ships a speed of 34½ knots.

They could carry 90 planes and the crew consisted of 1,788 men, 672 of which were flight personnel. The main armament, which was intended for defence against cruisers and destroyers, was eight 8-inch guns. Including aircraft the ships cost $45 million each, and when they were modernised in 1939 another $15 million was necessary. This was much money, even for the United States, and other carriers built before 1943 were considerably smaller than the *Lexington* and the *Saratoga*.

The Forrestal, 1955

The U.S. carrier *Forrestal* (643, 644) together with her five sister ships is, at the time this book was written, the largest warship in the world. In February 1958, however, construction was begun on a nuclear-powered carrier whose dimensions will be: length 1,100 feet, width of flight deck 252 feet, fully loaded displacement 85,000 tons. She will be able to carry over 100 planes and has been calculated to cost $435 million.

The dimensions of the *Forrestal* are: length 1,039 feet, width of the hull 129·5 feet, greatest width of the flight deck 252 feet, draught 37 feet, displacement 75,900 tons. The 280,000 H.P. engines give a speed of 34 knots. Depending on type and size she can carry some 90—100 planes, and the peacetime crew amounts to 3,412 men. Apart from normal guns for warding off attacks from the sea and the air she also carries guided missiles. Planes can land and take off at the same time on her deck which is fitted with four large lifts. She cost $218 million.

255

646

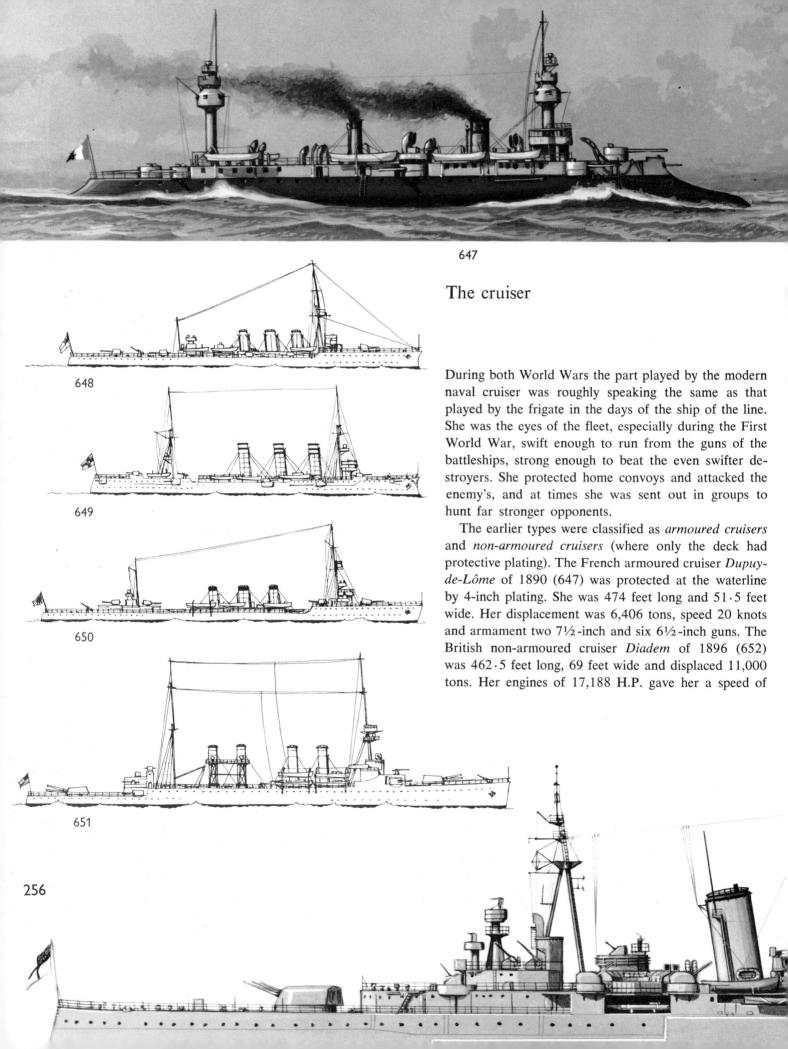

647

The cruiser

648

649

650

651

During both World Wars the part played by the modern
naval cruiser was roughly speaking the same as that
played by the frigate in the days of the ship of the line.
She was the eyes of the fleet, especially during the First
World War, swift enough to run from the guns of the
battleships, strong enough to beat the even swifter destroyers. She protected home convoys and attacked the
enemy's, and at times she was sent out in groups to
hunt far stronger opponents.

The earlier types were classified as *armoured cruisers*
and *non-armoured cruisers* (where only the deck had
protective plating). The French armoured cruiser *Dupuy-
de-Lôme* of 1890 (647) was protected at the waterline
by 4-inch plating. She was 474 feet long and 51·5 feet
wide. Her displacement was 6,406 tons, speed 20 knots
and armament two 7½-inch and six 6½-inch guns. The
British non-armoured cruiser *Diadem* of 1896 (652)
was 462·5 feet long, 69 feet wide and displaced 11,000
tons. Her engines of 17,188 H.P. gave her a speed of

20½ knots and the armament was sixteen 6-inch and twelve 3-inch guns. Battleships of the times could make 18—19 knots.

Armoured cruisers lost their importance when the battle-cruiser was introduced, and during the First World War the light, non-armoured cruiser of 3,500—5,000 tons was the most common type. The German *Königsberg* of 1907 (649) was of 3,470 tons. She was 383 feet long, 45·3 feet wide and had a speed of 25·7 knots. Her armament was ten 4-inch guns, two machine guns and two torpedo tubes. — The British *Galatea* built in 1914 (648) measured: length 410 feet, width 39 feet, draught 13·4 feet, displacement 3,560 tons. Her speed was 29 knots and armament two 6-inch and six 4-inch guns, four machine guns and four torpedo tubes. — A Japanese cruiser, the *Tatsatu* (650), built in 1918 made 33 knots having the same displacement.

As early as 1920 a U.S. cruiser of the *Omaha* class (651) had been launched which in size, 7,600 tons, and armour plating came close to the old armoured cruisers, but after the 1922 Washington Treaty — where it had been decided that cruisers were not to be greater than 10,000 tons or be armed with guns larger than 8 inches — nearly all cruisers had been built to the full limits allowed for tonnage and armament. The new classification was to be into *heavy cruisers* and *light cruisers*.

As the fastest battleships and battle-cruisers were soon to reach speeds of over 30 knots it became clear that the "Washington cruisers" were abortive. A new class of armoured cruiser thus appeared, many of which were slower than the fastest battleships, being the reason why most countries ceased to build these heavy cruisers, going over to the "light" type although the name did not stop some of them coming up to the 10,000-ton mark.

The Sheffield, 1937

A typical representative of these heavy "light" cruisers is the *Sheffield* from 1937, shown here as she appeared after rebuilding 1949—51 (653). Her dimensions are: length 591·5 feet, width 64 feet, draught 21 feet, displacement 9,100 tons (12,400 tons fully loaded). The plating at the waterline amidships is 4 inches thick, thinning out to 3 inches. The deck armour is 2-inch and the gun turrets' 1—2-inch. The 75,000 H.P. engines give her a speed of 32½ knots. The armament is nine 6-inch guns, eight 4-inch and eighteen 40 mm anti-aircraft guns and six torpedo tubes.

653

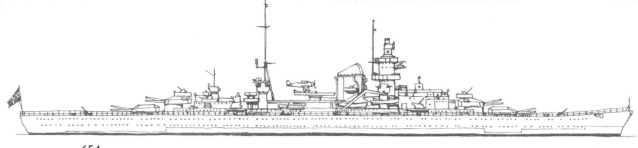

654

The Prinz Eugen, 1940

The German heavy cruiser *Prinz Eugen* (654) which was begun in 1936 and was ready for operations in 1940 was outwardly different from the pocket battleships such as the *Admiral Scheer* only in armament. Her displacement, officially given as 10,000 tons, seems in fact to have been 19,800 tons when fully loaded, and her 3-inch side plating was thicker than on most other heavy cruisers. The Italian *Bolzano* which had a speed of 38 knots was protected by 3-inch armour, and the Italian light phantom-cruisers of the *Regolo* class which had a speed of 41 knots were not fitted with armour plating at all. The 132,000 H.P. engines of the *Prinz Eugen* gave her a speed of only 32 knots, but she was made for service in more difficult waters.

Her dimensions were: length 639·6 feet, width 69·6 feet, draught 15·5 feet. Her armament consisted of eight 8-inch guns, twelve 4-inch and twenty-eight 20 mm anti-aircraft guns and twelve torpedo tubes. She also carried three aircraft which were launched by catapult. The total crew was 1,600.

The Cleveland, 1942

The U.S. light cruiser *Cleveland* (656) was the first-launched of the largest class of cruisers ever built. Before the end of 1946 twenty-seven vessels had been built according to the same plans. Their dimensions are:

length at the waterline 600 feet, width 61·5 feet, draught 20 feet, displacement 10,000 tons (12,000 tons fully loaded). The plating at the waterline is 5-inch. The 100,000 H.P. engines bring the speed up to 33 knots. The armament comprises twelve 6-inch and twelve 5-inch guns, twenty-four 40 mm and nineteen 20 mm anti-aircraft guns. They carry three aircraft, launched by catapult, and some of the cruisers are today equipped with helicopters.

The anti-aircraft cruiser De Grasse, 1955

Construction had already begun on the French cruiser *De Grasse* (657) in Lorient in 1938 but was stopped by the German occupation and was not resumed until 1946. After a further pause for the most modern anti-aircraft equipment to arrive she was finally completed in 1955. Her dimensions are: length 617·2 feet, width 61 feet, draught 18·3 feet, loaded displacement 11,545 tons. The armour at the waterline is 5-inch and on the deck 2½-inch.

She is not fitted with missiles as yet but all her guns are controlled by radar. The French are at the moment in the process of experimenting with different types of anti-aircraft, anti-ship and anti-submarine missiles. The *De Grasse* is armed with sixteen 5-inch and twenty 2¼-inch anti-aircraft guns. She has a speed of 33½ knots and a crew of 966.

655

258

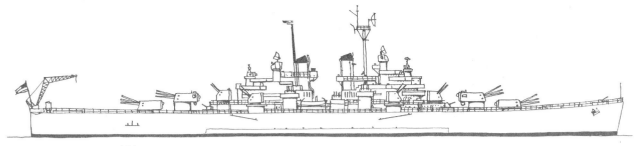

The guided missile cruiser Boston, 1955

656

The heavy cruiser *Boston* (655) had already been launched in 1942 as one of the large *Baltimore* class but was refitted together with the *Canberra* in 1955 to be the first *guided missile cruiser* in the world. She was equipped with anti-aircraft missiles, special radar apparatus and other arrangements for guiding the weapons.

The *Boston* is a step towards a wholly new type of warship. She is still only considered as a half missile-equipped cruiser and an experiment because part of the old armament in the form of conventional guns was retained. She mounts six 8-inch guns, ten 5-inch and twelve 3-inch anti-aircraft guns, yet it is possible that the four guided missiles that can be fired simultaneously are her main weapon.

They are missiles of the type called *Terriers,* 27 feet long, narrow with a very pointed nose and a speed of 1,600 m.p.h. They are made to hit and destroy aircraft in all weather conditions at a range and height greater than that attained by any previous anti-aircraft weapon. The radar finds the target and an electronic apparatus guides the missile. Four missiles can be fired every half minute. The *Boston* carries 144 of them.

The dimensions of the remarkable vessel are: length 673·5 feet, width 71 feet, draught 26 feet, displacement 13,600 tons (17,200 when fully loaded). The sides are protected by 6-inch and the deck by 3-inch plating. The crew consists of 1,730 men.

The Long Beach, 1961

The first nuclear-powered, guided missile cruiser was launched on 14th July 1959 and is to be completed in 1961. Her total cost has been calculated to $250 million of which $18,335,305 go to the reactor. She has been christened *Long Beach* and will appear more or less as in the picture (658); the camouflage painting is for wartime service of course.

Her dimensions are: length 721 feet, width 73 feet, draught 26 feet, displacement 14,000 tons (18,000 tons when fully loaded). Her nuclear-powered engines are calculated to give her a speed of 45 knots. She will probably not carry any guns at all but will be armed with different types of missile weapons.

The *Long Beach* is an attack ship and will operate independently of other units, and she is believed to be capable of successfully countering attacks by all types of aircraft, guided missiles, surface and underwater vessels armed either with conventional or nuclear weapons.

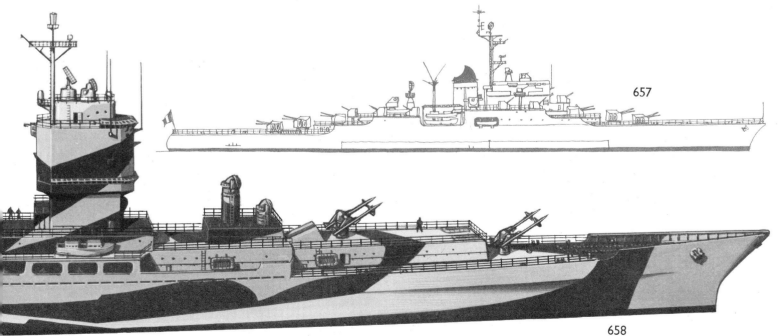

657

658

The torpedo boat

It is thought that the prototypes of the torpedo boat were the small steam sloops that operated in the American Civil War of 1861—65 fitted with one or two *spar* or *outrigger torpedoes,* an explosive charge with a detonating arrangement on the end of a long pole. The idea was later developed by various designers who built low, narrow boats offering the smallest target, the mine on its pole being placed on a support in the bow (659). When the torpedo boat went in to attack, the mine was pushed as far forward as possible, some 27 feet or so, and course was set on the target until the mine exploded under the waterline of the enemy ship. Another construction (661) shows a torpedo boat with a mine at each end, theoretically being able to make two attacks. In reality the first mine was almost as dangerous for attacker as attacked.

It is said that the first torpedo in the modern sense came into being when an Austrian naval officer contacted Robert Whitehead, an English engineer, to obtain his help for the realisation of an idea for sending an unmanned, steerable boat filled with explosives and fitted with a

659

660

661

662

663

664

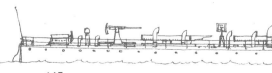

665

667

detonator at an enemy. Whitehead then hit on the idea of constructing the missile so that it could travel underwater, and in 1868 his first torpedo was ready. It was 10 feet long, 14 inches in diameter and was propelled by compressed air.

During the 1870's experiments were made with different methods of discharging the torpedoes, and with these the torpedo boats became longer and faster. The British *Lightning* of 1876 was 84·5 feet long and had a speed of 18 knots. The torpedo was fired from a tube on the foredeck. Boats were constructed where the torpedoes could be dropped over the sides (662), and finally the firing tubes were built into the bows (663). The French built a series of torpedo boats during the 1890's which had two tubes, the one built into the bow and the other, which could be rotated, on the after deck (664). They were also armed with two small guns and their speed was 23 knots.

The new weapon had caused a certain amount of panic among those who decided how warships were to be constructed, and attempts were even made to persuade admiralties that the age of the expensive and easily damaged battleship was already past. But new large ships continued to be built, they were made stronger at and under the waterline and were protected with torpedo nets, double bottoms and a system of cells and watertight compartments.

The British had learned of the speedy French torpedo boats at the beginning of the 1890's and as usual replied with something better. Two boats were built, 180 feet long, 18·5 feet wide, with a draught of 5·2 feet and a displacement of 260 tons (665). The boats were armed with three torpedo tubes and four small guns and made over 27 knots. They were called *torpedo boat destroyers,* but the name was later changed to *destroyers* simply.

The *Nembo* (667) was a typical destroyer from the turn of the century. She was built for the Italian Navy in 1901 and her dimensions were: length 208 feet, width 19·3 feet, draught 7·5 feet, displacement 330 tons. The 5,200 H.P. engines gave her a speed of 30 knots.

The Turbinia, 1897

At the 1897 Spithead Review a small private vessel created a sensation by weaving among the other ships with a speed greater than any yet seen on water. This was the way Charles A. Parsons, the inventor of the steam turbine, demonstrated the value of his invention for the previously sceptical Admiralty with his boat the *Turbinia* (666). Her engines developed 2,000 H.P., and nine propellers on three shafts gave her the sensational speed of 34½ knots.

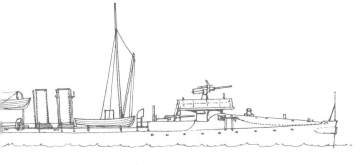

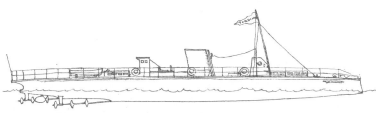

666

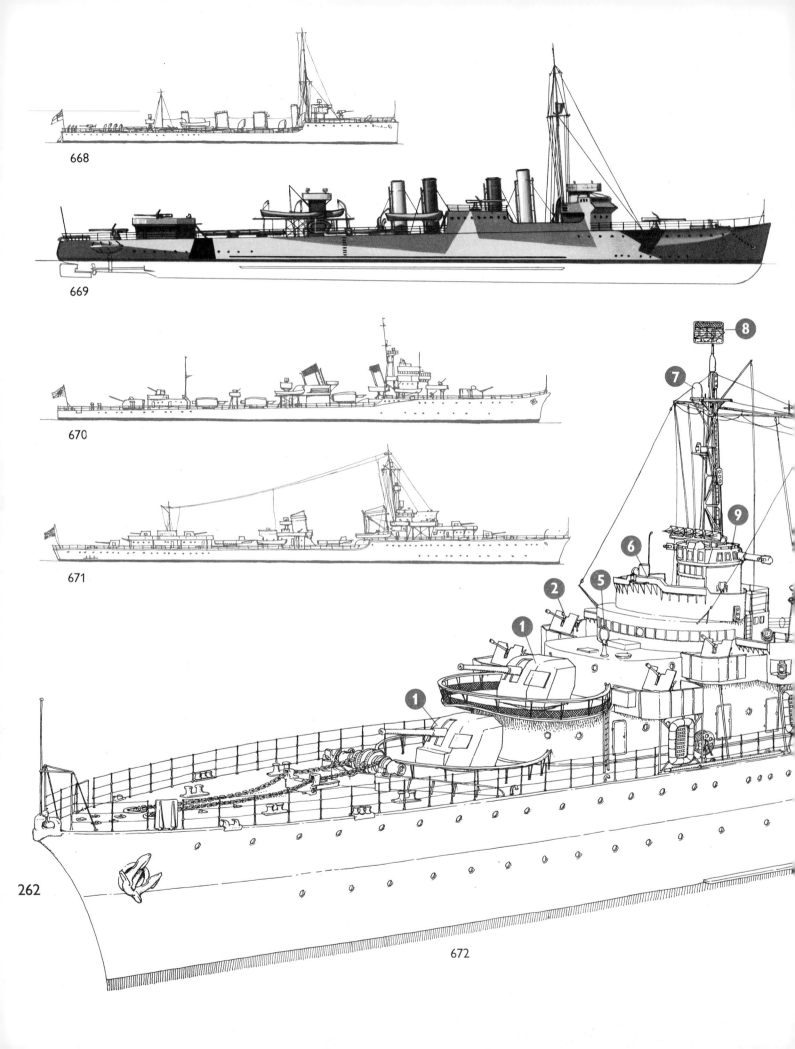

668

669

670

671

1

1

2

5

6

7

8

9

262

672

Destroyers

Britain then began to build destroyers with turbines, but the light hulls were no longer able to stand the stresses the swift craft were exposed to, and after one of the first turbine-driven destroyers was smashed by a storm in the North Sea in 1901 it was decided to build them larger and stronger in the future. Destroyers of 540 tons were launched by 1903, and those of the *Tribal* class 1907—09 (668) had the following dimensions: length 270 feet, width 26 feet, draught 8 feet and displacement 870 tons. They did over 33 knots and were armed with five 3-inch guns and two torpedo tubes.

The much spoken of U.S. destroyers that came to Britain in exchange in September 1940 were built 1917—20 (669) and had the following dimensions: length at the waterline 311 feet, width 30·4 feet, draught 9·2 feet, displacement 1,190 tons. Their speed was 35 knots.

During the period between the wars many countries built vessels of about 3,000 tons which were a cross between a cruiser and a destroyer — the displacement of destroyers proper was between 1,000 and 1,800 tons as a rule. The Japanese destroyers of the *Hibiki* class (670) had the following dimensions: length 371.5 feet, width 33·7 feet, draught 9·7 feet, displacement 1,700 tons (2,300 tons fully loaded). The 40,000 H.P. engines gave them a speed of 34 knots. The armament consisted of nine torpedo tubes, six 5-inch guns and four anti-aircraft guns.

The 1938 *Karl Galster* (671) was a typical representative of the German heavy destroyers and had the following data: length 410 feet, width 38 feet, draught 14·8 feet, fully loaded displacement 3,415 tons, speed 38 knots. The armament comprised eight torpedo tubes, five 5-inch guns, eighteen anti-aircraft guns of various calibres and sixty mines.

The French *Le Terrible* from 1933 (672) could reach the fantastic speed of 45¼ knots. Dimensions: length 434·3 feet, width 39·3 feet, draught 14 feet, displacement 2,569 tons (3,230 tons when fully loaded). The engines developed 100,000 H.P. at top speed.

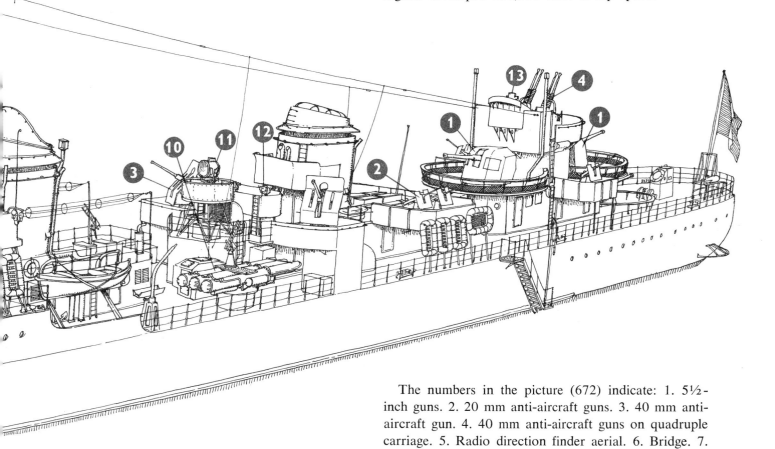

The numbers in the picture (672) indicate: 1. 5½-inch guns. 2. 20 mm anti-aircraft guns. 3. 40 mm anti-aircraft gun. 4. 40 mm anti-aircraft guns on quadruple carriage. 5. Radio direction finder aerial. 6. Bridge. 7. Radar for sea spotting. 8. Radar for air spotting. 9. Range finder for 5½-inch guns. 10. Torpedo tubes. 11. Searchlight. 12. Range finder for 40 mm guns. 13. Range finder for the quadruple 40 mm guns.

673

The modern destroyer

During the Second World War and after, development has made the destroyer into an all-purpose weapon, and it seems as if a displacement of over 3,000 tons has become the rule — the technical equipment increasing and becoming more complicated with the new duties, increasing the size of the ship in turn. All guns on board are intended to be used on both sea and air targets. Torpedoes and depth charges are standard fittings, and the most modern destroyers are equipped with anti-submarine missiles and guided missiles for use against aircraft and other ships.

Over a hundred destroyers of the *Gearing* class (673) were built in the United States 1944—46, and many of them have since been rebuilt for various kinds of special duty and fitted with guided missiles, anti-submarine rockets and special radar equipment. Their dimensions are: length 390·5 feet, width 40·9 feet, draught 12·5 feet, fully loaded displacement about 3,500 tons. Their 60.000 H.P. engines give them a speed of 35 knots.

The standard type is armed with six 5-inch, six 3-inch or sixteen 40 mm guns, all intended to be used both against ships and aircraft, five torpedo tubes, two "hedgehogs" (a kind of mortar system for submarine hunting) and depth charges.

The eight British destroyers of the *Daring* class (675) were completed 1952—54. They are more than ten times as large as the first British destroyers and the largest to have been built in the country. The most expensive of them cost £2,880,000. Their dimensions are: length 390 feet, width 43 feet, draught 17 feet, fully loaded displacement 3,600 tons. The six 4½-inch guns are wholly automatic and, like some of the 40 mm guns, are radar-controlled. They are fitted with five torpedo tubes and various anti-submarine weapons. The 54,000 H.P. engines give them a top speed of about 35 knots.

Britain, the U.S.S.R. and the United States are building destroyers whose main armament will consist of guided missiles. The British will be of about 4,000 tons (5,500 tons fully loaded) and about 500 feet long. The U.S. guided missile destroyers will be fitted partly with conventional and partly with nuclear-powered engines. The nuclear-powered destroyer *Bainbridge* (674) is calculated to be ready in 1962. It will be about 550 feet long and its fully loaded displacement 7,600 tons.

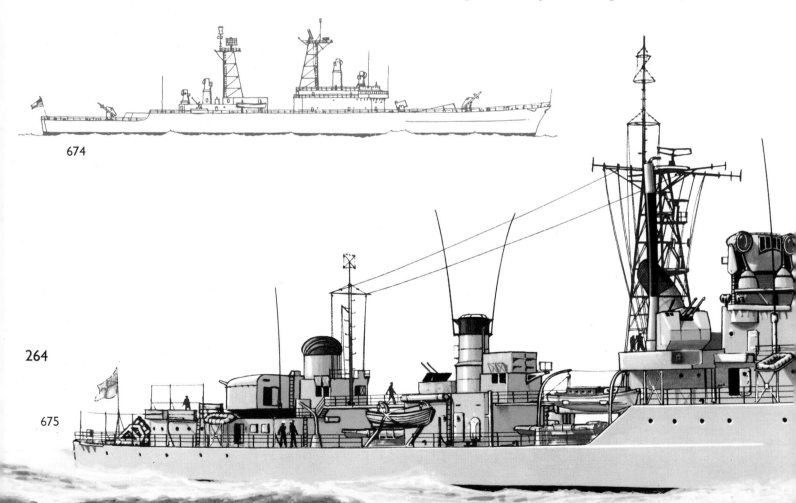

674

675

Motor torpedo boats

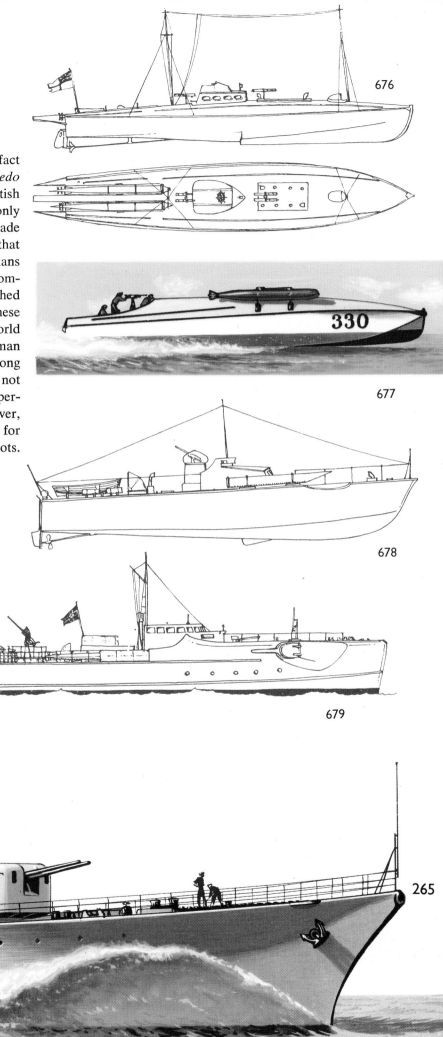

When the internal combustion engine had become a fact Britain began in 1904 to build so-called *motor torpedo boats,* and during the First World War several British cruisers carried such 40-foot craft, but it was only towards the end of the war when the craft were made larger and were allowed to operate independently that they became of real use (676). After the war the Italians began to build their M.A.S. boats (Motoscafi Anti Sommergibili) which carried two torpedoes and reached speeds of 40 knots with their 1,500 H.P. engines. These were further developed, and during the Second World War were capable of reaching 50 knots. The German "Schnellboote" were large and heavy (679), 90 feet long and weighing 100 tons. Their speed was probably not more than 39 knots. MTB performances, like the performances of all warships, are military secrets, however, and it is likely that the British pre-1939 MTB, for example, (678) could do more than the official 40 knots.

676

330

677

678

679

265

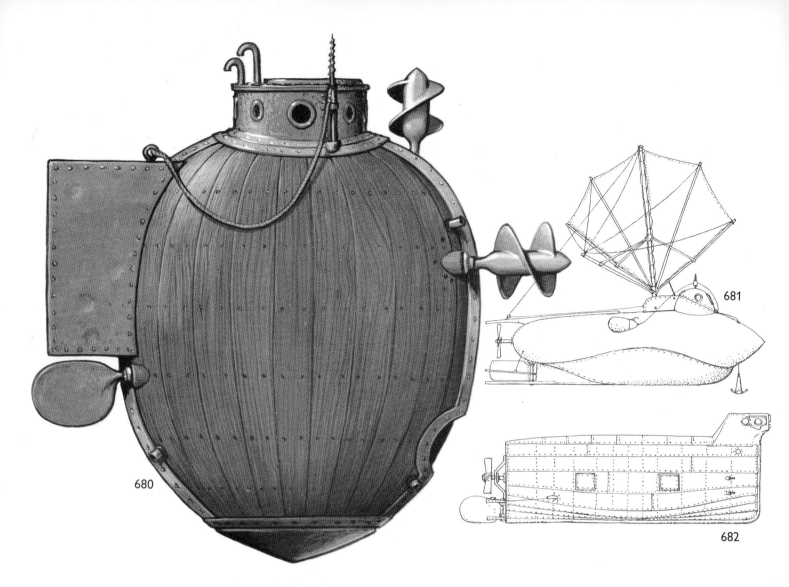

680

681

682

The submarine, 1775-1900

The first working submarine (680) was built in 1775 by an American named David Bushnell and was called the *Turtle* as it looked like the shells of two such animals joined together. It was used a year later when Sergeant Ezra Lee tried to blow up the British blockade ship *Eagle* with it. There was only room for Lee on board, and he alone had to turn the screws and manage the valves, pumps and changes in ballast which brought the *Turtle* to and under the *Eagle*. He tried to attach the mine which hung over the *Turtle's* rudder to the underside of the *Eagle* with a long screw, but the hull was protected with copper sheeting and he failed. He then managed to return safely to base in the *Turtle*.

In 1801 Robert Fulton built a submarine of copper (681) which was fitted with a ballast tank in the lower part of its hull so that it could dive and return to the surface. He tried to interest Napoleon in his craft and demonstrated it on the Seine, but the Emperor showed no enthusiasm. The German inventor Wilhelm Bauer built a curious vessel (682) in Kiel in 1850 which was 26 feet long and had a crew of three, one at the helm and two driving the propeller. It made a successful trip underwater, but on a second attempt the sides were pressed in and the crew only just managed to save their lives.

The submarine *El Ictineo* (685), designed by Monturiol, a Spaniard, in 1862, was long before its time. It had a double hull of modern form, and the ballast tanks between the hulls could be pumped out with compressed air. It was driven by a steam engine even when submerged, and the air used in combustion was replaced with oxygen from a chemical plant. — *Le Plongeur* (683), constructed in France a year later by Bougois and Brun, had its ballast tanks in the double bottom and the propeller was driven by compressed air. The armament

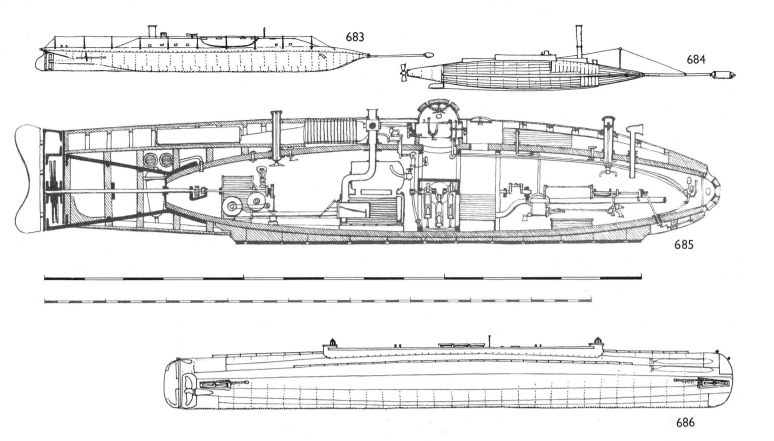

683

684

685

686

consisted of a mine on a long pole. The craft, however, was difficult to keep on an upright keel when submerged.

During the American Civil War the Confederate Navy used small, so-called "Davids" (684) which could not dive but were so-trimmed from the start that only the funnels and hatches to the ladderways were above water. — During the 1880's a Swede, Torsten Nordenfelt, designed a number of submarines armed with the newly invented Whitehead torpedo, and on the large vessel he built for Russia (686) the torpedo tubes were for the first time fitted inside the hull which meant that they could be loaded while the vessel was submerged. The submarines of those days manoeuvred badly when submerged as they were disposed to plunge. This was first overcome on the French *Gymnote* (687), constructed by Dupuy de Lôme and Gustave Zedé, which had been fitted with two further horizontal rudders in the bow.

John P. Holland, an American, had been experimenting with submarines since the 1870's, and having won a constructional competition, his boat the *Plunger* came to be built in 1896. Four years later the U.S. Navy ordered six of his boats (688). A 50 H. P. petrol engine gave the vessels a surface speed of 7 knots and an electric motor of the same power gave them 6 knots when submerged. They had a ballast tank amidships (690) and trimming tanks in the bow and the stern.

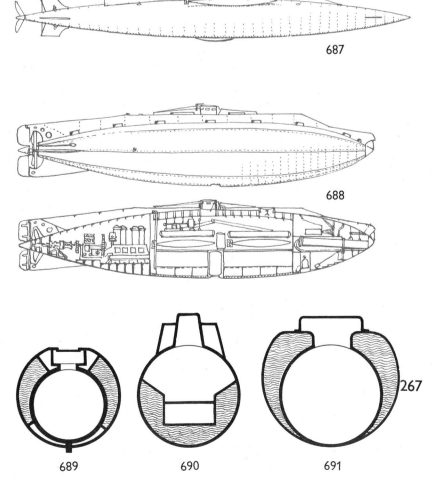

687

688

267

689

690

691

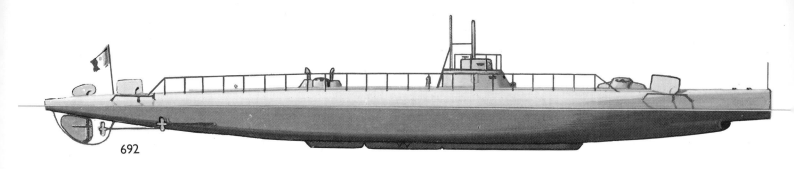

692

The submarine during the First World War

The French designer Max Laubeuf had already built submarines during the 1890's whose ballast tanks lay outside the powerfully constructed hull, the *pressure hull,* and he gave the outer shell a shape which made the submarine when surfaced look like a contemporary torpedo boat (691). This basic type was to be common for a considerable time to come. As during the whole of their history the French Admiralty were not shy of innovations and they showed wholehearted interest in the new weapon. The British Navy were given their first submarines in 1902 and the German in 1905.

The method of propulsion was still a difficulty as the steam engine was unsuitable and the petrol engine, because of the risk for explosions, too dangerous. It was only when the diesel engine had been developed that the problem was solved to satisfaction. The various types that existed at the outbreak of the First World War such as the Italian (692), the German (697) and the British

(698) roughly functioned according to the same principles.

The vital parts of the craft were all contained in the pressure hull which was strong enough to withstand the pressure at depths of 35—40 fathoms. The fuel and ballast tanks lay between the pressure hull and the outer hull. The outer hull was either built right round the pressure hull (692, 697) or as long blimps along its sides (698). As the lower valves of the ballast tanks were open when the vessel was submerged the pressure was the same on both sides of the outer hull irrespective of the depth and could therefore be of relatively light construction.

The numbers in the illustration of the German U-boat (697) indicate: 1. Periscope. 2. Pressurized conning tower with navigational and manoeuvring apparatus for both surface and underwater operations. 3. Torpedo tube. 4. Trimming tank. 5. Tank for flooding the tor-

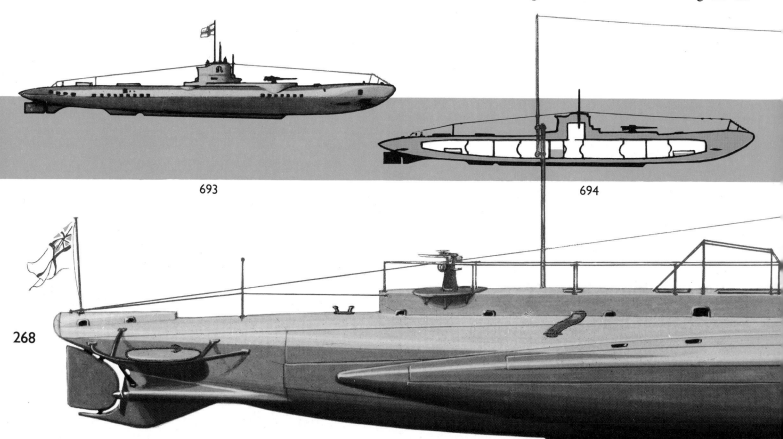

693

694

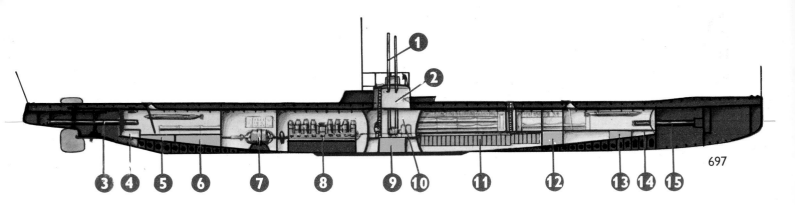

697

pedo tubes. 6. Torpedo tube blowing tank. 7. Electric motor for submerged propulsion. 8. Diesel motor for surface propulsion. 9. Regulating tank. Under this a false keel. 10. Control room. 11. Accumulators for the electric motor. 12. Freshwater tank. 13. Tube filling tank. 14. Trimming tank. 15. Forward torpedo tube.

Illustrations 693—696 show the principle functional features of a submarine. They are of a large German U-boat from the First World War, 275·5 feet long, 25 feet wide and with a surface displacement of 1,175 tons. The speed on the surface was 17½ knots and 7 knots when submerged. It had six torpedo tubes and a crew of 46. — When travelling on the surface (693) the ballast tanks are empty and the vessel is propelled by the diesel motor. When the U-boat is to dive the diesel motor is stopped and the electric started. The lower valves of the ballast tanks are opened, and when the air ports in the upper halves of the tanks are also opened

water pours in and the boat sinks. — When submerged (694) the ballast tanks around the pressure hull are filled and the water in the trimming and regulating tanks so adjusted that the vessel has the same weight as the surrounding water and therefore "floats freely". In this position the boat is very sensitive to change in weight in the fore-and-aft direction. — If the boat is too heavy, starts to sink too deep and has forward trimming (695) this is counteracted by blowing the regulating tank and the trimming tanks from fore to aft. The horizontal rudders in the bow and the stern also help to reattain stability. — If the boat is too light and has aft trimming (696) more water is let into the regulating tank and water pumped from the aft trimming tank to the fore. The horizontal rudders are also of help here. — Finally if the boat is damaged so that the ballast water cannot be pumped out it can still be brought to the surface by releasing the heavy false keel.

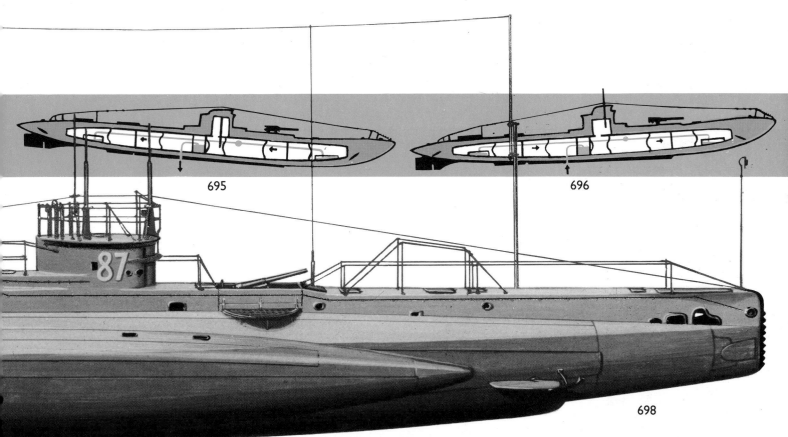

695

696

698

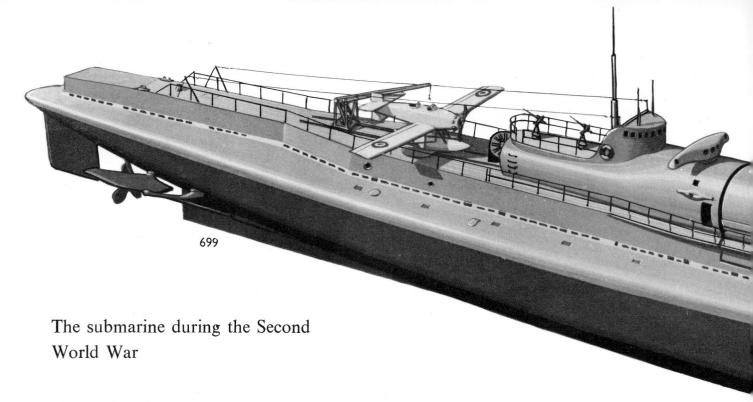

699

The submarine during the Second World War

The French underwater cruiser *Surcouf* of 1929 (699) was the largest submarine in the world until she was sunk in 1942. She was 361 feet long, 29·5 feet wide and her surface displacement was 2,880 tons. She was armed among other things with two 8-inch guns, ten torpedo tubes and she carried a scouting aircraft in a special hangar.

The Versailles Treaty forbade Germany to build submarines, but Hitler already chose to ignore the prohibition by 1935, and during the war the German U-boat fleet was the foremost in the world. Dwarf submarines (701, 702) were used by all leading sea powers. In the section of a large German one-man submarine (701) the numbers indicate: 1. Diving tank. 2. Electric motor. 3. Petrol motor. 4. Oxygen container. 5. Snorkel. 6. Periscope. 7. Mirror compass. 8. Batteries. 9. Diving tank.

An important German invention, or rather an improvement of an old idea, was the *snorkel,* an air intake which made it possible for the diesel motors to be used even in the submerged position. The German snorkel-fitted U-boat of type *XXI* (700) has been called the first submarine proper as opposed to all earlier types which were really only "diving craft". The *XXI* boats were 251·2 feet long, 21·3 feet wide, and their surface displacement 1,621 tons. The whole construction of the hull was for speed under water, and the very efficient electric motors gave them an underwater speed of 17½ knots.

Another German war invention was the Walther turbine which was based on the heat energy obtained when very concentrated hydrogen peroxide is mixed with water. The engines were very efficient, and the Walther U-boats that were being experimented with in 1945 attained an underwater speed of 25 knots. The very expensive hydrogen peroxide, however, made the cost of running almost a thousand times as high as for a conventional U-boat. — The numbers in the section of a Walther U-boat (703) indicate: 1. Diving tank. 2. "Silent" machinery. 3. Fuel oil tank. 4. Walther turbine room. 5. Engine room. 6. Snorkel. 7. Periscope. 8. Conning tower. 9. Torpedo room with crew quarters. 10. Trimming tank. 11. Lubricating oil tank. 12. Regulating tank. 13. Ingolin tank. 14. Batteries. 15. Fuel oil tank. 16. Commander's cabin. 17. Hydrophone room. 18. Radio room. 19. Control room. 20. Side torpedo tubes.

700

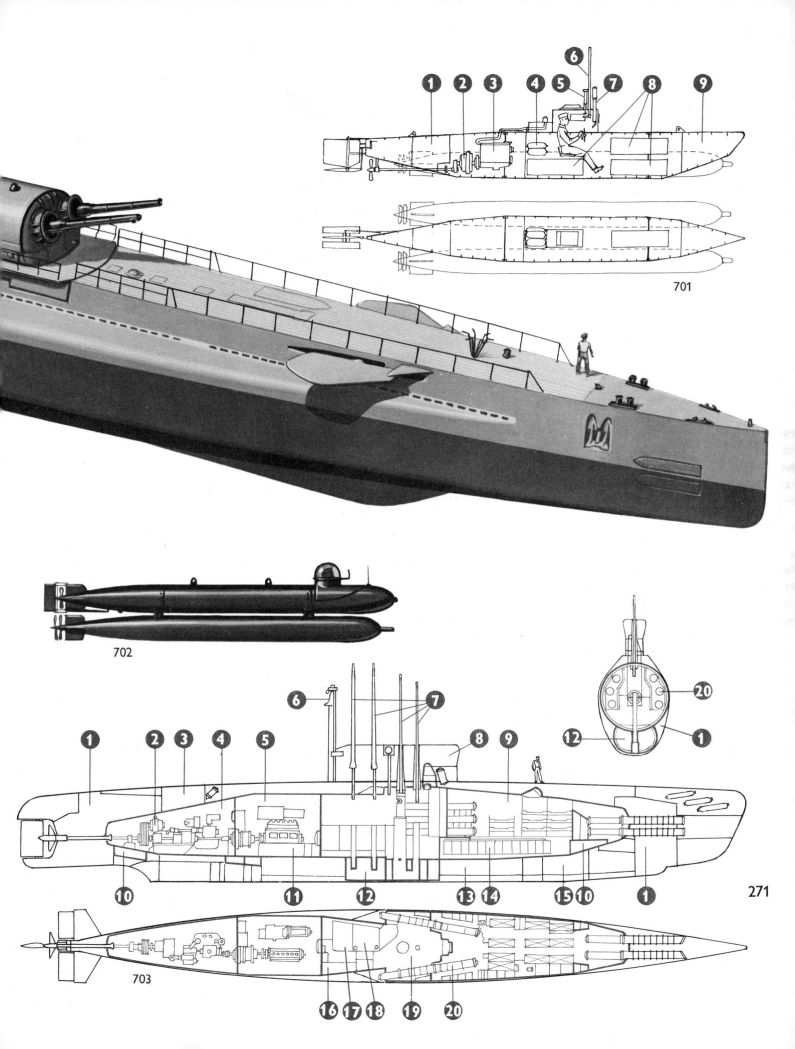

701

702

271

703

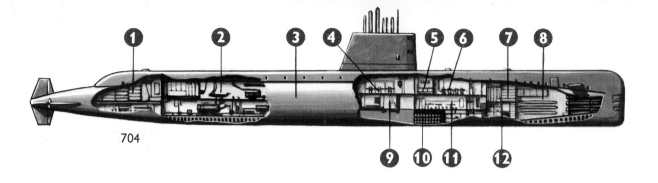

704

The nuclear-powered submarine

Warships have always been accorded great secrecy, especially so in the case of submarines, and there is perhaps nothing as secret as the actual data and performance of nuclear-powered submarines. The following information which has been released is therefore to be taken with a great deal of reservation.

The U.S. *Nautilus* (704) which was launched in 1954 and was ready for trials a year later is the first nuclear-powered vessel in the world. She is 323·6 feet long, 27·6 feet wide and her surface displacement 3,200 tons. Apart from the nuclear-powered engines which at 13,400 H.P. give her a speed of 21 knots, she has both diesel and electric motors as well. Her radius of action is stated to be 40,000 nautical miles and her crew consists of 101 men. She can dive to a depth of over 120 fathoms, and with a single refuelling of the reactor she has covered 91,324 nautical miles, 78,885 of them under water. On 3rd August 1958 she reached the North Pole after a voyage under the ice.

The numbers in the drawing (704) indicate: 1. Crew quarters. 2. Engine room. 3. Reactor room. 4. Operations room. 5. Commander's cabin. 6. Officers' mess. 7. Crew quarters. 8. Torpedo room. 9. Control room. 10. Batteries. 11. Crew mess. 12. Store room.

When this was written Britain's first nuclear-powered submarine the *Dreadnought* had not been completed. Information about the nuclear-powered submarine being built in the U.S.S.R. is not available. The United States has already launched several dozen nuclear-powered submarines. The largest of them, and the largest submarine ever to be built, is the *Triton* (705). She was launched in 1958 and measures 447 feet long and 37 feet wide. Her surface displacement is 5,900 tons and she has three decks inside the pressure hull. Two reactors can hold enough fuel for two years' operations and her main duty is as a warning and scouting vessel working in co-operation with carrier units. For this purpose she is fitted with long-distance radar and other electronic spotting equipment. She has a crew of 148 and is stated to do 33 knots. She cost $ 100 million.

The fastest submarine in the world is the drop-shaped *Skipjack* (opposite page and title-page) which is said to do over 35 knots under water. She is 252 feet long, 31·5 feet wide and has a displacement of 2,850 tons. The *George Washington* which was launched in 1959 (706) has the following dimensions: length 380 feet, width 32 feet, displacement 5,600 tons. She is armed with sixteen Polaris missiles which are some 30 feet long, 50 inches in diameter and have a nuclear warhead. These missiles can be fired when the vessel is submerged and are stated to have a range of 1,500 miles.

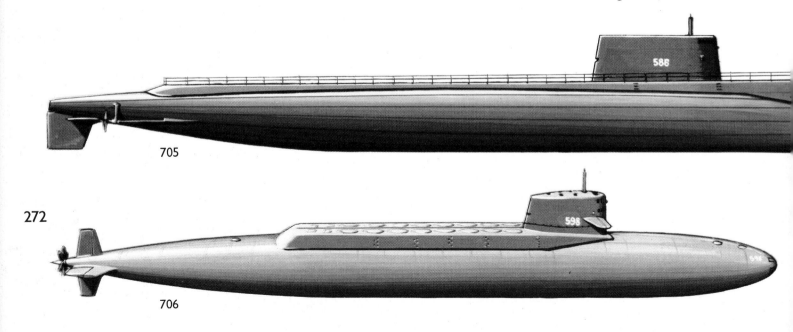

705

706

272

708

Frigates and corvettes

Just before the outbreak of the Second World War when Britain was preparing herself for defence against the U-boat war that was to be expected, the chief naval designer was given the job of constructing a suitable anti-submarine craft. Before, mainly destroyers and minesweepers had been equipped for submarine hunting, but other duties were thought necessary for them now and another vessel had to be constructed. It is said that a firm who specialised in whale fishing suggested the idea that a submarine hunter ought to look like a whale catcher, and the new craft were built with lines and shape based on the small whaling vessels.

The vessels were called *corvettes* as they were equivalent to the smallest class of fighting craft from the days of the sailing-ship. They were of 925 tons and about 195 feet long, were equipped with listening apparatus and armed with light guns and, of course, mainly depth charges.

Such a corvette of a slightly more advanced type and launched in 1943 was the *Hedingham Castle* (709) of the large *Castle* class which were later promoted to frigates. It had the following dimensions: length 252 feet, width 36·7 feet, draught 15·8 feet, fully loaded displacement 1,630 tons. The armament was one 4-inch gun, two 40 mm and two 20 mm anti-aircraft guns, one depth charge mortar and two depth charge throwers.

During the war the United States built hundreds of so-called *destroyer escorts,* vessels which in their use corresponded to the British frigates. The units in the large *Buckley* class (710) had the following dimensions: length 306 feet, width 36·9 feet, draught 10·4 feet, fully loaded displacement 2,170 tons. They were as a rule more strongly armed than the early British frigates.

Together with the destroyer the frigate is today one of the most all-round types of warship. The new kind of warfare that is foreshadowed by all new weapons has caused the technical equipment of ships to become larger, and with this the frigate has also grown, both in size and importance. Anti-aircraft and anti-submarine frigates are being built, the latter often carrying a helicopter to aid spotting. The british frigate *Salisbury* (711) from 1957 is a so-called *aircraft direction frigate,* but it is armed and equipped as a destroyer and submarine hunter. Its dimensions are: length 340 feet, width 40 feet, draught 11·5 feet, fully loaded displacement 2,180 tons. — The French anti-aircraft and anti-submarine frigates of *Le Normand* class from 1956 are 327·5 feet long and have a displacement of 1,700 tons (712).

Corvette still remains as a name for small submarine hunters in Italy for example where a corvette of the *Airone* class (708) is 249·3 feet long and has a displacement of 950 tons.

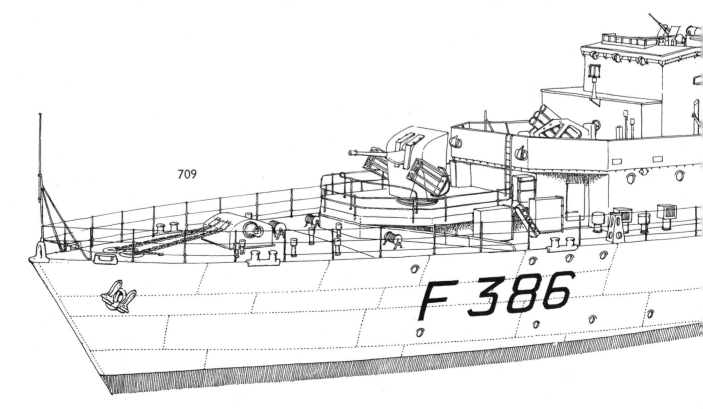

709

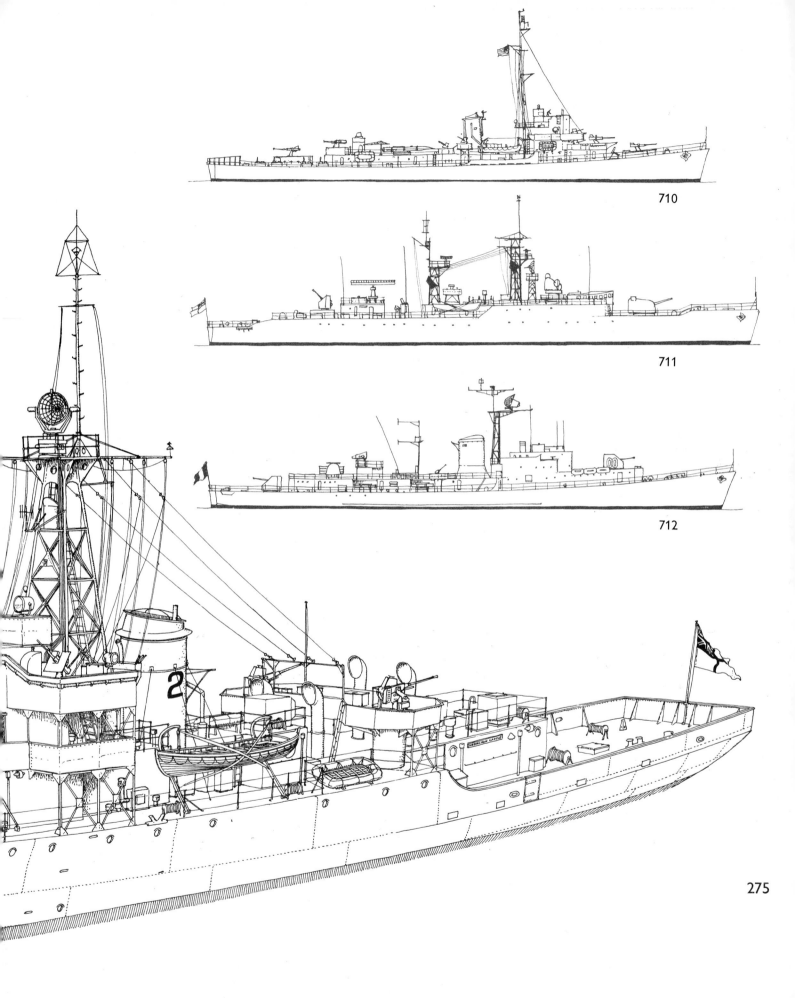

710

711

712

275

713

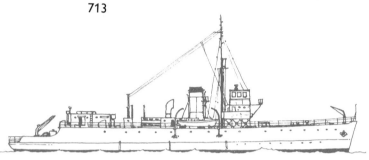

714

Minelayers

The vessels that have been and still are used for mine-laying have had very diverse shapes. Ordinary warships have been used, cruisers, destroyers and submarines which have had minelaying as a secondary duty, old warships and merchantmen have been rebuilt for the job, and finally different sorts of craft have been built with the main object of minelaying. As a rule it seems to be that the navies which operate in waters especially suited to mine warfare such as the Baltic and its bays have equipped nearly all types of warships for mine-laying, whereas in the British and French navies for instance each vessel type is constructed for a special purpose.

A specially built minelayer of the largest sort is the U.S. *Terror* (713) of 8,650 tons, 453·8 feet long, 60 feet wide and 20 feet draught. She can carry 800 mines and is armed with four 5-inch and nine 20 mm anti-aircraft guns. She was launched in 1941 and during the war carried a crew of 400. — The British minelayers are smaller. There are vessels of 4,000 tons which have a speed of 40 knots, but the ordinary coastal minelayers (714) are of about 1,000 tons and have speeds of no more than 14—15 knots.

Minesweepers

During the Russo-Japanese War of 1904—05 mines came into greater use than before. This was when the Japanese began *minesweeping* which was carried out by two boats towing between them a long sweep of stout wire held underwater by two anchors. In this way the mines were reaped and disarmed. The method was not particularly efficient, however, and a few years later the British began experiments on the trawler principle using a water kite which held the wire sweep down and gave it better spread. But as long as two vessels were used for sweeping — both having to pass through unswept water — the risk was great. Many British minesweepers were lost during the First World War.

715

716

717

In 1918 the British brought in the so-called *oropesa sweep* which was towed by only one vessel. The wire was forced out to the side by a water kite supported by a buoy, and the sweeper behind could travel in the edge of the swept water without much risk and itself broaden the swept path. Different ways have developed from this, and the magnetic and acoustical mines of the last war have necessitated very advanced methods.

Difference is made between deep-sea sweepers, coastal sweepers and harbour sweepers. Typical deep-sea sweepers are the vessels of the British *Algerine* class built in 1942 (715) which have the following dimensions: length 235 feet, width 35·5 feet, draught 11·5 feet, displacement 1,335 tons. During the war many of them had to serve as escort vessels, and some of them are equipped as anti-submarine corvettes. — The German minesweepers built in 1935 (717) were very shallow-draught in spite of their size and weight and were therefore well-suited for sweeping in different depths of water. Their dimensions were: length 232·3 feet, width 27 feet, draught 8·5 feet, displacement 874 tons. — The U.S. coastal minesweepers of the *Bluebird* class (716) which have been widely distributed among the NATO countries measure: length 144 feet, width 28 feet, draught 8·3 feet, displacement 378 tons.

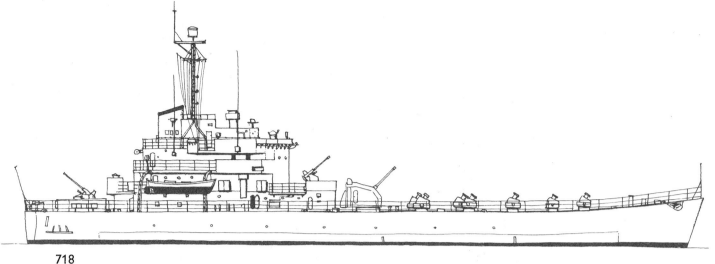

718

Landing craft

For the large amphibious operations made during the war in the Pacific and Normandy, the United States in particular built a number of different landing craft, from the smallest carrying a platoon to the large vessels that landed tanks and other heavy material. Since the war many countries have continued to develop the construction of landing craft, the most modern probably being those intended for the landing of troops by helicopter.

In 1955 the United States introduced a vessel intended to give fire support to invasion troops at close range, popularly called a "bobtailed cruiser" (718). Its dimensions are: length 245 feet, width 39 feet, draught 10 feet, displacement 1,500 tons. It is armed with one 5-inch gun, two 40 mm anti-aircraft guns and eight rocket throwers.

The large, modern L.S.T.s (Landing Ship Tank) have a fully loaded displacement of 8,000 tons (720), then carrying 700 troops and 20 amphibious tanks apart from the crew of 124. Their dimensions are: length 442 feet, width 62 feet, draught 18 feet.

A common type from the Second World War is the L.S.M. (Landing Ship Medium) of 1,095 tons fully loaded (721). A French L.C.T. (Landing Craft Tank) built in 1957 (722) has the following dimensions: length 187 feet, width 38·7 feet, draught 4·5 feet, fully loaded displacement 642 tons. The small L.C.U.s (Landing Craft Utility) are in the main as during the war, 118 feet long and fully loaded displacing 360 tons (719).

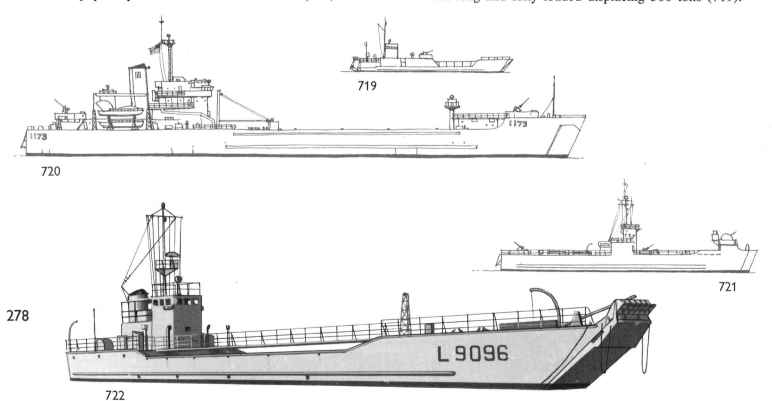

719

720

721

722

L 9096

723

724

Coastal vessels

Various countries had begun to build smaller, heavily armed vessels for coastal defence as early as the 1870's, and according to their construction they were called gunboats or armed coastal vessels.

The Finnish armed coastal defence ship *Väinämöinen* (723) was launched in 1930 and had the following dimensions: length 305 feet, width 55·5 feet, draught 14·7 feet, displacement 3,900 tons. The protective plating around the turrets was 4½-inch and at the waterline 2¼-inch. She was armed with four 10-inch guns, eight 105 mm, four 40 mm and six 20 mm anti-aircraft guns. The speed was 15½ knots and she had a crew of 329.

During the Second World War Britain built two so-called monitors for coastal defence. They looked more like bobtailed cruisers than anything else. The *Abercrombie* (724) had the following dimensions: length 373·3 feet, width 89·7 feet, draught 11 feet. She was armed with two 15-inch, eight 4-inch and twelve 2-pounder guns and twenty 20 mm anti-aircraft guns. Her speed was about 12 knots. — Towards the end of the war a series of small wooden anti-submarine craft (726)

was built for France in the United States. They were 110·9 feet long, 17 feet wide, had a draught of 6·5 feet and a displacement of 110 tons. The armament consisted of one 40 mm and three 20 mm anti-aircraft guns and two depth charge mortars. Their speed was 15 knots and they carried a crew of 25.

Under construction in Sweden at present is a vessel of new type, an armoured motor gunboat (725) of about 100 tons, armed with 75 and 40 mm guns and probably with guided missiles for surface targets as well.

There are of course many other different types of vessels in service in the navies of today that are not shown here. There are, for instance, special craft for the laying of submarine nets, parent ships for submarines and almost every conceivable type of smaller craft, floating hangars for seaplanes, repair and depot craft, troop transports, tankers, icebreakers, tugs, hospital ships, various sorts of life boats and cargo vessels. — In many cases these do not differ so much from their civil equivalents, in others they are so modified that it is not yet possible to discern any clear types. Countries are consciously arming under the supposition that the next war, if it comes, will be fought in the air. The future importance of the surface vessel still remains to be seen.

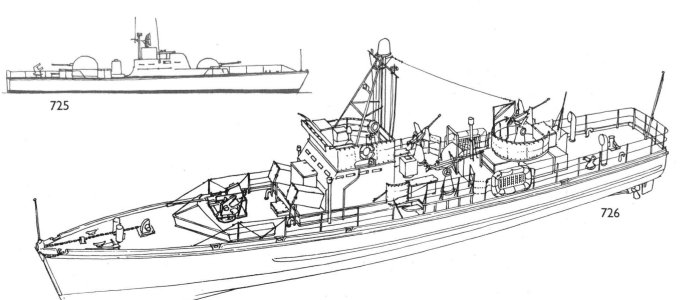

725

726

727

The Oceanic, 1871

The *Great Eastern* had been the very expensive and unsuccessful experiment of a gifted man, and the vessels closest in her wake were more carefully proportioned. The days of sailing were not quite yet over and many details of the sailing-ship were still retained on even the newest steamships. And for that matter the time was not quite ripe for abandoning the sail completely:

The passenger ship *Oceanic* (727) which was put into traffic on the Transatlantic line in 1871 was a revolutionary vessel in many respects. Earlier passenger steamers had lounges and the better cabins in small wooden deckhouses, but the *Oceanic* had a new deck and the lounges extended under it right out to the sides of the ship. The cabins were placed fore and aft of the lounges and were better lighted and ventilated than on any ship

before. The earlier bulwarks had been done away with and replaced by an iron railing which did not hinder water from running off in stormy weather. The dimensions of the *Oceanic* were: length 420 feet, width only 41 feet, draught 31 feet.

The City of Paris, 1888

The sister ships the *City of Paris* and the *City of New York* were the first Transatlantic steamers to be driven by two propellers. They were built of steel, and the *City of Paris* (728) which was launched in 1888 had the following dimensions: length 560 feet, width 63·2 feet, moulded depth 41·9 feet. Her gross tonnage was 10,499 tons and displacement 14,500 tons.

Tonnage

The tonnage of a vessel is expressed in many ways. For warships it is usually given in *tons displacement* which

729

728

is the weight of water displaced by the vessel (exactly the same as the weight of the vessel itself). — *Tons gross* indicate the total volume of a ship, and such a "ton" is equivalent to 100 cu. feet. This is the usual way of stating the size of a passenger ship. — *Tons net* express the volume of the cargo space after the space for engines, crew and navigation has been subtracted from the gross tonnage. — *Tons deadweight* is once again a measure of weight and expresses the amount of cargo a vessel can carry.

The Mauretania, 1906

In 1899 a ship which was longer than the *Great Eastern* was built. This was the second *Oceanic* of the following dimensions: length 704 feet, width 68·4 feet, depth 49 feet. The gross tonnage was 17,040 tons and the displacement 28,500 tons. People were no longer afraid of large vessels, and as the machinery was now more or less relied on no sails were carried.

The construction of the sister ships the *Mauretania* and the *Lusitania* was begun in 1904. The *Mauretania* (729) was to be the most fortunate and successful passenger ship of all. She was launched in 1906 and was ready for service by the following year. Her dimensions were as follows: length 790 feet, width 88 feet, draught 36·2 feet, gross tonnage 37,938 tons. — She had seven decks amidships and in all fifteen bulkheads and 175 watertight compartments. Her 70,000 H.P. turbine engines with their four propellers gave her a speed of 27·4 knots. She won the so-called Transatlantic blue ribbon from the German steamer *Kaiser Wilhelm II* and held it for 22 years until the *Bremen* rewon it for Germany in 1929.

She could accommodate 560 passengers 1st class, 475 2nd class and 1,300 3rd class. Her total crew was 812 officers and men.

The Normandie, 1932

In the period between the two World Wars, before the existence of the Transatlantic airlines, the most important items in the competition between the Transatlantic passenger shipping companies were luxury and speed. In the long run luxury cost the companies much less than speed.

The French Atlantic giant *Normandie* (731), launched in 1932, was of 86,496 tons gross and required a 160,000 H.P. engine to reach a new record with an average speed of 31·3 knots. Her dimensions were: length 1,029 feet, (the first ship over the 1,000 mark), width 117·8 feet, draught 36·6 feet. She had eleven decks and her three accommodation classes could take a total of 2,170 passengers. She had a crew of 1,320.

The Queen Mary, 1934

The *Queen Mary* (730, 733) was launched in Scotland in September 1934, and together with her sister ship the *Queen Elizabeth* of 1938 she still covers the route Southampton—New York. Her dimensions are: length 1,019·5 feet, width 118·7 feet, draught 39·6 feet, gross tonnage 81,235 tons. She has twelve decks. The numbers in the section indicate: 1. Sport deck. 2. Sun deck. 3. Promenade deck. 4. Main deck. 5. A deck. 6. B deck. 7. C deck. 8. D deck. — The 1st class can accommodate 776 passengers, the tourist class 784 and the 3rd class 579, making a total of 1,939. She has a crew of 1,101. Her 160,000 H.P. turbine engines brought the average speed of her record crossing up to 31.7 knots.

Both the *Queen Elizabeth* and the *Queen Mary* served as troop transports during the war, the *Queen Elizabeth* making her first real maiden voyage as a passenger liner in 1946. As her bow leans a little further out over the water than that of her sister ship she is the largest mercantile vessel in the world today with a length of 1,031 feet and a gross tonnage of 83,673 tons. Her engines of 181,700 H.P. have not yet been used for a greater average speed than 28 knots.

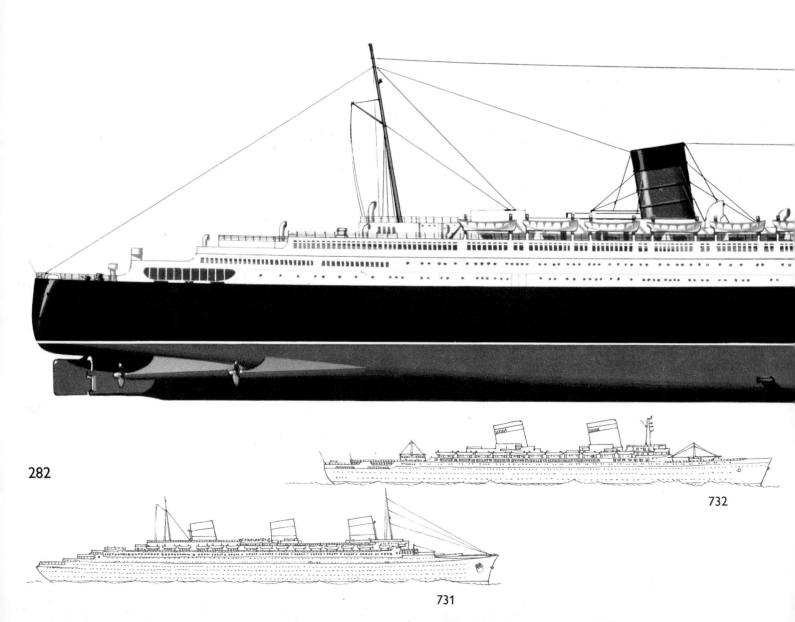

282

732

731

The United States, 1951

It was only after the war that the United States first built a vessel large and strong enough to take part in the fight for the blue ribbon. The keel of the *United States* (732) was laid in February 1950 and on her maiden voyage in the summer of 1952 she won the coveted symbolic ribbon with an average speed of 34·48 knots. Her dimensions are: length 990 feet, width 101·5 feet, depth (from the top of the funnel to the keel) 175 feet, gross tonnage 53,329 tons.

She cost $72 million, has accommodation for a total of 2,008 passengers and for a crew of 1,093. She is easily convertible to a troop transport, then being able to carry a whole division. She is air-conditioned throughout and a novelty is that nearly all her superstructure is made of aluminium. Her 165,000 H.P. engines ought to be able to give her a speed of about 36 knots, but her normal speed is only about 30.

733

734

The Rotterdam, 1958

Those who today wish to cross the Atlantic quickly choose to go by air, and the new passenger liners which are built for the Transatlantic route try no longer to compete for speed, offering relaxation in much luxury and comfort instead. Atlantic giants larger than ever are under construction, yet the elegant passenger ship launched in Holland in 1958 is perhaps not enormous by modern standards.

Nevertheless the *Rotterdam* (734) is considerably larger than the *Great Eastern*. She is 748 feet long, 94 feet wide and has a gross tonnage of 38,645 tons — thus shorter and more roomy than the *Mauretania* of 1906. She differs from all previous large liners in having no funnel. The turbine engines, which are situated in the stern to give more passenger space amidships, develop only 35,000 H.P. (as opposed to *Mauretania's* 70,000), giving her a normal speed of about 20 knots.

She has twelve decks and accommodation for 1,456 passengers. Normally she carries 647 passengers in the 1st class and 809 in the 2nd. The *Rotterdam* has no 3rd class. She has a crew of 776 officers and men. Like all newly-built Transatlantic passenger liners she is fully air-conditioned. A further novelty is that she carries no fresh water, distilling it instead from seawater in three evaporators with a capacity of 700 tons per day.

The Santa Rosa, 1958

The *Santa Rosa* (735), launched in the United States in 1958, is a combination of passenger and cargo liner and covers the route from New York to the west coast of S. America via the Panama Canal. She has accommodation for 300 passengers, all 1st class, and the lounges and cabins occupy three decks. She has a crew of 246.

Her dimensions are: length 583·5 feet, width 84 feet, draught 26 feet, displacement 19,364 tons, gross tonnage 15,366 tons. Her 20,000 H.P. engines give her a normal speed of 20 knots. She has a cargo capacity of 337,000 cu. feet as well as refrigeration space of 81,000 cu. feet.

735

736   Postal and passenger motor vessel *Kronprins Frederik* on the route Esbjerg—Harwich was built before the war, is of 3,895 tons gross and does 20½ knots.

737   The Fishguard—Cork cross channel ship *Leinster* which can take 2,600 passengers on her daily crossings. She is of 2,600 tons gross and does over 20 knots.

Passenger vessels

On these two pages we see medium-sized passenger vessels from different parts of the world. Some are ultra-modern, others are from the period before the Second World War. The Finnish ship *Bore III* (739) which runs between Stockholm and Turku (or Helsinki) has the following dimensions: length 298·5 feet, width 46·5 feet, draught 16·4 feet. She accommodates 63 passengers 1st class, 185 tourist class and 169 on deck. The bows are reinforced and shaped so that she can break through moderate ice. The numbers indicate: 1. A deck. 2. Fan room under the boat deck. 3. Deck lounge. 4. Radio room. 5. Boat deck. 6. Officers' accommodation. 7. Lifeboat for 50 passengers. 8. Owner's private accommodation built into the funnel housing. 9. Cabins for the long-distance pilots. 10. Room for the radar and gyro compass. 11. Chart room. 12. Radio direction finding aerial. 13. Radar aerial. 14. Captain's cabin. 15. Bridge. 16. Forecastle deck. 17. Tourist café. 18. 1st class dining room. 19. 1st class smoking lounge and bar.

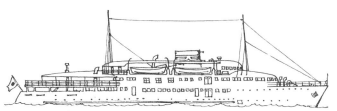

738   The streamlined, diesel-propelled *Sirogane Maru* was built in 1939 for traffic between the Japanese islands.

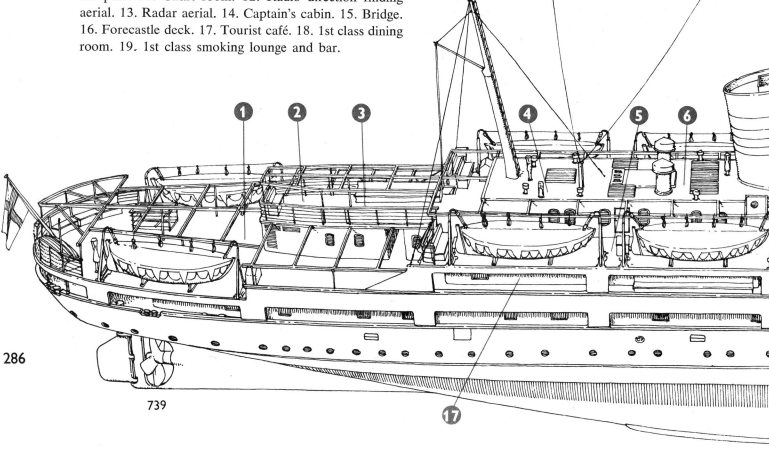

739

740 The train ferry *Trelleborg* began on the route Trelleborg—Sassnitz in 1958. She is of 6,476 tons gross, takes 40 railway carriages, 30 cars and 1,500 passengers.

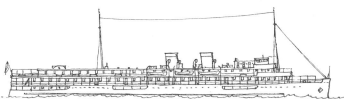

741 A shallow-draught motor vessel from Rio de la Plata capable of running in both coastal and river traffic.

742 The 1958 car ferry *Compiègne* runs between Calais and Dover. It is of 3,473 tons gross, has space for 164 cars, about 1,000 passengers and does 20 knots.

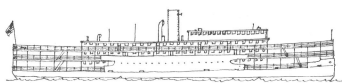

743 A steamer of 1,700 tons from the Hudson River. — During the last few years fast hydrofoil craft (744) have begun to compete with the conventional vessels.

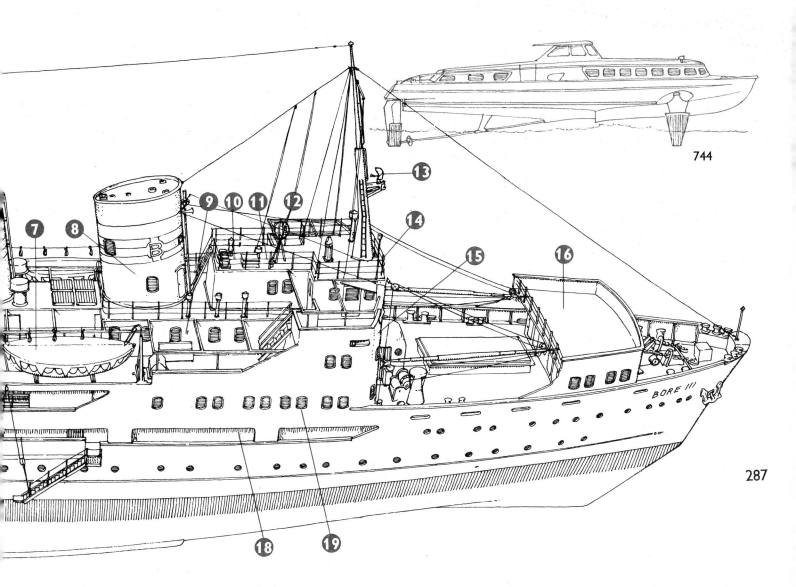

744

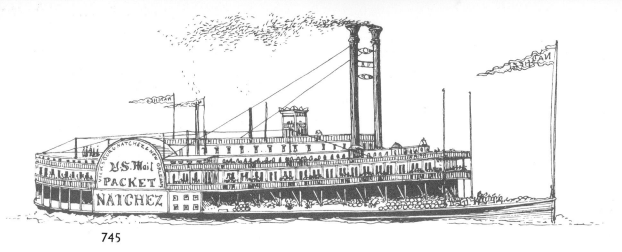

745

Paddle steamers on the Mississippi

Paddle steamers had already begun to dissappear from the seas by the middle of the nineteenth century, outclassed by the more efficient, propeller-driven vessels, and yet they are still in use today on rivers, shallow inland waters and in shallow harbours where the conventional type of propeller with its need for depth of water is unsuitable.

The type of paddle wheeler which has become more well-known than any other is the Mississippi steamer — long and low with a high superstructure of three or four storeys, often with carved pillars and balustrades, a wheelhouse sometimes decorated to pagoda-like lengths, two long funnels splayed at the top and of course the splashing paddle wheels; this was how Mark Twain saw her, and this is how many generations of Americans have seen her and still see her today.

The first steamer for traffic on the river was built as early as 1811. This was the *New Orleans,* but she was not strong enough to make the return journey upstream. The *George Washington* was built five years later with paddle wheel in the stern, two funnels and two decks. She was to become the model for the more than five thousand steamers which have been built since then for traffic on the Mississippi.

The stern-wheeler was for a long time the ugly duckling of the Mississippi, the swans being the large, fast

746

side-wheelers with a paddle wheel on each side. The captains of these side-wheelers called the others "wheelbarrows". Up to the middle of the nineteenth century the boilers were fired with wood, then came a transitional period when both wood and coal were used, and by about 1880 the wood was dropped. In order to increase the speed of the large, competitive dandies high-pressure boilers were soon brought into use, but as the materials were not yet of the best quality many serious accidents occurred when boilers exploded and caused fires on board.

One of the largest and most elegant of the side-wheelers was the *Natchez* (745) which in 1870 lost the great race for the title "the fastest boat on the river" (and by this was meant the fastest boat in the world) to the *Robert E. Lee*. She was 307 feet long and 43 feet wide. The *Robert E. Lee* made the journey New Orleans —St Louis in 3 days, 18 hours and 14 minutes.

Stern-wheelers were from the very beginning more economical to run, and when steel boilers started to appear, making it possible to raise the pressure without much risk, they even attained satisfactory speeds. By the time the railroads had established themselves the reign of the elegant side-wheelers came to an end and the golden age of the stern-wheeler began. The wooden *Chaperon* (746) was built in upper Ohio in 1884. Like Pharaoh Sahure's and Queen Hatshepsut's ships (cf. 24, 33) the long low hulls of the *Chaperon* and all other Mississippi steamers were strengthened fore-and-aft with sturdy supporting trusses stretched over spars. Her dimensions were: length 121 feet, width 27 feet, draught 4 feet. Her machinery normally turned the wheel 20 times per minute, but there is no information as to her speed.

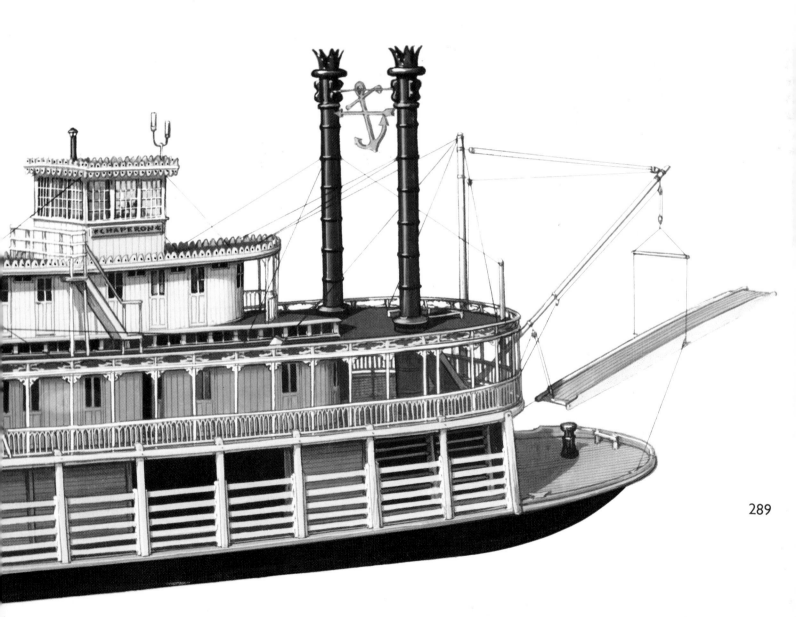

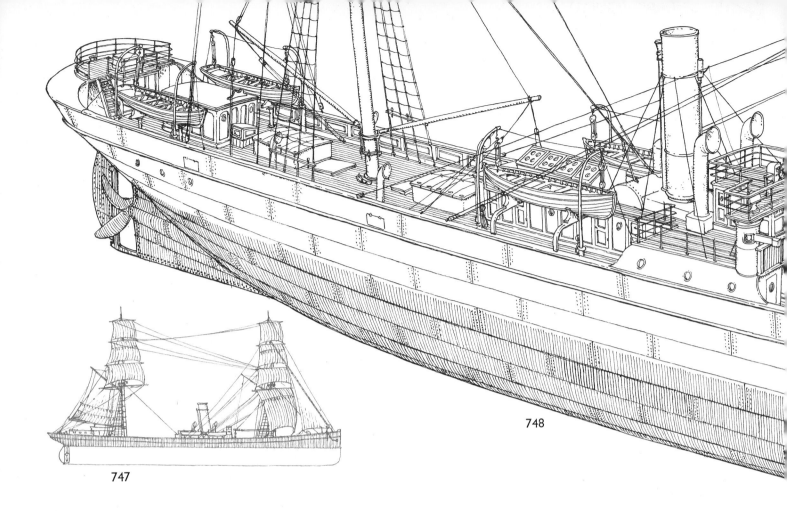

748

747

The cargo ship

Cargo ships are usually classified according to their main duty and use but it is also possible to differentiate them into types by various details of appearance and construction. The *flush-decked* type (747) is the oldest where the deck runs unbroken from fore to aft as on many nineteenth century sailing-ships. The bridge and wheelboxes amidships seem to have been common about the middle of the nineteenth century, and it is possible that the bridge which joined the wheelboxes (cf. 588) was an important link in the development.

Early on, when the steering wheel was positioned furthest aft and it could happen that both wheel and helmsman were washed overboard, a small poop deck was constructed to raise both man and wheel to a safer level. It was found practical to build an anchor deck in

the bow which was later to grow into a forecastle. The light bridge gradually became a platform connected to the vessel by a wide deckhouse which acted as a breakwater in heavy weather. The schooner-rigged steamer *Iberia* of 1881 (748, 749) had the following dimensions: length 254·6 feet, width 36 feet, depth 19·5 feet, gross tonnage 1,331 tons.

As it was shown that ships which carried a homogeneous cargo went too deep in the bow, vessels were constructed with a *raised quarter-deck* (750) making it possible for more cargo to be placed in the stern. The officers and any passengers would be accommodated in the deckhouse amidships, the crew quarters being in the fo'c'sle. Vessels on which the half deck had been extended forward were called *well-decked* (751). This well deck, however, which was situated between the fo'c'sle and the half deck, when swamped could retain the water so long that the stability of the vessel was endangered. Because of this the half deck and fo'c'sle deck were

290

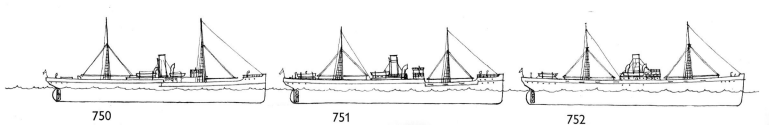

750   751   752

749

IBERIA

753

joined into a single deck called the *hurricane deck* (752), completing the cycle to the flush-decked ship although now the height of the deck above water made the vessel safer.

On certain vessels the poop was joined to the bridge, these being called *long poopers* (754), which in reality were almost well-deckers (751). A *shelter deck* vessel (755) has a lighter, protective deck above the main deck. The hatches of the shelter deck may not be battened down and the space between the two decks is considered to belong to the superstructure and is not included in the tonnage. If the shelter deck is made of more sturdy construction and the hatches are battened down the ship is then referred to as a *closed shelter-deck vessel* (756) and the whole of the space under this shelter deck is included in the tonnage.

Many vessels which have their machinery furthest aft are built without a bridge, having only one long poop and a fo'c'sle above deck. Smaller tankers and coastal vessels (753), especially, are of this type.

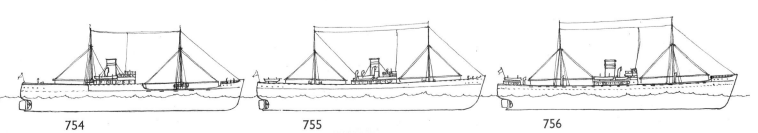

754   755   756

Cargo liners

A vessel is said to be a *tramp* when it does not run a regular line between definite ports but takes on transport duties where they are offered. Tramping has become less profitable since the war and the majority of the world's cargo vessels are now liners. Seventy-five years of development have taken place between the *Iberia* (748) and the Swedish *Rio de Janeiro* (757) which plies the route Sweden—S. America.

The *Rio de Janeiro* has three decks, a poop and a long, high fo'c'sle. The hull is all-welded and fitted with

The French vessel *Magellan* (758) of 9,600 tons dead weight and 7,200 tons gross for work in the S. Pacific has the following dimensions: length 490·5 feet, width 61·7 feet, draught 26·9 feet. Her diesel engines give her a speed of 16 knots. She carries a crew of 57 and has accommodation for twelve passengers.

The German *Santa Inés* (759) on the Hamburg — S. America route measures: length 479 feet, width 61 feet, fully loaded draught 28 feet and is of 11,710 tons deadweight. The 4,000 H.P. diesel engines give her a speed of 13 knots. She can accommodate 28 passengers and has a crew of 54.

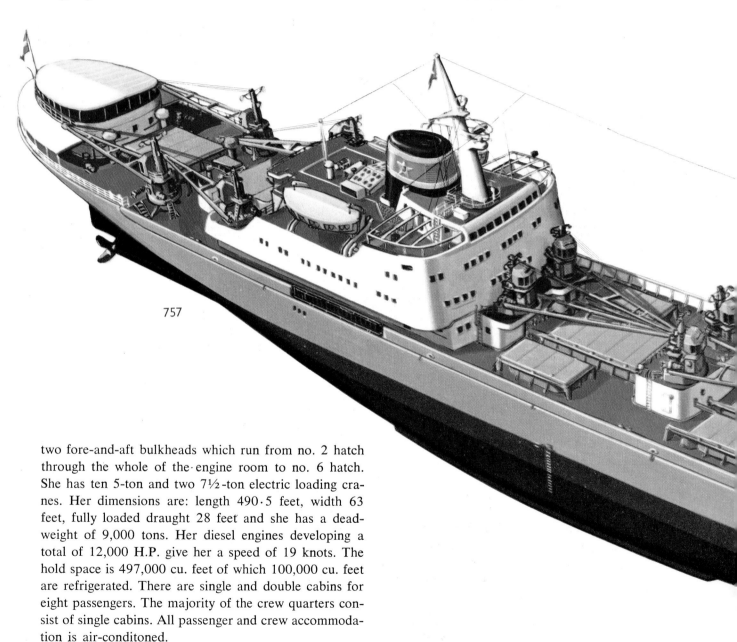

757

two fore-and-aft bulkheads which run from no. 2 hatch through the whole of the engine room to no. 6 hatch. She has ten 5-ton and two 7½-ton electric loading cranes. Her dimensions are: length 490·5 feet, width 63 feet, fully loaded draught 28 feet and she has a dead-weight of 9,000 tons. Her diesel engines developing a total of 12,000 H.P. give her a speed of 19 knots. The hold space is 497,000 cu. feet of which 100,000 cu. feet are refrigerated. There are single and double cabins for eight passengers. The majority of the crew quarters consist of single cabins. All passenger and crew accommodation is air-conditoned.

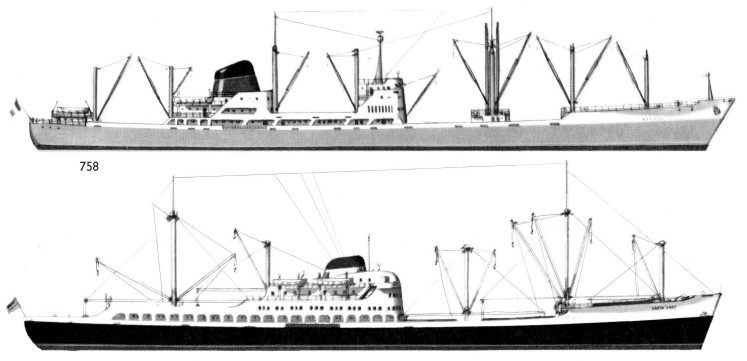

758

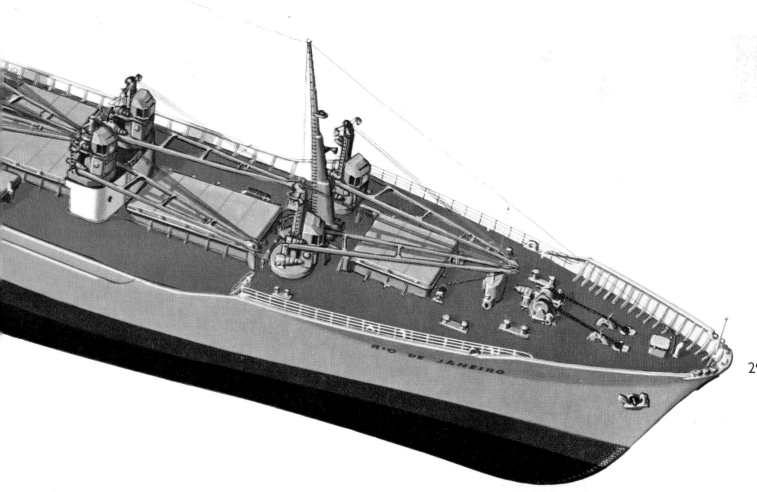

759

293

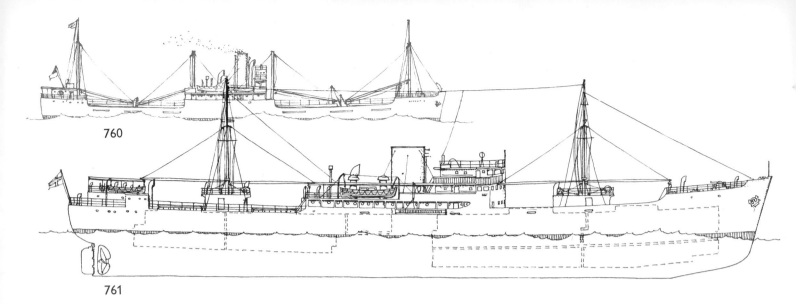

760

761

Cargo vessels

A freighter which has fo'c'sle, bridge and poop is called a *three island vessel* (760, 762). The name has come about because the three superstructures look like three islands when the lower part of the hull is hidden behind the horizon. A common type that does both line and tramp freighting is the 6,000 tonner illustrated (762) where the numbers indicate: 1. Poop deck with warping capstan. 2. Deckhouse with crew mess. The poop contains rudder machinery and crew quarters. 3. No. 4 hatch open. 4. No. 3 hatch with beams. 5. No. 2 hatch with hatch covers fastened down with a tarpaulin and iron battens. 6. No. 1 hatch with covers. 7. Boat deck. The deck below this is called the bridge deck. 8. Skylight to the engine room. 9. Bridge with wheel and navigation houses. 10. Captain's cabin. 11. Fo'c'sle deck with windlass. 12. Mainmast. 13. Five-ton cargo boom. 14. Maintop. 15. Foremast. 16. Thirty-ton cargo boom. 17. Foretop.

The vessels which run on the timber routes between Scandinavia and most often British ports are generally of the *three island* type (760). The masts and cargo booms are situated on top of the superstructure to give all possible space to the deck cargo.

On *refrigerator vessels* which are intended for the transport of meat, fruit, fish and dairy products, the holds are wholly or partly equipped as refrigerators.

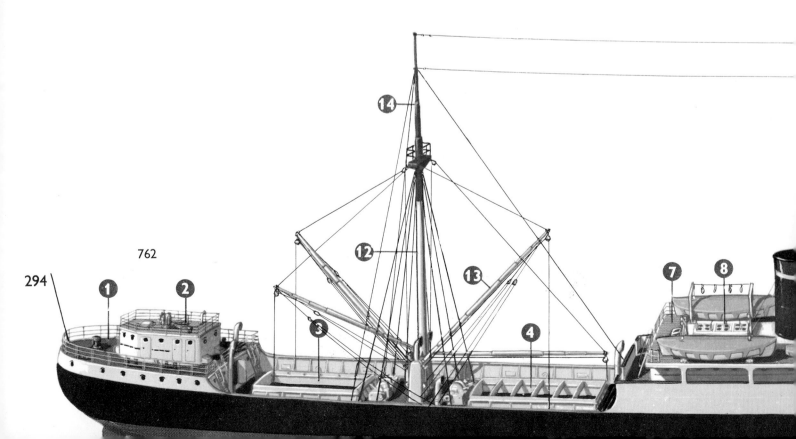

762

294

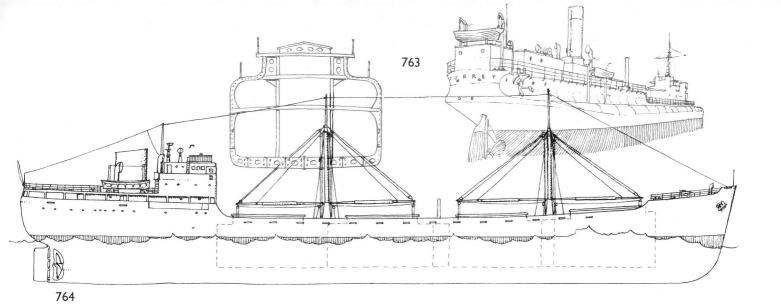

763

764

They are generally fast vessels, and because the holds are not very deep and the expensive insulating material can easily be damaged they seldom take other cargoes than those they are intended for. The refrigerator vessel portrayed (761) carries citrus fruits. It is 315 feet long, 45 feet wide, and the diesel engines give it a speed of 16 knots.

Bulk cargo is homogeneous and unpacked such as coal, ore and grain. As such cargo is both heavy and can easily shift to one side special types of vessel have long been constructed for the purpose. The ship *Turret* (763) was built in 1892 and gave its name to the whole family of such vessels. A *turret vessel* or *turret-decked vessel* has sides which first sweep inwards to form a side deck and then pass upwards to the narrow deck

proper where all hatches, ladderways and ventilators are situated. Turret vessels were mainly intended for carrying ore, and the advantage of the construction was that it combined the necessary hold volume with a high deck and yet relatively small gross tonnage.

Turret vessels are no longer built, but related to them are the *trunk-decked* vessels (765) which are used for the transport of oil and grain.

The British *Thackeray* of 6,600 tons gross (764) is a modern bulk cargo vessel. The engines and the whole of the crew quarters are situated in the stern. Under the four holds there are large tanks for water ballast.

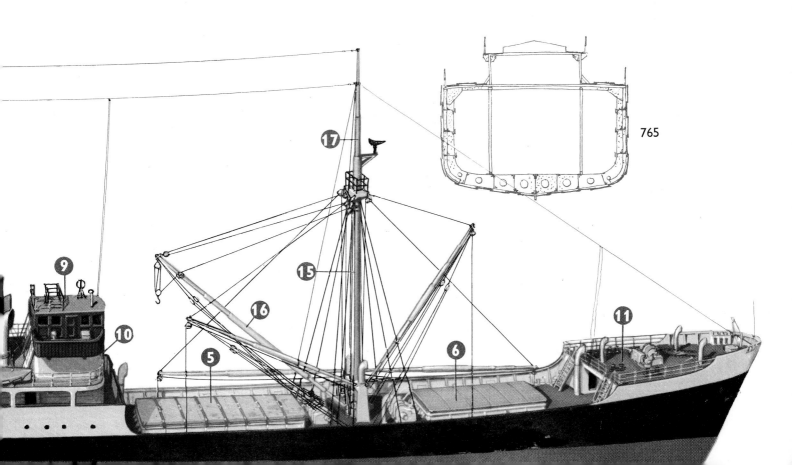

765

766

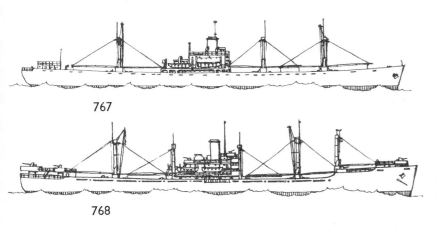

767

768

Standard U. S. ships

In order to replace the shipping losses suffered by the Allies at the beginning of the Second World War the United States began to build large series of a cargo vessel of about 7,000 tons gross, the so-called *liberty ships* (767). They were of very simple design, facilitating serial construction, and their dimensions were: length 441·5

feet, width 57 feet, draught 26·5 feet. The 2,500 H.P. steam engines gave them a speed fully loaded of 11 knots. All in all about 2,600 liberty ships were built, the superstructure varying somewhat with the different duties.

Towards the end of the war the so-called *victory ships* (768) began to be built. They were of 7,500—8,500 tons gross and had the following dimensions: length 455 feet, width 61·5 feet, draught 27·6 feet. They were stronger and faster than the liberty ships, and during the years 1943—45 a total of 531 were built. One type had 6,000 H.P. turbine engines which gave a speed of 15½ knots and another 8,500 H.P. engines which brought the speed up to 16½ knots.

After the war the United States set up a gigantic constructional programme in which it was planned that all possible vessel types were to be built in standardised series. The ships in the new merchant navy were to be faster and to have better cargo space than before, and two variations were planned for each type: a normal type with the usual first-class fittings and a wartime type with a minimum of fittings and crew, without passenger accommodation and easy to arm and fit with protective plating.

769

A standard vessel of type C3-S-A2 (766) has the following dimensions: length 465·3 feet, width 69·6 feet, draught 33 feet, gross tonnage 7,940 tons, dead weight 12,470 tons. The 9,350 H.P. turbines give a speed of 17 knots.

Bulk cargo vessels on the Great Lakes

The earlier transport of grain and ore on the Great Lakes of N. America was carried out by so-called *whalebacks* (770) on which the juncture between the sides and deck was rounded like the back of a whale. It had been thought that such vessels would be stronger and more seaworthy than the more common types, but it proved that the heavily laden whalebacks were easily swamped by waves which caused damage to the superstructure.

A modern ore freighter from the Great Lakes (769) can have the following dimensions: length 618·7 feet, width 61 feet, draught 24 feet. About 80 % of the total length is taken up by four holds with many broad hatches. The engines are situated in the stern and the bridge in the bow. In order that the helmsman may more easily see in which direction the vessel is turning, a steering pole has been rigged up like a sort of bowsprit.

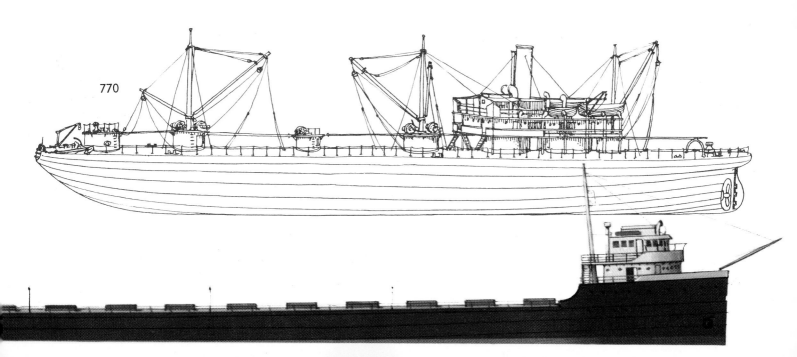

770

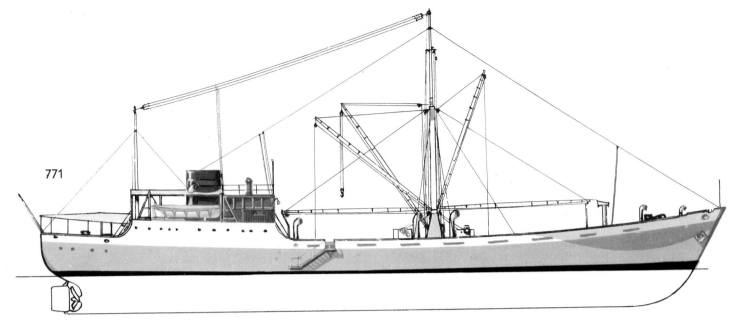

771

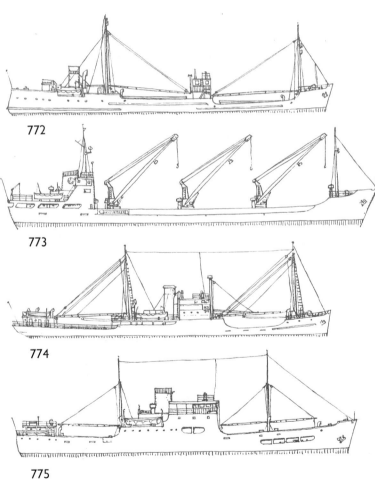

772

773

774

775

776

Small craft

Hundreds of different types of small freighters are to be found along the coasts of the world and on its inland seas, lakes and rivers. Since the war many of the small coastal vessels have disappeared as they have no longer been found to be economical. A modern European coastal vessel of the traditional type (771) might have the following dimensions: length 188·6 feet, width 29·9 feet, draught 11·5 feet, dead weight 680 tons.

A British coastal vessel from the 1930's (772) has its engine in the stern but the bridge is situated at the forward edge of the long poop. A modern Swedish bulk cargo vessel of 1,055 tons deadweight (773) has an open shelter deck and three electric-hydraulic 3-ton cranes. The 960 H.P. diesel engine gives her a speed of 12 knots. In the waters around Australia and New Zealand there are steamers with a raised half deck (774) built for the transport of sundries. They are of about 1,000 tons deadweight and do 12 knots. The merchant vessel from the Caribbean (775) ought to be looked on as a well-decker with a bridge and open shade deck above the well deck.

The paddle steamers on the Rhine and other European rivers have begun to be replaced with vessels driven by Voith-Schneider propellers (776) which rotate around a vertical shaft and by means of their adjustable blades function as a rudder at the same time. The propeller was invented by Ernst Schneider, a German, and from 1926 onwards was developed by J.M. Voith.

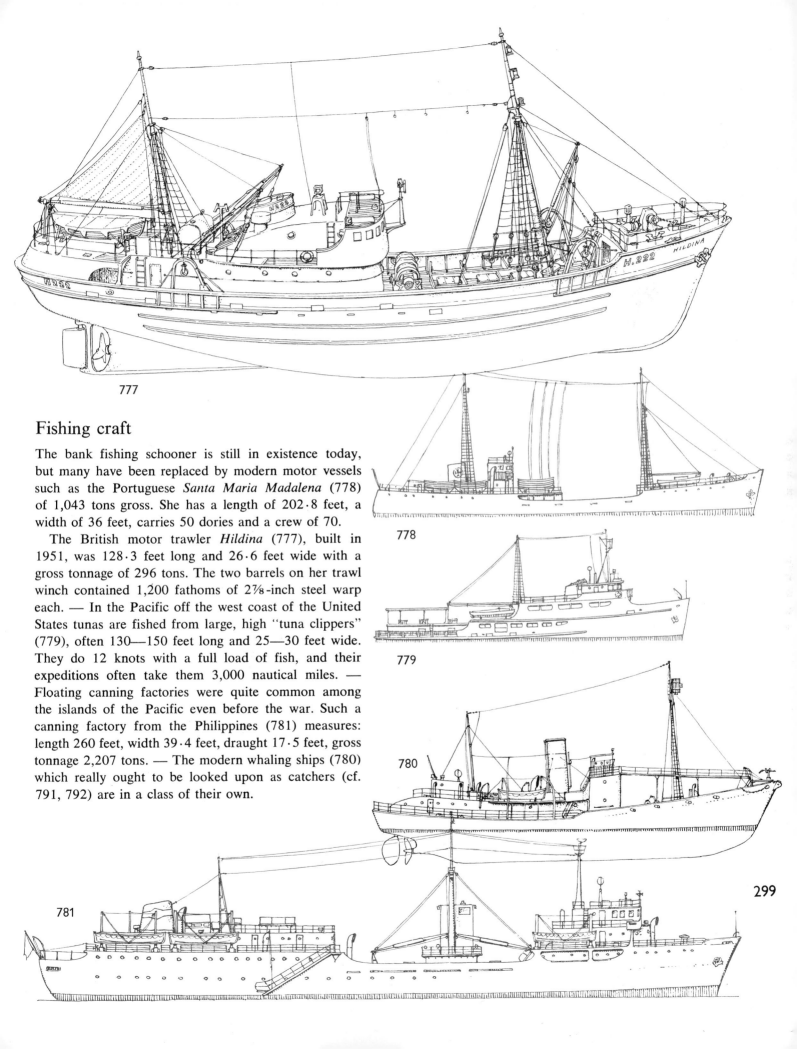

Fishing craft

The bank fishing schooner is still in existence today, but many have been replaced by modern motor vessels such as the Portuguese *Santa Maria Madalena* (778) of 1,043 tons gross. She has a length of 202·8 feet, a width of 36 feet, carries 50 dories and a crew of 70.

The British motor trawler *Hildina* (777), built in 1951, was 128·3 feet long and 26·6 feet wide with a gross tonnage of 296 tons. The two barrels on her trawl winch contained 1,200 fathoms of 2⅞-inch steel warp each. — In the Pacific off the west coast of the United States tunas are fished from large, high "tuna clippers" (779), often 130—150 feet long and 25—30 feet wide. They do 12 knots with a full load of fish, and their expeditions often take them 3,000 nautical miles. — Floating canning factories were quite common among the islands of the Pacific even before the war. Such a canning factory from the Philippines (781) measures: length 260 feet, width 39·4 feet, draught 17·5 feet, gross tonnage 2,207 tons. — The modern whaling ships (780) which really ought to be looked upon as catchers (cf. 791, 792) are in a class of their own.

777

778

779

780

781

782

783

300

784

Tankers

It is possible that the Chinese were the first to build tankers. It is known that in the eighteenth century they carried oil in junks which were about 55 feet long, 13 feet wide and had a hold capacity of 50 tons. Sailing tankers began to appear in Europe during the 1860's, the first steam tanker was built during the 70's and in 1886 the prototype of the modern tanker, the S.S. *Glückauf* (782), was built in Britain for a German company. She was of 2,307 tons gross, 300·5 feet long and 37·2 feet wide, had the engine in the stern and a long poop. The hold space was divided fore-and-aft with a bulkhead in the centre line and transverse bulkheads further divided the space into eight tanks. They were separated from the coal bunkers and the engines by the pump room which also served as a cofferdam, and above them was a long trunk to allow for the expansion of the oil.

Tankers of 16,000 tons deadweight were built before 1914, and in 1921 the United States built the *William Rockefeller* of 22,600 tons deadweight and 14,054 tons gross (783). She was 572·5 feet long, 75 feet wide and had a speed of 10·3 knots.

These supertankers were exceptions however. In the period between the wars large tankers were usually of 10,000—15,000 tons deadweight and their speed was seldom more than 11 knots. It was only after 1945 when the world demand for oil had become even greater that full steam was applied and ships of a size before undreamed of were built. In 1950 the *Velutina* of 28,000 tons deadweight was launched, and three years later the *Tina Onassis* (784) of 45,750 tons deadweight and 25,101 tons gross. She is 775 feet long, 95 feet wide and has a draught of 37·5 feet when fully loaded. Her 17,000 H.P. turbines give her a speed of 16½ knots.

The supertanker *W. Alton Jones* (785) was launched in 1959. Her dimensions are: length 824·6 feet, width 116 feet, draught 43 feet, dead weight 68,840 tons. When developing 20,000 H.P. her turbines give her a speed of 16½ knots. The hold space is divided into a total of 51 tanks by three longitudinal and a number of transverse bulkheads. Eight side tanks are for ballast water and six are dry. The cargo oil tanks can contain a total volume of 3 million cu. feet. She has a crew of 60 and can accommodate 4 passengers.

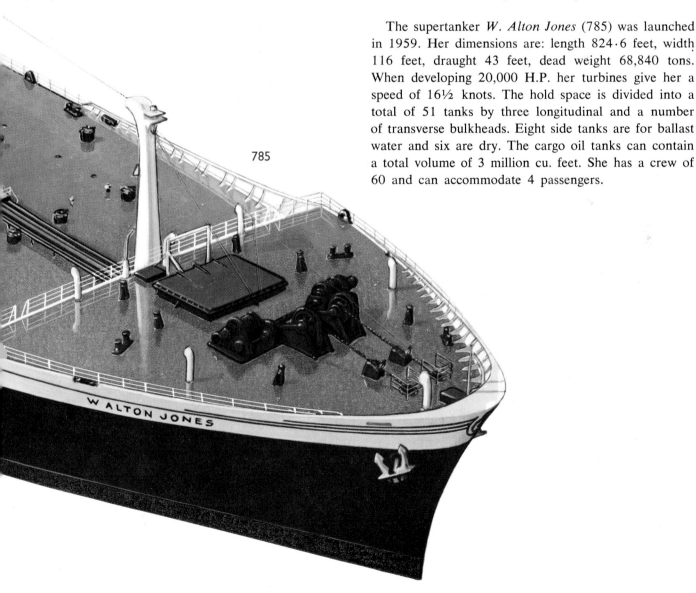

785

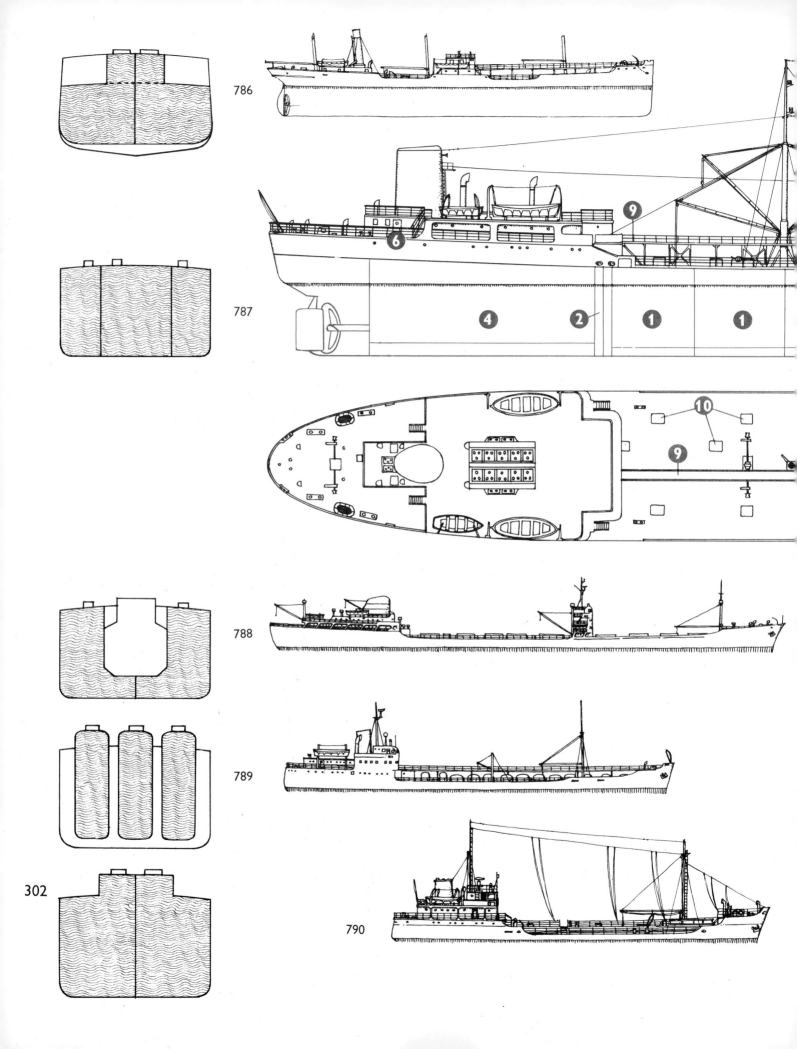

786

787

⑥ ⑨

④ ② ① ①

⑩ ⑨

788

789

302

790

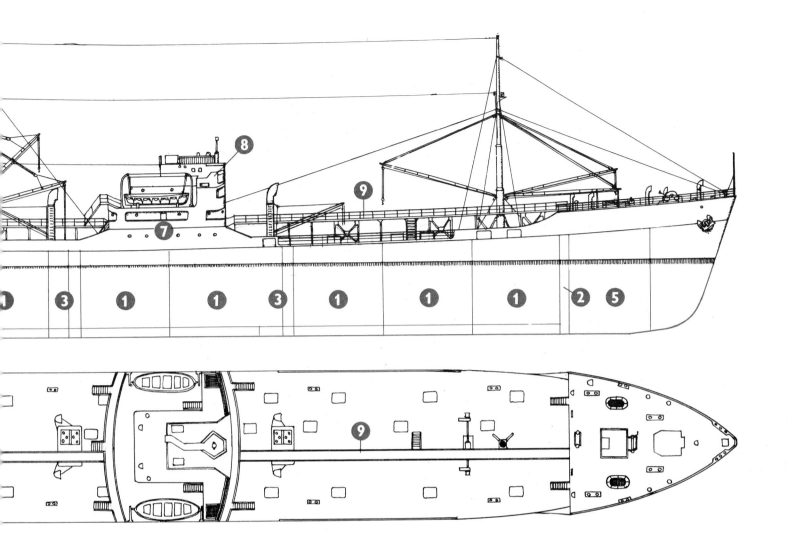

Tankers

The system of tanks which had been introduced with the *Glückauf* in 1886 including an expansion tank in the centre of the vessel is to be seen in the tanker from 1905 (786) and was in principle to be retained for another twenty years. Even the space on both sides of the trunk began to be used as so-called summer tanks where lighter oils were sometimes carried.

Today the hold space of most larger tankers is divided by two longitudinal and a number of transverse bulkheads except on the very largest (785) where there are three longitudinal bulkheads. In the illustration of a modern tanker of about 12,000 tons deadweight (787) the numbers indicate: 1. Oil tanks. 2. Cofferdam which isolates the tanks from the engine room and dry cargo hold. 3. Pump room. 4. Engine room. 5. Dry cargo hold.

6. Poop with crew accommodation. 7. Bridge with officers' accommodation. 8. Navigating bridge. 9. Monkey bridge. 10. Hatches to the cargo oil tanks.

An *ore tanker* (788) is so constructed that it can carry ore in a hold between two longitudinal bulkheads on the outward journey and oil in the tanks on either side of the ore hold on its return. It is usually a large vessel, and the first ore tanker, the *G. Harrison Smith*, was built as early as 1921 and was of 14,305 tons gross.

When transporting chemicals it has not been found advisable to have only a single wall between the tanks, and the ships have therefore been built with wholly insulated tanks (789) with the result that a chemical tanker has only about 54 % of the hold capacity of a normal tanker.

The ordinary type of coastal tanker (790) of 500—600 tons gross has its tanks arranged in principle as on the *Glückauf* with a trunk which decreases the free fluid surface area.

303

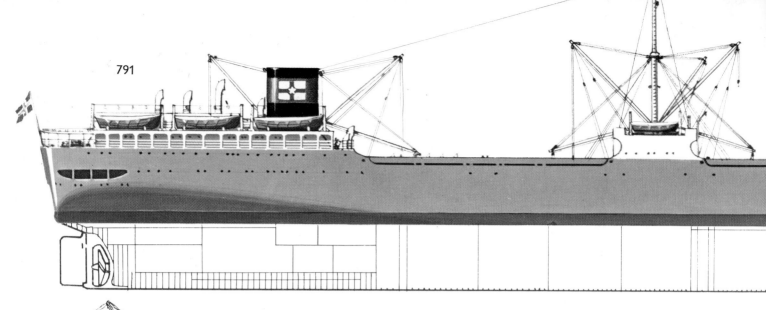

791

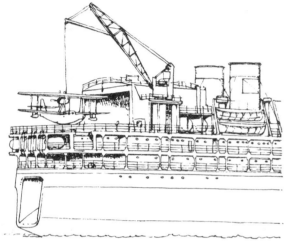

792

Whale-oil factory vessels

Whales are captured with harpoons which are shot from a gun on the small whale catchers (780). The carcasses are hauled up through the stern of the large whale-oil factory vessels onto their flensing decks with winches where they are cut up (791, 792). A modern whale-oil factory vessel is a combination of factory and tanker where the dismembering and utilization of the different parts of the catch are largely carried out by machine. The Norwegian whale-oil factory vessel *Kosmos III* (791) measures: length 638·5 feet, width 78 feet, draught 35 feet, dead weight 25,100 tons. The cargo tanks have a volume of about 1¼ million cu. feet.

Tugs

Roughly speaking it may be said that there are two main types of tug, those for work in ports and those which work out to sea. Within these groups, and even between them, there are naturally a number of local types, as well as types of different size and strength. A modern French sea-going tug (794) built in 1956 is of the traditional European type with deckhouse far forward, towing hook almost amidships and the after deck without superstructure. The displacement is of 1,050 tons, length 175 feet, width 32 feet, draught 14 feet. The 2,500 H.P. engines give a speed of 16 knots.

The New York tugs are quite different from their European sisters. Their duty is most often not to tow but to "push" the Atlantic giants, to "butt" them into the quays, and for this purpose they are fitted with a very large fender in the bow (793). They can be about 80 feet long, 24 feet wide, have a draught of 8 feet and a gross tonnage of 150 tons.

The Voith-Schneider propeller has come into use on harbour tugs of modern type (795, cf. 776). Their measurements are roughly: length 65 feet, width 20·5 feet, draught 9 feet, displacement 95 tons.

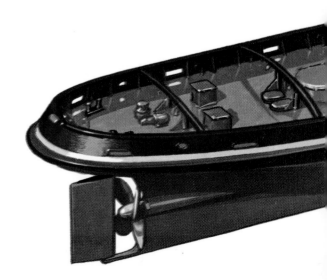

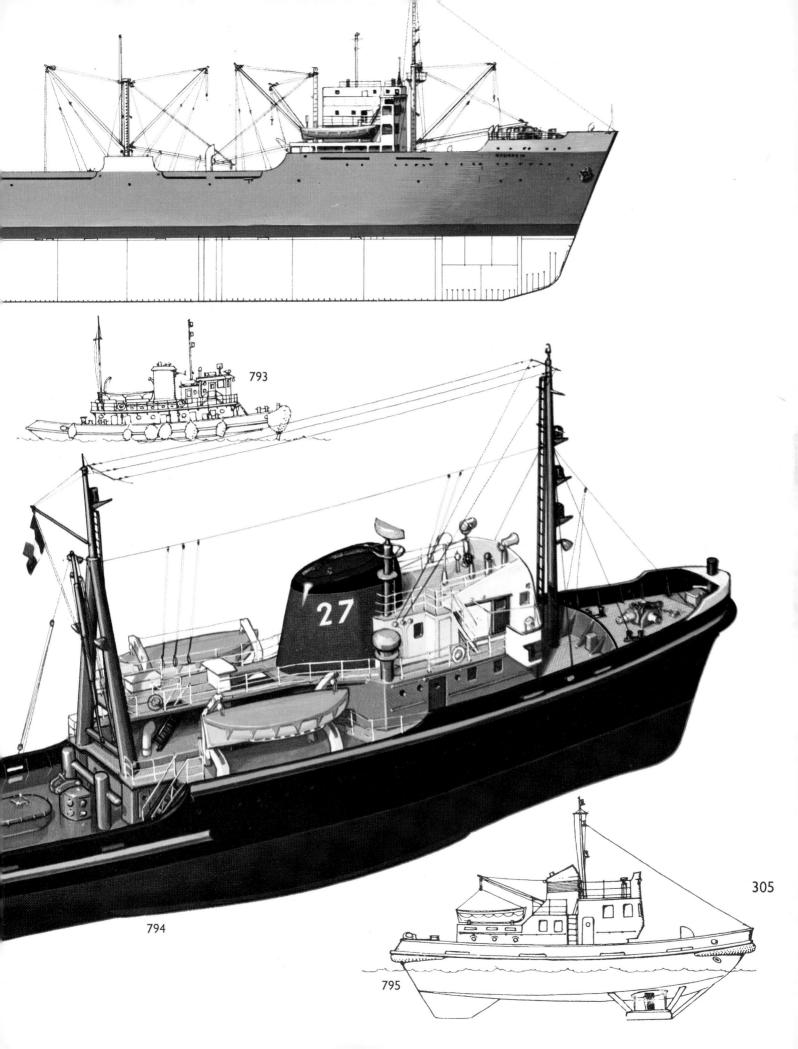

793

794

795

305

796

797

Icebreakers

Vessels which break a path through ice for merchant traffic in waters which are usually icebound during the winter are to be found in such countries as Canada, Denmark, Finland, the U.S.S.R., Sweden and the United States. The first practicable icebreaker appears to have been built in Hamburg in 1871, and the illustrations 798—802 show how the icebreaking bows developed from 1871 to 1924. The propeller in the bow draws the smashed ice aft. Icebreakers intended for operation in the very thick ice of the Arctic such as the Russian 15,000-tonners of the *Moscow* class (803) have no bow propeller. Their engines develop 22,000 H.P. and they are 400·5 feet long, 80·3 feet wide and have a draught of 34·4 feet.

The Finnish icebreaker *Karhu* from 1957 (804) is built to be able to assist merchantmen through relatively narrow, shallow waters and is therefore of moderate dimensions: length 243 feet, greatest width 57 feet, width at the waterline 55 feet, draught 19 feet, displacement 3,370 tons. The engines develop 7,500 H.P. Like the most modern icebreakers the *Karhu* has two stern and two bow propellers. She is fitted with two heeling tanks at the sides, and 100 tons of water can be pumped from the one to the other in 90 seconds so that the vessel heels over and in this way can free herself should the ice hold her. All four propellers can be manoeuvred directly from the bridge, wheelhouse and aft bridge.

Lightships (796) and *pilot vessels* (797) are of such variety around the coasts of the world that the two illustrations ought not to be taken as representative by any means.

306

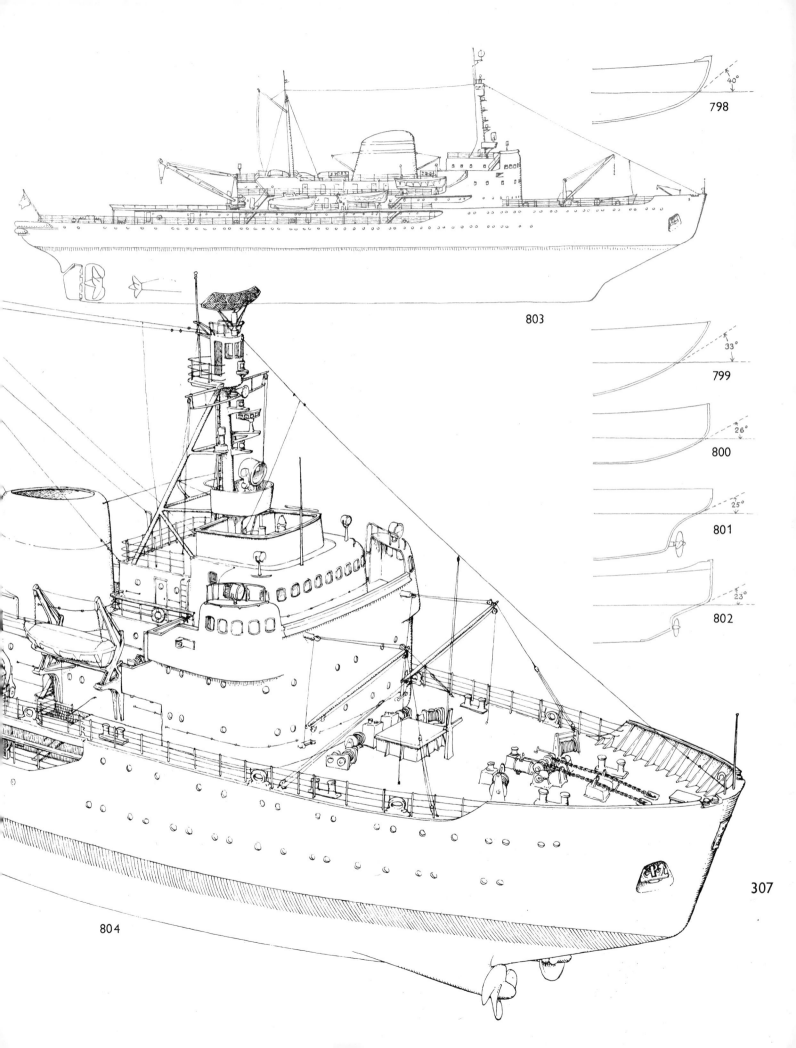

798

803

799

800

801

802

307

804

805

Ships in the Nuclear Age

We are on the threshold of a Nuclear Age. The situation is not so different from that of a little more than a hundred years ago when the first steamships began to ply the oceans. Nuclear-powered engines are in no way perfected, and the vessels which have been built so far with a nuclear reactor as a source of energy are experimental boasts that are highly uneconomical to run. The wise men of the world are agreed that what has been built is only the tiny beginning of great revolutionary development. Significant of the fear and ignorance of people in general towards all that has to do with nuclear power was the little intermezzo a few years ago when a European capital refused to receive a visit by a U.S. nuclear-powered submarine because it was feared that it would expose the public to radiation.

In the U.S.S.R. the nuclear-powered icebreaker *Lenin* has been put into service. She has three reactors, two of which are in use at the same time while the third is in reserve. The nuclear machinery with its protective casing weighs 3,000 tons. The steam turbines which are driven by the heat generated in the reactors develop 44,000 H.P., and in ice-free water the *Lenin* can come up to 18 knots. She is 439·5 feet long, 88·5 feet wide and breaks ice 8 feet thick at a constant speed of two knots.

On 22nd May 1958 the keel of the first nuclear-powered merchantman in the world was laid in New York. She is named *Savannah* after the first ship fitted with a steam engine to cross the Atlantic (cf. 587). This new *Savannah* (806) was launched on 21st July 1959, and when this was written she had not come into service.

806

She is 585·3 feet long, 78 feet wide and has a displacement of 21,840 tons. Her hold capacity is 9,500 tons and she has accommodation for 60 passengers and a crew of 100. In order to eliminate the risk of leakage from the reactor should there be an accident the whole of the reactor housing has been encased in one-foot thick steel. The output of the reactor is 74 megawatts, and the 20,000 H.P. steam turbines give the *Savannah* through her five-bladed propeller a speed of 20½ knots.

It is stated that a single fuelling of the reactor is enough for journeys totalling 300,000 nautical miles, such a distance being normally covered over a period of three years. The *Savannah* has cost $ 41 million. She will never be a profitable concern, but the construction of her machinery has afforded much experience, and among other things she will be used as a training ship for the men who will soon be taking new and more profitable nuclear-powered ships across the seas.

Reed boats, hide boats, rafts and dug-outs still float on the waters of the world. The step from a Brazilian *jangada* (805) to the *Savannah* has perhaps taken more than 6,000 years, and yet it is possible that the jangada will outlive her. The nuclear reactor may not be the last word as a source of energy. Perhaps the ships of the future will be gigantic submarines independent of wind and weather (807) with a retractable conning tower for further streamlining, giving them, more than any vessel before, the appearance of the fish in the sea.

807

Sources

Åkerlund, H., Fartygsfynden i den forna hamnen i Kalmar, Uppsala 1951

Anderson, R. & R. C., The Sailing-Ship, London 1947

Anderson, R. C., The Rigging of Ships in the Days of the Spritsail Topmast, Salem 1947

— Seventeenth Century Rigging, London 1955

Artiñano, G. de, La Arquitectura Naval Española, 1920

Association des Amis des Musées de la Marine
    La Belle Poule
    Le Chébec
    Côte D'Emeraude
    La Flore
    Percé pour 86 Canons
    La Réale de France
    Remorqueur de Haute Mer
    Surcouf
    Le Terrible

Bangeau, Receuil de petites marines, Paris 1817

Bidault, J., Pirogues et Pagaies, Paris 1945

Bowen, F. C., The Sea, Its History and Romance I—IV, London

Bowness, E., The Four-Masted Barque, London 1955

Brito, N. de, Caravelas, Naus e Galés de Portugal, Oporto

Brøgger & Shetelig, The Viking Ships, Oslo 1953

Callender, G., The Portrait of Peter Pett and The Sovereign of the Seas, Newport 1930

Chapelle, H. I., The History of American Sailing Ships, New York 1936

— The History of the American Sailing Navy, New York 1949

Chapman, F. H. af, Architectura Navalis Mercatoria, Stockholm 1768, Facsimile, Magdeburg 1957

Chatterton, E. K., Sailing Models, Plymouth 1934

Crone, G. C. E., Nederlandsche Jachten, Binnenschepen, Visschersvaartuigen, Amsterdam 1926

Donnelly, I. A., Chinese Junks, Shanghai 1930

Dugan, J., The Great Iron Ship, London 1953

Dunn, L., The World's Tankers, Bournemouth 1956

Farrere, C., Histoire de la Marine Française, Paris 1956

Fletcher, R. A., Steam-Ships, London 1910

— Warships, London 1911

Furttenbach, J., Architectura Navalis, Ulm 1629, Facsimile, Paris 1939

Greenhill, B., The Merchant Schooners I—II, London 1951

Gröner, E., Die deutschen Kriegsschiffe 1815—1936, Berlin 1937

Halldin, G., Från Hajen 1904 till Hajen 1954, Malmö 1954

Hammar, H., John Ericssons Monitor, Stockholm 1937

Handels- og Søfartsmuseet på Kronborg, Aarbog, 1946—1957

Hardy, A. C., Kampen på haven, Malmö 1950

— The Book of the Ship, London 1947

— Seafood Ships, London 1947

— Ships at Work, Norwich 1939

Harnach, E. P., All about Ships and Shipping, London 1903—1959

Heinsius, P., Das Schiff der hansischen Frühzeit, Weimar 1956

Herzog, B., Die deutschen Uboote 1906 bis 1945, Munich 1959

Holmes, G. C. V., Ancient and Modern Ships I—II, London 1916

Hornborg, E., Segelsjöfartens historia, Helsingfors 1948

Jane's Fighting Ships 1915—1959

King, J. W., War-Ships and Navies of the World, Boston 1880

Klem, K., De Danskes Vej, Copenhagen 1941

Konijnenburg, E. van, Shipbuilding from Its Beginning I—III, Brussels

Ladage, J. H., Merchant Ships, Cambridge Mar. 1955

Laird Clowes, G. S., Sailing Ships I—II, London 1932 1952

Laughton, L. G. Carr, Old Ships, Figure-Heads and Sterns, London 1925

Lindqvist, S., Gotlands Bildsteine, Stockholm 1941

Lever, D., The Young Sea Officers Sheet Anchor, London 1819, Facsimile, New York 1955

Longridge, C. N., The Anatomy of Nelson's Ships, London 1955

— The "Cutty Sark" I—II, London 1933

Lubbock, B., The Blackwall Frigates, Glasgow 1924

— The China Clippers, Glasgow 1946

Magoun, F. A., The Frigate Constitution, Portland Maine 1928

Marques, V. de la, Diccionario de Arquitectura Naval (MS) 1719—1759

Marstrand, V., Arsenalet i Piraeus og Oldtidens Byggeregler, Copenhagen 1922

Moll, F., Das Schiff in der bildenden Kunst, Bonn 1929

Mollema, J. C., Geschiedenis van Nederland ter zee I—IV, Amsterdam 1939

Monleon, D. R., Construcciones Navales (MS) 1890

Mookerji, R. K., Indian Shipping, Calcutta 1957

Moore, A., Last Days of Mast and Sail, Oxford 1925

Morison, S. E., Admiral of the Ocean Sea, Boston 1951

Morton, N. R., Sailing-Ship Models, London 1949

Páris, E., Souvenirs de Marine I—VI, Paris 1882—1908

Paris, M., Essai sur la Construction Navale des Peuples Extra-Européens, Paris

Parkes, O., British Battleships, London 1957

Rålamb, Å. Classon, Skeps Byggerij eller Adelig Öfnings Tionde Tom, Stockholm 1691, Facsimile, Malmö 1943

Rimington, C., Fighting Fleets, New York 1943

Robinson, M. S., Van de Velde Drawings, Cambridge 1958

Roërie, G. La, Navires et Marins, Paris 1946

Ronciére & Clerc-Rampal, Histoire de la Marine Française, Paris 1934

Rooij, G. De, Practical Shipbuilding, Harlem 1953

Roscoe & Freeman, Picture History of the U.S. Navy, Wakefield Mass. 1956

Salisbury W. & Anderson R. C. (ed.), A Treatise on Shipbuilding and a Treatise on Rigging written about 1620—1625

Sjöhistorisk Årsbok 1943—1959

Sölver, C. V., Obelisk-Skibe, Copenhagen 1943

Spratt, H. P., Merchant Steamers and Motor Ships, London 1949

— The Birth of the Steamboat, London 1958

Steensen, S., Alverdens Krigsskibe, Copenhagen 1942

Stenton, F., The Bayeaux Tapestry, London 1957

Stevens, J. R., Old Time Ships, Toronto 1949

Svenska Flottans Historia I—III, Malmö 1942—1945

Ucelli, G., Le Navi di Nemi, Rome 1950

Underhill, H. A., Deep-Water Sail, Glasgow 1952

— Sailing Ship Rigs and Rigging, Glasgow 1938

Vocini, M., La Nave Nel Tempo, Milan 1942

Warrington Smyth, H., Mast and Sail in Europe and Asia, London 1929

Way, F., Mississippi Stern-Wheelers, Milwaukee 1947

Wetterhahn, A. & Schünemann, H., US Standard Fracht- und Passagierschiffe 1938—1956, Hamburg 1957

Weyers Flottentaschenbuch 1915—1960

Winter, H., Breydenbachs Pilgerreise nach dem heiligen Lande, 1486, Berlin 1948

— Die Katalanische nao von 1450, Magdeburg 1956

Periodicals:

The Mariner's Mirror

Sheet Anchor

Ships and Ship Models

Svensk Sjöfarts Tidskrift

Museums:

Altona, Altonaer Museum

Amsterdam, Nederlandsch Historisch Schepvaart Museum

Barcelona, Museo Maritimo

Elsinore, Handels og Søfartsmuseet, Kronborg

Genoa, Museo Navale

Gothenburg, Sjöfartsmuseet

Greenwich, National Maritime Museum

Hamburg, Museum für Hamburgische Geschichte

London, Science Museum

Madrid, Museo Naval

Mariehamn, Sjöfartsmuseet

Oslo, Vikingskipshuset, Bygdøy

Paris, Musée de Marine

Rotterdam, Maritiem Museum Prins Hendrik

Stockholm, Statens Sjöhistoriska Museum

Venice, Museo Storico Navale

Translated from SKEPPET (Bokförlaget Forum AB, Stockholm, 1961) by Michael Phillips.

Set with 10 pt Times New Roman type by Bohusläningens AB, Uddevalla, Sweden, and printed by Smeets Lithographers, Weert, on 115 gram wood-free offset paper from Lessebo AB, Lessebo, Sweden.
Design by Björn Landström